INTERDEPENDENT MINDS

DISTINGUISHED CONTRIBUTIONS IN PSYCHOLOGY
Susan T. Fiske, Series Editor

INTERDEPENDENT MINDS

The Dynamics of Close Relationships

SANDRA L. MURRAY
JOHN G. HOLMES

Foreword by Harry T. Reis

THE GUILFORD PRESS
New York   London

© 2011 The Guilford Press
A Division of Guilford Publications, Inc.
72 Spring Street, New York, NY 10012
www.guilford.com

Printed in the United States of America

This book is printed on acid-free paper.

Last digit is print number: 9   8   7   6   5   4   3   2   1

Library of Congress Cataloging-in-Publication Data

Murray, Sandra L.
  Interdependent minds: the dynamics of close relationships / by Sandra L.
Murray and John G. Holmes.
     p. cm. — (Distinguished contributions in psychology)
  Includes bibliographical references and index.
  ISBN 978-1-60918-076-8 (hbk: alk. paper)
  1. Couples—Psychology.   2. Interpersonal relations.   I. Holmes, John G.
(John Grenville), 1945–   II. Title.
  HQ801.M855 2011
  646.7'8—dc22

                                                              2010045822

To Colin, Derek, and Lynda
—S. L. M. and J. G. H.

About the Authors

Sandra L. Murray, PhD, is Professor of Psychology at the University at Buffalo, The State University of New York. She has received numerous awards for her scholarship, including the Distinguished Scientific Award for Early Career Contributions to Psychology from the American Psychological Association (2003), the Theoretical Innovation Award from the Society of Personality and Social Psychology (2007), the Early Career Award from the International Society for Self and Identity (2001), and the New Contribution Award from the International Association for Relationship Research (1998, 2000). Dr. Murray's research has been supported by grants from the National Institute of Mental Health and the National Science Foundation.

John G. Holmes, PhD, is Professor of Psychology at the University of Waterloo in Waterloo, Ontario, Canada. He has received numerous awards for his scholarship and teaching, including a University Research Chair (2004), the Mentoring Award from the International Association for Relationship Research (2004), the Theoretical Innovation Award from the Society of Personality and Social Psychology (2007), and the New Contribution Award from the International Association for Relationship Research (1992, 1998, 2000). Dr. Holmes's research has been supported by grants from the Social Sciences and Humanities Research Council of Canada.

Foreword

"The smallest indivisible human unit is two people, not one; one is a fiction," writes the playwright Tony Kushner in the afterword to *Angels in America: Perestroika*. He continues, "From such nets of souls societies, the social world, human life springs." In this remarkable book, *Interdependent Minds: The Dynamics of Close Relationships*, Sandra L. Murray and John G. Holmes have dug deeply into Kushner's assertion, explaining how these "nets of souls" operate. They describe how interdependent minds working and living together create the fabric of human connections. Anyone interested in a thoughtful, integrative, and altogether contemporary analysis of how relationships work will find much to savor in these pages.

Murray and Holmes's theorizing begins with the simple idea that relationships are fundamental to human experience. This idea is gaining momentum in social psychology, but it was not always thus. As Reis, Collins, and Berscheid (2000) explain, psychological theories have historically emphasized the individual, be it the individual's inner psychodynamics (as in psychoanalytic theories), responses to environmental stimuli (as in behaviorist theories), or mental processing of events (as in modern cognitive theories). Reconciling this doggedly individualist emphasis with the manifest impact of relationships on nearly all aspects of human experience has often been challenging. After all, actions—or what we see—are produced by individuals. Yet perhaps more than any other species on earth, we humans are a social species. From birth throughout the lifespan, most human behavior depends on an individual's past, present, and anticipated future relationships. It takes a nimble theorist to make the leap from individual to dyad.

One theory that bucked psychology's preoccupation with the individual was interdependence theory, first presented by John Thibaut and Harold Kelley (both influential personal mentors for Murray and Holmes) in 1959. Interdependence theory is social psychology's classic statement of how certain properties of social situations—namely, how partners' interaction influences their outcomes—affect behavior. Murray and Holmes used their mentors' framework as a springboard for two decades' worth of theory and research into what might be called the fundamental dilemma of life in a close relationship: that partners must somehow coordinate their individual needs, wants, preferences, and anxieties in order to make their relationships work. This book summarizes in a clear, accessible manner that extraordinary body of scholarship.

The astute reader will have noticed that the title of this book refers to "interdependent minds." Minds reside within individuals, of course. Murray and Holmes's key insight is to define relationship dynamics in terms of how partners respond to the fact of their interdependence. Understanding these responses requires examination of the processes and products of the human mind, or the motives and goals that guide behavior and the cognitions and affects that result from the mind's activity. What makes the Murray and Holmes approach special (and more innovative than earlier individualistic approaches) is their emphasis on the interdependence of minds—a dyad-specific pattern that takes into account how each partner responds to the other and to the fact of their shared, ongoing relationship. Just as these patterns of interdependence make relationships more than the sum of their individual parts, so too do they make the Murray and Holmes approach more than the sum of prior theories and research.

A further innovation that Murray and Holmes have brought to the study of close relationships is their synthesis of conscious and unconscious (also called controlled and automatic by some researchers) processes. Although few scholars or professionals doubt, in principle, that much of significance in relationships goes on beneath the surface of our awareness, until recently researchers have not had the tools for studying those processes rigorously. Murray and Holmes's account is not an "either/or" approach; instead, they integrate both kinds of processes into a single, elegant model, explaining when one or the other predominates and how they complement each other, typically to the partners' constructive advantage but occasionally less so. This is an insightful, thoroughly modern approach to understanding the mind and how it directs behavior.

Many researchers study relationships today and, as is common in academic scholarship, the topics they pursue have become ever more specialized and narrowly defined. In this light, the broad scope of the authors' work is refreshing. Just a glance over the range of topics covered in these pages—responsiveness, trust, commitment, connection and rejection, compatibility, conflict, support, hurt feelings, the impact of personality on relationships, passionate love, relationship stability and breakup, social cognition, attachment, motivation, and more—reveals a range of phenomena that is truly impressive.

Researchers will find herein a way of thinking about relationships that inspires many new ideas for future work. But this is not just a book for researchers. In the current climate of seemingly impermeable boundaries between scientific research and clinical practice, the authors plainly aim to keep the real-world implications of their model and research on the front burner. Clinicians will find countless ideas that clarify problematic behaviors once considered inscrutable or dismissed as pathologies and numerous insights and suggestions for helping clients understand and improve their relationships; for example, the authors' description of the "smart unconscious," an idea that makes their guide for relationships (see Chapter 12) not just practical but also hopeful and helpful. The lucid, yet detailed, writing style of the entire book is part of its appeal, made even more compelling by the stories of Ron and Gayle, Harry and Sally, Hector and Helena, and Gunter and Lastri. These characters came to life for me, and I will confess to an itch of disappointment when I came to the end of the book: I wanted to know how things really turned out for these couples!

Readers not personally acquainted with Murray and Holmes may be interested to know that these two scholars have had a remarkably successful and enduring long-term collaboration—a circumstance that, in itself, may qualify them to write a book about close relationships! Ultimately, what makes their account of relationship dynamics unique is the way that it bypasses so many traditional accounts that stress the individual and his or her personal characteristics—for example, trying to explain relationship success or failure in terms of an individual's personality, social skills, emotional intelligence, or childhood experience; or attributing relationship problems to men and women "coming from different planets," to finding that one "perfect match" on Internet dating sites, to relying on self-help books, or to designing interventions that target one person in the relationship. Rather, Murray and Holmes suggest that we look to the unconscious habits and conscious reasoning that shape our responses to the interdependent situations in which life puts us. As you will see in the pages that follow, this book changes the playing field in thinking about close relationships.

HARRY T. REIS, PhD
Professor of Psychology
Department of Clinical and Social Sciences in Psychology
University of Rochester

REFERENCE

Reis, H. T., Collins, W. A., & Berscheid, E. (2000). The relationship context of human behavior and development. *Psychological Bulletin, 126,* 844–872.

Acknowledgments

We are tremendously grateful to the many students and colleagues who enriched the research we describe in this book. Their names populate the pages that follow. We also owe a special debt to the interdependence scholars whose work has inspired our own, including Ellen Berscheid, Harold Kelley, and John Thibaut, whose legacy infused the work of Caryl Rusbult (and students), Margaret Clark (and students), Harry Reis (and students), Jeffry Simpson (and students), Arthur Aron (and students), Mark Baldwin (and students), John Lydon (and students), and Nancy Collins (and students). Their research and thinking populates these pages as well. We are also grateful to Susan T. Fiske and Seymour Weingarten for their wise editorial counsel. A National Institute of Mental Health grant awarded to Sandra L. Murray (No. MH 60105-08) and a Social Sciences and Humanities Research Council of Canada Standard Research grant awarded to John G. Holmes supported the preparation of this book.

Contents

CHAPTER 1

Motivating Responsiveness

Why a "Smart Relationship Unconscious"?

Relationships are hard. A quick perusal of titles in the self-help section of any bookstore reveals just how difficult and taxing relationships can be. Titles promise guides for communicating with a spouse who is other-planetary by virtue of gender, strategies for prevailing in conflict, and tricks for keeping the embers of one's sex life from burning out. Do people really need this much tutelage? Are relationships really this complex to manage?

Yes and no. Think for a moment about everything couples do together. Imagine the lives of two busy lawyers, Ron and Gayle, coping with an infant and an energetic toddler. Their marriage has all the potential stresses and strains of running a small, understaffed company. On the factory floor, they change diapers, shop to put food in the fridge, cajole their toddler to eat his meals, do the laundry, juggle play-dates with work, mow the lawn, and balance trips to the doctor's office with court dates. In the offices of upper management, they manage relations between the employees—in their case, between their young children, between each other, and between themselves and outside friends and family. In juggling these executive roles, they can be called on to provide emotional

1

support, offer career counsel, quash conflicts with in-laws, tolerate each other's faults, and mesh Gayle's penchant for beer and football with Ron's proclivity for fine wine and foreign films. They depend on each other in so many situations that, inevitably, some will provide opportunities to disappoint each other. Gayle might be tempted to work rather than take the time to relax with Ron; Ron might be tempted leave too many of the diapers and too much of the cajoling to Gayle; Gayle might express her irritation with Ron's mother, much to his chagrin. Despite such potential for conflict, Ron and Gayle generally find ways of being responsive to each other's needs. Ron often takes on household responsibilities that Gayle finds onerous, he usually listens when Gayle wants to talk (and vice versa), and Gayle sacrifices football for Ron's subtitles often enough to make him feel appreciated and valued.

Relationships scholars agree that mutually responsive behavior is key to satisfying and stable relationships (Reis, Clark, & Holmes, 2004; Thibaut & Kelley, 1959). Responsiveness is ascribed this lofty status in large part because partners are *interdependent*. Interdependence refers to a structural feature of relationships: Partners influence and constrain one another's actions (Kelley, 1979). What Gayle does constrains how happy Ron can be with his outcomes, and what Ron does constrains how happy Gayle can be with her outcomes.

Because partners are interdependent, any relationship can be broken down into a series of situations involving social coordination. In each of these situations, one partner has a need or goal that he or she cannot reach on his or her own, and the other partner must adjust his or her own behavior to accommodate it (Kelley & Thibaut, 1978). In any relationship, partners typically coordinate their actions at three different levels of interdependence (Braiker & Kelley, 1979; Holmes, 2002):

1. Life tasks
2. Personal preferences and personality
3. Relationship goals

First, couples are interdependent at the level of life tasks. To live together happily, Ron and Gayle must ensure that someone predictably cooks, someone competently cleans, someone caringly tends to their children's needs, and someone promptly pays the bills. Second, couples are interdependent at the level of personal preferences and personality. To live together happily, Ron and Gayle must ensure that his introverted preference for solitude respects her gregarious desire to socialize. They must also mesh Gayle's forthright tendency to be blunt in her criticisms with the necessity of protecting Ron's easily bruised feelings. Third, couples are interdependent at the level of relationship goals. To live together happily, Ron and Gayle must adjust his wistful desire for a traditional family to accommodate her career, and Gayle must adjust her preference for independent hobbies with Ron's desire for shared leisure pursuits.

WHY A BOOK ON MOTIVATING RESPONSIVENESS?

Although mutual responsiveness is widely regarded as the holy grail of relationship life, exactly how mutually responsive behaviors emerge (or fail to emerge) in relationships remains a mystery. Our goal in writing this book was to unravel this puzzle. In the pages that follow, we detail the elements of a new theory of interdependence that we developed to explain why and how mutually responsive (and nonresponsive) interaction patterns emerge in relationships. The theory we articulate revolves around the following premise: People's general working models of relationships contain the unconscious "know-how" to motivate mutually responsive behavior.

We use the term *interdependent mind* to refer to the cognitive representation of this relationship know-how in memory (Murray & Holmes, 2009). Interpersonal scholars characterize relationship knowledge as working models (Baldwin, 1992; Collins & Read, 1994; Mikulincer & Shaver, 2003). These working models govern how people experience the self in relation to others (Andersen & Chen, 2002; Baldwin, 1992). For instance, Andersen and Chen (2002) contend that aspects of people's self-conceptions (e.g., traits and goals) are tied to their representations of significant others in memory. Such ties, they reason, control behavior in interpersonal situations. Similarly, Baldwin (1992) argued that working models include beliefs about the characteristics of the self in specific contexts, beliefs about the characteristics of others in these same contexts, and "if–then" or procedural scripts that specify the relation between the self and others (e.g., "If I depend on my spouse for support, then he or she will be comforting").

Following in this social–cognitive tradition, we conceptualize the *interdependent mind* as a system of interconnected procedural or if–then rules for interaction within adult romantic relationships. These unconscious rules coordinate partner interaction by linking specific features of the situation (i.e., "if Ron does X") to correspondent ways of feeling, thinking, and behaving (i.e., "then Gayle does Y"). For instance, one rule links Ron's good humor (i.e., "if") to Gayle's contingent tendency to seek his social support and counsel (i.e., "then") after a difficult day in court.

Another such rule links Gayle's criticism of Ron's introversion (i.e., "if") to his contingent tendency to withdraw from her in social situations (i.e., "then"). As we will see, these if–then rules function to coordinate mutually responsive partner interactions by matching specific features of the situation partners face to congruent behavior. In so doing, these if–then rules unconsciously function to make the best of specific interdependent situations.

This book has three main features that distinguish it from prior writing on close relationship dynamics. First, it articulates a new model of interdependence to explain how patterns of mutual responsiveness (and nonresponsiveness) develop in relationships. This model of the interdependent mind is based in the classic arguments John Thibaut and Harold Kelley (1959) advanced about the power of situations, but it also incorporates 21st-century knowledge about the power of the unconscious in directing behavior (Bargh, 2007). Second, this book reveals how breaking down partner interaction into underlying if–then rule structure can explain why some relationships succeed while others fail. From our perspective, relationships do not fail primarily because men are from Mars and women are from Venus, because partners are short on emotional intelligence, or because partners lack the skills to "fight fair." Instead, relationships fail because the if–then rules that become one's unconscious habit constrain responsiveness and thereby limit just how rewarding interacting with one's partner can be. Third, this book articulates a pivotal role for partner compatibility in relationships. The immense popularity of Internet services that promise compatible partners suggests that people fervently want to find a partner who understands and shares their interests, values, and personality. However, few people actually find such a compatible match (Lykken & Tellegen, 1993). Moreover, no existing scholarship articulates what it means for partners to be compatible or to explain what effects compatibility might have on relationships. This book does both.

When we began our collaborative work 20 years ago, we had no way of anticipating we would end up here. We started our research together talking about Brickman's (1987) book on commitment. Through this, we discovered a shared fascination with the motivational machinations that keep people in happy and committed relationships. For years we happily went about our research enterprise limiting our theorizing and research to the realm of the conscious mind. While we were doing business as usual, social psychology changed radically, with the advent of empirical research on the automatic regulation of social behavior first appearing in the early 1990s (see Bargh, 2007, for a review). It took a few years, but we finally caught the spark. At its core, the theory we develop in this book assumes that we cannot uncover how relationships work simply by asking people to complete self-report scales (or even by observing their behavior). Instead, it's only by looking at the operation of the unconscious in conjunction with the conscious that we can begin to understand why some relationships thrive while others falter.

In offering this book, we hope to reach academic researchers, clinicians working in the field, students curious about the scientific study of relationships, and the interested layperson hoping to find some relationship advice. Given the diversity of this audience, we offer both empirical data to support our arguments and examples to illustrate our main points. In weaving together the empirical and the hypothetical, we bring the marriages of four fictional couples to life: Ron and Gayle (whom you have already met), Harry and Sally, Hector and Helena, and Gunter and Lastri. Table 1.1 presents a thumbnail sketch of each of these couples. We fill in these sketches—articulating the nature of their compatibilities and incompatibilities in life tasks, personality, and relationship goals—as we proceed. Each of these couples will end up being responsive (and not

TABLE 1.1. Introducing Our Couples

Couple	Basic demographics	Life task preferences	Personality preferences	Relationship goal preferences
Ron and Gayle	African American Lawyers Two young children	Stay tuned . . .	Gayle more gregarious.	Stay tuned . . .
Harry and Sally	White Mechanic/customer service officer Three children, eldest 17	Stay tuned . . .	Stay tuned . . .	Stay tuned . . .
Hector and Helena	Hispanic Factory worker/ homemaker Three young children Catholic Economically stressed	Stay tuned . . .	Stay tuned . . .	Stay tuned . . .
Gunter and Lastri	Indonesian PhD student/ homemaker One toddler	Stay tuned . . .	Stay tuned . . .	Gunter wants another baby; Lastri wants to return to school.

responsive) to one another's needs in different ways. They will also end up more or less happy. In telling their stories, we use our model of the interdependent mind both to anticipate how each of these couples met their respective fates and to describe the circumstances that might have led them to experience a different relationship end.

We already introduced Ron and Gayle. They are a dual-career, African American couple coping with a young family. Ron and Gayle spent the initial years of their marriage in relative bliss, enjoying the spoils of their respective legal careers. They worked late, got promoted often, lived lavishly, and traveled to exotic locales to escape stress. Three years ago that changed. First they had a son, a happy but unexpected event; recently, they welcomed an infant daughter. Now they struggle to find the time to balance work with family, live frugally to save for college tuitions, and limit travel to often stressful trips to visit grandparents.

Later we will meet Harry and Sally, a white couple coping with the many challenges facing families entrenched in the middle class. Harry is a mechanic at a local automotive shop. Sally is a part-time customer service officer at a local bank. They have three children. Their youngest is 3; their eldest is 17. Their middle child has recently been diagnosed with attention-deficit/hyperactivity disorder. Sally spends most of her week squeezing her bank hours in between the demands of managing their household and shuttling their children between daycare, school, and soccer games. Harry spends most of his week wishing he had more time for his children and hoping he hasn't done something to disappoint Sally.

Hector and Helena face many of the same life tasks as Harry and Sally—but their challenges are greater still. Each the child of Hispanic immigrant parents, Hector and Helena had few privileges growing up. Hector managed to go to trade school, but Helena never finished high school. Hector now works as an assembly-line worker in an auto plant and he worries about his job security. Helena supplements his salary by babysitting for their neighbors when she can. Even though a shared Catholic faith cements their marriage, they don't spend as much time alone together anymore, constantly struggle to pay the rent, and Helena clips coupons every week to stretch their earnings far enough to support three very young children.

Gunter and Lastri, who married through the matchmaking of their parents, face a different set of challenges. They are recent immigrants from Indonesia. Gunter is an engineer and relocated to the United States to pursue an advanced degree while working full-time at an upstart biotech firm. Because Gunter works such long hours, Lastri tends to their toddler and manages their household full-time. Although this traditional division of labor has made it easy for them to coordinate their goals in the past, Lastri has been questioning this arrangement as of late. She thinks she might want to return to school herself. Gunter still is not sure how he feels about the turn of events, but he would like to have another baby, and he is reasonably sure that his parents would not approve of Lastri sacrificing time at home with their child to pursue her education. At this point in their marriage, uncertainty seems to be the only certainty.

As these examples attest, our hope is to offer a new model of interdependence that is general enough to explain close relationship dynamics in different economic and sociocultural contexts. No doubt future research will prove some of the hypotheses and arguments we advance incomplete (if not altogether wrong), but in advancing the ideas, we hope to spur new thinking and further research. In terms of general organization, this book is divided into two main sections, one more conceptual, the other more applied. The first two-thirds of the book outline the conceptual model and its empirical support. We do this in progressive stages. In the remainder of this chapter, we set up the basic elements of our model. We start by describing why it can be difficult for partners to be responsive. Then we describe the essential elements of the relationship "know-how" needed to motivate mutuality in responsiveness. We present the model formally in Chapter 2. In Chapters 3 through 8, we break the model down into its constituent elements. In the last third of the book (Chapters 9 through 12), we outline applications of the model. (We provide more detail about the contents in the "Book Overview" section at the end of this chapter.)

WHY RESPONSIVENESS IS HARD:
THE TWIN TEMPTATIONS OF SELF-INTEREST

Some situations make it easy to be responsive. Being responsive to a partner's goals is easy in situations where partner interests converge. Imagine that Ron's preference for doing car maintenance converges with Gayle's distaste for it. In such a situation, Ron does not even need to recognize Gayle's preferences to be responsive to her needs. He can meet her needs simply by acting in his own interest and taking care of the car maintenance himself. But here's the problem. Behavioral coordination is going to be hard in many of the situations couples face. Couples are interdependent in so many different ways that at least some incompatibilities or conflicts of interest arise for even the happiest and most compatible couples. We use the term *conflict of interest* to refer to a "mixed-motive" situation (Kelley et al., 2003). Such situations offer the potential for mutual gain (if partners put aside self-interested concerns to be either selfish or self-protective), but also the risk of potential loss (if one or both partners accede to the temptation to pursue self-interested concerns).

The number and severity of the conflicts of interest that partners face depend on their compatibility at each of the levels of interdependence they share. Consider the tasks life imposes on a couple. At this level of interdependence, the likelihood of a conflict of interest arising depends on the task itself and the degree of correspondence between partners' task preferences (Kelley, 1979). Some life tasks are objectively more appealing than others. Popping dirty clothes into the washing machine is not the most enticing activity. However, it is probably more appealing than driving endlessly around the neighborhood at 3 A.M. trying to lull a colicky infant to sleep. Both tasks need to be done, but coordinating responsibility for the colicky infant is likely to generate more conflict because being responsive to a partner's needs for sleep requires sacrificing one's own sleep. Some life tasks are also objectively more difficult for some couples. If money is abundant, deciding whose material needs to prioritize is not likely to be a source of conflict. If Ron loses his job, budgeting household finances is likely to require at least one partner to sacrifice because there is not enough money to go around. The available options in such life tasks also generate more or less conflict because of the attitudes and preferences each partner brings to the relationship. If Gayle prefers being a night owl, being the 3 A.M. chauffeur may be an easy sacrifice for her to make. If both Ron and Gayle need to arrive early at work, deciding who gets to sleep may be a source of great contention. Thus, complementary interests can make it easier to be responsive in specific situations because one partner finds the tasks the other finds onerous to be desirable. Couples who find the same tasks onerous are going to face more situations where responsiveness is hard because it requires more personal sacrifice.

Next consider the personal attitudes, preferences, goals, and personality each partner brings to the relationship. At this level of interdependence, the likelihood of conflicts of interest arising depends on the compatibility or correspondence between partners' personal attitudes, preferences, goals, and personality (Braiker & Kelley, 1979; Kelley, 1979). In some domains, being similar minimizes conflict and makes coordination easier. If Ron and Gayle are both disavowed Baptists, being responsive to one another's goals for Sunday morning activities is easy because their personal goals converge in a shared desire not to go to services. However, it would be much harder for Ron to respond to Gayle's needs for them to go to church if he would rather sleep in. If Ron and Gayle are both outgoing and sociable, it will also be easy for them to coordinate their shared goals to spend some of their time together with friends. It would be more difficult for Ron to meet Gayle's needs to socialize if he prefers solitude to parties. In other domains, being opposite minimizes conflict and makes coordination easier. It is easier for Ron to meet Gayle's need to exercise her controlling and compulsive nature if he is an easygoing person who really does not mind being bossed around. It would be much harder for him to meet Gayle's need to be controlling if he would rather control her. In that case, Gayle's exercise of her dominance would thwart Ron's capacity to be his controlling self.

Now consider the relationship goals couples need to negotiate. At this level of interdependence, the number of conflicts of interest likely to arise depends on the extent to which partners aspire to convergent or divergent goals for their relationships. Here, convergent goals make coordination easy. If both Ron and Gayle want to increase the amount of time they spend together, they can easily meet each other's needs for greater closeness. However, if Ron wants to start trying to have a third child at the time Gayle wants to devote more energy to her career, greater sacrifices will be necessary for both of them to meet their relationship goals.

The many ways in which partners are interdependent make incompatibilities and conflicts of interest inevitable. Because both onerous and pleasurable tasks need to be done, Ron and Gayle will encounter specific situations where they would both rather play with their toddler than vacuum and do the dishes. Because they are different people, Ron and Gayle will encounter situations where they are going to want different things. In fact, the idea that birds of a feather flock together does not quite capture the romantic reality. Partners do match on basic dimensions such as age, socioeconomic status, ethnicity, and basic attitudes (Berscheid & Regan, 2005). However, on many of the preference and personality dimensions that control behavioral interactions in close relationships, mismatches are just as common as matches. In a large study of twins and their spouses, Lykken and Tellegen (1993) examined whether couples sorted themselves out on the basis of personality. The authors reasoned that if people selectively choose partners who are a good personality fit, the personalities of real couples should be more similar than the personalities of couples the authors randomly paired. What they found was astonishing. Real couples were no more similar in personality than random couples. This element of randomness in romantic choice ensures that couples will experience conflicts because extroverts are paired with introverts, neat freaks are paired with slobs, and obsessive planners are paired with free spirits. In fact, conflict is inevitable even for those couples lucky enough to choose more compatible partners and face more easy than hard tasks. Because social perception is biased, Ron and Gayle are also going to make mistakes discerning exactly what each other actually wants out of specific situations (Griffin & Ross, 1991). Sometimes they will see conflicts where none exactly exist because emotions in the heat of the moment and stereotypes about what men and women want can bias perception in ways that exaggerate any differences.

Risk and the Twin Temptations of Self-Interest

Conflicts of interest make it hard to be responsive because these situations make *risk* a central facet of interdependent life (Murray, Holmes, & Collins, 2006). In reaching out to a partner to meet their needs, people have to risk not having their basic physical, emotional, and psychological needs met. Why would that be the case?

Imagine that it is Gayle's turn to take 3 A.M. chauffeur duty, but she's due in court early the next morning. In this situation, she needs Ron to sacrifice his own need for sleep so she can get a good night's rest in advance of her appearance. However, asking Ron to take an extra turn at chauffeur duty leaves her vulnerable to his refusal. Such a situation is risky because Gayle cannot get what she wants without Ron's help, and Ron has a real reason not to cooperate because he would rather sleep than drive. Now imagine that Gayle just got reprimanded at work, putting a promotion in jeopardy. Disclosing her failure to Ron is risky because he might ignore her real need for social support and instead chastise her for her failure to get the raise if he's upset at the prospect of needing to put in more work hours himself.

The self-interested concerns Gayle and Ron each bring to these situations create risk and present a major barrier to responsiveness. We use the term *self-interest* to refer to twin motivations: (1) one partner's motivation to be selfish and (2) the other partner's corresponding motivation to self-protect. In each of these situations, Ron faces the temptation to pursue his own goals without regard for Gayle's welfare. He can selfishly refuse to chauffeur to preserve his own sleep and he can chastise Gayle for her job failure to vent his own frustration. Consequently, in each of these situations, Gayle faces the temptation to protect herself from being vulnerable to Ron's lesser nature. To keep herself safe, she can decide just to suffer through her turn at chauffeuring or she could decide to confess her failures to her friends instead of to Ron. For Ron to meet Gayle's needs for a chauffeuring reprieve and a sympathetic ear, each of them must set aside their own specific self-interested concerns. That is, she must be willing to ask and he must be willing to give. If either of them fails to do so, her needs will go unmet.

This reality informs the central premise of this book: Coordinating patterns of mutual responsiveness to need requires mechanisms for trumping self-interested concerns on each partner's part. To coordinate mutually responsive behavior, Ron's temptation to be selfish needs to be tempered when Gayle sets aside her motivation to protect against his exploitation; similarly, Gayle's temptation to be selfish must be tempered when Ron sets aside his motivation to self-protect. When this happens, partner interactions can be fluid and easy.

MOTIVATING RESPONSIVENESS: FIVE ELEMENTS TO RELATIONSHIP KNOW-HOW

The model of the interdependent mind we formalize in Chapter 2 revolves around the following assumption that tempering partners' self-interested temptations in a way that promotes mutually responsive behaviors requires effective *motivation-management*. When partner motivations are effectively managed, Gayle generally solicits the type of care Ron is willing to provide and she also provides the type of care that Ron needs. Managing partner motivations is central to motivating responsiveness, because it provides a mechanism for keeping the goal conflict inherent to conflict of interest situations from thwarting action. Namely, in putting her outcomes in Ron's hands, Gayle stands to gain the benefits of his care, but she also risks being hurt and disappointed by his nonresponsiveness. Essentially, conflicts of interest put the fundamental goals to approach what is good and to avoid what is bad in opposition (Elliot & Church, 1997; Gable, 2005; Higgins, 1998). In relationship terms, these situations put the goal to connect to the partner in conflict with the goal to self-protect against rejection. Because people cannot act with any direction in such a state of indecision or ambivalence (Cacioppo, Gardner, & Berntson, 1999), behaving responsively requires the know-how to resolve this goal conflict. There are five elements that are basic to this relationship know-how:

1. Trust
2. Goal direction
3. Commitment reciprocity
4. Efficient but flexible goal implementation
5. Suitability for the relationship circumstance

Trust

For Gayle to know when it is safe to approach Ron, she needs to know when putting her outcomes in his hands is likely to be more or less risky. For this reason, gauging the partner's responsiveness is central to our model. The inherent difficulty of disambiguating the partner's motivations is probably obvious: It is impossible for anyone to have direct insight into the contents of another person's consciousness (Griffin & Ross, 1991). Gayle cannot know Ron's motivations because she cannot insert herself into his mind to discern where the truth lies. Instead, she must rely on an indirect barometer. Trust functions as this barometer.

Gayle's level of trust in Ron captures her expectations about the strength of his commitment to her, and thus the strength of his motivation to respond to her needs (Holmes & Rempel, 1989). As traditionally defined, trust involves meta-perspective taking, that is, discerning how the partner feels about oneself (Holmes & Rempel, 1989). Through her level of trust in Ron, Gayle can discern what she can safely risk asking of him. Our model of the interdependent mind's structure assumes that five interrelated if–then rules govern Gayle's expectations about the strength of Ron's commitment to her.

These five rules comprise the if–then rules for trusting. These rules tell Gayle when it is reasonable to expect Ron to be responsive. They basically set the conditions that warrant Gayle's worthiness of Ron's care. In so doing, they tell Gayle when she needs to be vigilant and when she does not. For instance, one of these rules links Gayle's worry that she is too competitive for Ron to her occasional concerns about his rejection. Another rule links Gayle's belief that she's kinder and more intelligent than Ron's college girlfriend to her general confidence in his acceptance. By linking specific conditions (e.g., being kinder and more intelligent, being too competitive) to more or less trusting expectations, these rules help signal risk. They help Gayle fill in the blanks in conflicts of interest by revealing when Ron is safe to approach and when putting her outcomes in his hands is likely to yield the fulfillment versus disappointment of her needs. In so doing, they govern Gayle's chronic need to be vigilant for the possibility of Ron's nonresponsiveness.

Goal Direction

The second element of people's unconscious relationship know-how involves two if–then rules that provide a general guide for action. These rules answer the basic question: Should I stay or should I go? In technical terms, these rules turn the risks Gayle perceives in a specific conflict of interest into a general direction for her actions. In so doing, these rules orient Gayle toward approaching situations that offer the hope of Ron's responsiveness and avoiding those situations that threaten his nonresponsiveness. One rule links Gayle's anticipation of Ron's acceptance to her desire to approach good outcomes. The other rule links Gayle's anticipation of Ron's rejection to her desire to avoid bad outcomes. These rules link risk appraisal to directed action by using the interpersonal goals Gayle adopts in specific conflicts of interest as an intermediating force. In particular, the "approach" rule links Gayle's expectations of Ron's acceptance (i.e., low risk) to her goal to connect to him (i.e., approach Ron). The "avoid" rule links Gayle's expectations of Ron's rejection and nonresponsiveness (i.e., high risk) to her goal to self-protect against his possible rejection (i.e., avoid Ron).

Commitment Reciprocity

Fluid and responsive interactions involve the goals of both partners. To reap the best outcomes Gayle needs to take the risk of putting her outcomes in Ron's hands, and Ron needs to forego the temptation to best his own personal outcomes. Therefore, fluid, mutually responsive interaction involves coordinating the interpersonal goals partners jointly pursue. For mutually responsive interactions to develop, both partners must be equally willing to set aside self-interested concerns (Drigotas, Rusbult, & Verette, 1999). Any asymmetry in their willingness to do so invites coordination difficulties (Drigotas et al., 1999; Sprecher, Schmeeckle, & Felmless, 2006). Imagine the difficulty of coordinating mutually responsive interaction patterns in a marriage where Gayle is more committed to Ron than Ron is committed to her. Being less invested in the relationship gives Ron greater power and disproportionate license to behave selfishly and disappoint Gayle. Not needing Gayle as much as she needs him frees him from having to care about her reactions to his behavior. In such a marriage Ron would face the constant temptation to be selfish, and Gayle would faces the constant need to protect against his possible exploitation. Waller (1938) described this adaptive problem in terms of the "principle of least interest." With unequal commitment, Waller reasoned, the power to be selfish resides disproportionately with the person who benefits least from the relationship (i.e., most powerful), and the demand to sacrifice falls largely on the person who benefits most (i.e., least powerful).

Fortunately, people's unconscious relationship know-how also includes if–then rules for minimizing the chance of such power imbalances developing in the first place. Our model of the structure of the interdependent mind posits three further "if-then" rules for keeping Gayle's commitment to Ron commensurate with Ron's commitment to Gayle (Drigotas & Rusbult, 1992). As traditionally defined, commitment captures the strength of one's motivation to respond to the partner's needs. Commitment regulates the motivation to behave selflessly or selfishly (Rusbult & Van Lange, 2003). In knowing his commitment to Gayle, Ron has a heuristic ready to tell him whether Gayle is valuable enough to him in the long term for him to take over her chauffeur duty or listen sympathetically to her failures. Reciprocity in commitment eases interactions by putting partners on a level playing field where each is similarly motivated to be responsive to the other's needs.[1] These three rules follow.

Matching Commitment to Trust

Because Gayle cannot see directly into Ron's head (or heart), her trust in Ron functions as her "best guess" as to the strength of his commitment. One of the if–then rules for coordinating commitment across partners makes trust a stepping stone for commitment. In particular, this if–then rule makes the expression of one's own commitment contingent on trust (Murray, Holmes, & Collins, 2006; Wieselquist, Rusbult, Foster, & Agnew, 1999). How might such a rule coordinate partners' goals in conflicts of interest? Being more committed means that Gayle puts more of her outcomes (whether practical or symbolic) in Ron's hands. She might depend on Ron for his help with child care, seek his advice about a work-related stressor, forgive his caustic comment about her new hairstyle, or take on extra child care responsibilities so he can have more time to work. These behaviors leave her vulnerable to disappointment (should he not be similarly responsive), but she can minimize such risks by extending herself only when she has good reason to trust him to be responsive. In other words, the interpersonal mind can keep Gayle's commitment (i.e., dependence) calibrated to Ron's likely commitment by motivating her to risk only as much commitment as she anticipates Ron will extend (Murray, Holmes, & Collins, 2006). But the success of such a matching rule assumes a perfect world in which Gayle's trust in Ron and Ron's commitment to Gayle never wavers (and never errs). Neither of these possibilities is likely to be the case. To coordinate partner commitment, the interpersonal mind also has two further rules for avoiding the problems that could arise if trust were misplaced or commitment derailed.

Ensuring Trust Is Not Misplaced

No matter how responsive Ron is in general, Gayle will find herself in situations where she needs something from him that he is not inclined to provide. In such situations, Gayle's unconscious relationship know-how motivates her to take some kind of remedial action to make Ron "owe" her. By putting Ron in her debt, Gayle effectively leverages the power to motivate Ron to do what he does not necessarily want to do. Imagine that Ron has no desire to take the children to the park on a Sunday afternoon to indulge Gayle's penchant for watching a football game. If Gayle wants to ensure her uninterrupted viewing, she needs to take some kind of pre-emptive action to motivate Ron to indulge her. Therefore, the interpersonal mind contains an if–then rule for putting subtle pressure on him—one that ensures he has little choice but to be responsive. Making sure that he "owes" her—by laundering his clothes in the morning and making his favorite dinner in the evening—could provide just the motivation he needs. Once he's become more dependent on her, he loses some of his power to antagonize her, a state of being that keeps his motivation to be responsive in check with Gayle's willingness to put her outcomes in his hands. In this state, he might readily head off to the park with children in tow and let her watch football in peace to ensure that he will have clothes to wear and a meal to eat the next day. In this way, Gayle's efforts to leverage Ron's dependence on her give Ron all the more reason to be responsive in situations where his commitment to being responsive is starting to flag (Murray, Aloni, et al., 2009).

Ensuring Commitment Is Not Derailed

No matter how responsive Gayle is in general, she will also find herself in situations where Ron needs something from her that she is not inclined to provide. Such situations might peak at moments when Ron's desire to try a new wine interferes with her enjoying her beer at day's end. In such situations, people's store of procedural knowledge also contains a back-up rule for motivating people to do things that they just do not want to do for their partner (Murray, Holmes, et al., 2009). After all, commitment inevitably imposes undesirable costs or restrictions on one's own goal pursuits. Married to someone who prefers subtitles to second downs, Gayle will miss games or plays she was just dying to see. Because Ron cannot help but thwart some of Gayle's independent goal pursuits, the mind needs a mechanism in place to motivate Gayle to be responsive to Ron when petty annoyances and frustrations threaten to derail her commitment (Murray,

Holmes, et al., 2009). By making Ron more valuable to her precisely when he thwarts her goals, this if–then rule gives Gayle renewed motivation to be responsive, keeping her commitment in check with Ron's willingness to put his outcomes in her hands. Imagine that tripping over Ron's shoes on the kitchen floor actually makes Gayle think about the last time he made her laugh. If it did, she might willingly listen to his complaints about his job even as she applies ice to her shoe-assailed ankle. Her mind compensates for the experienced costs of coordinating their lives by underlining his virtues.

Efficient, but Flexible, Goal Implementation

Because partners are interdependent in multiple respects, the complex demands of social coordination could foreclose other goal pursuits (Enfield & Levinson, 2006). Our model of the interdependent mind also attributes the if–then rules with the power to efficiently but flexibly regulate affect, cognition, and behavior (Bargh, 2007; Dijksterhuis & Nordgren, 2006).

By *efficient*, we mean that the if–then rules are implicit or unconscious features of people's general working knowledge of relationships (Baldwin, 1992). Because the mind cannot afford the luxury of thinking through every decision it needs to make, social cognition scholars assume that ongoing and complex problems underlying social life have automatic and effortless solutions (Bargh, 2007; Bargh & Ferguson, 2000; Bargh & Williams, 2006; Dijksterhuis, Chartrand, & Aarts, 2007; Dijksterhuis & Nordgren, 2006). The "efficiency" criterion stipulates that the if–then rules that comprise the interdependent mind are implicit procedural features of relationship representations (Baldwin, 1992; Holmes & Murray, 2007; Murray, Aloni, et al., 2009; Murray, Derrick, Leder, & Holmes, 2008; Murray, Holmes, et al., 2009; Tooby & Cosmides, 1996). By *implicit*, we mean that these rules can operate without conscious mediation (Bargh, 2007; Dijksterhuis et al., 2007). Situations that activate the "if" elicit the propensity to engage in the "then" without any conscious intent, thereby freeing needed self-regulatory resources for other pursuits (Finkel et al., 2006).

Evidence for such nonconscious mediation of social behavior is now ubiquitous (see Bargh, 2007, for a review). Activating the construct of politeness without awareness increases patience (Bargh, Chen, & Burrows, 1995); priming the stereotype of African Americans increases aggressiveness (Bargh et al., 1995); priming the expectations a beloved mother holds elicits greater achievement strivings (Fitzsimons & Bargh, 2003); and priming Einstein (an imposing exemplar) eclipses intellectual performance (Dijksterhuis & van Knippenberg, 1998).[2] Such automatic behavior facilitates the complex and ongoing task of social coordination. Indeed, the mind automatically elicits the behavioral propensity likely to produce social interactions that facilitate one's goals. The desire to affiliate automatically increases the tendency to gain interpersonal favor by mimicking the expressions and gestures of others (Lakin & Chartrand, 2003). Research examining intergroup relations further reveals striking evidence of the automatic tuning of one's behavior to match the goals of others. For instance, priming stereotypes activates behavioral goals that facilitate one's desired interactions with stereotyped group members (Cesario, Plaks, & Higgins, 2006; Gunz, Sahdra, Holmes, Fitzsimons, & Kunda, 2006; Sinclair, Huntsinger, Skorinko, & Hardin, 2005). Priming the stereotype of being advanced in age slows walking speed for those people who anticipate harmonious interactions with the elderly; it speeds the pace (and departure) of people who anticipate more disagreeable interactions (Cesario et al., 2006).

By *flexible*, we mean that the power of these rules to compel overt behavior should also shift with motivation and opportunity to correct or override the rules (Olson & Fazio, 2008). Flexibility implies that an automatic urge to think, feel, or behave in a particular way is less likely to translate into correspondent action if people are motivated *and* able to correct it (Murray, Aloni, et al., 2009; Murray, Derrick, et al., 2008; Murray, Holmes, et al., 2009). Consistent with this logic, models of attitudes, impression formation, and stereotyping assume that such automatic propensities control behavior unless people have the motivation, opportunity, and capacity to override them (Fazio & Towles-Schwen, 1999; Fiske & Neuberg, 1990; Gilbert & Malone, 1995; Kunda & Spencer, 2003; Olson & Fazio, 2008; Wilson, Lindsey, & Schooler, 2000). In fact, the behavioral effects of automatically activated goals can be overridden by situational cues that suggest pursuing such goals might preempt more important goal pursuits (Aarts, Custers, & Holland, 2007; Macrae & Johnston, 1998). For instance, people primed with helpfulness pick up clean pens for a clumsy colleague. However, they leave ink-stained pens at her feet because the now more pressing goal of staying clean trumps the goal to help (Macrae & Johnston, 1998). Similarly, people who are generally motivated to be egalitarian avoid applying stereotypes that are activated unconsciously when these distasteful thoughts enter their minds. People who experience no such goal conflict make no such effort (Kunda & Spencer, 2003).

Applying this flexibility criterion to relationships means that partners can be motivated to correct or overturn "in-the-moment" impulses that conflict with broader goal pursuits. As we see in Chapter 2, trust in the partner's responsiveness supplies the motivation to correct if–then rules that provide a bad "fit" to broader goal pursuits. Trust supplies this motivation because being more trusting generally allows people to connect (i.e., approach), and being less trusting generally motivates people to self-protect (i.e., avoid). Now imagine a highly trusting Gayle in a situation where her automatic impulse is to self-protect. Perhaps Ron transgressed and refused to take their kids to the doctor so she could meet an important client. Her impulse to retaliate for his selfishness (by shouting at him or slamming a door) isn't likely to feel "right" because such an impulse compromises her general desire to be close. Not comfortable with her impulses, she might then instead decide to give Ron another chance. However, a less trusting Gayle would have no reason to correct her automatic impulse to distance herself from him because such an inclination provides a good or comfortable fit to her chronic goals.

Suitability for the Relationship Circumstance

Relationships are different. Some are just riskier than others. Therefore, our model of the interdependent mind assumes that the if–then rules that partners make a habit come to match the character of the risks encountered in a specific relationship. Not all couples are the same, obviously. Partners differ in compatibility, and as a result, the type and degree of conflict partners face at each level of interdependence varies across relationships. Some relationships are riskier than others because some partners face more serious and more frequent conflicts of interest at the level of life tasks. Coordination might be difficult because there are too many chores to do with too little time. Some relationships are riskier than others because partners' preferences and personal goals are less compatible. Deciding what to do together simply will be harder for partners whose basic interests and inclinations take them in different directions. It's hard for a coach potato to keep an exercise addict happy. Some relationships are riskier than others because partners' goals for the relationship are harder to reconcile. Someone who wants a constant companion is going to struggle feeling close enough to someone who prefers to flit and flutter from friend to friend. To coordinate mutually responsive interaction patterns, the structure of the interdependent mind also adjusts to these vast differences in partner compatibility, and thus to the level of risk encountered in a given relationship. In relationships, as in shoes, one size does not fit all.

The relationship specificity of risk introduces the final consideration: Some of the if–then rules are more useful (and more used) for some couples than others. Therefore, the ease with which particular if–then rules can be activated needs to shift to match the character of the risks in a specific relationship (Wood & Neal, 2007).[3] As we see in Chapter 2, the interpersonal mind does something different to coordinate responsiveness when partners face or perceive many high-risk situations than it needs to do to coordinate responsiveness when partners face many low-risk situations. Therefore, partners in a high-risk relationship are likely to develop different if–then rule habits than partners in a low-risk relationship. In fact, we'll argue that the capacity to develop idiosyncratic habits is what distinguishes patterns of responsiveness in one relationship from another. In some relationships, partners rely on each other primarily for the exchange of small favors; in others, they largely restrict interaction to coordinating instrumental roles like caregiver and provider; in still others, they rely on each other for emotional support and negotiate shared identities. Our model assumes that relationships develop such different "personalities" in how responsiveness is expressed because if–then rules adapt themselves over time to match the risks common to a particular relationship. Our model also assumes that such "personalities" control how satisfying the relationship becomes because the ways in which partners are responsive (and not responsive) to each other's needs control the rewards (and costs) of interaction.

Summary

Figure 1.1 summarizes the five elements underlying effective motivation-management. These considerations all derive from the coordination problem posed by negotiating conflicts of interest situations. Such situations offer the twin temptations of self-interest (i.e., selfishness and self-protection). To promote mutually responsive interaction in the face of such self-interested concerns, the interdependent mind has (1) if–then rules for telling Gayle when to trust Ron; (2) if–then rules for giving direction to Gayle's actions; (3) if–then rules for equalizing commitment by coordinating Gayle's expression of trust with Ron's expressions of commitment; (4) the capacity to run without power (i.e., efficiently) most of the time (i.e., flexibly); and (5) the capacity to match the if–then rules it relies on to suit the risks characteristic to a given relationship circumstance.

In this way, the rules that come to energize or "run" this smart unconscious shape the developing "personality" of the relationship by controlling what types of responsive behaviors partners do (and do not) exchange as they coordinate their interactions. In attributing such functionality to an interdependent mind, we should also clarify what we do not mean. We are not proposing the existence of a relationship homunculus. We do not think there is a little person or "mini-me" inside Gayle's head telling

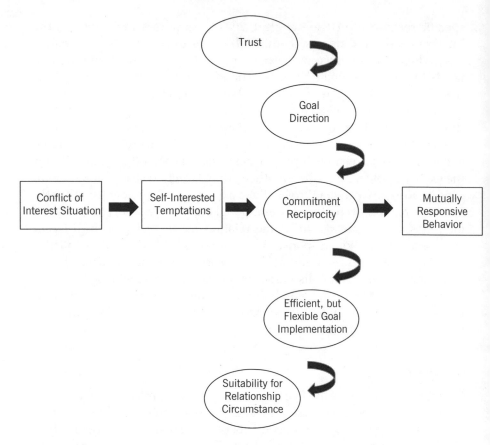

FIGURE 1.1. The basic requirements for effective motivation-management.

when to feel, what to think, and how to behave (Wegner, 2002). We use the term "interdependent mind" in the sense that philosophers, social scientists, and cognitive scientists use the term the "social mind" (Bargh, 2007; Dennett, 1991; Tetlock, 2002; Tomasello, Carpenter, Call, Behne, & Moll, 2005). Such scholars argue that the mind evolved certain capacities to foster the interpersonal connections required for basic physical survival. One such capacity is consciousness and the related capacity to distinguish one's own goals from the goals of others (Dunbar & Shultz, 2007; Hare, 2007; Herrmann, Call, Hernandez-Lloreda, Hare, & Tomasello, 2007). We believe that the if–then rules comprising the interdependent mind similarly developed to ease the difficulties inherent in maintaining a stable adult romantic relationship. These rules collectively function as a "smart relationship unconscious" that motivates mutually responsive behavior

(Bargh & Morsella, 2008; Dijksterhuis & Nordgren, 2006). Second, in arguing that the interdependent mind eases partner interactions, we are not about to argue that it also makes every relationship the picture of domestic bliss. In later chapters, we instead describe how applying the if–then rules in certain circumstances might make some relationships the picture of domestic misery.

BOOK OVERVIEW: IN DETAIL

Before we proceed to the next chapter, we introduce a few more points of housekeeping about organization. Chapter 2 formalizes our model of the interdependent mind. In this chapter, we describe how the if–then rules within the interdependent mind control trust (i.e., if–then vigilance rules), shape interpersonal goals (i.e., if–then goal-orientation rules), and direct behavior (i.e., if–then implementation rules). We then describe how the particular if–then rules the interdependent mind relies on most heavily create the relationship's "personality" by controlling how responsiveness is expressed. In Chapters 3 through 8, we break the model of the interdependent mind down into its component elements.

Chapters 3 and 4 introduce trust and commitment, the psychological foundation for coordinated and mutually responsive behavior. In these chapters, we elaborate on what it means to be trusting and what it means to be committed. Chapter 3 defines the experience of trust in the partner by outlining the if–then rules that gauge and maintain this sentiment. The if–then rules for vigilance link signs of one's value to the partner (i.e., "if") to the contingent response to trust or distrust (i.e., "then"). The if–then rules for trust insurance link any concerns about the partner's trustworthiness (i.e., "if") to behavioral efforts to ensure that one's trust is not misplaced (i.e., "then"). Chapter 4 defines the experience of commitment to the partner by outlining the if–then implementation rules that gauge and maintain this sentiment. The if–then rules for commitment link signs of one's greater (or lesser) value to the partner (i.e., "if" trust) to the contingent response to increase (or decrease) connection to the partner (i.e., "then"). The if–then rules for commitment insurance link the costs that come from such connection (i.e., "if") to the contingent response to value the partner more (i.e., "then").

Chapters 5 through 8 describe how the if–then rules operate in concert in specific conflicts of interest to extract as much responsiveness as the situation allows. Chapter 5 introduces the idea that situations afford the opportunity to pursue different interpersonal goals. Imagine that Ron and Gayle both face busy weeks at work but someone needs to forego work to stay at home to nurse their toddler through his flu. The goal to connect (i.e., approach) or self-protect (i.e., avoid) each pursues in this situation depends entirely on the situation's perceived risks. Is sacrificing one's own work an opportunity to demonstrate caring for the partner or an invitation to the partner's exploitation? Chapter 5 both describes the process of risk appraisal and details how subjective perceptions of risk control the interpersonal goals that people pursue in specific situations. In this context, we detail if–then goal-orientation rules that link expectations of acceptance (i.e., low risk) and expectations of rejection (i.e., high risk) to the goals to connect and self-protect, respectively.

Chapters 6 and 7 reveal how the pursuit of specific interpersonal goals activates if–then implementation rules in memory that serve connectedness and self-protection goals, respectively, by eliciting goal-congruent behavior. Chapter 6 describes how the mind operates in situations that better afford the pursuit of connectedness goals. It explains how the goal to connect activates complementary if–then rules that motivate Gayle to depend more on Ron (the complementary commitment rule) and to justify any costs she incurs in doing so (the complementary commitment-insurance rule). Chapter 7 describes how the mind operates in situations that better afford the pursuit of self-protection goals. It shows how the goal to self-protect activates complementary if–then rules that motivate Ron to depend less on Gayle (the complementary commitment rule) while eliciting her greater dependence on him (the complementary trust-insurance rule). By wedding the goals in the situation to the propensity to feel, think, and behave in goal-congruent ways, the mind effectively reaps as much responsive (and as little nonresponsive) behavior as the situation affords.

Chapter 8 describes how this process of goal-congruent rule activation and expression creates the relationship's "personality." Relationships differ in risk. First, they differ in objective risk. Some partners face conflicts of interest that are easy to solve because their preferences are largely compatible; some partners face conflicts of interest that are difficult to solve because their preferences are largely incompatible. Second, they differ in subjective risk. Some partners simply trust that their conflicts are remediable, whereas other partners do not. Chapter 8 delineates how trust and the risks inherent to the relationship elicit its "personality" by controlling how often specific if–then rules get activated in memory and expressed in behavior. Such if–then rule habits control whether responsiveness resides in the exchange of small favors; the coordination of complementary roles;

the communal provision of support; or the mutual validation and negotiation of shared personal goals and identities.

In Chapters 9 through 12, we put the interpersonal mind back together again and develop applications of the model. Chapter 9 describes how the interpersonal mind works to coordinate trust and commitment during the earliest phases of a relationship's development. Chapter 10 describes how the interdependent mind adapts to meet the unique challenges faced when interdependence increases and conflicts of interest mount, such as happens with the birth of a first child. Chapter 11 tackles the problem of why particular dispositions—such as attachment style, neuroticism, or self-esteem—matter in relationships, whereas other dispositions do not. It also specifies how contextual factors, such as economic stress, change how the interpersonal mind coordinates mutuality in responsiveness. Chapter 12 spells out how the model might be applied to preempt relationship distress and promote relationship happiness. In this chapter, we use our model to offer a practical guide for relationship happiness.

In the next chapter, we formalize our motivation-management model of mutual responsiveness into a theory of the interdependent mind's structure—what essentially functions as a "smart unconscious" for relationships.

NOTES

1. We use the term *reciprocity in commitment* to capture equality in partners' experience of commitment across time and situations within the relationship. As a point to carry forward, it's important to note that reciprocity does not require equal expressions of commitment in a specific situation within the relationship. It does require that expressions of commitment generally balance out across partners over successive interactions (Holmes, 1981; Reis et al., 2004).
2. Priming refers to the process by which exposure to a particular stimulus affects responses to a subsequent stimulus without conscious mediation (Franzoi, 2009).
3. These risks may be either objective or perceived. Namely, some couples face objectively more difficult conflicts of interest (e.g., managing too little money vs. deciding how to spend a surplus of money). Other couples might perceive even easy-to-manage conflicts as intractable because being less trusting sensitizes them to the possibility of rejection (Holmes & Rempel, 1989). We return to this in Chapter 2 and explore these issues in depth in Chapter 5.

CHAPTER 2

Procedural Rules for Responsiveness

The Motivation-Management Model

> Consider the plight of [Ron and Gayle]. . . . When their
> eyes first met, the din of the party seemed to recede and
> the room to light up for the two of them with a glow of
> promise. After a few months of Friday and Saturday
> nights together, they moved in with each other. Within
> a year, marriage felt right for both of them.
>   But marriage turned out to be a good deal more
> than they had bargained for. As singles living together,
> they'd conducted their lives separately. When they
> dined together, it was usually in restaurants. Now
> someone had to shop and cook, clear the table and
> do the dishes. The garbage had to be taken out every
> night. Piles of bills mounted. There was the question
> of who got to sleep through the night and who was on
> call when their new baby's colic kicked up at 2 A.M. It
> became more and more difficult to find time for sex.
> They were both too tired anyway. . . .
> —MICHAEL VINCENT MILLER (2008)

In an article for *O, The Oprah Magazine*, Michael Vincent Miller recounted the experiences of a couple whose personal story tells a familiar tale. Like most couples, Ron and Gayle (not their real names) discovered that marriage was not exactly what they expected (Holmes & Rempel, 1989). Having committed to each other in the haze of infatuation, they later found themselves trapped in interdependence dilemmas that were anything but intoxicating. Who would take out the garbage? Who would shop? Who would sacrifice sleep? What needs to happen in relationships once infatuation accedes to reality? What psychological mechanisms keep relationships stable once coordinating responsibilities for life tasks, merging personalities, and negotiating compatible relationship goals take center

24

stage? In this chapter, we describe how the interdependent mind coordinates fluid and responsive partner interactions. We present a snapshot view of our model here. We expand on its basic premises in subsequent chapters.

Our model begins with the assumption we introduced in Chapter 1: Mutuality in responsiveness promotes stable relationship bonds (Reis et al., 2004). Responsiveness stabilizes relationships because having one's needs met makes interactions with the partner more rewarding (Kelley & Thibaut, 1978). We use the term *responsive* to refer to one partner's willingness to accommodate his or her own choices and goals to further the other partner's choices and goals. For instance, Gayle behaves responsively when she stops writing a legal brief to listen to Ron's complaints about his day. Ron behaves in a mutually responsive way when he takes care of their infant daughter in the wee hours of the morning so Gayle can get needed sleep in advance of a court date. We use the term *mutually responsive* to refer to the communal norm of extemporaneous give-and-take in which Ron and Gayle take care of each other's needs over the longer term in their relationship (Clark & Mills, 1993; Holmes, 1981; Kelley et al., 2003). This definition of mutuality precludes "tit-for-tat" exchanges of one consideration traded for another in a specific situation. Indeed, concerns with short-term reciprocity typically foster relationship distress (Grote & Clark, 2001; Holmes, 1981). Instead, this definition of mutuality involves reciprocity in what each partner seeks and provides to the other across time and situations. With this definition, Ron and Gayle's marriage could be mutually responsive if each generally met the other's instrumental expectations to fulfill agreed-upon roles of caregiver and provider. It could also be mutually responsive if they generally traded off onerous household tasks and met the other's expectations for socioemotional support. Their marriage might end up more satisfying in the latter than former case (as we will see), but it would fit our definition of a mutually responsive relationship in both cases.

THE VALUE OF PERSPECTIVE TAKING

The requisite cognitive capacity for behaving in a mutually responsive way is simple, yet remarkably sophisticated. People must be able to step outside themselves. Ron must recognize that Gayle has goals distinct from his own, and Gayle must recognize that Ron has goals distinct from her own (Kelley, 1979). This capacity to take perspective allows Ron to accommodate his personal actions to better Gayle's goals. But it also makes such social coordination risky. The knowledge that Gayle has goals distinct from his allows Ron to anticipate how her divergent personal interests might tempt her not to be responsive to him (Kelley, 1979).

Our model of the structure of the interdependent mind presupposes the basic capacity to consider another's perspective (no matter how faulty the capacity to gauge another's mind sometimes may be). Cognitive and developmental scholars use the term *mind perception* to refer to the capacity to simulate the plans and goals of another. Behaving responsively requires people to have a means of perspective taking, because coordinated social action requires knowledge of how one's goals intersect with the goals of another: Help is appreciated when needed, sacrifice is safe when reciprocated, competition is a reasoned response to selfishness, and fleeing is prudent when others are combative. For this reason, the capacity to form mental models or representations of the self in relation to others became an adaptive necessity. Indeed, many cognitive and developmental scholars contend that the capacity for insight into another's goals distinguishes humans from other animals (Dunbar & Shultz, 2007; Enfield & Levinson, 2006; Hare, 2007; Herrmann et al., 2007; Tomasello et al., 2005). The existence of mirror neurons provides a telling illustration of the adaptive significance of the capacity to take another's perspective. The neurons that fire when observing specific actions in others are the very neurons that fire when engaging in that action oneself (Carr, Iacoboni, Dubeau, Mazziotta, & Lenzi, 2003; Knoblich & Sebanz, 2006).

Functional analyses of attachment (Mikulincer & Shaver, 2003), self-esteem (Leary & Baumeister, 2000), and social exchange (Tooby & Cosmides, 1996) similarly assume that the social mind evolved to solve the adaptive problems inherent in meshing one's own goals with those of others. Consider two examples of these dynamics. Early in development, the attachment system fosters complementary goals between infants and caregivers through a primitive mental architecture that links infants' biological needs to reflexive behavioral patterns (e.g., rooting, grasping) that elicit behavior from caregivers that satisfies these needs (Ainsworth, Belhar, Waters, & Wall, 1978). As development progresses, mental models of the self and others that assess and inform how best to relate one's own goals to the anticipated goals of others gradually replace such reflexive responses (Mikulincer & Shaver, 2003). In later periods of social life, the "sociometer" or self-esteem system ensures others will be willing to meet one's physical and psychological needs through a mental architecture that links self-assessed value to the goals of others. Within this system, drops in self-esteem, such as those posed by failure, signal the likelihood of others' impending rejection and motivate compensatory behaviors to develop more accepting social ties (Leary & Baumeister, 2000).

The interpersonal mind we envision co-opts this adaptive capacity to simulate others' orientation toward one's own goals (Thibaut & Kelley, 1959). In adult romantic relationships, trust is the reification of this adaptive capacity to take another's perspective. Trust is a meta-perspective (see Chapter 1). It captures Gayle's assessment of Ron's commitment or long-term orientation toward her (Holmes & Rempel, 1989). Gayle's trust in Ron thus reflects her best guess as to what he might be willing to do for her in any given situation. High levels of trust give her reason to expect his willingness to sacrifice his own interests to meet her needs. Low levels of trust give her reason to expect reasonably little. By allowing Gayle to simulate Ron's orientation toward her, trust functions as the mind's motivational director or coordinator. If the interdependent mind actually contained a homunculus, trust would be this inner voice.

Let us explain (and foreshadow the discussion to come). For patterns of mutual responsiveness to needs to unfold, Ron must curb his temptation to be selfish and Gayle must curb her temptation to self-protect against his exploitation. Put in terms of goal coordination across partners, Ron's expression of caring to Gayle must be met by her openness to accept his caring. In other words, Ron's willingness to meet Gayle's needs (i.e., his expression of commitment) must be met by Gayle's willingness to put her outcomes in his hands (i.e., her expression of commitment). Solving this coordination problem involves motivation management. When the mind effectively manages partner motivations, both partners experience the benefits and pleasures of connection without undue exposure to the costs and pains of rejection. The relationship know-how to elicit such seamless and fluid interactions involves (1) assessing the likelihood of the partner's responsiveness (through trust and the if–then vigilance rules); (2) directing the corresponding goal to connect or to self-protect (through if–then goal orientation rules); (3) coordinating partners' expressions of commitment (through if–then goal implementation rules); (4) being quick to act (i.e., efficient), but amenable to change (i.e., flexible); and (5) matching the if–then rules to the nature of the risks partners in a particular relationship routinely confront (i.e., develop a "relationship personality"). As we see next, trust considerations infuse each of the four elements involved in coordinating mutually responsive interactions (Murray & Holmes, 2009).

A MOTIVATION-MANAGEMENT THEORY OF MUTUAL RESPONSIVENESS

How exactly does the interpersonal mind manage partner motivations to produce fluid and mutually responsive interaction patterns? Figure 2.1

presents our model of mind in snapshot form (Murray & Holmes, 2009).
Table 2.1 summarizes the if–then rules that underlie its operation. This
table cross-lists the if–then rules we attribute to the interpersonal mind
by function (i.e., vigilance, goal orientation, goal implementation) and
content (e.g., "if inferior to partner, then distrust"). We describe only the
general tenets of the model in this chapter. We fully articulate its theoretical and empirical basis in subsequent chapters.

A quick glance at Figure 2.1 reveals that the model looks reasonably
complex on the surface. So let's break it down. First, we'll take a macroscopic view. We look to the beginning (trust) and to the end (commitment)
of the model and explain why: (1) the interpersonal mind uses trust and
commitment to motivate mutual responsiveness and (2) the interdepen-

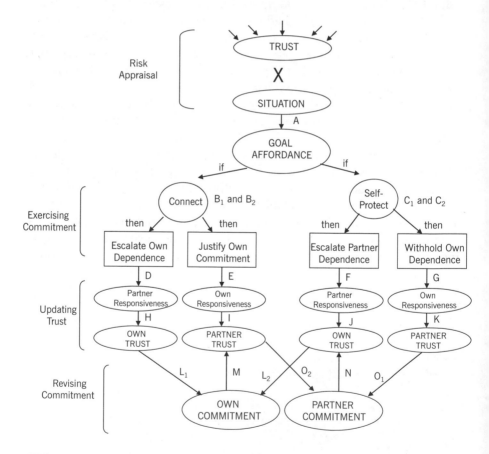

FIGURE 2.1. A motivation-management model of mutual responsiveness. From
Murray and Holmes (2009). Copyright 2009 by the American Psychological Association. Reprinted by permission.

TABLE 2.1. Procedural Rules for Motivation Management

Function	Content
Vigilance	If partner sacrifices, then trust.
	If partner values traits, then trust.
	If equal in worth to partner, then trust.
	If better than alternatives, then trust.
	If barriers, then trust.
Goal orientation	If partner accepting, then connect.
	If partner rejecting, then self-protect.
Goal implementation	If connect goal, then escalate own dependence.
	If connect goal, then justify own commitment.
	If self-protect goal, then escalate partner dependence.
	If self-protect goal, then withhold own dependence.

dent mind focuses on issues of trust and perspective taking to coordinate partners' expressions of commitment. Next, we take a microscopic view of the model. We look to its components to explain how the interdependent mind utilizes the if–then vigilance, goal orientation, and goal implementation rules to maximize responsiveness (and minimize nonresponsiveness) within conflicts of interest. Finally, we explain how such responsive (and nonresponsive) behaviors reinforce trust and commitment in ways that elicit the different types of mutuality in responsiveness. Such patterns of responsiveness define the relationship's "personality."

The Macroscopic View

Let's start with trust and commitment. Trust is the interdependent mind's monitor of the strength of the motivation to avoid rejection. Trust essentially tells partners when to risk approaching each other. It is Gayle's statement about Ron's anticipated willingness to meet her needs (Holmes & Rempel, 1989). Because Gayle cannot go inside Ron's head and directly access his commitment, she relies on five if–then rules to gauge the limits of his trustworthiness (indicated by the arrows descending into trust in Figure 2.1).

The if–then rules for controlling vigilance tell Gayle when it is safe to put her outcomes in Ron's hands and when she would be better off being wary. They essentially tell her when to trust Ron (and when not to trust him). The five vigilance rules detailed in Chapter 3 share a point of commonality. They all treat Gayle's self-assessed value, as reflected in her being more or less replaceable to Ron, as a marker of his motivation to be more or less responsive to her needs (Tooby & Cosmides, 1996). These if–then rules warn Gayle that Ron is not likely to be responsive if the grass on the other side of the fence looks greener to him. These rules caution that Gayle must be difficult enough for Ron to replace that he is motivated to sacrifice on her behalf. Therefore, the if–then rules for controlling vigilance dictate the conditions that reveal Gayle's likely value to Ron. Specifically, these vigilance rules let Gayle know that Ron is likely to find her harder to replace when Ron is: (1) willing to sacrifice self-interest on her behalf; (2) valuing of her personal qualities, such as her warmth and intelligence; (3) not superior in worth to her; (4) unlikely to be poached by other women; or (5) fettered to the relationship largely by constraints and obligation, such as their toddler son and infant daughter. Such signals strengthen trust. The opposite cues (i.e., not willing to sacrifice, not valuing of her personal qualities, superior in worth, likely to be poached, and free from constraint) suggest she could be easily replaced and threaten her trust in Ron. In this way, the vigilance rules link Gayle's detection of a specific trigger to the contingent response to trust or distrust Ron (Murray & Holmes, 2008, 2009; Murray, Leder, et al., 2009).

Commitment is the interdependent mind's monitor of the strength of one's motivation to seek connection. Commitment essentially tells partners how far to go in approaching each other. Commitment is a statement about one's own long-term orientation toward the future of the relationship and the partner. The more committed Gayle is to Ron, the more important he and the marriage are to her. Gayle's level of commitment captures her own willingness to draw closer to Ron and deeper into her relationship by both asking more of Ron and by providing more to him (Rusbult & Van Lange, 2003). For instance, Gayle expresses her high level of commitment through her reliance on Ron as a source of social support and the pleasure she takes in providing the same support to Ron (Collins & Feeney, 2004). In this way, her commitment "signals" Ron's value to her. As we introduced in Chapter 1, mutually responsive interactions are unlikely to develop when one partner in the relationship is more committed than the other partner (Sprecher et al., 2006; Waller, 1938). Reciprocity in commitment puts partners on an equal playing field where each partner depends on the other and each partner is similarly motivated to be responsive to the other partner's needs.

Trust as a Precondition for Commitment

The problem the interdependent mind faces in equalizing partner commitment is that Gayle cannot discern the true contents of Ron's mind.

Nor can Ron discern the true contents of her mind. Therefore, the interpersonal mind needs trusting sentiments—Gayle's meta-perspective on Ron's commitment—as an intermediary that matches Gayle's willingness to put her outcomes in Ron's hands (i.e., her expression of commitment) to Ron's reciprocal willingness to commit and meet her needs when it is costly to him (i.e., his reciprocal expression of commitment).

In making trust this intermediary, the interpersonal mind generally only allows Gayle to feel truly committed to Ron when she trusts in his commitment to her (Murray, Holmes, & Collins, 2006). This "trust comes first" aspect of our model makes it unique from prior models of interdependence (Kelley, 1979; Rusbult & Van Lange, 2003). It also makes it distinct from other models positing independent brain and behavior systems for approaching pleasure and for avoiding pain (see Elliot, 2008, for a review). In our model, trust is a precondition for commitment. In relationships, we suspect there is a strong motivational hierarchy. In this hierarchy, avoidance generally takes priority over approach. Avoiding rejection comes before seeking connection. That is, Gayle cannot risk approaching Ron for connection until it is safe (Murray, Holmes, & Griffin, 2000).

Why would this be the case? "Bad" experiences elicit greater pain than "good" ones elicit pleasure (Baumeister, Bratslavsky, Finkenauer, & Vohs, 2001). In relationships, this hedonic asymmetry suggests that the possibility of rejection must be avoided before the opportunity for connection can be approached. In making avoidance the gatekeeper of approach, we echo an assumption basic to attachment theory: A sense of safety or "felt security" in the world must come before infants can afford to risk exploration (Bowlby, 1969). The motivational imperative to satisfy avoidance before approach motivations has major implications for relationships. Namely, it suggests that an inability to get beyond the issue of trust sets the stage for a qualitatively different experience of commitment. It also reveals a fascinating paradox. Although people might believe they are willful agents in their relationships, the contingent nature of commitment limits the power of one's will to decide. If commitment emerges from experience with the partner rather than compelling it, the experience of consciously deciding to commit to a partner might be something of an illusion (Wegner, 2002). We return to these themes in later chapters.

The Microscopic View

So let's look now at the guts of the model: How the interdependent mind automatically coordinates solicitations and expressions of responsiveness when a conflict of interest develops. These mixed-motive situations arise when partners negotiate responsibilities for life tasks, when they attempt to merge divergent personal preferences and personality, and when partners try to forge shared goals for their relationship. For instance, at the level of life tasks, Ron and Gayle must manage two young children while they each pursue their own legal careers. Given that both would rather catch up on work than cook or clean once the children are asleep, they could face frequent conflicts of interest over the allocation of household responsibilities.

Situations such as these pose an acute "conflict," or quandary, because they offer both the potential for gain and the potential for loss in putting one's outcomes in the partner's hands. These situations put people in an acute approach–avoidance conflict. The benefits that might be gained motivate people to seek connection (i.e., approach)—and put their outcomes in their partner's hands. The costs that might be incurred motivate people to self-protect (i.e., avoid)—and keep their outcomes within their own hands. Imagine that Gayle wants to ask Ron to take her turn as the 3 A.M. chauffeur. In such a situation, Gayle stands to benefit from Ron's sacrifice by getting the sleep she needs to prepare for her court appearance the next morning. She also stands to gain the benefits that come from feeling loved. She stands to lose both sleep and her confidence in his caring if Ron decides to be selfish and sleep rather than drive. Because Ron might succumb to self-interest, Gayle has the temptation to drive herself—thereby losing the sleep she needed, but sparing herself the hurt of being rejected—or the cost of being in debt.

In short, conflicts of interest such as this one involve mixed motives. They offer the gains of cooperative exchange that come from setting aside self-interest. Namely, they offer the gains that come from Ron's willingness to resist the selfish inclination to consider only his own outcomes and the gains that come from Gayle's willingness to set aside the urge to self-protect against being exploited by Ron. These situations also offer the potential losses that come from either partner's failure to set aside such self-interested concerns. Because predicting a partner's behavior involves uncertainty, mixed-motive situations such as the chauffeur dilemma put the goal of seeking connection, and the substantial gains that cooperation offers, in conflict with the goal of protecting oneself against rejection, and the prohibitive losses that exploitation and nonresponsiveness impose (Baumeister & Leary, 1995; Murray, Holmes, & Collins, 2006). The approach–avoid structure of this situation leaves Gayle caught—stuck between the goal of connecting and the goal of protecting herself against rejection.

From Risk Appraisal to Interpersonal Goals

Indecision is no recipe for action. Purposeful and directed action requires the resolution of acute goal conflicts (Cacioppo et al., 1999). The interdependent mind's first task in such situations is resolving the conflict Gayle experiences between her goal to connect to Ron and her goal to self-protect against his rejection. Resolving this quandary involves disambiguating Ron's motives in a way that gives Gayle a clear direction for action. Trust and the if–then vigilance rules that control vigilance and the if–then rules that control goal orientation are all central to this process.

So how does the interpersonal mind disambiguate the partner's motives? Classic models of social perception in social psychology rely on a person by situation logic (Griffin & Ross, 1991; Monson, Hesley, & Chernick, 1982). The interpersonal mind appraises risk in a similar fashion. Namely, the appraisal of risk is a joint function of what more or less trusting expectations predispose the perceiver to see and the objective situation itself (Holmes & Rempel, 1989; Murray, Holmes, & Collins, 2006). This person by situation logic further assumes that trust plays a larger role in shaping the perception of risk and the interpersonal goal pursued when the gains and costs afforded by the situation are more ambiguous than when they are more clear cut.

As we detail in Chapter 5, situations differ in the clarity of the gains and costs they pose because situations differ in their objective structure. Risk varies with situation features that mark the likelihood of experiencing gains or costs as a consequence of putting one's outcomes in the partner's hands. For instance, situations differ in risk because they differ in content. Coordinating a personality conflict in conscientiousness generally has larger and more far-reaching personal costs and benefits than resolving a conflict over washing the dishes. So negotiating the personality conflict poses greater risk. Ron might willingly take Gayle's turn at the dishes one night, but he's probably much less willing to give up on his lifelong need to be on time (indeed, early) just because Gayle likes to do things at the last minute. Situations also differ because they differ in structure. Opposite interests, such as those that arise when Gayle wants Ron to 3 A.M. chauffeur and Ron wants to sleep, make a high level of risk absolutely clear because Gayle knows that her gain is Ron's concrete loss. Nontransparent interests, such as those that arise when Ron won't tell Gayle why he is upset, make such risks more unknown because Gayle cannot be certain exactly what Ron wants out of the situation, making it difficult to gauge what she should do to elicit the best outcome (Holmes, 2002).

As these examples illustrate, some situations clearly offer more benefits than costs because of their features. For Gayle, asking Ron to trade chauffeur duties on a night when he's feeling relaxed because he has the next morning off work is objectively low in risk. In this situation, Ron has little incentive to be selfish. Other situations clearly offer more costs than benefits. Asking Ron to sacrifice a promotion to better Gayle's career is objectively high in risk. In this situation, Ron has strong incentive to be selfish. The interdependent mind we propose can detect these situational differences and it adaptively orients one's interpersonal goals in response to these clear situation features. In particular, situations that clearly offer more to gain than lose (i.e., low risk) strengthen the complementary goal of seeking connection. By contrast, situations that clearly offer more to lose than gain (i.e., high risk) strengthen the goal of self-protection.

When Trust Steps In to Disambiguate Risk. Few of the situations that partners confront are likely to be so clear. Therefore, trust and the if–then rules for vigilance step in as a barometer of risk for the approach–avoid conflicts that fall within the ambiguous range of the risk spectrum. In ambiguous situations, incidental cues to trust in a specific situation and chronic levels of trust in a partner's responsiveness together function as a heuristic guide to risk. How does trust infuse the appraisal of risk? As we detail in Chapter 3, high levels of trust in a partner's responsiveness make the prospect of rejection by the partner less hurtful and esteem threatening and less likely to foretell further costs (Holmes & Rempel, 1989; Murray, Griffin, Rose, & Bellavia, 2003; Murray, Pinkus, et al., 2010).

Why would this be the case? People who generally trust in their partner's responsiveness can afford to see more opportunity for gain than loss in ambiguous conflicts of interest. Being high in trust is akin to having excess money in the bank. People with abundant cash can make frivolous purchases and risky investments without putting an undue strain on their bank balance. Similarly, people who are already banking an abundant reserve supply of their partner's goodwill can better afford to be spendthrifts when it comes to trust. They can afford to risk being hurt because one bad experience puts such a small dent in their responsiveness reserves. Practically speaking, being "flush" with trust means that any one instance of nonresponsiveness hurts a lot less and has a lot less significance for the relationship. Being more trusting, Gayle can easily put any anxieties she might have about disclosing to Ron aside because the gains of having a sympathetic ear to confide her problems outweigh the risk of his criticism. For her, being more trusting strengthens the pull of connectedness goals (relative to the push of self-protection goals) in conflicts of interest because she can afford to take the risk of being hurt.

This is not at all true for people who question their partner's motivations to be responsive to their needs. Being less trusting is akin to having too little money in the bank. For people with few funds, even minor expenditures put a big dent in their existing bank balance. Similarly, being less trusting means that any specific instance of nonresponsiveness hurts more because there is no large reserve store of the partner's responsiveness available to soften or cushion the blow. Because rejection is so painful, people who are less trusting have little choice but to be vigilant to the possibility of rejection in the hopes of avoiding it. As we see in later chapters, Sally is one such distrusting person. Disappointed by Harry on more than one occasion, she can no longer afford to miss the potential for being hurt. She sees the most minor of critical remarks by Harry as a direct attack. Being less trusting, she is vigilant to rejection and sees more opportunity for loss than gain in ambiguous conflicts of interest. Such vigilance then strengthens the push of self-protection goals (relative to the pull of connectedness goals) in conflicts of interest because Sally cannot afford to risk being hurt once again (Murray, Holmes, & Collins, 2006).

So now let's turn to the link between risk appraisal and goal affordance. The relative risks Gayle perceives in putting her outcomes in Ron's hands (or keeping her outcomes out of Ron's hands) then control whether the goal to seek connection or the goal to avoid rejection is more motivating (Path A in Figure 2.1). Gayle's appraisal of risk controls her motivations through two if–then *goal-orientation* rules. The "approach" version of these rules links expectations of partner responsiveness (i.e., low risk) to the activation of the goal to connect. The "avoid" version links expectations of partner nonresponsiveness (i.e., high risk) to activation of the goal to self-protect. For instance, expecting a good-humored Ron to be accepting of her needs (i.e., low risk) activates her goal to approach him and ask him to drive (i.e., connect). Expecting an already overtired and irritable Ron to reject her needs (i.e., high risk) activates her goal to avoid him and simply do the chauffeur duty herself (i.e., self-protect). In this way, the if–then rules for goal orientation link Gayle's expectations for Ron's behavior in a given situation to the activation of her goal to secure or avoid that outcome.

Before proceeding, here's something to keep in mind for future chapters. We've been describing the interdependent mind as a smart relationship unconscious, but in the last few pages we've made the process of risk appraisal seem quite calculated. Indeed, interdependence theories typically describe the appraisal of risk in terms of an active process of inference and attribution (Kelley & Thibaut, 1978). But that does not mean that automatic processes play no role in the appraisal of risk. As we see in Chapter 3, some situations may simply feel safer than others because being in the partner's presence automatically elicits a positive and automatic evaluative response. In these situations, Gayle simply wants to approach Ron regardless of any calculated deliberations she might make. In Gayle's case, Ron has always been so supportive of her anxieties about her weight and appearance that she goes to him for reassurance without even thinking about it. She has a conditioned and positive evaluative association to him in this context that simply compels her to act.

This brings us to a fascinating possibility we explore in later chapters: The unconscious mind might know something about risk that escapes the attention or notice of the conscious mind. We argue that the interpersonal mind actually uses two barometers to signal the safety of approach—one trust barometer that is reasoned (i.e., relatively conscious and reflective) and one trust barometer that is associative (i.e., relatively unconscious and impulsive). As described in this chapter, the conscious or reflective barometer of trust captures a thoughtful assessment of the strength of the partner's commitment—one that comes from applying the if–then rules for vigilance. The unconscious or impulsive barometer of trust (described in Chapter 3) captures automatic evaluative associations to the partner that emerge through a history of being treated well or poorly by one's partner (Murray, Holmes, & Pinkus, 2010). Because these gauges of the partner's commitment are based on different sources of information, the reflective and impulsive barometers of trust sometimes send conflicting messages about the safety of approach. We explore these complications in Chapters 10 and 11. For the rest of this chapter (indeed, the rest of the book), we use the unqualified term "trust" to refer to conscious expectations about the partner's responsiveness (i.e., reflective trust). When we wish to draw a parallel (or contrast) between the conscious and unconscious trust barometers, we do so by referring to the reflective and impulsive trust, respectively.

From Interpersonal Goals to Reciprocity in Commitment

Now let's look at the next phase of the model. Here the interpersonal mind marshals the goal to connect (or self-protect), once activated, into an action plan for promoting reciprocity in commitment. It does so through if–then implementation rules for matching commitment to trust, ensuring trust is not misplaced, and ensuring commitment is not derailed. Let's take this step by step, beginning with the activation of the goal to connect or self-protect.

Implementation rules involve an association between a goal (i.e., "if") and a congruent commitment intention (i.e., "then") in memory. We use the term *commitment intention* to refer to both the concrete and symbolic ways in which partners can both put their outcomes in each other's hands and tend to each other's outcomes. As traditionally defined, the experience of commitment comes from the objective state of dependence and the subjective state of attachment (Rusbult, Martz, & Agnew, 1998; Rusbult & Van Lange, 2003). For instance, Ron expresses his commitment to Gayle (through dependence) when he relies on her for her computer prowess. He also expresses his commitment to Gayle (through dependence) when he volunteers to help her bathe the children. He similarly expresses his commitment to Gayle (through attachment) when he feels better in her company (or when he finds a way to make her feel better in his company). Because the interpersonal mind has two major goals to pursue (connect or self-protect), it has two general action plans or strategies at hand for coordinating one partner's commitment intentions with the other partner's commitment intentions.

Action Plan 1 satisfies the goal to connect (i.e., approach) by maximizing the chance for partners to behave responsively in situations perceived to be low in risk (Paths B_1 and B_2 in Figure 2.1). Action Plan 2 satisfies the goal to self-protect (i.e., avoid) by minimizing the chance for partners to behave nonresponsively in situations perceived to be high in risk (Paths C_1 and C_2 in Figure 2.1). Each of these action plans contains two if–then implementation rules, one for matching commitment to trust, and one for ensuring such matching does not go awry. We discuss the action plans for connection (Plan 1) and self-protection (Plan 2) in turn.

Action Plan 1. The action plan for implementing the goal to connect motivates Gayle to put her outcomes in Ron's hands. It also motivates Ron to justify the costs he incurs in being responsive when Gayle takes the risk of putting her outcomes in his hand. The "if connect goal, then escalate own dependence" rule matches Gayle's short-term or state feelings of trust in Ron to willingness to commit in a particular situation. This implementation rule automatically links Gayle's anticipation of gains from putting her outcomes in Ron's hands to the propensity to behave in a way that increases Ron's opportunity to be responsive to her. Namely, anticipating his responsiveness motivates Gayle to increase her commitment to Ron and put her personal outcomes more squarely in his hands (Murray, Bellavia, Rose, & Griffin, 2003). Such expectations might motivate her to disclose secrets, seek his support in coping with a crisis, solicit an onerous favor, reciprocate his disclosure, or let Ron make career decisions for her. In escalating her dependence, Gayle gives Ron more opportunities to prove his responsiveness (which, as we will see, creates a self-perpetuating cycle for the growth of trust).

However, Gayle's heightened dependence on Ron can have unfortunate and unintended costs for him. When Gayle increases her commitment to Ron, he loses some autonomy to pursue his own goals. Gayle also exposes him to more situations in which she can interfere with his goals (whether she intended to or not). The frustrations that result could undermine his commitment and threaten his motivation to be responsive to Gayle (Clark & Grote, 1998). The "if connect goal, then justify own commitment" rule helps keep Ron's commitment in check with Gayle's evident commitment to him. This rule essentially keeps commitment from being sidetracked or derailed by the inevitable autonomy costs that come with interdependence, ensuring reciprocity. This implementation rule automatically links Ron's experience of costs to his compensatory tendency to value Gayle more. Wanting to stay connected effectively makes him value Gayle more when being with her costs him time with friends to be with her or when her attempts to be socially supportive are more clumsy than skilled (Murray, Holmes, et al., 2009).

Action Plan 2. The action plan for implementing the goal to self-protect motivates Gayle to take her outcomes out of Ron's hands until she's taken remedial action to ensure his dependence (i.e., his commitment). The "if self-protect goal, then withhold own dependence" rule matches Gayle's short-term distrust and anticipation of Ron's rejection to her reluctance to commit. That is, anticipating (or experiencing) Ron's rejection automatically motivates Gayle to withdraw her commitment by lessening her practical and psychological dependence on him (Murray, Bellavia, et al., 2003). Such expectations might motivate her to divulge only superficial details of her day or spend more time at work or with her own friends. In so doing, she makes it more difficult for Ron to be nonresponsive because she asks relatively little of him. Feeling less committed in turn restricts her own responsiveness, increasing the likelihood that if she sacrifices self-interest it will be at a level and type commensurate with Ron's willingness to sacrifice (e.g., taking his turn at the dishes over providing a receptive ear). In implementing this rule, Gayle limits her dependence on Ron and thus minimizes his opportunity to be nonresponsive.

Of course, interdependence does not allow Gayle to completely escape her dependence on Ron. Therefore, the action plan for self-protection also motivates Gayle to take remedial action to ensure Ron's future motivation to be responsive. The "if self-protect goal, then escalate *partner* dependence" implementation rule helps ensure Gayle's trust in Ron is not misplaced. It automatically links Gayle's anticipation of Ron's rejection to behavioral propensities that give her more control over him. That is, anticipating costs motivates Gayle to make sure that Ron needs her or "owes" her. Gayle can unilaterally increase Ron's dependence on her by escalating the instrumental benefits Ron gains from the relationship and limiting his freedom to find such benefits elsewhere. For instance, anticipating Ron's rejection might motivate Gayle to make his appointments, cook his favorite meal, or limit his time with friends. In escalating Ron's practical or concrete dependence on her in these ways, Gayle gains control over Ron and thereby limits his power to be selfish because he cannot afford to lose her (Murray, Aloni, et al., 2009). His indebtedness to her acts a kind of glue or barrier that gives him little choice but to be responsive to her. This implementation rule thus ensures Gayle's trust in Ron is not misplaced by allowing Gayle to draw Ron closer to her before she takes the risk of putting her outcomes in his hands.

A quick caveat before we move onto the next phase of the model. The implementation rules provide a general or generic guide to action. By linking specific "if" inputs to contingent "then" responses, these rules essentially "tell" people how to feel, think, and behave in specific contexts. In this book, we argue that the general structure of these rules is invariant across relationships because interdependence poses the same general problems in different relationships and sociocultural contexts. However, the specific translation of these rules might depend heavily on the relationship context. Consider the "if self-protect goal, then escalate partner dependence" rule. Motivating a partner to be responsive to one's needs presents a fundamental adaptive dilemma because personal deficiency (e.g., illness, distress) turns people into costly liabilities when they most need another's support. Making oneself indispensable to the partner solves this "bankers' paradox" (Tooby & Cosmides, 1996). But the most salient and effective means of promoting dependence might depend on the sociocultural context. Imposing barriers to dissolution, such as closer ties to in-laws (Levinger, 1976), might foster loyalty in the arranged marriage between our Indonesian couple, Guntur and Lastri. In Ron and Gayle's more voluntary and egalitarian marriage, Ron's upping the instrumental benefits he provides, from making Gayle's appointments to updating her iPod, might be more effective in fostering her loyalty.

From Responsiveness to Reciprocity in Commitment. By matching commitment to trust, ensuring trust is not misplaced, and ensuring commitment is not derailed, the implementation rules supply the opportunity and motivation needed for behavioral expressions of responsiveness. Paths D through G in Figure 2.1 capture these displays. These if–then implementation rules govern what Gayle is willing to do for Ron, what Gayle needs Ron to do for her, what Ron is willing to do for Gayle, and what Ron needs Gayle to do for him. For instance, the "if connect goal, then escalate own dependence" rule might motivate Gayle to disclose a personal worry to Ron—a behavior that gives him the opportunity to be responsive. The "if connect goal, then justify commitment rule" in turn motivates Ron to listen to Gayle's disclosure even though he'd rather continue reading his paper. These behavioral displays of responsiveness provide the experiential base needed to coordinate commitment across partners. How so?

Trust functions as the crucial intermediary in this coordination process. As we detail in Chapters 6 and 7, witnessing the partner's responsiveness bolsters one's own trust in the partner, in both its unconscious and conscious forms (Paths H and J in Figure 2.1). Greater trust in the partner in turn solidifies one's own commitment and motivation to be responsive (Paths L_1 and L_2). One's own greater responsiveness then reinforces the partner's trust (Path M) and strengthens the partner's commitment (Path O_2). In contrast, experiencing the partner's nonresponsiveness decreases one's own trust, in both its unconscious and conscious forms. Decreased trust in turn compromises one's own commitment and motivation to be responsive. One's own reduced responsiveness then decreases the partner's trust and weakens the partner's commitment (Path O_1). Through such mutually reinforcing patterns, trust reinforces the reciprocal expression of commitment (Wieselquist et al., 1999). In longitudinal research, Wieselquist et al. (1999) revealed such a dynamic. Their study of how trust and commitment develop over time revealed that Gayle's witnessing Ron's sacrifices and willingness to forgive her transgressions (i.e., his responsiveness) predicted her own greater feelings of trust in him. Gayle's greater trust in Ron then foreshadowed increases in the strength of her own commitment. Gayle's strengthened commitment then increased her own motivation to be responsive, which in turn, provided Ron with greater reason to be more trusting of her. Ron's greater trust then allowed him to extend his commitment, making his responsiveness more likely, and thereby reinitiating the commitment reciprocity cycle.

Through such dynamics, a fourth level of interdependence develops:

1. Life tasks
2. Personal preferences and personality
3. Relationship goals
4. Trust and commitment

This highest level of interdependence—trust and commitment—transforms risk. It does so because the feelings each partner has for the other can both magnify and dampen the conflicts evident at other levels of interdependence (Kelley, 1979). Think about how the interdependence between Gayle's commitment and Ron's commitment might shape the experience of risk within their relationship. Committing to Ron is a pretty good bet when Ron is highly committed to Gayle. It's a good bet because Ron's commitment transforms conflicts of interest in ways that make responding to Gayle's needs rewarding to him. Commitment is not a safe bet when Ron is less committed to Gayle. Being overly committed could result in Gayle seeking favors, sacrifices, and accommodations that Ron would be hesitant to provide. Such missteps would escalate the risk posed in even objectively low-risk conflict situations by making Gayle less trusting. Because mutuality in responsiveness requires reciprocity in commitment, the interdependent mind functions in a way that coordinates these sentiments. In so doing, it sustains the relationship bonds that are so critical to physical and psychological well-being, indeed to survival itself (Baumeister & Leary, 1995).

But Automatic Impulses Might Not Be Enacted . . .

To this point in our discussion, the interdependent mind has been running relatively seamlessly and efficiently. To simplify our logic, we've acted as if the if–then rules that are automatically activated are always carried out in behavior. Most of the time, they are. But the interpersonal mind's flexibility means that automatic impulses will not always be enacted. There will be circumstances when people are both motivated and able to correct or "check" one of the rules the mind supplies, and instead, do exactly the opposite of what the mind suggests.

The MODE (motivation and opportunity as determinants) model of the attitude–behavior relation suggests that automatic propensities may not turn into actual behavior when people have the motivation and opportunity to override them (Olson & Fazio, 2008). Similar flexibility governs the functioning of the interdependent mind. Gayle is highly trusting in part because Ron is almost always considerate, attentive, and willing to sacrifice on her behalf. Given her relationship circumstance, acting on an impulse to self-protect would probably do Gayle more harm than good. She might hesitate to ask him for a sacrifice that he would have happily provided. Because some if–then rules fit better in some relationship circumstances than others, the interpersonal mind needs a mechanism for tagging potentially destructive or self-defeating impulses. It has just this mechanism in trust.

Just as trust infuses the process of risk appraisal and goal orientation, it infuses the process of turning implementation intentions into action. Specifically, trust in the partner's responsiveness provides the motivation to correct the impulses compelled by if–then implementation rules that run counter to a person's more chronic goal orientation toward the relationship (Murray, Aloni, et al., 2009; Murray, Holmes, et al., 2009). Some degree of conscious or executive control over behavior supplies the opportunity to correct (Gilbert & Malone, 1995; Muraven & Baumeister, 2000; Murray, Derrick, Leder, & Holmes, 2008).

How does this happen? General levels of trust in the partner determine one's chronic goal habits, one's overall agenda. High levels of trust in the partner's responsiveness foster the chronic pursuit of connection in relationships (Mikulincer & Shaver, 2003; Murray, Holmes, & Collins, 2006). People who are more trusting can afford to set aside worries about being exploited in conflicts of interest because the partner's nonresponsiveness is not that likely or that hurtful (Murray, Griffin, et al., 2003). Low levels of trust in the partner's responsiveness foster the chronic pursuit of self-protection in relationships. People who are less trusting cannot afford to set aside worries about being exploited because the partner's nonresponsiveness is more likely and more hurtful (Holmes & Rempel, 1989; Murray, Holmes, & Collins, 2006). Because trust shapes chronic goal habits or pursuits, trust also changes how it feels when the goal to connect or self-protect is activated in a specific situation.

Because Gayle is highly trusting, her chronic habit is to connect to Ron. Being in a high-risk situation where she instead wants to self-protect might not feel quite right because this state goal is a bad "fit" to her chronic goal habits, to borrow a turn of phrase from the theory of regulatory fit (Higgins, 2000). Therefore, her chronic habit to seek connection motivates her to correct this foreign impulse. In more formal terms, trust (and its associated chronic goal habits) can change the psychological utility or consequences of enacting the state goal to self-protect (or connect) when this state goal is activated or provoked in a given situation. By making some state goals a better "fit" than others, trust basically provides the motivation to correct poorly fitting rules once they become accessible and begin to exert some influence. How does this happen?

Each of the action plans for implementing commitment in specific conflicts of interest is goal-specific; one prioritizes connection, the other self-protection. Therefore, each of these dual action plans for behavior also fits chronic desires to approach or avoid the partner to a greater or lesser degree. Consider how the climate of trust in the relationship changes the benefits and costs of the "if connect goal, then justify commitment" implementation rule. Valuing a costly partner more has the benefit of promoting one's own responsiveness, but the personal cost of making rejection more painful (because losing a valued partner hurts more than losing a less valued one). This implementation rule is not a good "fit" for those who are less trusting because their chronic habit is to protect themselves against such an outcome. Therefore, being less trusting motivates people to over-turn the automatic reaction to value a costly partner more when they have sufficient executive or conscious control (i.e., opportunity) to do so.

As we mentioned earlier, Sally is not that trusting. In her relation-ship circumstance, she cannot afford to invest more in Harry when he thwarts her goals (whether such infractions were intentional or not). One day recently, Harry changed the TV channel to watch a hockey game just when Sally was about to see the last few minutes of her movie. Her autonomy infringed and her goals thwarted, her automatic impulse is to compensate, perhaps by remembering how much she values Harry's athleticism (Murray, Holmes, et al., 2009). However, such an automatic response escalates the psychological costs of rejection to an uneasy level because rejection hurts more as she attaches greater value to Harry. When such compensatory thoughts slip into her mind, she might try to dismiss them—perhaps countering her impulse to connect with thoughts about Harry's selfishness. Being less trusting would essentially motivate Sally to counter or "check" her automatic reaction to value a costly Harry more. However, valuing a costly partner more does not have the same costs for people who are more trusting. Therefore, a more trusting Gayle would have no reason to second-guess her compensatory musing about Ron's patience as he switches the channel from the last few plays of her football game to his movie.

An example from one of our experiments might help to illustrate how the conscious mind can sometimes correct the leanings of the smart rela-tionship unconscious (Murray, Holmes, et al., 2009). In this study, we first primed people in dating relationships with all of the ways in which their partner thwarted their goals on a daily basis. We had experimental par-ticipants indicate everything their partner had done recently (e.g., chang-ing the TV channel) to interfere with them. Control participants thought about how the world itself sometimes interfered with their goal pursuits. We then measured how quickly people associated their partner with posi-tive traits on a reaction time task (which taps impulsive responses) and we measured how positively people described their partner when they had lots of opportunity to think about it.

Because reaction time tasks limit people's opportunity to correct, we expected to see evidence for the smart relationship unconscious here. That is, we expected participants primed with the many ways in which their partner thwarted their goals to be faster to associate their partner with positive traits (i.e., the "justify commitment" implementation rule). They were. Being reminded of costs automatically elicited the tendency to value the partner more. This automatic reaction was just as much in evidence for people who were less trusting as it was for people who were more trusting. But explicitly evaluating the partner's merits gives less trusting people the opportunity to correct what could be an uncomfortable impulse. On this conscious measure, we expected less trusting people who were primed with the ways in which their partner thwarted their goals to evaluate their partner less, not more positively. That is, we expected them to contradict the contents of their unconscious. They did! We return to this study in Chapter 6. For now, the important message to take forward is a simple one. In situations where a less trusting Sally has the opportunity to correct, her automatic reaction to Harry might be positive, but her lingering sentiment might be all the more negative!

The climate of trust in the relationship also changes the subjective utility of the "if self-protect goal, then withhold own dependence" implementation rule. Withdrawing from risk minimizes the potential pain of a partner's rejection, but it might also weaken one's own commitment needlessly. Because Gayle is highly trusting, withdrawing from Ron when she has the urge to do so would have compromised utility for her because keeping her distance forfeits some of the gains of his responsiveness she has every reason to anticipate (Murray, Bellavia, et al., 2003). This implementation rule is not a good "fit" for people who are highly trusting because their chronic goal habit is to approach such outcomes. Therefore, being more trusting motivates Gayle to curb such inclinations. Specifically, when self-protective inclinations arise, being more trusting motivates people to correct for the automatic reaction to self-protect by reacting with anger, retaliating for a transgression, or withdrawing one's support (Cavallo, Fitzsimons, & Holmes, 2009; Murray, Derrick, Leder, & Holmes, 2008). Much like Sally, Gayle's automatic and impulsive response to her spouse's failure to buy groceries as he promised is anger and the urge to chastise him. But Gayle's greater trust essentially allows her to "bite her tongue" in situations where the automatic inclination might be to retaliate and push Ron away. In fact, such "good manners" are critical in fostering satisfying interaction patterns (Rusbult, Verette, Whitney, Slovik, & Lipkus, 1991).

The Relationship's Personality

Because partners vary in compatibility, relationships vary in risk. The relationship's "personality" emerges as the mind adapts to the differences in the risks partners in a specific relationship experience (Mischel & Shoda,

1995). In this process, the interdependent mind "discerns" that some of the if–then rules better fit the relationship circumstance. Consider the relationship circumstances Ron and Gayle and Harry and Sally faced. Table 2.2 updates each of the couple profiles. As it turns out, Ron and Gayle were fairly compatible, sharing similar preferences for life tasks and similar relationship goals. Harry and Sally were not as fortunate. As we will see, each of their marriages developed unique personalities as a result.

How does the "discerning" process that shapes the relationship's personality unfold? Experience creates habits (Wood & Neal, 2007). Because Ron and Gayle are compatible in most respects, Gayle repeatedly encountered low-risk situations as her marriage progressed. Such situation exposure repeatedly activated the implementation rules for escalating her dependence and justifying her commitment. These if–then rules became stronger and more accessible as a result. She essentially developed the habit to connect because she had so much practice relying on these rules. By contrast, Sally repeatedly encountered high-risk situations as her

TABLE 2.2. Updating Ron and Gayle and Harry and Sally

Tasks	Basic demographics	Life task preferences	Personality preferences	Relationship goal preferences
Ron and Gayle	African American Lawyers Two young children	Ron likes washing cooking; Gayle likes dishes. Both enjoy child care.	Gayle more gregarious.	Both value Gayle's working.
Harry and Sally	White Mechanic/customer service officer Three children, eldest 17	Harry dislikes all things domestic.	Sally more gregarious. Sally more fastidious.	Sally wanted to work; Harry wanted her at home.
Hector and Helena	Hispanic Factory worker/ homemaker Three young children Catholic Economically stressed	Stay tuned . . .	Stay tuned . . .	Stay tuned . . .
Gunter and Lastri	Indonesian PhD student/ homemaker One toddler	Stay tuned . . .	Stay tuned . . .	Gunter wants another baby; Lastri wants to return to school.

marriage progressed because Harry wanted her to stay at home and she wanted to work, because she wanted to socialize when Harry wanted to stay in, and because she wanted Harry to be fastidious and compulsive when he wanted to be carefree. Such situation exposure repeatedly activated the procedural rules for vigilance, withholding her dependence, and promoting Harry's dependence. These rules then became stronger or more accessible mental habits (again, through practice).

By creating if–then rule habits that match the situational risks, interaction experiences shape each relationship's unique personality. We use the term *relationship personality* in a dual sense. One: We use the term to refer to an adaption or tuning process that makes particular if–then rules a habit. Through experience, the interdependent mind adjusts the ease with which specific procedural rules are activated, corrected, and enacted to match the character of the risks in the conflicts of interest partners repeatedly encounter. In this first sense, relationships differ in personality because partners have different rule habits. Two: We also use the term to refer to the type of mutuality in responsiveness that results when the interdependent mind makes some rules a habit (and not others). In this second sense, relationships differ in personality because some partners rely on each other primarily for the exchange of small favors, some partners largely restrict interaction to coordinating instrumental role responsibilities, and some partners instead seek emotional support and shared goals and identities. Both senses of the relationship's "personality" emerge as the interdependent mind adjusts its rules to match differences in risk.

Figure 2.2 illustrates how the personality of the relationship emerges through experience. In the process of personality development, situations, trust, and correction determine which particular if–then rules become stronger habits (Paths A_1, through A_3 in Figure 2.2). The specific if–then rule habits that preoccupy the mind in turn control how partners experience the meaning or purpose of their relationship (Path B in Figure 2.2). The attributions for trust and commitment that emerge from this sense-making process then control exactly what particular behavioral expressions of mutuality in responsiveness entail (Path C in Figure 2.2). We provide a brief overview of these dynamics next. Chapter 8 thoroughly describes this process. In foreshadowing how relationship personality emerges, we begin with the three main sources of variability in relationship personality:

1. Situations
2. Trust
3. Correction

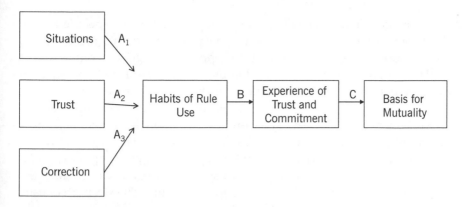

FIGURE 2.2. The development of relationship personality.

Situations

Situations matter in the development of the relationship's personality because objective risk varies across relationships. Partners can be more or less interdependent at the level of life tasks, personality, and relationship goals. Partners can also face more or less easily resolvable conflicts at each level of interdependence (Kelley, 1979). This means that the typical content of the situation depicted in Figure 2.1 differs across couples. Because situation exposure varies across relationships, relationships differ in their objective *risk profile*. We use the term risk profile to refer to the type (e.g., life tasks, personality, relationship goals) and tractability of the conflicts (e.g., magnitude of conflict, transparency of interests) partners repeatedly encounter. As we see below, the risk profile of the relationship provides a window to the ways in which partners are compatible and the ways in which partners are incompatible.

In relationships with a low risk profile, partners face fewer conflicts of interest at each level of interdependence and the conflicts they do face are relatively easy to coordinate (e.g., equal power, largely correspondent outcomes, easily discernable interests). In relationships with a high risk profile, partners face more frequent and more serious conflicts of interest at each level of interdependence, and the conflicts they face are comparatively difficult to coordinate. In lower-risk relationships, partners encounter more situations in which the outcomes each prefers are largely compatible (signaling the potential for gain by putting one's outcomes in the partner's hands). In higher-risk relationships, partners encounter more situations in which the outcomes each prefers are largely incompatible (signaling the potential for loss through such dependence).

How do situations elicit relationship personality? For people to feel, think, or behave in a particular way, some provocation is required (Bargh, 2007). Simply put, something needs to happen for the goal to connect or the goal to self-protect to be activated. Let us explain. The "if self-protect, then promote partner dependence" rule motivates Gayle to respond to fears of Ron's rejection with behaviors that make him need or "owe" her. For this rule to be activated, Gayle must encounter a situation that makes her worry about Ron's motivation to be responsive to her needs. The degree to which this rule preoccupies Gayle's mental life depends on how often she encounters such situations. Variability in situation exposure thus provides the first source of variability in relationship personality. The strength of each if–then rule varies across partners because situation exposure strengthens the accessibility of information in memory, and such exposure varies across relationships (Fazio, 1986; Wood & Neal, 2007).

In relationships with an objectively low risk profile, partners encounter more situations with the clear or real potential for gain. Such situation exposure strengthens the accessibility of the action plan for seeking connection (i.e., "if connect goal, then escalate dependence"; "if connect goal, then justify commitment"). The selective activation and enactment of these implementation rules makes a certain type of responsiveness habitual, one that does not restrict opportunities for closeness on the basis of risk. Namely, these rule habits tend to elicit a bold type of responsiveness, one that involves the communal giving of benefits, the provision of major sacrifices, and the solicitation and provision of identity support. In relationships with an objectively high risk profile, partners encounter more situations with the clear potential for loss. Such situation exposure strengthens the accessibility of the action plan for self-protection (i.e., "if self-protect goal, then escalate partner dependence"; "if self-protect goal, then withhold own dependence"). The selective activation and enactment of these implementation rules elicits a cautious type of responsiveness, one that puts firm boundaries on the amount of risk encountered. Namely, it tends to elicit the tit-for-tat exchange of practical benefits and minor sacrifices and the coordination of rigid roles, such as caretaker and provider. As these examples illustrate, the if–then rules that become a habit in a particular relationship in part reflect a process of social learning (Bargh, 2007). Through this process, partners learn styles of interacting that best match the objective risks they face.[1]

Trust

Variability in situation appraisal provides a second source of variability in relationship personality. Overall feelings of trust in the partner help disambiguate the partner's motives. Therefore, people who differ in their chronic level of trust in their partner's responsiveness are likely to perceive different levels of risk in ambiguous conflicts of interest. Such differences in perceived risk call different if–then rules into play. For people who are less trusting, being chronically uncertain of the partner's motives strengthens the accessibility of the if–then vigilance rules. Being less trusting motivates Sally to scrutinize Harry's every behavior for what information it might reveal about his motivation to be responsive. Her greater vigilance then makes it hard for Sally to connect because looking for signs of rejection almost guarantees finding them. After all, even the best-behaved partner is going to slip up from time to time. The hyper-accessibility of the if–then vigilance rules results in Sally being quick to perceive rejection in even the most innocuous of Harry's comments. Such an appraisal bias strengthens the accessibility of the if–then rules for implementing the goal to self-protect in memory. She has become quick avoid Harry and promote his instrumental dependence on her because she had so much practice self-protecting (because she perceives so many occasions that seemed to warrant it). In this way, a less trusting Sally's tendency to perceive risk tends to elicit a more cautious style of responsiveness, such as exchanging dishwashing for grocery shopping rather than making major sacrifices on Harry's behalf.

Being more trusting instills the opposite set of if–then rule habits and promotes a bolder style of responsiveness. Being more trusting frees Gayle from actively gauging Ron's motivations. Such insensitivity to rejection then makes it easy for Gayle to connect because she so seldom sees cause for concern in even those situations where Ron had some incentive to be selfish. Such an optimistic appraisal bias strengthens the accessibility of the if–then rules for implementing the goal to connect in Gayle's memory. Her considerable practice increasing and justifying her connection then motivates her to provide Ron with emotional support, sacrifice on his behalf, and share her own fears and concerns with him.

Correction

Variability in the motivation and opportunity to correct the if–then rules that are automatically activated by the situation provides the third source of variability in relationship personality. Chronic feelings of trust in the partner's responsiveness determine how well the state goal to connect or self-protect "fits" with one's broader goal agenda. For this reason, trust in the partner's responsiveness provides the motivation to correct ill-fitting if–then rules. The capacity for such a gap between rule activation and rule enactment (i.e., the mind's flexibility) can steer people from an automatic propensity to react in one way to an exactly opposite behavioral expression. Relationships thus differ in personality because some people have more frequent opportunities and greater motivation to correct the leanings of the smart unconscious. Some people more often decide to connect (i.e., approach) in situations that motivate self-protection (i.e., avoidance). For instance Gayle, being more trusting, might decide to throw caution to the wind and ask Ron for a major favor (e.g., sacrificing his whole day at work) when he only seems disposed to provide a more minor favor (e.g., sacrificing half a day at work). In contrast, some people more often decide to self-protect (i.e., avoid) in situations that motivate seeking connection (i.e., approach). For instance Sally, being less trusting, might decide not to tell a sympathetic Harry about her child-related stresses even when he asks whether something is bothering her. Let us elaborate.

The "if rejected, then distance" rule motivates Gayle to respond to feeling hurt by withdrawing from Ron. However, the degree to which lashing out at Ron typifies Gayle's response to feeling hurt depends on her trust in Ron. Sufficient trust motivates her to curb, and even reverse, such automatic impulses when she can. Correcting the temptation to retaliate allows a more trusting Gayle to decide to be forgiving at least some of the time. In fact, with repeated experience correcting, she might unlearn the urge to retaliate (Murray, Derrick, Leder, & Holmes, 2008). Having a new "forgive Ron" rule in place then might condition her more positive association to Ron and make it easier for her to trust him in the future. Quite a different eventuality might unfold if a less trusting Sally got practiced in correcting the automatic inclination to compensate for Harry's interference with her goals by valuing him more. In such a scenario, being quick to chastise Harry for minor gaffes would then elicit her more negative conditioned association to Harry and make it all the harder for her to trust him.

To correct, though, the motivation supplied by one's beliefs about the partner's responsiveness itself is not sufficient. People also need the strength of will (i.e., opportunity) to do so (Olson & Fazio, 2008). For this reason, people may not always be able to overturn an automatic reaction, no matter how motivated they may be to do so. Models of attitudes, impression formation, and stereotyping assume that some degree of executive control over behavior supplies at least the initial opportunity to correct (Gilbert & Malone, 1995; Muraven & Baumeister, 2000; Murray, Derrick, Leder, & Holmes, 2008). Distracted by other tasks at hand, however, Sally might not have the cognitive resources needed to curb her impulse to connect and to be generous in her attributions. For this reason, the state goals that are activated in a particular situation might still contradict or subvert people's more chronic relationship goal pursuits. Even a distrusting Sally might end up drawing closer to Harry in situations where she cannot help but connect. We explore this possibility in detail later. As we will see, the inherent difficulty in curbing the leanings of the interdependent mind provides a crucial but never before considered point of leverage in making dissatisfying relationships more satisfying (or vice versa).

Shaping the Basis for Mutuality in Responsiveness

So how exactly do the if–then rules that become a mental habit elicit substantively different styles of mutual responsive interactions? Why do some couples rely on each other for everything while others rely on each other for only the most superficial of favors? To answer this question, we need to draw in the conscious mind's musings. People can explain their relationships to themselves in different ways. They can attribute commitment to intrinsic factors such as the value the partner places on one's inherent qualities (e.g., sense of humor, intelligence, athleticism). They can attribute commitment to instrumental factors such as the value one puts on the tangible benefits provided (e.g., cooking, child rearing, social support). They can also attribute commitment to extrinsic factors such as pressures from family or religious prohibitions against divorce. The if–then rule habits that come to preoccupy the mind make some of these reasons for commitment more salient or compelling than others.

What Gayle comes to believe about her relationship depends on how her (and Ron's) mind adapts to suit the risks endemic in their relationship. Ron and Gayle are both reasonably secure in attachment style. They encounter multiple situations where behavioral coordination is easy because they would both rather do things together than do things apart. For them, something as mundane as dishes might represent an opportunity for togetherness. Their easy sense of trust in each other fosters the frequent activation of the "if connect goal" rules. The frequent activation of the "if connect goal, then escalate own dependence" rule results in each being willing to seek each other out for support. The second rule, rather paradoxically, results in Ron's inherent qualities becoming more special and valuable to her the more she is exposed to the costs of her interdependence and commitment. In a sense, the second rule eases the smooth implementation of the first. In this way, the pattern of rule use likely in "compatible" relationships flags the intrinsic factors motivating Gayle's commitment while deemphasizing the instrumental or extrinsic factors governing Ron's commitment.

Now imagine a relationship in which partners' goals diverge often. Perhaps Harry is avoidant and Sally is anxious-ambivalent in attachment style. They are going to encounter many situations in which behavior coordination is difficult because Harry wants his autonomy and Sally wants to cling. In such a relationship, Harry might even view Sally's request that he dry the dishes as she washes as an affront to his independence. Frequently encountering risky situations makes Sally worry more about Harry's rejection. Such worries frequently activate the "if self-protect goal" implementation rules. Preoccupation with ensuring Harry's trustworthiness compels Sally to do many things for him, from packing his lunch to placating her in-laws. Such compulsive efforts to curry his favor make the constraints and instrumental reasons governing Harry's commitment salient to Sally. Holding herself back because of her worries, perhaps by finding whatever fault in Harry she can, also stalls the strength of her own intrinsic motivation to be responsive to him by making him less valuable to her. Harry's resistance to closeness prompts him to react to any infringements on his autonomy by distancing, which makes the barriers keeping him in the marriage (e.g., children) all the more salient to him.

The attributions Ron and Gayle make for commitment in turn shape their orientation to future situations of risk. In so doing, such residues of past if–then rule habits determine exactly what mutuality in responsiveness comes to entail, and thereby, control satisfaction. Imagine that Gayle trusts in Ron's commitment because she believes he values her personal qualities and that Ron similarly trusts in Gayle's commitment because he believes she values his personal qualities. They readily enter situations in which each partner has the opportunity to support each other's personal goals. As we see in Chapter 8, practicing responsiveness at such high levels of interdependence maximizes the rewards each can gain from the relationship, making it easier for both to stay satisfied in the marriage (Reis & Shaver, 1988). Now imagine that Sally believes that Harry only stays with her because of the instrumental benefits she provides. Because she centers their interactions on instrumental activities (e.g., trading laundry for car maintenance), she experiences the marriage as a cooperative partnership, but not a communion. As a result, she might limit what she asks of Harry to such instrumental tasks. Because Harry believes that Sally only needs him for car maintenance, he only asks her for similar concrete favors because he doubts her willingness to provide any other kind of care (Berscheid, 1983). Practicing responsiveness at such low levels of interdependence limits the reward each can gain from the relationship, making it difficult for either of them to be highly satisfied.

Relationship Resilience and Stability: A Recap

In positing a procedural basis for personality, we echo Mischel and Shoda (1995). These scholars define individual "personality" in terms of situation-specific patterns of behavior (Mischel & Morf, 2003). Their person-by-situation analysis states that deeming a child "aggressive" reveals little about the child because it takes the child out of the situation. More apt depictions of this child's personality come in knowing when a child is likely to be aggressive—when responding to a peer's taunts, reacting to a teacher's demand, or rejecting of a parent's affection. According to Mischel and Shoda (1995), personality is a system that adapts affect, cognition, and behavior to match the characteristics of interaction partners in specific situations. The applied chapters in this book (Chapters 9–12) advance a similar narrative about a functional relationship personality that adapts itself to changing relationship situations.

Our hope is that the arguments we advance will put a new spin on basic questions. What makes a relationship satisfying? What makes it stable? Existing models assume that satisfaction and stability are a function of what partners think and do. Resilience thus depends on where partners end up in terms of conscious sentiment and overt behavior. Overall sentiments of trust (Holmes & Rempel, 1989), commitment (Rusbult & Van Lange, 1993), or satisfaction (Karney & Bradbury, 1995) or ratios of positive to negative behavior (Gottman, 1994) determine resilience in most existing models. As valuable as these approaches have been, they take the relationship out of the situation. They also assume that what people consciously experience presents a complete picture of their relationships.

We think that much more generative understanding of relationships comes in knowing exactly how partners got to particular sentiments or behaviors. In this book, we put situations back into relationships because we think it is crucial to understand the process that governs when Ron is likely to be sarcastic—for example, in response to Gayle's pointed criticism or unintended gaffe. The analysis of relationship stability we advance in this book is unique in making satisfaction and stability a function of the process by which partners feel, think, and behave. By underlining the power of procedural knowledge (i.e., if–then rules), our model positions the workings of a generally smart, but not infallible, relationship unconscious as a central factor in forecasting exactly where a relationship ends up. It also raises the fascinating possibility that the unconscious mind may know something about the relationship that escapes the attention of the conscious mind. Why? Because the unconscious mind better tends to situational risks.

SUMMARY AND CAVEATS

This chapter overviewed our theory of the interdependent mind. This smart relationship unconscious uses trust as an intermediary to coordinate mutually responsive partner interactions. In this process of motivation management, the interdependent mind matches Gayle's willingness to put her outcomes in Ron's hands (i.e., to commit) to Ron's willingness to be responsive (i.e., to commit himself). This chapter had two main points. First, we introduced the if–then rules (Table 2.1) and explained how these rules coordinate mutual displays of responsiveness. This procedural core to the interdependent mind involves: (1) if–then rules for vigilance that govern trust and disambiguate the partner's motives; (2) if–then rules for goal orientation that link the perception of risk to the goal to connect or self-protect (as is appropriate); and (3) if–then rules for goal implementation that match commitment to trust, ensure trust is not misplaced, and ensure commitment is not too easily derailed. Second, we introduced the relationship personality. We explained how the interdependent mind develops different if–then habits in relationships characterized by high-risk situations than it develops in relationships characterized by low-risk situations. In the process of making particular if–then rules a habit, the interdependent mind elicits behavioral displays of responsiveness that are sensitive to risk. Therefore, different relationship personalities (i.e., responsiveness displays) emerge because partners vary in: (1) the objective situational risks they face, (2) the situational risks trust disposes them to perceive, and (3) how often they correct the automatic will to connect or self-protect in a given situation when that state goals runs counter to their chronic goal pursuits.

We must bring up two caveats before we proceed. First, early in this chapter, we suggested that one's sense of having a "conscious will" emerges from relationship experience rather than compelling it. By this we meant that one's experience of the relationship emerges from situations. Because these situations are tied to procedural knowledge within the smart-relationship unconscious, partners come to behave in some ways over others. Later in this chapter, we described partners as conscious sense-makers who reflect on the meaning of their interactions. This imposes a thoughtfulness or willfulness to the interdependent mind. In later chapters, we will see exactly how the unconscious and the conscious influence each other in creating the couple's behavioral history and orientation toward the future. We return to this in Chapters 9 through 12 as we explain why some relationships thrive while others falter.

Second, the if–then rules are not meant to be circumscribed to the minds of an egalitarian Western couple, as our Ron and Gayle example might imply. We expand the breadth of our examples and provide evidence that the if–then rules are evident across cultures in the chapters that detail how the if–then appraisal and implementation rules both inform and motivate trust and commitment. We also make no claim on one type of mutuality being inherently better than another type of mutuality. Different cultures impose different expectations about the roles and responsibilities of relationship partners (Berscheid & Regan, 2005). In our model, relationships that revolve around the exchange of instrumental roles (e.g., traditional marriage) are not inherently any more or less stable than ones that revolve around shared interests and personal goal pursuits. Instead, instability results when the procedural rules fail to compel some type of mutuality because partners experience excessive exposure to situations that are high in risk, have chronic difficulty establishing trust, or both. Now let's proceed to Chapter 3. There we develop our conceptualization of what it means to be more or less trusting in relationships in detail. We start there because trust plays such a crucial role intermediary role in directing or orchestrating the functioning of the interdependent mind.

NOTE

1. The social learning perspective that has dominated clinical perspectives on close relationships assumes that satisfaction is controlled through the rewards and costs of interacting (Gottman, 1994). However, no existing theory or research specifies how this learning process occurs. As we will see, understanding how situations elicit particular if–then habits of thought may help elucidate exactly what social learning entails in adult close relationships.

CHAPTER 3

Trust

When to Approach?

> Don't accept a partner who wanted you for rational
> reasons. . . . Look for someone who is emotionally
> committed to you because you are you. If the emotion
> moving that person is not triggered by your objective
> mate value, that emotion will not be alienated by
> someone who comes along with greater mate value
> than yours.
>
> —STEVEN PINKER (2008, p. 83)

In a *Time* magazine article, Steven Pinker offers advice to people searching for a trustworthy romantic partner. His advice is pointed—and surprising, both in what he said and what he didn't say. He didn't advise
something most people do (or at least think they do): He didn't instruct
people to choose a partner by consulting their own personal checklist for
an ideal mate. He didn't even instruct people to choose by stacking themselves up against the qualities on the prospective partner's wish list. In his
estimations, such rational calculations only ensure the eventual alienation
of the partner's affection. Instead, Pinker advised people searching for
lasting love to select the special someone who loves them for the most
irrational of reasons—someone who thinks they are truly unique.

Why should discerning such irrational motives in the partner be a
priority for the interdependent mind? The romantic marketplace is inherently competitive (Gangestad & Simpson, 2000). Because it is competitive,
no rational accounting process can guarantee a partner's commitment.
No matter how desirable one's qualities, somebody younger, warmer, or

smarter might lure one's partner away. The key to establishing a stable bond rests in finding someone whose commitment can be trusted precisely because it is not so calculated rational. It rests in believing that one's partner could not imagine finding anyone else quite as special as oneself (Murray & Holmes, 2008; Murray, Leder, et al., 2009; Tooby & Cosmides, 1996). People seem to know this implicitly. In a speed-dating situation of 5- to 10-minute dates with multiple prospects, people gravitate toward the choosy—they want to pursue relationships with the suitors who find them uniquely fascinating. Suitors who like everyone do not get a second look (Eastwick, Finkel, Mochon, & Ariely, 2007).

This chapter begins our exploration of how the interdependent mind gauges trust in the partner's commitment, and thus their responsiveness, and keeps such trust from being misplaced. In illustrating these processes, we take the reader through some of the day-to-day dynamics in Hector and Helena's marriage. As we introduced in Chapter 2, trust is the interdependent mind's pulse or monitor for the strength of one's motivation to avoid rejection. By signaling the strength of the partner's commitment, trust signals the extent to which it's safe to approach and when it's wise to be cautious. We think of trust as a dynamic and evolving statement about one's special or unique value to the partner. Hector's trust in Helena signals how much caution is appropriate by tracking how valuable he is to her. Why would the interdependent mind rely on such a metric to gauge a partner's commitment? The interpersonal marketplace is competitive. Therefore, partners must worry more about the possibility of being replaced when the "goods" they offer are readily available from other alternative partners. To be blunt, people need to know when their partner might be thinking about greener pastures. For Hector, filling a special niche in Helena's life—whether it is by virtue of his simpatico sense of humor, mechanical expertise, skill in calming their three young children, or his approving mother-in-law—makes it all the more difficult for Helena to replace him. Filling a special niche gives Hector greater reason to trust that Helena has good reason to be responsive to his needs when it costs her more to do so.

The interdependent mind uses the ease of being replaced to gauge the partner's commitment because being hard to replace solves the adaptive problem that being in objective need of the partner's responsiveness creates. When something is wrong—when people are sick, or distressed, or fearful—they need the aid afforded by close interpersonal ties. However, when something is wrong, people are least able to repay or reciprocate any help they receive. Tooby and Cosmides (1996) describe this adaptive problem as a "bankers' paradox." The paradox refers to the fact that people most need "loans" of interpersonal sacrifice and goodwill when they are bad credit risks. This paradox led Tooby and Cosmides (1996) to this insight: For people to survive to reproduce, there must be some mechanism in place for discriminating good and sacrificing friends from fair-weather ones. These theorists contend that specific cognitive mechanisms evolved to track which specific others perceive one's qualities as special because they could not imagine finding those qualities in others. Securing a niche among friends—possessing some quality that makes one unique and thus valuable to one's social ties—ensures the responsiveness of these friends when it is costly. Why? Because filling a niche guarantees that others have some reason to be loyal in just those circumstances when one is a bad credit risk. Being irreplaceable basically provides liability insurance that someone will be there to meet one's needs in times of crisis. Securing such loyalty minimizes the chance of rejections that could otherwise threaten survival and the ultimate transmission of one's genes (Bowlby, 1969; Gilbert, 2005; Reis et al., 2004; Tooby & Cosmides, 1996).[1]

This chapter builds on the logic of the bankers' paradox to delineate how the interpersonal mind measures and motivates the partner's commitment. That is, it describes how the interdependent mind regulates trust. We argue that Hector gauges the status of Helena's commitment by monitoring how easily he could be replaced—that is, by estimating how valuable he is in Helena's eyes. In disambiguating Helena's motivation to be loyal to Hector, the interdependent mind employs if–then rules for both controlling vigilance and for promoting the partner's dependence. These complementary if–then rules work to assess and restore Hector's value to Helena. The rules for controlling vigilance signal Hector's overall value to Helena and thereby control trust. When his self-assessed value drops, the if–then rule for promoting Helena's dependence then restores his value to her and thereby repairs trust. In Hector's case, generally believing that Helena values his sense of humor, his contributions to the finances, his Catholic values, and his strong work ethic provides Hector with good reason to trust Helena's overall commitment. However, on days when factory layoffs put his financial contributions in jeopardy, doubting his value motivates him to take compensatory steps to put her in his debt and thereby ensure Helena needs him for some additional reason. On those days, he might sometimes find himself dissuading Helena from babysitting to make sure that she depends on him alone to pay for her occasional, but much-enjoyed, manicure.

This chapter advances four main points central for understanding trust. Table 3.1 summarizes these arguments, addressed in sequence in the chapter. In the first part of this chapter we describe the if–then rules

TABLE 3.1. The Main Arguments

1. If–then vigilance rules govern explicit expectations of responsiveness (i.e., reflective trust).
2. Sustaining trust involves ignoring the if–then rules (at least sometimes).
3. If–then rules are error ridden; mind keeps supplementary, unconscious barometer of the safety of approach (i.e., impulsive trust).
4. If–then rule for promoting the partner's dependence keeps trust from being misplaced.

that govern reflective trust. These rules gauge the ongoing state of the partner's commitment and consequently signal how much vigilance is necessary. These procedural rules automatically link signs of one's value to the partner (i.e., "if") to the contingent tendency to be more or less trusting or vigilant (i.e., "then"). These if–then rules tell Hector that Helena's responsiveness is more likely to be forthcoming when she is: (1) willing to sacrifice for him, (2) admiring of Hector's personal qualities that make him special, (3) not superior in worth to him, (4) not likely to be attractive to other men, and (5) tied to the marriage by barriers or constraints.

In the second part of this chapter we describe a paradox in how the interdependent mind applies the if–then vigilance rules: It seems to know that less is more. Sustaining trust in Helena requires Hector to take advantage of the interpersonal mind's flexibility to ignore the if–then rules at least some of the time. Why would that be the case? Trust is a statement about a future state of affairs. Hector's trust in Helena tells him whether he can expect her to be responsive tomorrow, the next day, and the day after that (Holmes & Rempel, 1989). The problem is that no amount of evidence (gained by applying the vigilance rules) can fully justify Hector's trust in Helena's responsiveness in the future because it might not mirror the past. Even if a 30-year-old Hector measures up to Helena's value, he has no guarantee that his 40-year-old self will stack up nearly as well. The intervening decade invites uncertainty. His six-pack abs might slip into a middle-aged paunch while Helena steps up her outings to the gym. He might lose his job, while she advances her education. More problematic still, the present is bound to give Hector reason for concern. Helena will inevitably behave badly no matter how responsive she is to his needs. Given that the present is not always reassuring in the moment at hand and the future invites uncertainty, the interpersonal mind has no choice but to relax the if–then vigilance rules to maintain trust in the partner's responsiveness. The interpersonal mind's flexibility in this regard motivates people who are already confident of their partner's commitment to overturn the if–then rules on occasion. Unfortunately, people differ substantially in their capacity to suspend caution and disbelief. Therefore, some people have a harder time than others taking advantage of the mind's flexibility in this regard (as we will see).

In the third part of this chapter we describe how the interpersonal mind compensates for the perspective-taking errors that come in the process of applying the vigilance rules. Because Hector cannot get directly inside Helena's mind, he relies on the contents of his own mind to gauge her commitment. For instance, he might consider how much Helena values his mechanical expertise (i.e., "if partner values traits, then trust") or remind himself that he's a much better father to their children than any of Helena's past boyfriends would have been (i.e., "if better than partner's alternatives, then trust"). But in trying to delve into Helena's mind, Hector cannot help but be biased by the contents of his own mind. People are egocentric (Griffin & Ross, 1991). They assume that others, including their romantic partners, see the world just as they do (Kenny, 1994). Such egocentrism makes the if–then vigilance rules a less-than-perfect barometer of the strength of the partner's commitment. For instance, a low self-esteem Hector is likely to miss the fact that Helena thinks he's intelligent and attractive because he underestimates how attractive and intelligent he is in actuality (Murray, Holmes, & Griffin, 2000).

Because the interdependent mind cannot escape its own egocentrism, it also keeps a secondary barometer of the strength of the partner's commitment. This barometer does not encode trust in terms of reflective or conscious expectations of the partner's responsiveness (i.e., how we described trust to this point). Unlike reflective trust, this impulsive barometer of trust is not formed through if–then inferential rules that are themselves subject to error. Instead, impulsive trust is formed through simple processes of associative learning (Bargh, 2007). Through interaction, the interdependent mind "learns" the extent to which the partner is safe to approach or better off avoided. Positive interactions condition a more positive automatic evaluative association to the partner; negative interactions condition a more negative automatic evaluative association. With this unconscious barometer of safety in place, being in the partner's presence is sufficient to compel the associated reflex to approach or to avoid.

In the fourth part of this chapter we describe the if–then procedural rules the interpersonal mind employs to ensure that trust is not misplaced. Helena's alternatives to her marriage—whether the allure of a life alone or the temptation of a life with someone else—give her the option not to commit. Being able to imagine such greener pastures basically gives her the freedom not to be responsive to Hector's needs. But she has little choice but to be responsive if she cannot imagine managing her life without Hector. For this reason, the interpersonal mind also works to ensure that Hector has a means of making himself indispensable to Helena. The "if self-protect goal, then escalate partner dependence" implementation rule links Hector's doubts about his value to Helena to his efforts to leverage Helena's greater commitment to him. For instance, he might escalate the instrumental benefits he provides (e.g., fixing Helena's car) or impose greater barriers to leaving (e.g., limiting Helena's income). Through such tactics, Hector makes Helena depend more on him for the satisfaction of her goals. By making her need or "owe" him in some way, he gains control over Helena and effectively limits or forecloses her option to be selfish. In so doing, his actions help ensure his trust in her will not be misplaced. We use the remainder of this chapter to describe each of these four points in greater depth.

GAUGING THE PARTNER'S COMMITMENT: IF–THEN VIGILANCE RULES

The arguments advanced to this point beg this question: Why does the interpersonal mind use "cues" to discern the partner's commitment? Isn't it clear how to discern what a partner is thinking? One can ask. And one can listen. Hector can ask Helena whether she loves him. He can also express his feelings of love to her in the hope of eliciting her reciprocated expression of affection. Hector can listen to what Helena reveals spontaneously in both her nonverbal expressions and verbal sentiments. People do treat such direct disclosures as a window to their partner's mind. A partner's spontaneous expressions of love and commitment bolster trust in that partner's responsiveness (Holmes & Rempel, 1989). In daily life, newlyweds report greater trust when their partner is more physically affectionate, verbally supportive, and expressly complementing (Murray, Derrick, Pinkus, Aloni, & Leder, 2008). The intimacy and affection Helena communicates simply in reciprocating Hector's self-disclosures similarly bolsters his trust in her affection and love for him (Collins & Miller, 1994).

Nonetheless, an information gap remains. What partners say is at best a partial indicator of their true motivations. Partners might not know how they really feel or why they feel the way they do (Wilson, 2002). Partners can also be reluctant to reveal how much (or how little) they care even when directly asked. Partners might also be reluctant to show caring in the most obvious ways—with a hug or a kiss or a smile—for fear of being rebuffed or rejected (Murray, Holmes, & Collins, 2006). They can also send mixed messages. The anguish of having love go unrequited happens in part because the beloved conveys disinterest in ambiguous and indirect ways out of the desire to be polite or kind (Baumeister, Wotman, & Stillwell, 1989). Partners can also send deliberately misleading messages. The physical desire for sex has motivated more than one person (often male) to overstate his affection or commitment. The practical need for support for offspring has motivated more than one person (often female) to overstate her affection or commitment. Consider the different evolutionary dilemmas men and women face (Haselton & Buss, 2000). Women risk investing 9 months in gestating a child with a man who then shirks responsibility as a provider. Men risk being cuckolded because they can never be certain of their biological connection to a child (barring the results of DNA tests, an innovation that has occurred too late in our evolutionary history to have a behavioral effect). Men and women both need a means of detecting duplicity, albeit for different reasons. Women need to discern men's inclination to cheat to ensure the material resources and physical protection required for the welfare of their immature young is available. Men need to discern women's inclination to cheat and deceive to avoid wasting their hard-won resources and protection by unknowingly raising another man's offspring (Haselton & Buss, 2000).

The if–then vigilance rules fill the information gap left by the partner's direct and possibly incomplete revelations of his or her mind. They link specific indirect and less readily feigned cues to one's value as hard to replace (i.e., "if") to the strength of the partner's commitment and motivation to be responsive (i.e., "then"). The interdependent mind has five if–then rules for signaling one's special value to the partner, and thus the state of reflective trust. Table 3.2 summarizes these rules. These rules govern inferences drawn from: (1) the partner's behavior in diagnostic situations, (2) the partner's perceived regard for one's traits or qualities,

TABLE 3.2. The If–Then Rules
for Controlling Vigilance

If partner sacrifices, then trust.

If partner values traits, then trust.

If equal in worth to partner, then trust.

If better than partner's alternatives, then trust.

If partner has barriers, then trust.

(3) comparisons of one's worth relative to the partner, (4) comparisons of one's worth relative to the partner's potential alternative partners, and (5) the constraints or barriers that cement partners to the relationship. We detail each of the five if–then vigilance rules in turn.

Rule 1: If Partner Sacrifices, Then Trust

The clearest way to discern a partner's true commitment and willingness to be responsive is to look to what he or she actually does. However, behavior is not always equally diagnostic in this regard (Kelley, 1979). Imagine that Hector and Helena are deciding which apartment to rent—a choice between one in an older duplex in a quiet neighborhood and one that was newly refurbished, but in a noisy high-rise. Helena prefers the duplex. If Hector is just as happy with the duplex as the high-rise, choosing the duplex reveals little about his willingness to be responsive to Helena. His choice is nondiagnostic because it required no sacrifice on his part. But if Hector chose the duplex despite dreading the repairs he knew would consume his weekends, his choice of the duplex clearly signals the premium he puts on Helena's happiness.

As this example illustrates, some situations are more diagnostic of trustworthiness than others. Mixed-motive situations offer the clearest trust prognostication when they offer the partner a choice between behaving in his or her own interest and behaving in the other's interest. In simple terms, situations that give the partner the most opportunity to be selfish best diagnose the partner's trustworthiness. Such mixed-motive situations fall into three general types: (1) coordination dilemmas, (2) exchange dilemmas, and (3) zero-sum conflicts (Kelley et al., 2003; Thibaut & Kelley, 1959). Coordination dilemmas offer the least opportunity to be selfish (and the least diagnostic information); zero-sum conflicts offer the greatest opportunity to be selfish (and the most diagnostic information). Let us explain.

Coordination dilemmas are least revealing of the strength of the partner's commitment. In a coordination dilemma, Hector and Helena must rely on each other to get something done that they both want. They might both want to paint their new apartment. This situation is low in risk because it requires coordinating their respective strengths to do something they both desire (e.g., choosing the paint color, moving the furniture, washing and painting the walls). Helena's offer to choose the paint (given her flair for decorating) while Hector moves the furniture (given his greater bulk) reveals little about her motivations because her choice facilitates a mutual goal.

Exchange dilemmas are somewhat more revealing of the strength of the partner's commitment. In an exchange dilemma, Hector and Helena each need something from the other to achieve some personal objective. To get some quiet time for reading, Helena might ask Hector to bathe and put their children to bed. She might solicit his willingness to do so by promising him a prized Friday night out with his friends. Although such a trade gets Hector something he wants, making this trade is risky because Helena could back out of her end of the bargain. Once she's had her night to herself, she loses the self-interested motivation she had for sending Hector out on a night with his friends later in the week. Keeping her promise by fulfilling her end of the bargain even though she has already gotten what she wanted reveals the strength of her commitment and motivation to be responsive to Hector's needs.

Of all the mixed-motive situations, *zero-sum conflicts* are the most diagnostic of the partner's commitment. In such a conflict situation, one partner's preferences oppose the other partner's preferences. The choice between the duplex and the high-rise captures a conflict. If Helena gets her way, Hector loses, but if Hector gets his way, Helena loses out. The partner's behavior in such situations strongly signals the strength of his or her commitment motivations because responsiveness requires the sacrifice of self-interest (Simpson, 2007). Hector's willingness to put Helena's desires for the duplex ahead of his desire for the high-rise reveals her value to him.[2]

Does the research literature suggest that the interdependent mind picks up on the greater import of diagnostic than nondiagnostic behavior? Witnessing evidence of the partner's willingness to meet one's needs in exchange and conflict situations does strengthen trust in the partner (Holmes, 1981; Kelley, 1979; Simpson, 2007; Wieselquist et al., 1999). For instance, people in both dating and marital relationships report greater trust in their partner's caring when they witness signs of their partner's commitment, such as selfless responsiveness to their needs or willingness to excuse their transgressions (Wieselquist et al., 1999).

The informative effects of self-sacrificing and responsive behaviors are evident where one might not expect to find them—the daily lives of newlywed couples (Murray, Derrick, Pinkus, et al., 2008). We return to this study for examples throughout this book. In this study, newlywed couples visited the Murray laboratory within 6 months of their marriage. They completed a battery of questionnaires about their marriage and then they returned home to complete standardized, electronic diaries each day for 2 weeks. Among other questions, they rated how valued they felt by their partner each day (e.g., "My partner sees the best in me"). They also described their behavior by indicating which of several specific events had happened that day (e.g., "We had a major argument"; "My partner was affectionate"). These newlyweds had just made a dramatic public testament to their commitment. Making this commitment is so powerful that it can even lessen anxieties about rejection that people have carried with them since childhood (Davila, Karney, & Bradbury, 1999). Nonetheless, these newlyweds still used what might seem like minor behaviors to gauge their value to their partner. These newlyweds reported feeling more valued and loved by their partner on days when their partner reported sacrificing to meet their needs. Acts of sacrifice as small as Hector cooking Helena's dinner, going out of his way to take her clothes to the dry cleaner, or acceding to her point of view when they had a disagreement made Helena feel more valued.

The information revealed about a partner's willingness to be responsive in such diagnostic situations even predicts how couples fare over the first 5 years of marriage (Markman, 1979, 1981). In an inventive early study of marital discord, Markman (1979) asked couples planning to marry to sit down at his laboratory "talk table" and converse. In these conversations, couples talked about risk—unbeknownst to them. Markman gave these couples vignette descriptions of various marital conflicts and asked them to decide who (husband or wife) was at fault. He also got them to talk about conflicts couples might have in their sex lives. He also asked them to pinpoint the biggest problem they faced in their relationship and find a solution to it. As they talked, each member of the couple rated their partner's motivations (on a 5-point scale ranging from super-negative to super-positive). This rating constituted a barometer of partner responsiveness because it captured how gratified or hurt the partner's statements made people feel. Markman then recontacted these couples 2.5 years and 5.5 years after they married. He found something remarkable. Perceiving a partner as responsive in these risky situations actually predicted greater satisfaction over 5 years later. Although the sample was small, the strength of this predictive correlation was striking ($r = .59$). Detecting greater reason to trust in the partner's responsiveness in these risky situations sealed marital fate!

Rule 2: If Partner Values Traits, Then Trust

Hector's perception of how positively Helena views his specific qualities— such as his intelligence, attractiveness, or warmth—also signals his value to her (Murray, Holmes, & Griffin, 2000). The interpersonal mind tends to such assessments because being valued by others generally fosters stronger social ties. The sociometer model of self-esteem assumes that people utilize the desirability of their own personal qualities to gauge others' dispositions toward them (Leary & Baumeister, 2000; Leary & MacDonald 2003). In the sociometer metric, the salience of one's strengths signals the likely acceptance of others; the salience of one's weaknesses signals likely rejection by others (Leary, Tambor, Terdal, & Downs, 1995). A parallel rule shapes and constrains inferences about how accepting and valuing one's romantic partner is likely to be.

There is solid cross-sectional and experimental evidence to suggest that the interpersonal mind possesses an "if partner values traits, then trust" rule (Murray, Holmes, & Griffin, 2000; Murray, Holmes, Griffin, Bellavia, & Rose, 2001). In cross-sectional studies, we assessed the "if" component of this vigilance rule by asking Hector how Helena sees him on 22 different interpersonal qualities, such as warm, critical, intelligent, demanding, lazy, patient, and sociable. We assessed the "then" component of the rule by asking Hector how much he generally trusts in Helena's love and commitment (e.g., "I am confident my partner will always want me to stay with him"). We then examined the overall strength of the "if partner values traits, then trust" rule by correlating Hector's perception of Helena's regard for his interpersonal qualities with his trust in Helena's responsiveness. In doing this, we also controlled for how Hector sees himself on the interpersonal qualities.[3] The results of these studies revealed that Hector trusts more in Helena's commitment when he believes she sees his traits more positively. Conversely, Helena trusts less in Hector's commitment when she believes he sees her traits more negatively.

One of our favorite laboratory experiments revealed a parallel dynamic. In this study, we brought dating couples into the Murray laboratory (Murray, Rose, Bellavia, Holmes, & Kusche, 2002). In the experimental condition, we manipulated the "if" part of the vigilance rule. We led one member of the couple to believe that their partner had a laundry list of complaints about their personal qualities. How did we do this? First we told experimental and control couples that they would each be completing the same measures in tandem throughout the study. We then sat partners back to back at two separate tables. In the experimental condition, we gave the target participant, let's call him Hector, a one-page questionnaire asking him to list important qualities in Helena that he disliked. The instructions also stipulated, in capital and bold-face type, that Hector did not need to list more than *one* quality if that was all that readily came to mind. So typically, Hector listed one of Helena's faults, stopped, and sealed his questionnaire in an envelope. Then he had to wait for Helena to finish before he could start the next experimental task. But as he sat,

Helena kept writing, and writing, and writing, and writing! Helena wrote so copiously because she was *not* asked to list faults in Hector (like Hector thought). Instead, she was asked to list at least 25 items in her bedroom. Inevitably, Helena took much longer to complete the writing task than Hector—which gave him considerable time to worry that Helena did not perceive him all that positively. In the control condition, both partners completed the one-fault listing task at the same time, and as a result, neither had any reason to think the other had a long list of complaints. Next we measured or dependent variable—trust in the partner's commitment and responsiveness. As we expected, threatening Hector's perception of Helena's regard for his traits (i.e., "if") elicited the contingent tendency to question her commitment to him (i.e., "then"). Experimental participants reported significantly less trust in their partner's commitment than control participants.[4]

Rule 3: If Equal in Worth to Partner, Then Trust

People also compare their own worth to the partner's perceived worth to judge their special value to their partner. The interpersonal mind relies on such comparisons as a further if–then rule for vigilance because fair-trade principles constrain one's romantic options. Indeed, social life makes the power of fairness or equity norms in limiting romantic options hard to escape (Berscheid & Walster, 1969; Feingold, 1988; Rubin, 1973; Walster, Walster, & Berscheid, 1978). Social exchange theorists argue that people implicitly understand "fair-trade" principles, so they limit romantic aspirations to those who have an equivalent "social net worth" (Berscheid, Dion, Walster, & Walster, 1971; Montoya, 2008; Murstein, 1970). People seem to know there is little point aspiring to a partner they do not deserve (and whose respect they would have trouble inspiring). Consequently, in thinking about what they want in a partner, people set aside hopes of the most desirable partner for a retainable one. People who perceive themselves less positively on traits such as warm, intelligent, attractive, and sociable expect less out of partners. They expect less perfection from their ideal partner. In contrast, people who perceive themselves more positively on traits expect more from their ideal partner (Campbell, Simpson, Kashy, & Fletcher, 2001; Murray, Holmes, & Griffin, 1996a, 1996b). Similar pragmatism governs people's choices on dating websites advertising "hot" prospects. Despite a plethora of options, people hesitate to pursue anyone whose physical attractiveness outstrips their own. Instead, they calculate and maximize the odds of success by pursuing equal matches (Lee, Loewenstein, Ariely, Hong, & Young, 2008). Such pragmatism is prudent. The real-world pressure toward matching is so powerful that dating partners who are unfairly matched on physical attractiveness are more likely to break up than fairly matched partners (White, 1980).

Because fairness constrains one's options, the interpersonal mind tracks one's special value to the partner by comparing one's own worth to the partner's worth (Derrick & Murray, 2007; Murray et al., 2005). To gauge Helena's commitment to him, Hector needs to know whether he measures up. He needs to know whether he deserves her. In this social comparison, believing one's own contributions to the relationship fall short of the partner's worth (i.e., "if") undermines one's status as hard to replace and threatens trust (i.e., "then"). In contrast, believing the worth of one's own contributions matches or exceeds the partner's enhances one's value to the partner. In applying this variant of the vigilance rule, the interpersonal mind attends to Hector and Helena's relative traits and behavioral skills. Hector's positive qualities, such as his greater patience and intelligence increase the value of his contributions relative to Helena's contributions; his negative qualities, such as his greater moodiness, subtract from it. Skills, such as his greater skill in disciplining their children, his income, and wizardry with a wrench, further bolster his relative value. Ineptitudes and negative behaviors, such as his inability to boil water, subtract from it.

A collection of direct and indirect evidence supports the existence of the "if equal in worth to partner, then trust" rule. First, violating the equality rule predicts greater concern about the partner's commitment in both dating and marital relationships. For instance, people who believe their contributions to the relationship are inferior to their partner's contributions report less confidence in their partner's love and commitment (Murray et al., 2005). Partners who believe their relationship contributions are inequitable also report less satisfaction in their relationships (Sprecher, 1988, 2001). Second, people generally use the perception of similarity (and thus the hint of equality) as a barometer of the strength of the partner's commitment. A voluminous literature suggests that the perception of similarity is one of the most powerful triggers of interpersonal attraction (Berscheid & Reis, 1998). Perceiving similarity fosters attraction in large part because people assume that people who are similar to them are also equal to them, and consequently, will want to commit to them (Condon & Crano, 1988).

Third, people who are already committed to their partner engage in considerable cognitive gymnastics to maintain the belief they made an equal match (and, thereby, abide by the equality vigilance rule). For instance, couples in committed relationships believe their own level of physical attractiveness matches their partner's attractiveness even if it does not (Feingold, 1988). In marriage, people who are more trusting also exaggerate how much their spouse shares the same traits, values, and feelings (Murray, Holmes, Bellavia, Griffin, & Dolderman, 2002). In fact, an already committed Helena will eventually come to believe that Hector is not that brilliant, hilarious, and gorgeous if she worries about her own intelligence, wit, and appearance. In so doing, she keeps him well within her league (Murray et al., 1996a). People also go out of their way to avoid threatening comparisons. For instance, people who feel committed to their partner compensate for the partner's greater aptitude or skill in a particular domain by affirming the general strength of their relationships (Lockwood, Dolderman, Sadler, & Gerchak, 2004). Satisfied couples also compensate for the threat posed by one partner outperforming the other by deciding they complement, rather than eclipse, each other (Beach et al., 1998; Beach, Whitaker, Jones & Tesser, 2001). Such equalization isn't a viable option for Helena when Hector outperforms her in a domain (e.g., child care) that is more important to Helena than it is to him. In such situations, the "if equal to partner, then trust" vigilance rule asserts its ugly influence, trust is compromised, and conflict and negative interactions between partners result (O'Mahen, Beach, & Tesser, 2000).

Rule 4: If Better Than Partner's Alternatives, Then Trust

People also compare their own desirability to the desirability of potential competitors for their partner's affections (Murray, Leder, et al., 2009). Such comparisons further cue the strength of the partner's commitment because fair-trade norms also constrain the partner's romantic options (Thibaut & Kelley, 1959). Partners' commitments are constrained by their alternatives to the current relationship (Rusbult & Van Lange, 2003; Thibaut & Kelley, 1959). Their affections can waver when the life that might be had with a possible alternative partner looks better than the life with the current partner (Rusbult, 1983). People most need to worry about such fleeting affections when the partner's value exceeds their own. In such circumstances, partners are likely to be poached precisely because others take such mismatches as an open invitation. The experience of couples mismatched in physical attractiveness presents a case in point. In such circumstances, the more attractive partner is more often the target of the advances and flirtations of others than the less attractive partner (White, 1980). Because the entreaties of available and better-matched alternatives can pose real temptation, gauging responsiveness also requires tracking how one stacks up against the partner's best options. In this social comparative metric, believing one's own worth or contributions exceeds the partner's most viable alternatives signals trust because one's relative superiority makes one harder to replace (Murray, Leder, et al., 2009). No matter how flawed Hector perceives himself to be, he still has some reason to trust in Helena's responsiveness if he thinks his most obvious competitors are even more flawed. He also has reason to trust in her responsiveness if he does things for Helena that competitors would be either unable or unwilling to do. He might secure his niche by shopping for shoes with Helena, an order of business her prior loves never entertained. However, the perception that his best qualities pale in comparison to these alternatives undermines trust because his commonness makes Helena's interest in pursuing a more deserving fit much harder to preempt.[5]

Rule 5: If Partner Has Barriers, Then Trust

Social life also reveals the factors that make ending relationships difficult (Levinger, 1976; Rusbult & Van Lange, 2003). Some barriers are inherent. For instance, if Hector cannot stand life as a single man, his distaste for solo status helps cement him to Helena. Because Hector is a devout Catholic, his faith also makes dissolving his marriage a less than viable option. Other barriers are engineered. Helena might ensure that Hector needs her in particular for instrumental and emotional support by isolating him from his friends. She might further increase her value to him by insinuating herself in his social network, making his friends her friends. She might also derogate his alternatives to the current relationship (Simpson, 1987), perhaps finding subtle ways to remind him that he's lucky she's willing to put up with his faults. Still other barriers are engineered to become inherent (Levinger, 1976). The more children they decide to have together, the harder it is for either Helena or Hector to dissolve their union. Burdened by child care, neither has the time, financial wherewithal or physical appeal to attract alternatives. In combination, such engineered and inherent barriers signal one's status as hard to replace because such constraints foreclose options to look elsewhere. Thus the salience of such barriers (i.e., "if"), such as Hector's need for emotional support (Drigotas & Rusbult, 1992), his eroding romantic appeal (Rusbult et al., 1998), and religious prohibitions against divorce (Levinger, 1976) all strengthen Helena's trust that Hector has little recourse but to stay committed to her and continue to meet at least some of her needs (i.e., "then").

Applying the If–Then Vigilance Rules across Cultures

Through applying the five if–then vigilance rules the interpersonal mind tracks the partner's commitment by signaling how readily one could be replaced. When the "if" triggers signal that the partner is willing to sacrifice, admiring of one's qualities, not superior in worth, not likely to be poached by alternatives, and confined by circumstance, they increase trust in the partner's commitment. When these "if" triggers instead convey that the partner is unwilling to sacrifice, dismissing of one's qualities, superior in worth, desirable to alternatives, and unfettered by constraints and obligations, they decrease trust in the partner's commitment.

There is a reason the interpersonal mind relies on at least five indicators (rather than one or two) to understand the complete basis for the partner's commitment. As we introduced in Chapter 2, people can attribute a partner's commitment to intrinsic (i.e., the value the partner places on one's inherent qualities, such as kindness or sense of humor), instrumental (i.e., the value the partner places on the tangible benefits one provides, such as emotional or instrumental aid), and extrinsic factors (i.e., the constraints imposed by circumstance, such as pressures from family or religious prohibitions against divorce). Each of the if–then vigilance rules addresses these different reasons for the partner's commitment to varying degrees. Applying these rules in combination thus offers a fuller picture of the likely true strength of the partner's commitment. Imagine Hector believes that Helena values him for his greater acumen in fixing her car and computer. Making an instrumental attribution, he might worry that her commitment would waver if she bought extended warranties (and no longer needed his expertise). He would have fewer such worries if applying the vigilance rules revealed that she valued him for his intrinsic ability to laugh at her jokes that nobody else found funny.

Cultures differ in the conditions that govern when and why romantic partners can be replaced. Therefore the utility of having intrinsic, instrumental, and extrinsic reasons for trusting in a partner's commitment varies as a function of the sociocultural context. Cultures generally differ along an individualism–collectivism dimension (Triandis, 1995). More individualistic cultures put a premium on independence and distinguishing oneself from others, whereas more collectivistic cultures put a premium on group harmony. In more independent cultures (e.g., Western), personal choice defines and sustains romantic bonds (Berscheid & Regan, 2005). Individuals decide whom to love; they decide when to marry; and they decide whether to bother marrying at all. In more interdependent cultures (e.g., Eastern), necessity and obligation also define and sustain the bond (Berscheid & Regan, 2005). Parents and kin help people decide whom to love and when to marry.

The priority placed on personal choice in independent cultures makes if–then rules that signal one's intrinsic value to the partner primary to trust (Murray & Holmes, 2008; Rempel, Holmes, & Zanna, 1985; Seligman, Fazio, & Zanna, 1980). In Western cultures, attributions to intrinsic, instrumental, and extrinsic factors form a hierarchy in shaping trust. Rempel et al. (1985) provided the first evidence for this assumption. In their study, they asked couples in ongoing dating and marital relationships to complete measures tapping trust and perceptions of the partner's motivations. The motivation items tapped the perceived reasons underlying the partner's commitment, including intrinsic ones (e.g., "We love each other and care more for each other than for ourselves"; "It gives my partner joy to offer me support"), instrumental ones (e.g., "With me around, my partner has someone to lend a hand"; "I keep my partner informed of things he/she should know about"), and extrinsic ones (e.g., "His/her parents would approve of me"; "I give him/her the kind of lifestyle I want to have one day").

The correlations between trust and each type of motivation revealed the hierarchy the researchers anticipated. Attributions to intrinsic motivations afforded greater trust in the partner than attributions to instrumental motivations, which in turn afforded greater trust than attributions to extrinsic motivations (Rempel et al., 1985). A further experimental study revealed that priming the extrinsic reasons for their partner's commitment actually decreases trust in the partner's responsiveness (Seligman et al., 1980). The predominance of intrinsic motivations in regulating trust in Western culture suggests that Western minds might most need to see certain cues to trust over others. In such cultures, attributing intrinsic motivation to the partner seems to require the inference that the partner values one's traits (Murray, Holmes, & Griffin, 2000) and willingly sacrifices on one's behalf (Wieselquist et al., 1999).

The priority placed on obligations to the social group in interdependent cultures increases the diagnostic value of the if–then rules that convey such social constraints. In such contexts, "if" triggers that support intrinsic attributions for a partner's commitment only signal trust when combined with "if" triggers that convey outside constraints (Berscheid & Regan, 2005). In Indonesia, believing the partner values one's traits is necessary, but not sufficient for trust. The partner's family must also value one's traits (MacDonald & Jessica, 2006). In such cultural contexts, trust requires confidence in both the partner's intrinsic and extrinsic motivations. The combined belief that the partner (i.e., intrinsic motivation) and the partner's family (i.e., extrinsic motivation) both value one's traits predicts greater trust in the partner's responsiveness.

DECIDING NOT TO BE VIGILANT

As we introduced early in the chapter, Hector is always going to have some reason to question the strength of Helena's commitment. He can't literally get inside her head to see what she is thinking, and he knows it. He cannot see into the future to know exactly how she is going to feel about his receding hairline and expanding waistline in 10 years' time. Helena also retains the capacity to hurt and disappoint him on occasion even though her past responsiveness rightly earned his trust. She'll get angry; she'll yell; she'll forget to get his beer at the grocery store; she'll lose their tickets to the basketball finals. This all happens in the best of the relationships. Because interdependence creates so many potential such red herrings, the interdependent mind must use its flexibility to ignore the if–then rules at least some of the time. Without such a capacity to decide not to worry, Hector's trust in Helena would be constantly buffeted about by the whims of ongoing events. Such reactivity is no friend to mutually responsive and stable interactions (Arriaga, 2001), and the interdependent mind seems to know it.

In interacting, partners who are highly trusting seem to stay that way by taking advantage of the mind's flexibility to correct the if–then vigilance rules. Practicing trust in the partner's responsiveness involves a leap of faith (Holmes & Rempel, 1989). In making this leap, people decide that they do not always need to trouble themselves with the evidence revealed by the automatic functioning of the if–then vigilance rules. Fortunately for him, Hector has a lot of faith in Helena's commitment to him. He has no real need to heed the vigilance rules because he has already answered the question they address: He is confident that she cares for him. He knows if would be hard, if not impossible, for Helena to find someone quite like him, so why pay attention to the evidence? For Hector the goal of disambiguating Helena's regard for him is rarely primed or called into action. The infrequent activation of this goal renders the associated vigilance rules less accessible (but still available) in his memory (Chartrand & Bargh, 1996). Less accessible knowledge structures (i.e., vigilance rules) are less likely to color inferences (Fazio, 1986; Holmes & Rempel, 1989). Therefore, slight shifts in Hector's perceived value to Helena, such as those prompted by her compliment on his dieting efforts, go unnoticed, assimilated to his positive expectations. He's not entirely immune, though. Because the vigilance rules are still available, but not highly accessible, within his procedural store of relationship knowledge, it just takes bigger events to make him think about Helena's motivations (Higgins, 1996). Strong cues that his value to Helena might be slipping, such as seeing her flirting with the neighbor, can still make him worry.

Unfortunately, Helena does not have the same level of faith in Hector that he has in her. She's never been able to answer the question of why Hector stays with her to her full satisfaction. Such a state of uncertainty has left her preoccupied with the if–then vigilance rules because they provide the key to the question she is trying to answer (Holmes & Rempel, 1989). Her overarching goal to disambiguate Hector's regard for her chronically primes the associated structures in memory (i.e., the vigilance rules) for satisfying such an appraisal goal (Chartrand & Bargh, 1996). Needing to discern Hector's trustworthiness acts like a constant situational nudge, priming the vigilance rules in a way that renders them highly accessible in her store of relationship knowledge. As a result she cannot escape wondering: Is she good enough? Is Hector taking her for granted? Did he just flirt with a neighbor? The hyperaccessibility of these rules results in a kind of signal-amplification bias. Events, no matter how mundane, are scrutinized for what might be gleaned about Hector's caring because Helena cannot afford to overlook any potentially diagnostic evidence (Murray, Bellavia, et al., 2003).

As Hector and Helena's contrasting experiences illustrate, trust in the partner's commitment changes the accessibility of the if–then vigilance rules. It does so in much the same way that faith in one's own value changes the sensitivity of the sociometer that gauges one's general value to others. That is, Leary and Baumeister (2000) argue that *state* self-esteem exists as a sociometer for garnering interpersonal acceptance. State drops in self-esteem alert people to the possibility of rejection and thus the need to take action to repair one's social ties. But when people have stronger social ties, the practical need for a highly sensitive alarm system decreases. When social ties are abundant, as they are in the eyes of people with high chronic self-esteem, the alarm can be sloppy. It can miss invitations to acceptance and warnings of rejection without imperiling a high-self-esteem person's strong social ties. When existing social ties are meager, as they are in the eyes of people with low chronic self-esteem, the alarm cannot afford to miss any potentially diagnostic evidence. Needing stronger social ties essentially sets a hair-trigger on this alarm. Such a goal state renders the "if succeed, then accepted" and "if fail, then rejected" rules that signal interpersonal value highly accessible in memory. This happens because people with weak social ties cannot afford to miss any sign that social circumstance might change (Baldwin & Sinclair, 1996; Ford & Collins, 2010; Nezlek, Kowalski, Leary, Blevins, & Holgate, 1997; Sommer & Baumeister, 2002).

Some People Are Probably Better Rule Breakers Than Others

Ignoring the if–then vigilance rules (at least some of the time) involves suspending disbelief. To sustain high levels of trust in the partner's commitment, people pretend to have a complete answer to a question that can never fully be answered: Will my partner always be there for me? In a sense, this level of faith in a partner is akin to religious faith (Brickman, 1987).

Some people have an easier time than others setting aside the need to be wary. Consequently, sustained faith or trust in the partner's commitment seems to come more readily to people of certain personality dispositions. Consider how the residue left by prior relationships with parents, friends, and past loves might affect people's capacity to decide not to be vigilant. Attachment theorists argue that people develop general expectations about relationships that start in the infant–caregiver relationship (Mikulincer & Shaver, 2003, 2007). Experiences with a consistently available and responsive caregiver in infancy provide a basic sense of felt security. This state of felt security communicates that one is worthy of the love that others are willing to provide. Experiences with inconsistently available or nonresponsive caregivers make such a state of felt security elusive. Such experiences make people doubt their own value and hesitate to trust in the responsiveness of others. The capacity for felt security developed early on in relationships then shapes subsequent experiences with new relationship partners (Collins & Read, 1994).

In this light, it's not surprising that people high in self-esteem or secure in attachment style have an easier time deciding to ignore the vigilance rules (i.e., deciding not to be wary). In fact, people who are low in self-esteem or insecure in attachment style are so prone to vigilance that they even underestimate how much long-standing romantic partners love them (Murray et al., 2001). They look at the history of their partner's commitment and decide rejection must be right around the corner. In a study that revealed how people's dispositions limit the capacity to trust, we asked members of dating and married couples to complete measures tapping their own feelings of love toward their partner and their perception of their partner's feelings of love toward them (Murray et al., 2001). Obtaining both sets of perspectives allowed us to examine whether some people are better at detecting how much their partner loves them than others.

Figure 3.1 presents the association between self-esteem and accuracy in perceiving the partner's feelings of love using the perceptions of dating men as an example. The results for dating women and married men and women were parallel. This figure breaks down the association between self-esteem and accuracy into two effects: (1) the association between self-esteem and perceptions of the partner's love, and (2) the association between self-esteem and the partner's actual feelings of love. The magni-

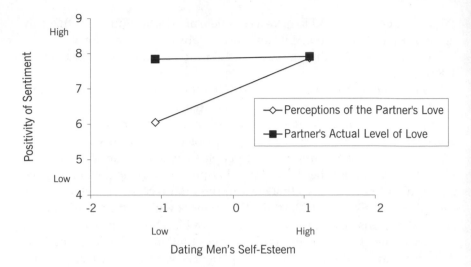

FIGURE 3.1. Accuracy in discerning a partner's love as a function of self-esteem. Adapted from Murray, Holmes, Griffin, Bellavia, and Rose (2001). Copyright 2001 by Sage Publications, Inc. Adapted by permission.

tude of the gap between these lines captures bias (in this case, the degree to which perceivers underestimate their partner's love for them). As Figure 3.1 reveals, people with lower self-esteem evidenced greater bias. That is, people who felt more negatively about themselves dramatically underestimated how much their partner loved them! Troubled by self-doubt, they could not make the leap of faith required to trust even though they routinely witnessed the most telling of cues—the constant presence of a loving and committed partner. Similar findings abound. People who chronically worry that others will reject them (i.e., those high on rejection sensitivity) underestimate their dating partner's satisfaction (Downey & Feldman, 1996). People who worry more about being rejection because childhood experiences left them anxious about their parents' love (i.e., those preoccupied in attachment style) also underestimate their dating partner's commitment (Tucker & Anders, 1999).

We return to the issue of how personality constrains faith in subsequent chapters. The theme we follow is straightforward. Practicing trust involves optimism in the specific and the general. It involves trust in the specific partner's responsiveness and faith in the general responsiveness of one's loved ones. Deciding not to be vigilant involves making a leap of faith that is eased by optimistic generalized expectations about oneself and one's relationship to others (Baldwin, 1992; Collins & Read, 1994; Rholes, Simpson, Campbell, & Grich, 2001). For instance, witnessing Hector's willingness to sacrifice sports to spend time with their children gives a low self-esteem Helena reason for faith in his responsiveness in this domain. But the rejection anxieties she carries forward from past failed relationships make her hesitant to ignore the vigilance rules in new domains. We return to the theme of how specific and generalized expectations interact in Chapter 10 and 11 discussions of relationship development.

Deciding Not to Be Vigilant: How Trust Inspires Rule Breaking

So let's now look to the empirical literature for the evidence that bears on the hypothesis that sustaining trust involves deciding not to be vigilant. The evidence on this point is substantial. High levels of chronic trust in the partner's commitment renders partners relatively immune to the if–then rules for vigilance. Low levels of chronic trust in the partner's responsiveness keeps these rules highly accessible and influential. To summarize the evidence to come: Smaller variations in "if" signals controlling vigilance trigger stronger state shifts in trust for people who are low on chronic trust in the partner's commitment (Derrick & Murray, 2007; Holmes & Rempel, 1989; Murray, Bellavia, et al., 2003; Murray, Holmes, MacDonald, & Ellsworth, 1998; Murray, Rose, et al., 2002; Murray et al., 2005). We do two things in reviewing this evidence. First, because personality dispositions like self-esteem can limit one's capacity to decide not to be vigilant, we use both indirect (e.g., self-esteem, attachment style, rejection sensitivity) and direct (e.g., trust, perceptions of the partner's regard for one's traits) barometers to capture chronic trust in the partner's commitment. Second, we limit our discussion to the vigilance rules involving the partner's respect (Rule 2), equality in worth (Rule 3), and the partner's alternatives (Rule 4). There is not yet good evidence on relaxing the barriers rule (Rule 5). The partner sacrifices and transgressions rule (Rule 1) is central to disambiguating the partner's goals in specific conflicts of interest, so we reserve discussion of this vigilance rule for Chapter 5.

Partner Respect

In daily life, partners do and say myriad things that convey information about how much they value each other's qualities and skills. Hector might frown when Helena tells him about the difficulties she had bathing their son. Helena might grimace when Hector asks her whether he's getting too heavy and roll her eyes when he regales her with his win at the poker table. People who question their partner's commitment to them grasp at such cues as evidence relevant to caring. For instance, people who are low in self-esteem interpret a dating partner's bad mood as clear evidence that their partner is upset or annoyed with them (Bellavia & Murray, 2003). Even people who have been married for a decade read rejection into a spouse's bad mood if they question how positively their partner regards them as a person on traits such as warm, intelligent, patient, critical, and demanding (Murray, Bellavia, et al., 2003). In a daily diary study, people who generally believed their partner saw less than positive qualities in them felt all the more rejected on days after their partner reported being in a bad mood. This happened even though the partner's mood had nothing to do with them!

Direct evidence that the partner is irritated or annoyed with oneself also amplifies *state* anxieties about the partner's commitment for people who are low in self-esteem. In two experiments, we gave participants in the experimental condition a reason to worry, an invitation to vigilance that low self-esteem people should take up more readily given that they have chronic concerns about the strength of their partner's commitment (Murray, Rose, et al., 2002). In Experiment 1, we asked experimental participants to focus on those dark, seamy, or secret sides of themselves they would rather their partner not see. We then told them their partner was likely to find them out. In Experiment 2, we led experimental participants to believe their partner had a complaint about their behavior or personality they had not yet expressed. We did this by having experimental participants complete a biased inventory that led them to think their partner often showed nonverbal signs of being distressed. We then told them that such signs meant their partner was itching to complain about something. Control participants were not given this worry. We then measured trust in the partner's responsiveness using a composite of measures that tapped the partner's anticipated willingness to forgive one's transgressions, reliance on the partner for support, and perceptions of the partner's love and acceptance. Figure 3.2 illustrates the effects on this composite measure in the secret selves experiment. When primed to think about their seamy secrets, low self-esteem participants reported less confidence in their partner's ongoing commitment than did control participants. They followed the vigilance rule. However, high self-esteem participants ignored the rule. They read nothing into the possibility that their partner might dislike certain of their qualities. In this instance, high self-esteem people could afford *not* to be concerned because they already "knew" that their partner valued their qualities.

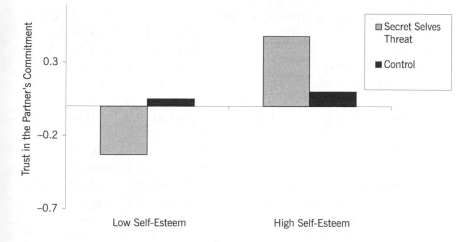

FIGURE 3.2. Trust in a partner's commitment as a function global self-esteem and threat.

Downward and Upward Social Comparisons

In day-to-day life, partners cannot escape comparing themselves to each other. Who is the better cook, parent, or driver? Who is more responsible, more pressured with tasks, more taken for granted, more controlling, more selfish, more forgiving, better in bed? Comparisons of relative contributions rarely escape the notice of people who trust less in their partner's commitment. For them, being better than the partner (i.e., a downward social comparison) increases state feelings of trust in the partner's commitment. Being worse than the partner (i.e., an upward social comparison) decreases trust.

The social comparative element of the equality in worth vigilance rule can have an immediate and paradoxical effect on the relationships of people who chronically question their partner's commitment. A flawed partner can actually be a more reassuring one! Imagine someone low in self-esteem like Helena. People who are low in self-esteem generally feel eclipsed by their partner (Murray et al., 2005). Helena thinks that Hector is a better person than she—smarter, warmer, more attractive, funnier, and so on. Feeling eclipsed makes it difficult for her to believe that Hector truly values her. Consequently, any hint that Hector might not be quite so exemplary gives her a little reason to hope. Such downward social comparisons bring him a little more within her grasp and make his commitment to her a little easier to explain.

In one relevant experiment, we led participants to believe that their partner was not behaving considerately. We created this downward social comparison by having experimental participants complete a biased partner behavior inventory. Items on this inventory focused on minor, but typically frequent, inconsiderate partner behaviors (e.g., "Have you ever had to say the same thing twice to your partner because he/she wasn't listening the first time? Have you ever felt like your partner was being selfish?"). As we expected they would, experimental participants readily agreed that such events had happened. We then reinforced this message by informing them their partner was not behaving particularly considerately. Control participants completed a neutral inventory. We then measured confidence in the partner's long-term acceptance and commitment using a combination of measures that tapped overall perceptions of the partner's commitment (e.g., "I am confident my partner will always want to stay in our relationship"), perceptions of the partner's closeness (e.g., "My partner feels extremely attached to me"), and predictions for the partner's future commitment-relevant behaviors (e.g., "My partner will want more independence and pull away from me," reverse-scored). Figure 3.3 presents the results for this composite dependent measure. As expected, low self-esteem participants actually reported greater confidence in their partner's commitment when their partner was behaving badly (Murray et al., 2005; Experiment 2)! No such effect emerged for high self-esteem participants.

In later research, we replicated the effects of closing the comparison gap among people insecure in attachment style (Derrick & Murray, 2007).

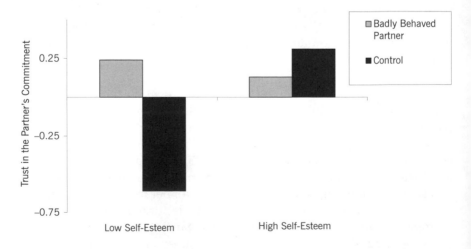

FIGURE 3.3. Trust in a partner's commitment as a function of global self-esteem and a badly behaving partner.

In a laboratory experiment, we simply asked experimental participants to list a few domains in which they outperformed their partner. Helena, for instance, might mention that she has a better sense of humor and a better sense of direction than Hector. When thinking about these relative strengths, people high in attachment anxiety actually report greater confidence in their partner's love and commitment (Derrick & Murray, 2007; Experiment 1). We also replicated this dynamic when we examined how married couples bring events at work home with them and then use these events as a gauge of their partner's commitment (Murray, Griffin, Rose, & Bellavia, 2006). In a daily diary study, we found that low self-esteem people used events at work during the day to gauge their partner's later regard for them that evening. Work successes bolstered trust! On days when they closed the comparison gap (because they succeeded at work), low self-esteem men and women perceived their spouse as more accepting and loving (Murray, Griffin, et al., 2006).

Of course, the social comparative element of the trust rule has a more invidious effect. Experiences that put the partner even more out of reach by provoking an upward social comparison elicit corresponding declines in the partner's love and commitment. Because Helena has low self-esteem, simply contemplating her own weaknesses is sufficient to trigger doubts about Hector's trustworthiness. Why? Such weaknesses increase the social comparative chasm. People with low self-esteem report less trust in their partner's love and commitment when they are led to believe that they are less intelligent (Murray & Pinkus, 2008) or less considerate than their partner (Murray et al., 1998). On days when low self-esteem women failed at work, they also perceived their husbands as more rejecting when they returned home (Murray, Griffin, et al., 2006). Again, this effect emerged even though their husbands were no more rejecting of them when they failed than when they succeeded. People with high self-esteem evidence no such reactivity to such implied comparisons. Indeed, they do the opposite. People with high self-esteem compensate for self-doubt by embellishing how much their partner loves them (Murray et al., 1998; Murray, Griffin, et al., 2006). Such findings support our earlier contention that high self-esteem acts as a psychological resource in sustaining trust because it allows highs to decide *not* to worry. It gives them license to ignore the rules. Rather than following the vigilance rule, high self-esteem people in this experiment actually contradicted it. They decided their partner loved them more when they failed!

Directly invoking an upward comparison to the partner similarly induces differential application of the vigilance rule as a function of self-esteem. Imagine that Hector and Helena both take an exam to qualify for entrance to a community college, and Hector outperforms Helena by a wide margin. Would she bask in his glory? Probably not if she has low self-esteem. In an experiment simulating such an event, Murray and Pinkus (2008) brought dating couples into the laboratory. Both members of the couple completed an intelligence test. In the upward social comparison condition, Helena learned that Hector scored better. In the control condition, Helena learned she scored equally well. We then measured state feelings of trust in the partner's acceptance and love. Lows again applied the vigilance rule: They reported feeling less accepted and loved when their dating partner outscored them as compared to control. In contrast, high self-esteem people ignored the rule: Being outperformed did not undermine trust.

The Partner's Better Options

Once people leave the safe confines of home, it is also hard to escape noticing how one compares to other partners. Such comparisons are abundant. They might occur at a party when Helena notices Hector's eyes lingering a little too long on a new female neighbor. They might occur when Helena listens to her friend Augusta recount the special meals she cooks for her husband (meals that Helena has neither the time nor the culinary skill to prepare). To the extent that Hector regales her with tales about past flames and past relationships, such comparisons might be hard for Helena to escape in even the safe confines of home. Although the evidence is limited, people who question their partner's commitment to them do glean more trust-related information from comparing themselves to the partner's alternatives.

In one relevant experiment, we manipulated how people stacked up to their partner's alternatives. We did this using a rather elaborate ruse (Murray, Leder, et al., 2009). We brought both members of the couple into the laboratory. In the experimental condition, we sat the participants back to back at two separate tables. We then gave the target participant a one-page questionnaire. This questionnaire asked the participant to list one quality she valued in the partner because she could not imagine finding that quality in anyone else. The target participant believed her partner was completing the same questionnaire. He wasn't. He was actually listing at least 25 items contained in his home. So target participants finished their short "list" quickly and then listened as their partner continued to write and write. Control participants both received the same questionnaire. Knowing their partner perceived valuable, hard-to-find qualities in them dramatically buoyed the hopes of low self-esteem people. They reported significantly greater trust in their partner's love and commitment (as compared to controls). So again, low self-esteem people used an if–then rule for vigilance that high self-esteem people largely ignored.

MISAPPLYING THE RULES: WHY A SECOND BAROMETER IS NEEDED

So let's recap. The interdependent mind *flexibly* uses the if–then vigilance rules to answer basic questions about the strength of the partner's commitment. In applying these rules, the mind informs and updates expectations about the partner's responsiveness in ways that people can readily articulate. Helena knows that she worries about Hector's greater patience and intelligence and she also knows that she worries about the security of his affections (although she might not put two and two together in her mind). But these sentiments miss something central to her experience with Hector: Even though she does not express highly trusting sentiments, she still "feels" reasonably safe in his presence. It's trying to explain why she feels good with him that seems to get her into considerable trouble (Wilson, 2002). This dichotomy brings us to a further complication we introduced earlier: The interdependent mind keeps a supplemental barometer for the safety of approach, an impulsive barometer of trust that is not bound by the if–then rules for vigilance.

It needs such a barometer because people are egocentric. People project their own feelings and beliefs onto others because they assume there is one world to perceive, and so the world they perceive is the same world others perceive (Griffin & Ross, 1991). This means that there's room for error in applying the vigilance rules. Consider the "if partner values traits, then trust" rule. In applying this rule, Helena cannot escape the concerns imposed by her own self-views (Kenny, 1994). In fact, she has so much trouble understanding why he loves her because her weaknesses are so obvious to her that she cannot figure out why Hector doesn't see them.

Looking to the research literature reveals considerable evidence of egocentrism in relationships. People in both dating and marital relationships assume that their partner sees them just as they see themselves (Murray, Holmes, & Griffin, 2000; Murray et al., 2001; Murray, Rose, et al., 2002). In our first study of this egocentrism bias, we asked people to describe themselves on 22 different positive and negative interpersonal qualities, such as warm, critical, intelligent, demanding, lazy, patient, and sociable. This constituted our measure of *self-regard*. Participants also described how they believed their partner saw them on these same qualities. This constituted our measure of the partner's *perceived regard*. The associations we found between self-regard and perceived regard revealed striking evidence of egocentrism. People assumed that their partner saw them just as they saw themselves. That is, they self-verified (Swann, Hixon, & De La Ronde, 1992). In fact, the correlation between self-regard and perceived-regard exceeded .75! This was just as true in marital relationships as it was in dating relationships and it was just as true for women as men. People who perceived themselves as possessing more desirable and special qualities believed their partner shared their high opinion, whereas people who perceived themselves as possessing less desirable qualities believed their partner saw similar failings.

But such egocentric perceptions are biased. They are not perfect barometers of the partner's actual regard for people who are low in self-esteem like Helena. Figure 3.4 illustrates this point. It shows how accuracy in discerning a partner's regard shifted as a function of global self-esteem in one of our early studies (Murray, Holmes, & Griffin, 2000). The depicted results are for dating men; the results for dating women and married men and women were parallel. In this figure, the gap between the line for perceptions of the partner's regard and the line for the partner's actual regard captures accuracy. As this figure illustrates, people with high global self-esteem largely understood how positively their partner saw them on specific interpersonal qualities. They assumed that their partner shared their more positive view of their own traits, and they were largely correct. In

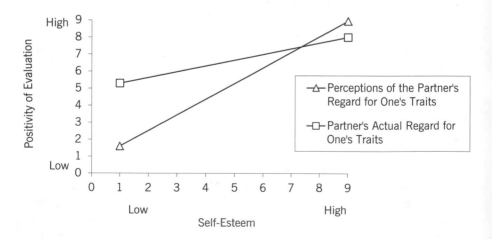

FIGURE 3.4. Accuracy in discerning the partner's regard for one's traits as a function of self-esteem. Adapted from Murray, Holmes, and Griffin (2000). Copyright 2000 by the American Psychological Association. Adapted by permission.

contrast, low self-esteem people dramatically underestimated just how positively their partner viewed them. They assumed that their partner shared their more negative view of their own traits. But they were largely wrong. Moreover, such unwarranted insecurities about their partner's regard for their personal qualities were more than sufficient to undermine overall levels of trust in their partner's responsiveness for lows (Murray, Holmes, & Griffin, 2000).

Impulsive Trust: Evaluative Associations to the Partner

Because applying the vigilance rules involves inferential processes that are themselves subject to error, their application provides a less-than-perfect barometer of the partner's commitment. Therefore, the interdependent mind also keeps a supplementary barometer of the safety of approach. This secondary pulse on the strength of the partner's commitment is not informed by the if–then vigilance rules. Instead, this impulsive barometer of trust is formed through processes of associative learning that are largely inaccessible to consciousness (Murray, Holmes, et al., 2010). Experiencing behavioral rewards (and few costs) in the partner's presence conditions a more positive evaluative association to the partner—one that can automatically signal the safety of approach even when applying the vigilance rules provokes caution.[6]

In positing an impulsive trust barometer for the interdependent mind, we share the philosophy advanced by a long history of research on attitudes. Conditioned evaluative associations (i.e., attitudes) automatically orient people toward their social worlds (Allport, 1935; Fazio, 1986). Positive evaluative associations automatically motivate behavioral approach; negative evaluative associations command behavioral avoidance (Alexopoulos & Ric, 2007; Baumeister, Vohs, De Wall, & Zhang, 2007; Chen & Bargh, 1999). For instance, priming positively evaluated objects automatically activates the behavioral tendency to draw objects in one's environment closer to oneself, whereas priming negatively evaluated objects automatically activates the behavioral tendency to push objects away (Chen & Bargh, 1999). Subliminally priming positive affect words (e.g., happy) also automatically activates the behavioral tendency (i.e., arm flexion) to draw closer; subliminally priming negative affect words (e.g., angry) activates the behavioral tendency (i.e., arm extension) to push away (Alexopoulos & Ric, 2007).

In relationships, the interdependent mind's capacity to form more or less positive automatic associations to the partner means that it also has a supplementary means of telling when it is safe to approach or wise to be cautious. Imagine that Helena has had a difficult day with her children and needs some comfort from Hector. Possessing a more positive automatic evaluative association to Hector makes her feel safe in his presence; she might then find herself confessing the stresses of the day despite her concerns about his responsiveness. Two experiments conducted in the Murray lab speak to this fascinating possibility.

Our general strategy in these experiments takes a little bit of explaining. We started with the assumption that positive evaluative associations to the partner (i.e., impulsive trust) automatically signal the safety of approach. If that's the case, people who possess such positive evaluative associations should still approach their partner even when there is reason not to approach. That is, they should still approach the partner when the "if-the" vigilance rules dictate caution. We gave experimental participants a reason not to approach by priming one of the if–then rules for vigilance.

In our first experiment, we brought dating couples into the laboratory (Murray, Pinkus, et al., 2010). We then used the Implicit Associations Test (IAT) to capture people's automatic evaluative associations to their partner and thus measure impulsive trust (Greenwald, McGhee, & Schwarz, 1998; Zayas & Shoda, 2005). In our version of the IAT, participants categorized words belonging to four categories: (1) pleasant words (e.g., *vacation, pleasure*); (2) unpleasant words (e.g., *bomb, poison*); (3) words associated with the partner; and (4) words not associated with the partner (Zayas & Shoda, 2005). We contrasted reaction times on two sets of trials to diagnose partners' unconscious evaluations of each other. In one set of trials, participants used the same response key to respond to pleasant words and partner words (i.e., compatible pairings). In the other set of trials, participants used the same response key to respond to unpleasant words and partner words (i.e., incompatible pairings). The logic of the IAT says reaction times should be faster when the nature of the task matches the nature of one's automatic associations to the partner. In particular, people who possess more positive evaluative associations to her partner (i.e., those high on impulsive trust) should be faster when categorizing words using the same motion for *partner* and *pleasant* than when using the same motion for *partner* and *unpleasant*.

We then primed the "if partner disregards traits, then distrust" vigilance rule for experimental, but not control subjects. As previously described, we led target participants in the *high-vigilance* condition to believe that their partner was spending a copious amount of time providing a long list of the participant's faults (when the partner was actually listing 25 items in their residence). Participants in the *low-vigilance* condition were led to believe their partner listed only one or two faults. "Seeing" the partner itemize numerous complaints leaves people feeling hurt and rejected, as we saw earlier in this chapter. Could being high on impulsive trust (i.e., possessing a more positive automatic association to the partner) actually keep the motivation to approach the partner intact in the face of a strong reason not to approach? To look at the strength of people's approach motivations, we measured how quickly experimental and control participants associated their partner with positive traits in a categorization task. The results astounded us: Possessing a more positive automatic evaluative association to the partner kept Helena's motivation to approach Hector completely intact when he seemed to be compiling a mammoth list of her faults! Figure 3.5 presents the significant interaction we found between impulsive trust as assessed by the IAT and the vigilance condition. Let's look first at the people who made *less* positive evaluative associations to their partner, that is, those low on impulsive trust (on the left): Thinking their partner had a laundry list of complaints automatically inhibited approach. They were significantly slower to associate their partner with positive traits than were control participants. Now let's look

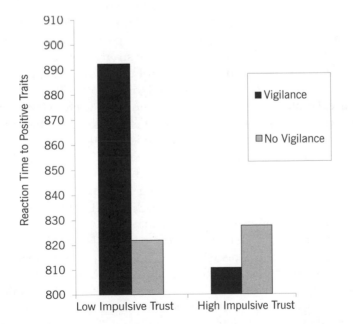

FIGURE 3.5. Implicit partner valuing as a function of vigilance salience and impulsive trust.

at the people who made more positive automatic evaluative associations, that is to their partner, those high on impulsive trust (on the right): Thinking their partner had a laundry list of complaints had absolutely no effect on approach. These high impulsive trust participants were just as quick to associate their partner with positive traits as were control participants.

In our second experiment, we gave experimental participants reason not to approach by indirectly priming the "if worse than partner's alternatives, then distrust" rule. We had all participants read a passage about relationships purportedly taken from a college textbook. In the *high-vigilance* condition, this passage stated that most people seriously overestimate the quality of their relationship (which should give Helena reason to think that Hector could find better fish in the sea). In the *low-vigilance* condition, this passage stated that most people underestimate the quality of their relationships. We then adapted a subliminal conditioning procedure developed by Dijksterhuis (2004) to condition positive automatic evaluative associations to the partner and thereby, manipulate impulsive trust. All participants completed a simple categorization task on computer. While completing this task, participants in the *high impulsive trust* condition were subliminally and repeatedly exposed to their partner's name followed by a positively valenced word (e.g., *warm, sweet, nice, sincere, honest, smart*). Participants in the *low impulsive trust* condition were subliminally and repeatedly exposed to their partner's name followed by a neutral word (e.g., *chair, bike*). To look at the strength of people's approach motivations, we then measured feelings of closeness to the partner (e.g., "My partner and I are strongly connected to each other").

Figure 3.6 presents the significant interaction we found between the vigilance and impulsive trust conditions. Let's look first at the low impulsive trust participants for whom we conditioned neutral evaluative association (on the left): Being primed with reason to be vigilant inhibited approach. Those participants who were led to think their partner might find better fish in the sea reported feeling less close to their partner as compared to controls. Now look at the high impulsive trust participants for whom we conditioned more positive automatic evaluative associations (on the right): Being primed with reason to be vigilant actually promoted approach! Those participants who were led to think their partner might find better fish in the sea reported feeling closer to their partner as compared to control participants. These two experiments raise a tantalizing possibility: Unconscious or automatic evaluations toward the partner— that is, impulsive trust—might actually provide a barometer of the safety of approach that can trump the if–then rules for vigilance. We return to

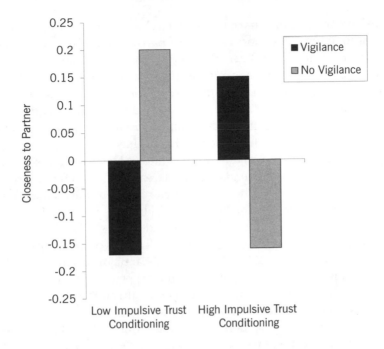

FIGURE 3.6. Closeness to the partner as a function of subliminally conditioned evaluative associations (i.e., low vs. high impulsive trust).

this possibility in subsequent chapters, hinting at the possibilities this creates in Chapter 5, but exploring this issue in depth starting in Chapter 10. Stay tuned.

MOTIVATING TRUST: FORECLOSING THE PARTNER'S OPTIONS

The findings reviewed to this point in the chapter point to a similar conclusion. People who chronically trust in their partner's responsiveness are less reactive to the vigilance rules. They are not as likely to code ongoing events as markers of the need for avoidance. This seems to be true whether deliberative expectations of the partner's responsiveness (i.e., reflective trust) or automatic evaluative associations to the partner (i.e., impulsive trust) signal the strength of the partner's commitment. Neither form of trust invokes complete immunity, though. Even a highly responsive partner can behave badly when the temptation to be selfish is too great to ignore. The most resilient of partners (e.g., high self-esteem, secure in attachment style) can also find themselves in situations where they question their partner's responsiveness. To coordinate mutually responsive interaction patterns, the interpersonal mind needs a mechanism to restore the partner's commitment when it is clearly in question. It has such a mechanism in the if–then implementation rule for promoting the partner's dependence. Imagine that Hector has a strong desire to go to a playoff basketball game on the same night that Helena had reserved for a rare night out with her friends. Hector faces a serious temptation to be selfish. His temptation will be all the greater if he's annoyed that Helena left the dishes for him the day before. It will be still greater if he remembers that Helena just went out with her friends 2 weeks ago.

Such a situation captures the essential elements of the bankers' paradox (Tooby & Cosmides, 1996): Helena needs a major sacrifice from Hector when he is not disposed to make a grand gesture. The interpersonal mind generally minimizes such eventualities through preemption. The "if self-protect goal, then promote partner's dependence" links Helena's anticipation of Hector's rejection in such a situation (i.e., "if") to behavioral efforts to make Hector "owe" or need her (i.e., "then"). This preemptive rule motivates Helena to take remedial action to gain greater control or power over Hector at the slightest hint that his commitment to her might be slipping. These "alarming events" are the ones that signal her potentially decreased value to him, such as happens when Hector criticizes her, has more success in calming their children, or spends a little too long staring at an attractive neighbor as she waters her lawn. In such situations, the interpersonal mind preempts the possibility of selfishness by making loyalty a necessity for the partner. It does so by linking one's own concerns about deservingness to preemptive behavioral efforts to put the partner in debt. This if–then rule essentially minimizes the threat of nonresponsiveness by finding ways to make the partner more practically dependent on oneself. That is, the mind has a mechanism for giving Helena the power to make Hector "owe" her. In behaving in ways that make Hector more dependent on her, Helena restores her special or unique value to him and increases Hector's commitment to being responsive.

A partner's commitment to the relationship stems in part from factors within one's personal control (Rusbult & Van Lange, 2003). Hector is more committed when he depends on Helena to fulfill more of his needs (Drigotas & Rusbult, 1992) and he cannot imagine fulfilling these needs in alternate relationships (Rusbult & Van Lange, 2003). Evidence suggests that the activation of deservingness concerns motivates Helena to make sure she fills such a niche in Hector's life (Murray, Aloni, et al., 2009). It prompts her to escalate the instrumental benefits Hector gains from the relationship and to limit his freedom to find such benefits elsewhere. To ensure that Hector needs her, Helena might become proficient in domains, such as cooking or cleaning, where Hector is weaker. She might also take responsibility for practical matters, such as managing Hector's schedule or appointments. She might make sure that all of Hector's friends come to like her and enlist his family as an ally in conflicts. By eliciting Hector's greater dependence on her when his commitment seems in question, Helena limits any future incentive that he has to be selfish because he cannot afford to lose her.

We found the first evidence of such trust-insurance dynamics unfolding in the Murray lab's daily diary study of newlywed couples (which we introduced earlier). We measured each component of the "if self-protect goal, then promote partner dependence" rule through electronic diaries. Each partner separately completed one of these diaries each day over a 2-week period. We tapped the activation of self-protection goals (i.e., "if") with items measuring Helena's fear that she might not deserve Hector (e.g., "I'm not good enough for Hector"; "Hector is a better person than I am"). We measured the activation of partner-dependence promotion (i.e., "then") through the instrumental favors Helena did for Hector each day. We targeted thoughtful and considerate behaviors that nonetheless usurped Hector's capacity to take care of himself (e.g., "I searched for something Hector had lost"; "I went out of my way to run an errand for Hector"; "I packed a snack/lunch for Hector to take to work"; "I did a chore that is normally Hector's responsibility").

Diary data such as these have two great advantages. First, these data allow us to examine within-person effects. As we mentioned earlier, people who are low in self-esteem are more likely to feel inferior to their partner than high self-esteem people. Diary data allow us to control for such individual differences among people by looking at the same person across time. Obtaining multiple measures from the same person across time allows us to see whether even high self-esteem people work to promote their partner's dependence on those days when their worries about deserving their partner spike (relative to their own mean). Second, because yesterday's events can determine today's experiences, but today's experiences cannot go back in time to determine yesterday's events, diary data can also shed some light on causality effects.

In this sample, we conducted analyses to see whether Helena's acute feelings of not deserving Hector (i.e., "if") generally triggered efforts to increase his dependence (i.e., "then"). That is, we examined whether Monday's anxiety about being inferior predicted increases in the effort to curry the partner's dependence on Tuesday. It did. These newlyweds responded to feeling undeserving one day by engaging in behaviors that made their partner need them more the next day (Murray, Aloni, et al., 2009). They worked to secure their partner's debt by doing practical things like searching for keys, packing lunches, picking up clothes, and running errands. Furthermore, currying Hector's dependence helped ensure that Helena's trust in him would not be misplaced. Namely, Helena's dependence-promoting behavior actually successfully increased Hector's commitment to his marriage the next day. People naturally seem to know how to make themselves more indispensable to their partner on those occasions when they have the greatest reason to question their value to their partner. We further discuss how the trust rule works efficiently and flexibly to escalate the partner's dependence in Chapter 7.

Before concluding, it is fascinating to consider a historical paradox concerning divorce rates in light of our argument that the interpersonal mind naturally seeks such trust insurance. The data suggest that social policies that make divorce easier to obtain actually strengthen marriages! Much to the chagrin of conservatives who warned no-fault divorce would destroy the nuclear family, the incidence of divorce has actually decreased since no-fault divorce laws were introduced (Matouschek & Rasul, 2008). Though not using our terms, political scientists explain this phenomenon using the logic of trust insurance. They reason, quite reasonably, that couples in more tenuous relationships should be hesitant to commit. (This assumption fits perfectly with our contention that commitment is predicated on trust.) However, the formal barrier to the partner leaving the relationship imposed by a formal legal contract gives vulnerable people the extra insurance they need to commit. But introducing no-fault divorce made the marriage contract not worth the paper on which it was written. Vulnerable couples then had considerably less reason to marry because the contract itself no longer bound the relationship. The divorce rate then declined because the couples whose distrust and dissatisfaction most increased their need for insurance never married in the first place (and could never divorce)!

SUMMARY AND CAVEATS

This chapter described how the interdependent mind gauges trust in the partner's commitment and keeps such trust from being misplaced. Trust functions as a window to the partner's mind. It signals the strength of the partner's commitment and the relative need for caution and vigilance. By using trust as an intermediary, the interdependent mind can then match Hector's expression of commitment to Helena's expression of commitment.

This chapter had four main points. First, we described the if–then vigilance rules. These rules convey the strength of the partner's commitment by signaling when the partner is willing to sacrifice, is admiring of one's qualities, not superior in worth, not likely to be poached, and confined by circumstance. We also explained how these if–then rules constrain trust across cultures by shaping the intrinsic, instrumental, and extrinsic attributions that Helena makes for Hector's commitment. Second, we described how the interpersonal mind uses its flexibility to "decide" to ignore the rules some of the time. By necessity, people who are more trusting are less sensitive to the vigilance rules, making it easier for them to sustain trust in the face of reason to be vigilant. We also saw that some people, such as those high in self-esteem or secure in attachment style, have an easier time suspending vigilance and disbelief than others.

Third, we described how the interdependent mind keeps a supplementary, unconscious, and associative barometer (i.e., impulsive trust) for the safety of approach. Through conditioning, the interdependent mind "learns" from the bottom up when the partner is likely to be responsive. More positive automatic associations to the partner give the interdependent mind further license to ignore the if–then vigilance rules on occasion. Fourth, we described how the interdependent mind keeps the partner's commitment from flagging by applying the "promote partner dependence" rule. With this rule for self-protection in place, Helena takes steps to ensure that Hector owes her in those situations where she has reason for concern about this willingness to be responsive.

One caveat: In this chapter, we sometimes saw people who were highly trusting do something surprising. They did more than just ignore a specific if–then vigilance rule; they drew conclusions opposite to the conclusion implied by the rule. A high self-esteem Hector can (and did) actually convince himself that Helena loves him more when he fails (not less). Such findings raise the possibility that people who are highly trusting might possess a modified or specialized set of rules. With repeated experience correcting, Hector might learn his own variant of the vigilance rules. This modified set of rules is one that practice has tailored to suit the situations he encounters most often in his relationship with Helena. If Helena simply has a hot temper by nature, he might come to ignore her occasional outbursts. Instead of taking her expressions of annoyance as a sign of devaluing (the original vigilance rule), he might take such passionate expressions of his sentiment as a sign of how much she values being herself with him (the modified vigilance rule). Observing her temper might then make him more convinced of her commitment to him.

Because such specialized rules take repeated experience with correction to develop, they are likely to have a shorter history of activation in memory than the original rules (Collins & Read, 1994). Consequently, when Hector worried about his job security, the original rules for vigilance could still prevail. In that instance, he could still question his value to Helena because stress elicits more familiar or rehearsed behavioral patterns (Mikulincer & Shaver, 2003). Consistent with this hypothesis, attitude theorists argue that new and old attitudes exist independently in memory, exerting distinct effects on judgment (Petty, Tormala, Brinol, & Jarvis, 2006; Wilson et al., 2000). We return to the issue of how specialized rules develop in our Chapter 8 discussion of how the relationship develops a distinct personality.

In our next chapter, we turn to commitment. There we detail what it means to be more or less committed. We also describe how the interdependent mind uses trust as an intermediary to match one partner's expression of commitment to the other partner's expression of commitment. Chapter 4 thus examines how the interpersonal mind captures commitment and keeps this sentiment from being derailed when it is tested.

NOTES

1. If being of unique value to certain others is an adaptive necessity, interpersonal perception should focus on discerning qualities in others that portend one's potential value to them. It is. Discerning qualities, such as interpersonal warmth, that strongly signal how much another person is likely to value oneself is more basic to social perception than discerning qualities, such as competence, that weakly signal such dispositions (Fiske, Cuddy, & Glick, 2006). Traits that convey how valuing another is likely to be, such as deceitful or cooperative, automatically capture attention (as evidenced by increased color-naming latencies in a Stroop task). Traits that fail to convey such orientations, such as powerless or happy, do not (Wentura, Rothermund, & Bak, 2000). In contemplating potential mates, men and women from 37 different cultures agree that "kind" and "understanding" are the qualities they value most. These cues to a spouse's capacity to be valuing and responsive are more important than even attractiveness or earning potential (Buss, 1989). In fact, people pinpoint trustworthiness as the quality they desire most in others across all different types of interdependent relationships (Cottrell, Neuberg, & Li, 2007).

2. The importance of sacrifice in diagnosing responsiveness reveals something paradoxical about relationships. Compatibility has a downside. The more partners' preferences correspond, the less often they encounter conflicts of interest (Murray & Holmes, 2009). The less often they encounter conflicts, the *fewer* the opportunities Hector has to sacrifice on Helena's behalf. The fewer the opportunities Hector has to sacrifice, the harder it is for him to prove his responsiveness to Helena (Holmes & Rempel, 1989; Simpson, 2007). In such compatible relationships, his responsiveness has all too salient an external attribution—acting in his own interest! We return to this paradoxical aspect of compatibility when we develop our arguments about relationship personality in Chapter 8.

3. As we see later in the chapter, Hector's self-regard strongly colors how positively he believes that Helena sees him (Murray, Holmes, & Griffin, 2000). We control for Hector's self-assessed traits in examining the "if partner values traits, then trust" rule to ensure that it is Hector's beliefs about how Helena sees him predict trust (not just his self-regard).

4. Some readers might wonder about the ethics of challenging people's perceptions of their partner's regard for them. We take such concerns very, very seriously and we only use manipulations that we feel confident can be easily undone. Indeed, the beauty of the manipulation we used in this study is the ease with which it can be undone. All it takes to alleviate Hector's concerns is to show him Helena's list of her room contents. And that's exactly what we did in debriefing our participants. To be sure this worked, we have also tracked participants over time to make sure that such manipulations have no long-term negative effects on their relationship's stability. They do not.

5. Our focus on comparisons to a partner's perceived alternatives is a variation on the classic interdependence notion of comparison level for alternatives (Thibaut & Kelley, 1979). From a classic perspective on interdependence, commitment depends on the comparison Hector makes between his outcomes in his marriage and the outcomes he envisions for himself in his most viable alternate relationship (e.g., Rusbult et al., 1998). The "if better than partner's alternatives rule" recognizes that comparisons to Helena's alternatives may also influence Hector's perceptions of her commitment (and thus constrain his trust in her).

6. We review evidence suggesting that automatic associations to the partner are conditioned through behavioral experience in Chapter 10.

CHAPTER 4

Commitment

How Close a Connection?

> When the time comes to act, the great
> advantage of having a set of internally
> consistent dispositions is that the individual
> is not forced to listen to the babble of
> competing inner voices.
> —JONES AND GERARD (1967, p. 181)

Commitment frees one from the paralysis of thought. Once people are committed to a line of action, they do not need to think. They act (Brickman, 1987). Such a capacity for mindlessness is critical in relationships. Because costs are a central feature of interdependence, something could always give one pause. On Monday, it might be Gayle's worries about Ron's spending habits. On Tuesday, it might be Ron's frustration with Gayle's sports obsession. On Friday, it might be the allure of weekend life as an unencumbered single. Such distracting inner voices need an effective counterweight. Commitment provides it. The sense of being tied to the partner for better or worse provides the motivation to persevere when inner voices might lead one astray. Think about Gayle asking Ron to take her turn as 3 A.M. chauffeur to their colicky infant. If Ron is committed to Gayle, he does not decide. He just drives. Without commitment, his desire to sleep, his frustration with Gayle's work schedule and obligations, and the resultant appeal of a more traditional wife could all dissuade him from being responsive to her needs.

This chapter begins our exploration of how the interdependent mind coordinates expressions of commitment across partners and keeps commitment from being derailed. As we introduced in Chapter 2, commitment is the interpersonal mind's pulse or monitor of the strength of one's motivation to approach connection. It basically tells Ron how far to go in drawing closer to Gayle. Ron can approach or draw closer to Gayle in two different but equally important ways: (1) he can solicit Gayle's care and responsiveness toward him and (2) he can provide his care and responsiveness to Gayle. Ron's commitment to Gayle reflects and motivates stronger (or weaker) approach overtures by revealing Gayle's inherent value to him. The more valuable Gayle is to Ron, and the more committed he is to her, the more he depends on Gayle for the satisfaction of his needs and the more psychologically attached to her he feels (Rusbult et al., 1998; Rusbult & Van Lange, 2003). Ron is highly committed to Gayle: He depends on her for most things, from her unerring ability to remember what he's about to forget at the grocery store to the ease with which she makes him feel sexy with a sideways glance. He's now grown so attached to her that he cannot imagine life without her. He's willing to do almost anything for her. He not only volunteers to take the children to the park so she can watch football in peace, but he takes on more than his fair share of household chores so she has enough time to further her career. In these respects, Ron's commitment has made his choices about his behavior in conflict of interest situations relatively mindless (Rusbult & Van Lange, 2003). Being more committed motivates him to minimize conflicts (Rusbult et al., 1991), seek and provide support (Collins & Feeney, 2004; Reis et al., 2004), and respond selflessly to Gayle's needs (Clark & Grote, 1998; Rusbult & Van Lange, 2003; Van Lange et al., 1997), all because she is more than worth it.

But approach invites the possibility of rejection. For approach overtures to be safe and met with caring or gratitude (as appropriate to the overture), partners cannot misstep in expressing commitment. Ron cannot let his commitment to Gayle get too far out of step with her commitment to him. Such a misstep would leave him vulnerable to Gayle's nonresponsiveness and even outright exploitation, because a less committed Gayle has no real incentive to reciprocate his dependence and responsiveness with similar overtures of her own. This is the "principle of least interest" we introduced in Chapter 1. People seem to implicitly understand the danger of putting themselves too far out on a limb. In ongoing relationships, the partner who is more committed and emotionally involved knows the fate of the relationship rests largely outside his or her hands (Sprecher et al., 2006). The worries that ensue from relative powerlessness increase the potential for conflict (Drigotas, Rusbult, & Verette, 1999; Grote & Clark, 2001), breed dissatisfaction, and forecast dissolution (Sprecher et al., 2006).

This chapter builds on the principle of least interest to delineate how the interpersonal mind tries to keep such destructive power imbalances from developing in the first place. It describes how the interdependent mind elicits reciprocity in commitment and thereby motivates Ron and Gayle to pursue correspondent goals for their marriage. In this task, the mind employs if–then rules for both (1) matching commitment to trust and (2) ensuring commitment is not derailed. The implementation rules that match commitment to trust make Ron's willingness to put his outcomes (practical or psychological) in Gayle's hands contingent on his anticipation of her responsiveness (Murray, Holmes, & Collins, 2006; Murray, Holmes, & Griffin, 2000). This matching rule applies in both the general and the specific case. Ron's chronic level of trust in Gayle controls his chronic level of commitment. His state anticipation of her acceptance (i.e., trustworthiness) in particular situations also controls his specific expressions of commitment in those situations. For instance, knowing that his wine obsession irritates Gayle motivates Ron to keep his enjoyment of a new bottle of Chianti to himself (i.e., "if self-protect goal, then withdraw own dependence"). Believing that Gayle values his contributions as a parent instead motivates Ron to seek her support when he's questioning his skills as a father (i.e., "if connect goal, then escalate own dependence"). However, as Ron draws closer to her, Gayle inevitably incurs costs. She simply no longer has the freedom she once had. Her resulting frustrations could then reduce her commitment and tip the balance of power in her favor. The interdependent mind wards off such an eventuality by making Ron all the more valuable to Gayle precisely when he thwarts her goals (i.e., "if connect goal, then justify own commitment"). With wine racks cluttering all of her available workspace on the kitchen counters, Gayle has come to value Ron's patience all the more (Murray, Holmes, et al., 2009).

This chapter advances four main points for understanding commitment. Table 4.1 summarizes these arguments, addressed in sequence in the chapter. In the first part of this chapter we define what it means to be committed in a structural sense. We describe how Ron gauges his commitment to Gayle through: (1) the benefits and costs he perceives, (2) the investments he has made, and (3) the alternatives he has and has foregone (Rusbult & Van Lange, 2003). In gauging his commitment, Ron notices Gayle's warmth, her stubbornness, his investments of time and energy, the women he cast aside, and the ones he might still attract. In the second

TABLE 4.1. The Main Arguments

1. Commitment based on satisfaction, investments, and alternatives.
2. Building commitment involves overstating the case—exaggerating the positives and minimizing the negatives.
3. If–then rules that match commitment to trust make willingness to solicit and provide care contingent on expectations of partner responsiveness.
4. If–then rule for justifying commitment keep feelings of commitment from being derailed by the experience of autonomy costs.

part of this chapter we define what it takes psychologically to approach and enact commitment. For commitment to push people forward, it needs an inertial, fixed quality. Ron cannot back away from closeness at the moment either his needs or Gayle's needs become too pressing. To stay connected when the going gets rough, Ron needs *resolve*. By this, we mean that Ron experiences his commitment to Gayle as a foregone conclusion. He cannot imagine being married to anyone who would better meet his needs, nor can he imagine finding anyone quite as worthy of his sacrifices. As we will see, building resolve requires that the interdependent mind play some perceptual tricks in assembling the case for commitment. To Ron, Gayle's stubbornness appears more courageous than curmudgeonly; his disclosures to her more revealing than concealing; the women foregone more aggravating than appealing.

In the third part of this chapter we describe how the interdependent mind matches Ron's expressions of commitment to Gayle's expressions of commitment. That is, we describe the if–then implementation rules that match commitment to trust (i.e., the partner's perceived commitment). These rules keep Ron (and Gayle) from missteps in expressing commitment. By making Ron's expressions of resolve in his commitment contingent on his anticipation of Gayle's commitment, these rules keep Ron from asking too much of Gayle. These rules also keep Ron from providing too much to Gayle. In the fourth part of this chapter we describe the if–then implementation rules that keep Gayle's resolve in her commitment to Ron from being derailed in the face of acute or situational costs. When Ron disrupts Gayle's plans for a night out with friends by insisting on staying home, her mind actually pushes her to value his need for quiet reflection and solitude more rather than less. We end by foreshadowing how the mechanisms that foster resolve and reciprocity in partners' commitments afford mutual behavioral expressions of responsiveness that further build trust and commitment.[1]

THE STRUCTURAL BASIS OF COMMITMENT

So what is commitment in a structural sense? Interdependence theorists root commitment in the history and quality of ongoing interactions. Three interaction features summarize Ron's need for his relationship with Gayle and thus his motivation to continue his marriage in the future (Kelley, 1979; Rusbult & Van Lange, 2003). These features include (1) satisfaction, how the balance of rewards and costs compares to his expectations; (2) the quality of his options or alternatives to the relationship; and (3) investments of time, energy, and resources that could be lost (Rusbult et al., 1998). When the balance of the rewards meets or exceeds expectations, alternate suitors or life alone pale in comparison to life with the partner, and irretrievable investments have been made, one's commitment to the partner and relationship is strengthened.

The investment model developed by Rusbult and colleagues details exactly how commitment emerges through interaction and experience (Kelley & Thibaut, 1978; Rusbult et al., 1998; Rusbult & Buunk, 1993; Rusbult & Van Lange, 2003; Thibaut & Kelley, 1959). Figure 4.1 illustrates its central tenets. The investment model makes two broad assumptions. First, commitment is rooted in the structural state of dependence. Ron is more dependent to the extent that he needs his marriage to persist to obtain outcomes he values. In this sense, commitment is fully rational. It captures what one is getting (and not getting) out of the relationship. Second, commitment goes beyond the simple state of dependence. Ron is more committed when he simply feels psychologically attached to Gayle, quite apart

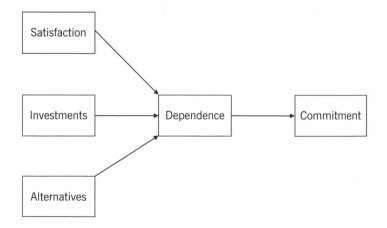

FIGURE 4.1. The investment model.

from any practical considerations about what he's getting out of his marriage. In this sense, commitment is not fully rational. It captures the incalculable value or meaning Ron has come to see in Gayle and the marriage itself. Let's break down each component of commitment in more detail.

Rooting Commitment in Dependence

The term *dependence* means that people need the relationship to persist to obtain specific outcomes they value. Three interaction features—satisfaction, investments, and alternatives—jointly determine dependence on the relationship. In the dependence calculus, *satisfaction* reflects need fulfillment. Satisfaction increases as the relationship fulfills more and more important needs, such as desires for self-esteem, intellectual companionship, dominance, support, sex, or recreation. For instance, Gayle's reasonably steady stream of compliments satisfies Ron's esteem needs; her occasional interference with his time playing basketball can frustrate his recreation needs. Her sharp wit and intelligence satiate his need for intellectual challenge; her occasional sloppiness sometimes thwarts his fastidiousness. Overall, Ron is highly satisfied in his marriage because interacting with Gayle fulfills more of his needs than it thwarts and because being with Gayle fulfills a larger variety of his needs than he expected his marriage to fulfill (i.e., his outcomes exceed his comparison level).

In the dependence calculus, *options* reflect the quality of one's available alternatives to the relationship. These options include the quality of the alternative partners one contemplates, the quality of the alternative partners one might pursue, and the anticipated pleasures and pains granted by a life alone (Rusbult et al., 1998). Ron's options are reasonably limited because the alternative partners he imagines (based on his dodgy experiences with past girlfriends) pale in comparison to Gayle. His options are further constrained because he finds the prospect of life as a single man completely unappealing.

In the dependence calculus, *investments* reflect all of the energies that bind people to relationships because of the psychological inertia created by sunk costs (Rusbult et al., 1998). Once invested, time spent with a partner cannot be recouped; once shared, friends cannot be easily realigned; once conveyed, secrets disclosed to a partner cannot be taken back; once public, promises are hard to break, and once foregone, opportunities to pursue a new school, job, or partner cannot be recaptured. Such irretrievable energies strengthen dependence by making relationship dissolution more personally costly and harder to justify psychologically. Ron has now put so much into his marriage—from sacrificing time on his career, to curtailing time with friends, to coming to enjoy Gayle's interests and passions—that he cannot imagine any other life.

The conceptual yield provided by the tenets of the investment model is evident in a wealth of empirical research (see Rusbult & Van Lange, 2003, for a review). In an exemplary series of studies, Rusbult et al. (1998) administered measures of the investment model constructs to people involved in dating relationships. The satisfaction items asked participants to indicate how well their relationship fulfilled their needs for intimacy, companionship, sex, security, and emotional involvement. The quality of alternative items asked participants to rate how well those various needs could be fulfilled in alternate relationships, such as those with a different dating partner, friends, or family. The investment items tapped how much time people had invested in the relationship, how many secrets they had disclosed, how much of an intellectual life they shared, how much of their personal identity was tied to the relationship, and how many memories they shared with their partner. The overall commitment items tapped future intentions toward the relationship (e.g., "I want our relationship to last forever").

Each structural aspect of dependence—greater satisfaction, less tempting or desirable alternatives, and larger investments—predicted greater commitment (Rusbult et al., 1998). When examined separately, greater commitment and greater dependence (i.e., greater satisfaction, less tempting alternatives, and more substantive investments) also predicted greater relationship stability over a period of 5 months. As Figure 4.1 implies, commitment explained (i.e., mediated) the effects of structural dependence on stability. When the researchers pit satisfaction, alternatives, investment, and overall commitment measures against one another in an analysis that examined the "unique" effects of each variable, only commitment emerged as a significant predictor of stability. These results suggest that greater satisfaction, fewer alternatives, and greater investment predict greater stability because these facets of dependence all strengthen commitment. A meta-analysis of studies testing the investment model has also revealed that the dynamics outlined above are characteristic of dating, marital, and nonromantic relationships. These dynamics are also evident for both men and women and they emerge across ethnic groups (Le & Agnew, 2003).

Going Beyond Dependence

The evidence that commitment predicts relationship stability controlling for its basis in dependence is especially revealing. It supports the second assumption of the model: Commitment captures something more than just the sum of its "dependence" parts. Commitment involves a sense of attachment to the relationship itself—an attachment that goes beyond Ron's rational considerations about what he gains from being in the relationship (or might lose as a consequence of leaving it). Commitment essentially transforms the objective reasons to be loyal to the partner (i.e., satisfaction, options, and investments) into attachment to the intrinsic importance of the partner and relationship. With commitment, the relationship becomes a valued end in and of itself—a state whose existence warrants no questioning. This sense of a higher meaning or purpose in his commitment motivates Ron to continue to put his outcomes in Gayle's hands and tend responsively to her outcomes on those occasions when satisfaction wanes, his options seem more appealing, and his investments become more costly.

EXPERIENCING COMMITMENT AS RESOLVE

This brings us to our second point about commitment. For Ron's commitment to push him forward, it needs to have an inertial, fixed quality. It cannot easily be undone. People are hesitant to undo decisions. They strenuously resist changing well-worn habits (Wood & Neal, 2007), beliefs and attitudes (Petty, Wegener, & Fabrigar, 1997), and prejudices (Kunda & Spencer, 2003). They most certainly resist changing romantic partners (Baumeister & Leary, 1995). In fact, merely contemplating alternatives to one's actions can be distressing, as the negative affect generated by counterfactual or "if-only" thinking reveals (Roese, 1997).

Decisions benefit from inertia because effectively implementing any chosen line of action requires certainty (Gollwitzer, 1990, 1999; Taylor & Gollwitzer, 1995). In fact, planning how to implement a chosen goal actually increases one's more general sense of meaning and purpose in life. Making plans increases self-esteem, self-efficacy, and optimism about the future, necessary ingredients for effective goal pursuit (Taylor & Gollwitzer, 1995). Maintaining certain or steadfast purpose in one's romantic commitment has similarly adaptive benefits in adult relationships. After all, Ron cannot move forward (and move closer) with purpose if he is constantly looking back and questioning his choice of Gayle as a mate. The problem is that the reality of interdependent life makes such unwavering resolve difficult to find. The conflicts of interest central to interdependence reveal grating aspects to the partner's behavior or qualities, the frustration of losing one's autonomy, and the sacrifices and compromises the future will bring (Murray, 1999; Murray, Holmes, et al., 2009).

But experiencing one's commitment as overjustified could provide the resolve to be responsive despite costs or doubts (Brickman, 1987). How so? When one's partner and relationship seem like the best, really the only, conceivable choice one could make, it provides a ready, relationship-affirming response to the angst provoked by questions such as: Can I really trust her? Is she really worth the sacrifice? Is the relationship worth strengthening? Ron's resolute belief that Gayle really is the only person for him energizes his commitment by making "yes" answers to such questions overdetermined. Being resolved in his commitment to Gayle keeps him willing to put his outcomes in Gayle's hands and willing to tend responsively to her outcomes come what may because he cannot imagine taking other courses of action.

Like a rudder on a ship, resolve functions to keep relationships on an even keel. Experiencing commitment as a foregone conclusion stabilizes relationships by neutralizing the costs that might otherwise undermine commitment. As a preemptive force, resolve makes it harder for people to see the costs inherent to their commitment. If Gayle's stubbornness is more disarming than dismaying to Ron, her most obstinate of actions might escape his attention (Balcetis & Dunning, 2007). Feeling resolved even blunts the import of those partner faults one cannot help but notice (Murray & Holmes, 1999). For instance, feeling committed protects people against declines in satisfaction when experimental feedback suggests their dating partner has serious personality weaknesses (Arriaga, Slaughterbeck, Capezz, & Hmurovic, 2007). As a postemptive force, resolve motivates people to justify the sunk costs that come from dependence on the relationship (Murray, 1999; Murray, Holmes, et al., 2009; Johnson & Rusbult, 1989; Rusbult & Van Lange, 2003). If Ron's interference with Gayle watching her football game actually causes Gayle to value Ron more (rather than less), his routine infringement on her goals might barely raise her eyebrow (Murray, Holmes, et al., 2009).

The Mind's Power to Rationalize

To keep partners moving forward, the interpersonal mind must deflect costs. It has just this capacity in the amazing ease with which people resolve troubling inconsistencies among thoughts, feelings, and behavior (Kunda, 1990). Consistency theorists have long argued that steadfast and purposeful action requires a clear or nonconflicted state of mind (Abelson, 1983; Brickman, 1987; Festinger, 1957; Harmon-Jones, 1999; Holmes & Rempel, 1989; Kelley, 1983; McGregor, 2003; McGregor, Zanna, Holmes, & Spencer, 2001; Rudman, Dohn, & Fairchild, 2007; Taylor & Gollwitzer,

1995). Dissonance theory typifies this assumption (Festinger, 1957). Consider someone in the unenviable position of making a difficult choice—the choice between two reasonable alternatives, such as two romantic partners, that each have significant pluses and minuses (Festinger, 1957). Choosing Option A and not Option B creates dissonance because it invites uncertainty. The negative features of Option A and the positive features of Option B provide reason to doubt the choice of option A—putting one's happy and efficacious pursuit of Option A in jeopardy. People typically resolve the dissonance that results from indecision by justifying the choice made. They make Option A the only conceivable choice by minimizing the costs of choosing Option A and the benefits of choosing Option B. In doing so, they imbue meaning, purpose, and clarity to ambivalent choices.

Recent evidence suggests that the capacity to sustain a clear and non-conflicted state of mind might have an evolutionary basis. It is evident in other primates and in young children who have not yet been socialized in the merits of justifying one's choices. Four-year-old children and capuchin monkeys both justify difficult choices—favoring hard-chosen stickers or M&M candies—over foregone ones (Egan, Santos, & Bloom, 2007). It is also evident across cultures. People from cultures that emphasize how the self is independent from others (e.g., Western cultures) justify choices that threaten their self-integrity as autonomous decision makers. They justify difficult choices they make for themselves (e.g., between coupons for two equally desirable items on a take-out menu). People from cultures that instead emphasize how the self is connected to others (e.g., Eastern cultures) justify the choices that threaten their integrity as thoughtful and considerate decision makers. They justify the choices they make for others (Hoshino-Browne et al., 2005). Maintaining resolve in action also biases processes as basic as visual perception, turning steep hills one volunteers to climb into gradual ascents and the long distances one chooses to journey into shorter and less arduous ones (Balcetis & Dunning, 2007). The interpersonal mind we envision co-opted this adaptive tendency to create value and meaning from conflicted action.

Overstating the Case in Relationships: Empirical Examples

In adult romantic relationships, the general drive to reduce uncertainty creates a specific tendency to overstate the case for one's commitment. In a fascinating book on meaning and value, Brickman (1987) argued that the negative aspects of his relationship make Ron all the more certain of his commitment to Gayle. Uncertainty has this effect because the negative aspects of one's endeavors motivate people to overstate how much positive value and meaning actually does exist in their actions.

In a treatise on motivated cognition, Kunda (1990) argued that people flexibly shift their memories, inferential strategies, and personality theories to accommodate their desired beliefs. However, people's capacity to believe what they want to believe is constrained by their desire to maintain that the weight of the objective evidence supports these beliefs. Imagine that Ron wants (indeed needs) to see Gayle as more patient and tolerant than the average spouse. His capacity to do this depends on his being able to define the criteria for patience and tolerance in ways that best suit Gayle's aptitudes (Dunning, Meyerowitz, & Holzberg, 1989). In forming his impression of Gayle's personality, Ron has a wealth of anecdotal evidence on which to draw. He can selectively pick and choose among the incoming evidence he perceives, focusing on how warmly she behaves when her work is going well and overlooking how curt she can be when she is tired. He can selectively recall the past, remembering how much fun they had trying new restaurants on a recent vacation and forgetting the argument they had about mislaid train tickets. He can believe that her intellect and sly sense of humor is simply more important to him than her casualness in the kitchen and matters domestic (Kunda, 1990).

The tremendous flexibility in social perception gives Ron the latitude he needs to overstate by amplifying the relationship's positives and downplaying its negatives (Murray, 1999). Brickman (1987) believed that the capacity for such overstatement breathes life into commitment. In his thinking, Ron is committed to Gayle not in spite of the costs, but precisely *because* of the costs. That is, discounting reasons to be unhappy, glorifying his investments, and derogating the attractiveness of his alternatives gives Ron resolve in his commitment. The evidence for such overstatement biases is robust (Boyes & Fletcher, 2007; Fletcher & Kerr, 2010; Gagne & Lydon, 2003; Hall & Taylor, 1976; Johnson & Rusbult, 1989; Levinger & Breedlove, 1966; Martz, Verette, Arriaga, Slovik, Cox, & Rusbult, 1998; Murray et al., 1996a; Murray & Holmes, 1997; Neff & Karney, 2002; Rusbult, Van Lange, Wildschut, Yovetich, & Verette, 2000; Van Lange & Rusbult, 1995). We review examples from this body of research next.

Provoking Doubts in the Lab

In our first foray into the empirical study of overstatement, we tried to "bottle" the process of building resolve in the laboratory. Our strategy was simple. We invited participants in dating relationships into the laboratory, threatened resolve, and then measured the compensatory tendency to overstate (i.e., rebuild resolve). In our favorite experiment, we threatened resolve by leading experimental participants to perceive a major, previously undiscovered, fault in their partner (Murray & Holmes, 1993, Experiment 1). To create this fault, we first enticed participants to describe their partner as rarely initiating conflict over joint interests. They did so happily on a three-item pretest tapping their partner's willingness to initiate conflicts. They also struggled to list recent examples of times when their partner had initiated such conflicts. Experimental participants next read bogus a *Psychology Today* article that turned their partner's cooperativeness into a fault (and thereby threatened resolve). This article argued that most dating couples were too hesitant to initiate conflicts over the choice of joint interests and activities. Control participants read a neutral article. Then we gave participants the opportunity to rationalize and overstate by turning this new fault back into a virtue. They first wrote the "story" of their relationships and then they rated how willingly their partner initiated conflicts in other domains (e.g., "My partner clearly expresses his/ her needs even when he or she knows that these needs conflict with my needs"; "My partner is willing to risk an argument by expressing attitudes or thoughts I oppose").

We reasoned that the *Psychology Today* article would be more threatening for participants who initially described their partner as most conflict avoidant on the conflict pretest. Accordingly, we expected low-conflict experimental participants to be in greatest need of some comforting and resolve-restoring overstatement. Therefore, we expected them to justify their commitments by exaggerating their partner's more general willingness to initiate conflicts. Figure 4.2 presents the results on the general conflict scale. These initially low-conflict experimental participants now described their partner as being significantly more willing to initiate conflicts (as compared with low-conflict controls). Similar overstatement emerged in the open-ended stories participants told about their relationships. Low-conflict experimental participants touted their partner's strengths in engaging conflicts. Their stories contained significantly more such references than low-conflict controls. They also rationalized their partner's weaknesses in engaging conflicts, often linking such faults to a greater virtue. These results suggest that the interpersonal mind has considerable latitude in turning negatives into positives. They further suggest that such mental contortions can take reasonable license with the available evidence. The participants who had the least objective evidence of conflict in their relationships were the ones who retold their stories in ways that

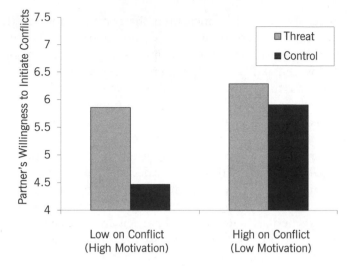

FIGURE 4.2. Partner's willingness to initiate conflict as function of motivation and threat.

provided a sense of resolve. In fact, the apparent ease with which people shifted their stories about their dating partner reinforced our confidence in the ease with which the committed mind can protect its resolve.

Positive Illusions In Vivo

This realization led to a series of studies on the existence of positive illusions in relationships (Murray et al., 1996a, 1996b; Murray & Holmes, 1997). Once we started this line of research, we ran into a problem. We wanted to argue that a committed Ron overstates Gayle's positives and understates her negatives—but claiming misstatement requires some benchmark for truth. Unfortunately, no benchmark for detecting reality is perfect when the reality to be judged involves subjective judgments (e.g., a partner's warmth or attractiveness, a relationship's likelihood of encountering unsolvable stressors). So we decided to start with a conservative benchmark—Gayle's self-perceptions. We chose this benchmark because people tend to see *themselves* more positively than objective standards warrant (Taylor & Brown, 1988). Using Gayle's self-perceptions as a benchmark for assessing Ron's tendency to overstate provides a hard test of our hypothesis because it requires Ron's illusions about Gayle to transcend her own tendency toward self-flattery.

In our first investigation, we asked both members of dating and married couples to describe themselves, their partner, and their ideal partner on interpersonal virtues and faults (e.g., kind and affectionate, critical and judgmental, stubborn, intelligent, responsive, sociable, patient, emotional). We then defined illusions as seeing positive qualities in the partner that the partner does not seem in him/herself. Figure 4.3 captures the assumptions underlying this definition. In this figure, Ron's illusions correspond to the qualities he sees in Gayle that she does not see in herself (i.e., the nonoverlapping variance in Ron's perceptions of Gayle). In analyses, we isolated this illusory or overstated aspect of Ron's perceptions by statistically controlling Gayle's perception of herself (i.e., removing the overlapping variance from Ron's perceptions).

The results of this first investigation pointed to both the existence and benefits of positive illusions (Murray et al., 1996a). Consider the evidence for overstatement at the level of mean or average perceptions. Even in marital relationships, wives saw husbands significantly more positively ($M = 6.61$) than husbands saw themselves ($M = 6.18$); husbands also saw wives more positively ($M = 6.40$) than wives saw themselves ($M = 6.30$). Dating women also rated men more positively ($M = 6.77$) than men saw themselves ($M = 5.93$). However, dating men were not as flattering to women (an aberration that Gagne & Lydon, 2003, later revealed to be a reflection of dating men's lesser commitment).

Where do such generally positive or inflated perceptions arise? Figure 4.4 presents a simplified version of the analytic model we used to examine directive biases on people's general tendency to overstate their partner's positives. In this model, Ron's perception of Gayle is a reflection of reality (i.e., Gayle's self-perceptions) and his motivation to overstate. Ron's tendency to overstate comes from his tendency to assume (indeed overassume) that Gayle possess the qualities he desires in his ideal partner. Our results supported this model. In dating and marital relationships,

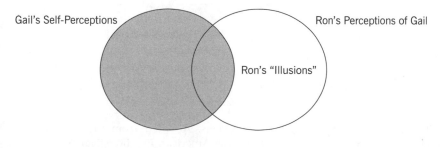

FIGURE 4.3. Conceptual definition of illusions.

perceptions of the partner in part reflected the "reality" of the partner's self-image. If Ron saw himself less positively, Gayle had a harder time overstating his positives; this kernel of truth did constrain her perceptions. Nonetheless, Gayle did still see Ron through idiosyncratic filters that were colored by her desire to see Ron's traits in the best possible light. In dating and marital relationships, people with loftier hopes for an ideal partner perceived their partner more positively than even their partner saw themselves (Murray et al., 1996a).

What happens in relationships when people overstate the case? The short-term outcomes of positive illusions are great. Possessing positive illusions predicted greater concurrent satisfaction for both men and women (Murray et al., 1996a). Ron reported greater satisfaction the more he overstated Gayle's positive (and understated Gayle's negative) qualities. In fact, Ron's resolve was contagious. Gayle also reported being more satisfied the more Ron overstated Gayle's positives. Gagne and Lydon (2003) found similar benefits. They hypothesized the existence of a commitment shift—a transformation in the need to overstate that comes with heightened commitment. Consequently, these researchers reasoned that those people who felt most committed to their dating partner would possess the strongest positive illusions. That's precisely what they found. The most highly committed dating women and men view their partners more positively than their partners view themselves. Less committed dating women are much less generous. The least committed dating men evidence no illusions at all!

We also found similar benefits of overstating the case for one's commitment in a further study utilizing a different reality benchmark (Murray, Holmes, Dolderman, & Griffin, 2000). In this study, we asked married

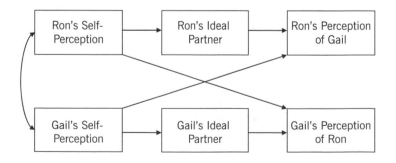

FIGURE 4.4. Sources of positive illusions. Adapted from Murray, Holmes, and Griffin (1996). Copyright 1996 by the American Psychological Association. Adapted by permission.

partners to nominate two friends who knew each of them well enough to rate both the husband and the wife on a series of interpersonal attributes. We then averaged the friends' ratings to provide an objective "reality" benchmark for detecting illusions. Satisfied men and women again overstated the case for commitment. They described their partner more positively than their friends did. Dissatisfied men and women actually understated the case for commitment. They described their partner less positively than their friends did.

Are the long-term outcomes of positive illusions just as great? An abundance of pop-psychology "evidence" would say no. Conventional lore suggests that overstating a partner's "real" strengths sets couples up for disappointment. But the empirical evidence does not bear this pearl of wisdom out. We conducted a longitudinal study of dating couples to examine long-term effects of positive illusions (Murray et al., 1996b). In this study, we examined whether possessing positive illusions about one's partner at Time 1 predicted satisfaction and commitment 12 months later at Time 2. The results revealed that people reported relatively greater satisfaction, less conflict, and fewer doubts about their commitment at Time 2 the more generously they perceived their partner at Time 1. Such resolve again proved to be infectious. People also reported less conflict and fewer doubts at Time 2 the more generously their *partner* perceived them at Time 1. Overstating the partner's strengths actually protected commitment in the face of the rising costs. For people who overstated the least, greater conflict at Time 1 predicted greater likelihood of relationship dissolution at Time 2. But, for people who overstated the most, greater conflict at Time 1 did not predict breakup!

Maybe though the long-term benefits of positive illusions fade in marriage once the passage of time reveals the ways in which a partner truly does fall short of one's hopes. Miller and his colleagues began to investigate this possibility in a 13-year longitudinal study of marriage (Miller, Niehuis, & Huston, 2006). They defined positive illusions as Ron perceiving Gayle as having a more agreeable personality than Ron's perceptions of Gayle's day-to-day behavior support. This type of bias involves Ron's perception that Gayle is a generally pleasant, cheerful, and friendly person despite her tendency to behave disagreeably (e.g., insulting him, criticizing him, yelling). The results yielded suggestive evidence for the long-term benefits of positive illusions. In fact, people who overstated the case for their spouse's agreeableness tended to stay more in love over the first 13 years of marriage.

While provocative, these findings leave a central question unaddressed: Is Ron ultimately better or worse off when he goes into his marriage believing that Gayle has the qualities he hoped to find in an ideal partner? The longitudinal study of newlyweds conducted in the Murray lab sheds some light on this question (Murray, Griffin, et al., in press). In this study, we asked each member of the couple to describe himself or herself, his or her partner, and his or her hopes for an ideal partner on a variety of interpersonal qualities (e.g., warm, intelligent, critical and demanding, responsive, lazy). Participants made these ratings at 6-month intervals seven times over the first 3 years of their marriage. They also reported their overall satisfaction in the marriage at each of these time intervals. These data allowed us to examine the long-term effects of Ron seeing Gayle as the image of his hopes.

As we see in Chapter 10, satisfaction typically declines over the initial years of marriage (e.g., Karney & Bradbury, 1997). These newlyweds were no different. Both husbands and wives evidenced steady declines in satisfaction. However, couples varied in the degree to which they evidenced more or less steep declines. Because declines in satisfaction varied significantly across couples, this gave us a great opportunity to see whether initially seeing one's partner as ideal set people up for declines in satisfaction or actually protected against it.

To do this, we first had to calculate a measure of idealization that captured our interest in bias or overstatement. We decided to calculate two sets of correlations for each couple. For the first set, we correlated Ron's ratings of Gayle's qualities across the 20 attributes with Ron's ratings of his ideal partner's qualities across the 20 attributes. We also correlated Gayle's ratings of Ron with Gayle's ratings of her ideal partner. In Ron's case, this "projection" index captures the degree to which Ron believes that Gayle has the qualities he hoped to find in an ideal partner. A strong positive correlation between these sets of ratings means that Ron ascribes the same profile or relative ordering of qualities to Gayle and to his ideal partner. For instance, Ron's ideal partner is more assertive than warm and more lazy than critical, and he also sees Gayle as more assertive than warm and more lazy than critical. For the second set, we correlated Ron's ratings of his ideal partner's qualities with Gayle's ratings of her own qualities. We also correlated Gayle's ratings of her ideal partner's qualities with Ron's perceptions of himself. In Ron's case, this "reality" index captures the degree to which Gayle's self-ratings match Ron's hopes for an ideal partner. That is, this index captures the degree to which Ron actually did find the qualities in Gayle he had hoped to find (at least according to Gayle).

We then predicted the satisfaction trajectory (i.e., declining, stable, increasing) from the "projection" and "reality" indices, both entered simultaneously in a multilevel regression model. In this analysis, the effects of "projection" represent the effects of Ron overstating Gayle's match to his ideals (because we removed the kernel of truth in his perceptions by statistically controlling for the match between Gayle's self-ratings and his perceptions of the ideal partner). Consistent with our emphasis on the importance of resolve, seeing one's partner as a match to one's ideals promoted relationship resilience. The more Ron idealized Gayle at the point of marriage, the less his satisfaction declined over the first years of his marriage (i.e., an intrapersonal benefit). Also, the more Ron idealized Gayle initially, the less her satisfaction declined over the same time period (i.e., an interpersonal benefit). Parallel effects emerged for women. In fact, partners who idealized each other the most initially did not evidence any decline in satisfaction (despite having farther to fall, given that they were more satisfied to start)! In contrast, partners who idealized each other the least initially evidenced steep declines in satisfaction. Furthermore, partners who initially idealized each other the most were less likely to separate within 3 years of getting married. Rather than setting partners up for disillusionment and distress, a sense of idealistic resolve that one's partner really is the "right" person seems central for sustained satisfaction and sustained commitment.

Perceived Superiority In Vivo

Rusbult and her colleagues found even more direct evidence for the link between overstatement and commitment in an inventive set of studies. These researchers reasoned that the push to overstate results in Ron seeing positive qualities in his marriage that he does not see in the marriages of others. Their results suggest that this type of overstatement—namely, perceiving one's own relationship as superior to the relationships of acquaintance, friends, or family—provides a critical impetus for commitment (Martz et al., 1998; Rusbult et al., 2000; Van Lange & Rusbult, 1995). To tap perceived superiority, these researchers had participants "list the positive and negative qualities that came to mind when thinking about their own and others' relationships" (Rusbult et al., 2000, p. 524). Then they defined "perceived superiority" in terms of Ron's tendency list more positives and fewer negatives for his own relationship than the relationships of others.

In a first experiment, Rusbult et al. (2000) tried to re-create the process of building resolve in one's commitment in the laboratory. To heighten the need for resolve, they told participants in the experimental condition that college dating relationships are dissatisfying and prone to dissolution.

Then they measured the tendency to overstate. As they expected, heightening the need for resolve increased overstatement. The tendency to see one's own relationship as possessing more positives and fewer negatives than others' relationships was more pronounced for experimental than for control participants. These researchers then looked to see whether such defensive tendencies to overstate might actually sustain commitment over time in marriage (Rusbult et al., 2000). This study revealed both short-term and long-term evidence for the benefits of overstatement. In the short term, the tendency to see one's own marriage as possessing more positives and fewer negatives than others predicted greater commitment. Over the long term, perceiving one's own relationship as superior to others even predicted lower risk of relationship dissolution over a 20-month period.

Not Just a Western Phenomenon

The motivation for resolve in one's commitment is so robust that cultural groups known for their general tendency to understate nonetheless still overstate when it comes to their relationships. People in more interdependent cultures (e.g., Japan, China) are self-effacing. They blame themselves for failure, credit others for success, and strive to fit in rather than stand apart (Heine & Lehman, 1995; Kityama, Markus, Matsumoto, & Norasakkunkit, 1997). In contrast, people in more independent (e.g., the United States, Canada) cultures are self-enhancing. They take credit for their success, blame others for failures, see themselves as better than average, and envision an especially good future (see Taylor & Brown, 1988, for a review). Despite the cultural tendency to be modest, people of Japanese heritage nonetheless overstate the case for romantic commitment just as Westerners do. In a telling set of studies, Endo, Heine, and Lehman (2000) asked Japanese, Asian Canadian, and European Canadian participants to rate their own relationship and the typical relationships on five dimensions (e.g., supportiveness, understanding, enjoyment). They also separately rated their partner and themselves on five traits (e.g., considerate, trustworthy, interesting). Participants described their own relationship more positively than the typical relationship regardless of culture. Participants from each culture also described their partner more glowingly than they described themselves.

Mind-Set and Resolve

All studies reviewed thus far suggest that overstating the case is critical in sustaining resolve in one's commitment. More direct evidence on this point comes from experiments examining the effects of mind-set on positive illusions (Gagne & Lydon, 2001a, 2001b). Research on mind-set distinguishes two phases in decision making (Gollwitzer, 1990; Taylor & Gollwitzer, 1995). The first is a predecision and preresolve deliberative phase. In this phase, people contemplate what they might do and open their minds to the evidence for and against each choice. The second is a postdecision implemental phase. In this phase, people shut out distractions and focus on how to carry out their plans.

Once Ron and Gayle are married, the big relationship decision (to commit) is made. In this postdecision phase, we reasoned that couples need illusions to carry out the plan to commit and be responsive to one another's needs. Is that indeed the case? Does thinking about implementing one's plans for action heighten overstatement? Gagne and Lydon (2001a) examined this question in a series of experiments where they manipulated mind-set and then measured optimism about the future of one's relationship. In the deliberative mind-set condition, participants identified a decision they still needed to make and listed its pros and cons. In the implemental mind-set condition, participants identified an already-made decision and described their plans for pursuing it. Participants then predicted how long their dating relationship would last. Six months later the researchers then contacted the participants to see whose relationships had lasted. Those in an implemental mind-set overstated the case. Compared with control participants, implemental participants made more optimistic predictions. Their greater need to see purpose in their actions resulted in their expecting their relationship to last longer than it actually did. Pretty surprisingly, this effect emerged regardless of whether implemental participants were thinking about how to carry out a decision within their relationships or not.

Even in stable and enduring relationships, events in and outside of the relationship can shift one's mind-set from the task of carrying out one's commitment back to the task of reconsidering the commitment itself. Gagne and Lydon (2001b) reasoned that such shifts back to a deliberative mind-set should result in people who were more committed rebuilding resolve—and defensively bolstering their positive illusions. In a creative experiment, they had dating participants who were about to graduate from college ponder their relationship futures. They asked some participants to ponder whether they should increase their commitment after graduation (i.e., deliberative mind-set). They asked other participants to plan how to maintain their relationship after graduation (i.e., implemental mind-set). All participants then rated their partner's status relative to the typical partner on physical attractiveness, intelligence, warmth, and sense of humor. This provided their dependent measure of positive illusions. The results revealed the power of resolve in instilling overstatement. First, planning the future of their commitment (i.e., implemental mind-set) increased the tendency to overstate the partner's virtues relative to the typical partner. Second, for those high in commitment, contemplating undoing that commitment (i.e., the deliberative mind-set) similarly strengthened illusions.

A Caveat: Bearing Risk in Mind

These collected findings suggest that overstating the case for one's commitment fosters resolve and stabilizes relationships. But we are not arguing that more illusion is always better (nor do these findings suggest that more illusion is always better). This takes us back to the basic principle of motivated cognition that started this section. People can believe what they want to believe without much consequence—up to a point (Kunda, 1990). This tipping point depends on the weight of contradictory evidence. As we introduced in Chapter 1, relationships differ in objective risk because partners face different types of conflicts at each level of interdependence. Glossing over real problems in the relationship is not likely to instill a lasting sense of resolve because such problems recur and challenge even the most creative thinkers. An instructive study of newlywed couples conducted by McNulty and Karney (2004) presents a case in point. These researchers reasoned that the satisfaction-instilling effects of overly optimistic evaluations of one's partner (i.e., resolve) depend on their fit to the reality of ongoing experience. They assessed resolve through items tapping (undue) optimism about the partner's future behavior (e.g., "My partner will rarely make mistakes"; "My partner will always agree with me about important things"). They assessed the risks inherent in ongoing experience by observing how positively or negatively partners behaved when they tried to resolve an ongoing conflict in their marriage. They tracked the resilience of these marriages by asking partners to complete measures of satisfaction every 6 months over 4 years.

This study revealed that the long-term effects of wives' resolve shifted according to the actual risks inherent in interacting with their husbands. When couples behaved relatively positively during their conflict discussion, more optimistic expectations stabilized the relationship. In this case, wives with more positive expectations (i.e., greater resolve) remained more satisfied in their marriages than wives with less positive expectations. However, the opposite effect emerged when the risks of interacting increased. When couples behaved relatively negatively during the interaction task, more realistic expectations stabilized the relationship. In this case, wives with less positive expectations remained more satisfied in their marriages than wives with more positive expectations. Such findings highlight our contention that the interpersonal mind cannot misstep in overstating the case for commitment.

THE IMPLEMENTATION RULES
FOR MATCHING COMMITMENT TO TRUST

So now it's time to back Ron up a bit before he missteps. The literature we reviewed might seem to suggest that Ron's capacity to justify his commitment is unlimited. It's not. For the interpersonal mind to elicit mutual responsiveness, it cannot let Ron's resolve outstrip Gayle's actual commitment. This brings us to our third point about commitment. It needs to be reciprocated by the partner. If Ron persistently asks more of Gayle than she is willing to give him or consistently provides more to Gayle than she is willing to ask of him, he leaves himself open to frequent disappointment and hurt. To avoid such unpleasant eventualities, the interpersonal mind makes Ron's expressions of commitment contingent on his anticipation of Gayle's reciprocal commitment. It does so through two if–then implementation rules that make his willingness to be farther out on a psychological limb in expressing his commitment contingent on the safety of the branch (Murray, Holmes, & Collins, 2006).

The implementation rules for matching make Ron's expression of his commitment contingent on his trust in Gayle's reciprocated commitment. These if–then rules contain a procedural association between a goal (i.e., connect vs. self-protect) and a congruent commitment intention in memory (e.g., seek support vs. shun support). As we introduced in Chapter 2, commitment intention refers to the two major ways in which partners can depend on each other. Ron can tie himself to Gayle by putting his outcomes in Gayle's hands (e.g., asking for her support) and by tending to Gayle's outcomes (e.g., providing support to her). The if–then implementation rules for matching use Ron's interpersonal goals as an intermediary to link his willingness to depend on Gayle to his level of trust in her commitment.

To understand how the matching rules work, we need to look back at the snapshot of the mind presented in Figure 2.1. Ron's interpersonal goal to connect (or self-protect) comes from his trust in Gayle's commitment to being responsive. Anticipating Gayle's acceptance in a given situation motivates him to connect; anticipating her rejection instead motivates him to self-protect. Therefore, his interpersonal goals reflect his trust in Gayle in that situation. The matching rules wed his trust-inspired goals to the contingent willingness to express his commitment to Gayle. The "if connect goal, then escalate own dependence" rule links his desire to be closer to Gayle to his intention to make himself more vulnerable to her. Namely, wanting to be closer motivates Ron to put more of his outcomes into Gayle's hands and take more of her outcomes into his own hands. For instance, anticipating Gayle's acceptance makes Ron want to connect and seek her support when he's had a difficult day at trial. It also makes him want to provide the same support to her. The "if self-protect goal, then withdraw own dependence" rule links his desire to avoid rejection to his intention to make himself less vulnerable to Gayle. Namely, wanting to avoid rejection motivates Ron to take his outcomes out of Gayle's hands and to leave Gayle to satisfy her socioemotional needs on her own (i.e., without relying on him). For instance, anticipating Gayle's nonresponsiveness motivates Ron to seek the company of outside friends when he needs distraction from his work woes. It also motivates him to avoid Gayle when she's had a bad day at work and needs support.

How Trust Restrains Resolve

The if–then implementation rules for matching commitment to trust control how partners express dependence in specific situations (e.g., seek/shun support). The investment model stipulates that global sentiments of commitment emerge from the culmination of these specific expressions. If that's the case, the if–then rules for matching should also leave an imprint on Ron's global feelings of commitment. Perceiving Gayle's commitment to be stronger should intensify his own commitment. To be more specific, Ron's overall level of trust in Gayle's commitment should dictate the strength of his resolve to put his outcomes in her hands and take her outcomes into his hands. We focus on how global or chronic trust constrains global or chronic commitment here. We detail how the matching rules constrain the state intentions to move forward (or backward) in expressing commitment when we describe the action plans for pursuing connection (Chapter 6) and self-protection (Chapter 7) in specific conflicts.

Let's consider how trust constrains the willingness to put one's own outcomes in the partner's hands. Experiencing one's commitment as a foregone conclusion puts one's overall life satisfaction squarely in the partner's hands. Ron's welfare is completely at Gayle's whim if he cannot imagine ever replacing her because she embodies his ideal partner. Because such resolve leaves Ron vulnerable to painful rejection, the interdependent mind should make its general tendency to overstate contingent on trust in the partner's commitment. We tested the hypothesis that Ron's trust in Gayle constrains his capacity to develop positive illusions about her in a series of follow-up studies (Murray, Holmes, & Griffin, 2000; Murray et al., 2001). In this research, we first had to decide upon metrics for assessing trust in the partner's responsiveness. Because trust depends on the perception that the partner values one's qualities (see Chapter 3), we asked participants in both dating and marital relationships to describe how they believed their partner saw them on a series of positive and negative interpersonal qualities (e.g., kind and affectionate, open and disclosing, intelligent, critical and judgmental, lazy, demanding). We then asked participants to describe themselves and to describe their partner on these same qualities.

In our analyses, we examined whether Ron's perception of how positively Gayle viewed him (our proxy for his trust in Gayle's commitment) constrained his capacity to possess positive illusions about Gayle. Figure 4.5 presents our analytic model. In this model, we examined whether Ron's perception of Gayle's regard predicted his tendency to overstate Gayle's strengths (i.e., Ron's perception of Gayle controlling for Gayle's perception of herself). As we anticipated, trust predicted illusions. People who believed their partner saw them more positively perceived their partner more positively. In contrast, people who believed their partner saw them more negatively perceived their partner more negatively. Of course, these cross-sectional data do not prove that trust in the partner's commitment constrains the tendency to overstate. Fortunately, longitudinal data we collected on our dating couples allowed us to examine the causality question. In the dating sample, we obtained repeat measures of positive illusions 4 months and then again 12 months after participants initially completed these measures. These data revealed that trust did indeed restrain illusions, especially for men. The more positively Ron believed Gayle regarded him initially, the more positively he regarded her over

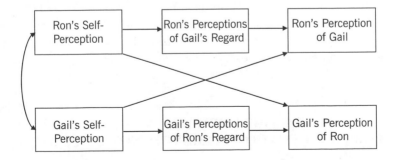

FIGURE 4.5. How perceptions of the partner's regard constrain illusions. Adapted from Murray, Holmes, and Griffin (2000). Copyright 2000 by the American Psychological Association. Adapted by permission.

time. In this way, the interpersonal mind matches commitment to trust, not letting Ron feel resolute in his commitment unless and until he trusts in Gayle's commitment to him.

Now let's consider taking the partner's outcomes into one's own hands. Resolved in his commitment, Ron generally tends to Gayle's needs without consideration of the personal costs involved in doing so (Reis et al., 2004). But such generosity also leaves him open to hurt and disappointment if Gayle does not reciprocate. Therefore, the interdependent mind also makes this expression of Ron's commitment contingent on his trust in Gayle's anticipated commitment.

Data from the Murray longitudinal study of newlyweds (Murray, 2010) speaks directly to this point. In this study, we again tapped trust in the partner's commitment through Ron's beliefs about how positively Gayle perceives his interpersonal qualities. We tapped Ron's general willingness to take Gayle's outcomes into his hands through communal strength (Mills, Clark, Ford, & Johnson, 2004). This measure taps how far Ron is willing to go in caring for Gayle's needs (e.g., "How far would you be willing to go to visit Gayle?" "How large a cost would you incur to meet Gayle's needs?"). We then looked at the association between Ron's perceptions of Gayle's regard for him (i.e., his meta-perspective on Gayle's commitment) and his willingness to respond communally to her needs. Trust again seemed to constrain the expression of commitment. This happened both concurrently and longitudinally. Just after marriage, those newlyweds who felt more positively regarded were willing to go further to tend to their partner's needs than newlyweds who felt less positively regarded. More important, this meta-perspective on the partner's commitment also predicted changes in communal motivation over 3 years of marriage. Newlyweds who felt more positively regarded initially were more willing to put themselves out to tend to their partner's needs 3 years later. As time passed, the interpersonal mind again matched commitment to trust. Feeling more valued by Gayle increased Ron's willingness to tend to Gayle's outcomes (i.e., the "escalate own dependence" rule); feeling relatively devalued curtailed it (i.e., the "withdraw own dependence" rule).[2]

THE IMPLEMENTATION RULE
FOR ENSURING COMMITMENT IS NOT DERAILED

By applying the implementation rules for matching, the interdependent mind helps ensure that Ron's expressions of commitment match Gayle's expressions of commitment. Of course, in drawing closer to Gayle, Ron exposes Gayle to costs that could reduce her commitment and disrupt this delicate balance of power. Ron is similarly exposed as Gayle draws closer to him. This brings us to the final point for the chapter. To ensure reciprocity in commitment, the interpersonal mind also needs a backup mechanism to ensure that commitment is not seriously derailed. In committing to Ron, Gayle gives up something precious. She submits to a life where she can no longer do exactly what she wants to do when she wants to do it. She cannot escape sometimes finding their life together constraining. Neither can Ron. Joined together, they necessarily restrict each other's options. On her part, Gayle does not understand why Ron insists on leaving the kitchen counters so spotless that she's uncomfortable even making a sandwich. Nor can she fathom Ron's taste in music or his tendency to constantly correct her misspoken words. She also still has trouble understanding why she is the one who always takes the time to call Ron's parents and keep them up to date on their children's activities. Ron has his own issues. Now that he's married, Ron knows he should not look sideways at his attractive—and doting—paralegal because he promised Gayle his fidelity. He sometimes bristles that he cannot sleep as late as he wants to on Saturdays because Gayle leaves him to tend to the children while she escapes to her weekly yoga class. It also annoys him that he can't even wear his favorite jeans out of the house because Gayle is too embarrassed for him to be seen in them.

Interdependence essentially guarantees the experience of autonomy costs that come through accommodating one's own goals and behavior to respect the partner's goals and behavior (Clark & Grote, 1998; Kelley et al., 2003). Interdependence restricts and sacrifices personal freedoms through its very structure. The resulting slights to one's autonomy involve the communal costs (Clark & Grote, 1998) one incurs in treating a partner well (e.g., Ron's sacrifice of personal time that comes from taking the children to the park so Gayle can watch her beloved football games in peace), the unintentional costs the partner's parallel existence creates (e.g., Gayle making a mess of Ron's just-cleaned kitchen, Gayle's blaring a televised football game while Ron tries to work), and the largely unintentional costs the partner imposes by satisfying his or her own goals (e.g., Gayle working late rather than keeping her promise to spend a quiet evening watching a movie with Ron). As these examples illustrate, autonomy costs are ones that even the best-intentioned partners cannot help but impose. In fact, exposure to autonomy costs is likely to be greatest in more satisfying relationships because the rewards of being connected to the partner elicit further efforts to increase interdependence, which in turn, creates greater exposure to costs![3]

The investment model states that costs subtract from the rewards the relationship offers (see Figure 4.1). If left psychologically unchecked, repeated exposure to autonomy costs could threaten satisfaction and undermine commitment. Indeed, if either Ron or Gayle obsessed about every slight to personal autonomy that the other imposed, their commitment to meeting one another's needs would invariably falter. Being preoccupied with costs would effectively short-circuit the single-minded focus on the value of one's commitment each needs to keep in mind to continue putting their outcomes in each other's hands and to continue to behave responsively. Fortunately, such ruminations are not likely to long preoccupy either one of them, provided the interdependent mind has its way (and gets the chance to justify the commitment).

Keeping Commitment on Track

The implementation rule for justifying one's own commitment makes a vexing partner more valuable. This if–then rule links costs that come with greater closeness to the tendency to value the partner all the more (i.e., "if connect goal, then justify commitment"). By turning adversity into statements of the partner's inherent value (Higgins, 2006), this procedural rule keeps commitment from being derailed. In so doing, this implementation rule effectively keeps Ron's commitment in check with Gayle's dependence on him. It maintains the implemental mind-set he needs to continue to behave responsively by making Gayle worth the sacrifices she asks of him (Abelson, 1983; Brickman, 1987; Festinger, 1957; Harmon-Jones, 1999; Holmes & Rempel, 1989; Kelley, 1983; Taylor & Gollwitzer, 1995).

Can the restrictions interdependence puts on one's freedoms actually cause people to value their partner more? Consider how people manage the implicit restraints interdependence puts on their freedom to pursue alternative partners. Alternatives threaten commitment (Rusbult, 1983). People in committed relationships seem to defend against such threats by deciding that even the most enticing of alternatives are not so tempting after all. It seems the interpersonal mind naturally lends itself to "sour grapes." This "derogation of alternatives" phenomenon first emerged in the literature in a set of intriguing studies conducted by Johnson and Rusbult (1989). Lydon and his colleagues later replicated it (Lydon, Fitzsimons, & Naidoo, 2003).

In a first study, Johnson and Rusbult (1989) asked people in newly established relationships to rate the quality of their alternatives (e.g., "How appealing are the people other than your partner with whom you could become involved?") and their commitment to their partner (e.g., "How likely is it that you will end your relationship in the near future?") for several consecutive weeks. They expected people in stable relationships to deny wanting the alternatives they chose not to pursue. They found strong evidence for such "sour grapes." People who stayed in their relationships reported less and less tempting alternatives from week to week. However, people who ended their relationships perceived more and more tempting alternatives from week to week. In a further experiment, Johnson and Rusbult (1989) found that highly committed people defensively derogate their alternatives. In this study, they utilized the guise of a dating service to expose participants to increasingly strong concrete temptations. Their participants viewed photographs of reasonably unattractive, moderately attractive or highly attractive alternatives and rated their attraction to each possibility. The most committed participants actually rated the most objectively desirable alternatives as least appealing!

Although foregoing alternatives objectively restricts one's personal freedom, it might not be experienced as a personal cost to one's autonomy. Forgoing alternatives is costly primarily for those people who desire to pursue them in the first place. For those who do not, derogation may essentially be an act of preemption—a cognitive trick that helps people avoid even considering this potential infringement on their freedom. The autonomy costs that likely most preoccupy the mind result from infringements on personal goals that one does hold dear. These costs also increase with one's own efforts to seek connection to the partner (rather than being imposed by others, as in the case with potential alternatives). With true autonomy costs, Ron loses the control to wear his favorite jeans out of the house because he cares about Gayle's opinions on his appearance. Gayle loses sleep as Ron snores because she lets him sleep in their bed rather than banish him to the couch. Such restraints on one's desired goals are unavoidable.

In a daily diary study of newlywed couples, we examined how fluidly the mind compensates for such costs (Murray, Holmes, et al., 2009). Coordinating patterns of mutual responsiveness requires a mechanism for keeping one's commitment on track in the face of distractions (see Chapter 2). Because costly partners pose a greater threat to one's own motivation to be responsive (Tooby & Cosmides, 1996), such a mechanism should make the partner more valuable precisely when they are more costly. Given the potential adaptive value of reenergizing commitment, we expected people to value their partner all the more when their partner infringed on more of their goals. In this study, newly wedded husbands and wives each completed an electronic daily diary for 14 days. Husbands and wives each indicated how often their partner's actions interfered with their personal goals that day (e.g., "Ron did something he wanted to do rather than what I wanted to do"; "Ron using the last of something I needed"; "Ron refused to talk about something I wanted to discuss"). They also reported on how much they valued their partner each day (e.g., "in love with Ron"; "Ron is a very special person").

We then conducted analyses that examined whether cost exposure elicited greater subsequent partner valuing. Specifically, we examined whether Gayle's reported autonomy costs on Monday predicted how much more (or less) she valued Ron on Tuesday. Cost exposure elicited compensatory cognition, as we anticipated. On days after people experienced greater levels of partner interference with their goals, they actually reported being even more in love with a special and essentially irreplaceable partner. Of course, there are a number of alternative explanations for such an effect. Perhaps Gayle values Ron more on days after he thwarted more of her goals because he compensates for one day's infringements with less infringing behavior the next day. Maybe he makes an extra effort to be responsive to Gayle's needs the next day. Perhaps he apologizes. We conducted analyses to control for such possibilities, and the tendency for Gayle to respond to the autonomy costs Ron imposes by valuing him more remained.[4]

The tendency to mentally compensate for costs even motivated people to behave more responsively toward their partner, which illustrates the great functionality of this implementation rule. Each day Ron also indicated how responsively Gayle behaved toward him (e.g., "Gayle listened to and comforted me"; "Gayle helped me solve a problem I was having"; "Gayle did something he/she didn't really want to do because I wanted to do it"; "Gayle put my tastes ahead of his/her own"). Ron actually perceived Gayle as behaving more responsively when she countered the costs he imposed by valuing him more (Murray, Holmes, et al., 2009).

Even more telling evidence of the functional value of commitment insurance emerged when we returned to these new marriages after a year. At this point, we asked each member of the couple to complete measures of satisfaction. We then looked to see whether the degree to which people compensated for autonomy costs predicted changes in their satisfaction over time. Because each participant provided reports on autonomy costs and partner valuing for multiple days, we could statistically derive an index of cost compensation for each person. This measure can be thought of as a kind of correlation (i.e., a within-person residual slope) that indexes how much (or how little) each person values the partner more in response to costs. We then used this cost-compensation index to predict changes in satisfaction over the year. We found something striking. Those newlyweds (both husbands and wives) who valued their partner more when their partner was most costly actually reported relatively greater satisfaction in their marriage 1 year later. Seeking commitment insurance hardened resolve and essentially sealed their bond.

RESOLVE MOTIVATES RESPONSIVENESS: A LOOK FORWARD

Commitment motivates responsiveness. To set aside one's own temptation to be selfish in conflicts of interest, people must prioritize their partner's welfare. Putting the partner first in situations where one's own needs are pressing requires the resolve commitment provides. Perceiving the partner as the best, and perhaps only, conceivable choice to be had puts a plan for action in hand. This action plan motivates people to provide support (Collins & Read, 2000), minimize conflicts (Rusbult et al., 1991), sacrifice (Van Lange et al., 1997), and behave in a generally communal way (Clark & Grote, 1998; Reis et al., 2004; Van Lange et al., 1997).

Our reasoning that purposeful action requires resolve suggests that resolute commitments might be more effective in fostering responsiveness than more equivocal ones. If commitment is essentially a foregone conclusion, one's state of commitment should be a chronically accessible part of consciousness. Merely raising the question should be sufficient to elicit a quick and resolute response (Fazio, 1986). Resolved commitment—that is, commitment that comes almost without thought—should be particularly powerful in compelling responsiveness. Research conducted by Etcheverry and Le (2005) suggests that this is the case. These researchers measured both commitment strength (e.g., "I am committed to maintaining my relationship with my partner") and commitment accessibility. They indexed accessibility by measuring how quickly participants responded to sentence stems querying their commitment (e.g., "I want our relationship to last"). Participants also completed scales tapping their willingness to sacrifice and accommodate (i.e., behave well) in response to their partner's transgressions. Resolved commitments were especially predictive of responsiveness. Being both committed and quick to assert one's commitment predicted the highest degree of accommodation and self-sacrifice. These results suggest that resolved commitment provides a critical platform for responsiveness.

SUMMARY AND A CAVEAT

This chapter described how the interdependent mind coordinates reciprocal expressions of commitment across partners and keeps commitment from being derailed. Commitment is the interpersonal mind's pulse on the strength of Ron's motivation to approach connection. Commitment essentially tells Ron how far to go in putting his outcomes in Gayle's hands and in tending responsively to her outcomes. We made four main points.

In the first half of the chapter we delineated what it means psychologically to be committed. We described the roots of commitment in the structural state of dependence. Ron is more committed to Gayle when she satisfies more of his needs, when he cannot imagine being happier with someone else (or alone), and when he has invested more of his time and energies into his marriage. However, we also noted that commitment also goes beyond the simple state of dependence. Ron is more committed the greater the value his marriage has to him (quite apart from any practical considerations). We then argued that enacting commitment involves resolve. We argued that being resolved in his commitment pushes Ron forward to approach stronger connections (when the realities of interdependence might pull him back). We also detailed a wealth of evidence suggesting that resolve results when the interdependent mind uses its capacity to rationalize to overstate the case. Ron not only sees virtues in Gayle that she does not see in herself, but he derogates his alternatives and minimizes his own sacrifices and costs.

In the second half of the chapter we described three of the four if–then implementation rules that the interdependent mind employs in the task of eliciting reciprocity in commitment. Two of these implementation rules match Ron's expressions of commitment to his trust in Gayle. The "escalate own dependence" rule motivates Ron to increase what he asks of Gayle and what he does for Gayle when he anticipates her acceptance. The "withdraw own dependence" rule motivates Ron to limit what he asks of Gayle and what he does for Gayle when he anticipates her rejection. In illustrating these rules, we described how Ron's trust in Gayle limits his resolve in his commitment and his willingness to be responsive to her needs. The third implementation rule keeps Gayle's commitment from flagging when Ron puts more of his outcomes in her hands. This "justify own commitment" rule motivates Gayle to value Ron all the more when he costs her, such as when she sacrifices needed work time to lend him a sympathetic ear.[5]

At caveat is in order before proceeding. The interpersonal mind lends itself to create commitments that are motivated from within. Because action requires certainty, the mind is ripe to imbue the partner and relationship with sufficient intrinsic value to motivate commitment. In such a state of commitment, Ron puts his needs in Gayle's hands and tends responsively to Gayle's needs because he wants to do so. He is resolved. However, the mind's capacity to exact this end varies with risk. In relationships where partners encounter more serious conflicts of interest, trust may prove elusive and restrain resolve. For relationships to endure in such circumstances, commitment may need to be imposed from without. In such a state of dependence, Ron tends to Gayle's needs because he must do so. He is resigned. The distinction between resolved and resigned commitments corresponds to the distinction between approach and avoidance commitment drawn by Frank and Brandstatter (2002). They revealed that people who are committed because they attach intrinsic value to the idea of the relationship itself (i.e., approach motivated) are more satisfied over time. People who are committed because they cannot afford not to be (i.e., avoidance motivated) are less satisfied over time. We return to a discussion of how resolved and resigned commitments arise and differentially affect satisfaction in our discussion of relationship personality in Chapter 8.

Now it's time to shift our focus away from a macroscopic toward a microscopic view of the interdependent mind. In Chapters 3 and 4, we detailed what it generally means to be more or less trusting and more or less committed. These macro sentiments begin and end the model of the interdependent mind we detailed in Figure 2.1. In Chapters 5 through 7, we take a microscopic look at how the interpersonal mind provides plans for action in specific conflicts of interest. We start with the process of disambiguating a partner's motives and orienting one's own interpersonal goals. This focus brings us back to Harry and Sally, who unfortunately have had more than their fair share of difficult domestic entanglements to disambiguate.

NOTES

1. In this chapter, we describe only how the procedural rules inform and motivate the global state of commitment. In Chapters 6 and 7, we make the situational translation of these rules concrete and describe their efficient (i.e., automatic) and flexible (i.e., controlled) operation.
2. Finding that trust restrains resolve in adult romantic relationships echoes effects first documented in the literature in terms of the "reciprocity of liking" principle (Berscheid & Walster, 1969). People like those others who like them. The phenomenon of people pledging

friendship allegiances to those who like them is so robust that Kenny (1994) described it as a "cultural truism." This effect is usually explained in terms of the pleasure principle. Liking is reciprocated because it is rewarding to be liked—but this logic does not fully explain the breadth of these data. In the platonic relationships typically examined, reciprocity of liking increases as relationships deepen in interdependence from acquaintances, to causal friends, to good friends (Kenny, 1994). However, perceiving another's liking should decrease in reinforcement value as partners become closer and more familiar. Our assumption that people first need trust in another's regard before they risk commitment anticipates exactly such an effect. As the strength of connection (and the negative consequences of rejection) increases, people are all the more in need of trust to risk extending themselves to potential intimates.

3. Autonomy costs do not include the more intentionally hurtful and rejecting acts, such as yelling, criticism, or physical abuse, that one partner can perpetrate on another. We discuss the effects of such behaviors in Chapter 7.

4. The tendency to compensate for costs was more pronounced for some people than for others (specifically, those high in global self-esteem). We return to this qualification in Chapter 6.

5. The fourth if–then implementation rule the interpersonal mind employs to elicit reciprocity in commitment is the "if self-protect goal, then promote partner dependence" rule, which we described in Chapter 3.

CHAPTER 5

The Situational Risks

Seek Connection or Avoid Rejection?

> The other day as I stood in front of the open freezer
> waiting for a dinner idea to strike, I noticed that the
> ice tray on top of the stack was empty. So I took it
> out. The second tray was empty too, as was the tray
> beneath it, and so on until the sixth and final tray,
> which held a single cube, spotted with grains of
> coffee. My husband had evidently been at it again.
> I was gearing up for a tirade when I heard a calm,
> reasonable voice at the back of my mind. . . .
> —FERNANDA MOORE, *CNN.com*

Sometimes an empty ice tray is just an empty ice tray. It is nothing more than unfortunate inconvenience at the moment one's drink needs cooling. Sometimes an empty ice tray is more than that. Think about the beleaguered Sally we introduced in Chapter 1. She struggles to manage the demands of housework, three children, and a part-time job. In 20 years of marriage to Harry, she has tried cajoling, teasing, bargaining, and begging to get Harry to take more responsibility for housework. Yet Harry loafs— he reaps the benefits of everything she does, from cooking to cleaning to grocery shopping—yet he seldom lifts a finger to help. For Sally, too often the victim of a free-riding Harry, the last cube of ice could be the proverbial last straw. To her, this coffee-flecked cube of ice could symbolize just how much Harry takes her for granted. By not taking a few seconds needed to fill even one ice tray, but instead leaving it for her once again, he thumbs his nose at her and everything she does for their family.

When is an empty ice tray full of ominous intent and when is it just empty? The issue of situational construal is central to understanding how interactions unfold in interdependent life. An ice tray that Sally simply perceives as empty invites her to solicit Harry's help. An ice tray that Sally fills with her disdain for Harry's loafing invites her to chastise him for his laziness. By revealing risk, the opportunities and costs Sally (and Harry) perceive in such conflicts of interest automatically shape their respective goals to connect or self-protect.

This chapter begins our exploration of how the interpersonal mind enacts "plans for action" that optimize responsiveness in specific conflicts of interest. As we introduced in Chapter 2, the interpersonal mind applies different if–then rules to coordinate responsiveness in low- and high-risk situations. Anticipating Harry's acceptance and responsiveness (i.e., low risk) motivates Sally to pursue the gains to be had in the situation by increasing her own dependence on Harry and justifying any costs she incurs in doing so (i.e., the action plan for pursuing connectedness goals). Anticipating Harry's rejection and nonresponsiveness instead motivates Sally to cut her potential losses by decreasing her dependence on Harry, perhaps until she's taken remedial steps to gain control over him by increasing his dependence on her (i.e., the action plan for pursuing self-protection goals). Because action plans are situation specific, the interpersonal mind's first step in coordinating interaction is to gauge situational risk.

This chapter describes how the interpersonal mind "decides" which specific situations should be approached and which specific situations should be avoided. In delineating how the interpersonal mind orients Sally's chosen goals in situations like the ice-tray dilemma, we begin by describing how the mind appraises risk. The term *risk* refers to two aspects of interdependent situations: objective risk and subjective risk. Let's consider each in turn.

Conflicts of interest vary in objective risk because such mixed-motive situations offer partners divergent gains and losses. As Sally mulls the one remaining ice cube, she has a decision to make. She can ask Harry, yet again, to take some responsibility. Or she can, resentfully, fill the trays herself. Harry, a witness to Sally's discovery of the empty ice trays, also has a choice to make. He can loaf or he can help. Figure 5.1 presents a 2 × 2 outcome matrix that illustrates the objective situation that Sally and Harry face. The horizontal axis captures Sally's options: She can ask for help or she can do it herself. The vertical axis captures Harry's options: He can loaf or he can help. Each combination of action results in differing gains and losses for Sally and Harry. The values on the top of the diago-

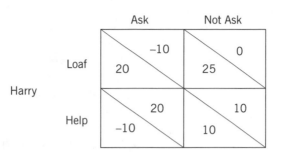

FIGURE 5.1. The ice-tray dilemma.

nal in each cell represent Sally's personal level of gain versus loss with each combination of choices. More positive numbers represent greater gain than loss; more negative numbers, greater loss than gain. The values on the bottom of the diagonal in each cell represent Harry's level of gain versus loss.

The objective gains and losses to be had in this situation can be practical or symbolic. In asking Harry to be more responsible, Sally stands to gain the practical benefits of a reliable source of ice and freedom from this chore. She also stands to gain the symbolic benefit of finally feeling like Harry really appreciates her efforts. However, in pleading her case to Harry once again, Sally also stands to lose. If he rejects her entreaty, she could incur his ire for nagging him about an inconsequential chore. The argument that results could also make her feel all the more exploited. By leaving the ice trays (and everything else) to Sally, Harry gains the practical benefits of cool drinks, cooked meals, and clean laundry without extending any effort himself. He also gains the symbolic benefits of feeling like the man and the provider. But by replenishing the ice tray, Harry stands to lose the extra time for TV and sleep he gains from the status quo.

What Sally stands to gain in this situation comes from Harry's capacity to behave in a way that is accepting and responsive to her needs. What she stands to lose comes from his power to behave in a way that is rejecting and nonresponsive to her needs. The situation Sally faces is high in objective risk because Harry has a strong incentive to be selfish. He can get both ice and freedom from work if he lets her fill the trays herself. In fact, the outcomes in Figure 5.1 reveal that Harry and Sally's objective interests in this situation are diametrically opposed. Sally gains the most if she asks Harry to help and he helps; she loses the most if she asks Harry for help and he loafs. In contrast, Harry loses the most if she asks him for help and he acquiesces; he gains the most if Sally stays silent and he continues to loaf. This objective situation puts Sally squarely in the middle of an approach–avoidance goal conflict. She can't get what she wants (i.e., Harry's help) without putting herself in the position of getting what she most doesn't want (i.e., Harry's refusal). That is, to obtain the best possible outcome Sally needs to risk being vulnerable to the worst possible outcome. This leaves her caught between asking (and its potential for huge gains and huge losses) and not asking (the safe, but not all that rewarding, bet).

Sally's subjective appraisal of the risks attached to each course of action (i.e., ask vs. not ask) makes the best course of action for resolving her goal conflict clear to her. In this situation, the risks Sally perceives in asking (and not asking) depend completely on her assessment of what Harry is likely to do. Expecting Harry to be selfish and continue to loaf makes asking for his help the higher-risk choice and filling the ice tray herself the lower-risk choice. Expecting Harry to happily acquiesce and fill the ice tray makes asking for his help the lower-risk choice and not asking the higher-risk choice. Because Harry has a strong objective incentive to be selfish in this situation, Sally must expect him to transform what he gains from loafing to take her needs into account to make soliciting his help her safe choice. Figure 5.2 illustrates such a caring transformation on Harry's part. The matrix on the left captures Harry's self-centered preferences: He has a strong inclination to continue being lazy because he gains the most when he does nothing. The matrix on the right captures his transformed preferences. The appeal of being recalcitrant in his laziness is lost when he takes Sally's hurt over being disappointed into account. As

| | Sally | | | Sally | |
	Ask	Not Ask		Ask	Not Ask
Loaf	20	25	Loaf	−10	15
Help	−10	10	Help	20	10

Harry

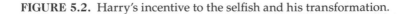

FIGURE 5.2. Harry's incentive to the selfish and his transformation.

we see in this chapter, Sally is more likely to expect Harry to transform if she generally trusts in his responsiveness or if she at least has a specific reason to trust him in this instance. In this instance, Harry's embarrassed smile as he sees her standing, ice tray in hand, might make his acceptance of her request for help seem more likely.

As this example illustrates, Sally's subjective appraisal of risk is akin to an expected utility function. This function weighs each gain and loss by the subjective probability of its occurrence. In this calculus, Sally's assessment of the probability of Harry helping or loafing depends on: (1) Harry's attachment to the status quo (a feature of the objective situation); (2) her chronic trust in Harry (a feature of the person); and (3) the incidental cues in the situation that give her more or less reason to be trusting in that specific instance (a feature of the person in the situation). By disambiguating Harry's goals, Sally's subjective appraisal of risk resolves her own goal conflict. This happens through the if–then goal orientation rules. These rules arbitrate approach–avoidance goal conflicts by using subjective risk as an "emotional tag," or cue to action. Expecting Harry to be solicitous motivates Sally to put her outcomes in Harry's hands and ask for his help (i.e., "if partner accepting, then connect"). Instead, expecting Harry to be recalcitrant motivates Sally to take her outcomes out of Harry's hands and fill the ice tray herself (i.e., "if partner rejecting, then self-protect). In this way, the goal orientation rules automatically motivate Sally to take the courses of action that offer the best hope of soliciting Harry's responsiveness or the most prudent means of avoiding his nonresponsiveness.

This chapter advances three main points for understanding how the interpersonal mind matches the risks Sally perceives in a specific situation to the interpersonal goal to connect or self-protect that she pursues in that same situation. Table 5.1 summarizes these arguments, addressed in sequence in the chapter. In the first part of this chapter we describe the structural features of situations that make some conflicts of interest higher in objective risk than others. In the second part we describe how the person and the situation interact to determine subjective risk. In this section,

TABLE 5.1. The Main Arguments

1. Structural features of situations make some situations higher in the objective risk of partner nonresponsiveness than others.
2. The perception of risk in a specific situation depends on the objective situation, incidental cues to trust, and chronic levels of trust.
3. The subjective appraisal of risk functions as an emotion tag, one that links anticipated acceptance to the goal to connect and anticipated rejection to the goal to self-protect.

we detail how incidental cues to trust (e.g., Harry's embarrassed smile) and chronic trust in the partner's responsiveness help disambiguate the partner's motivations in situations that offer unclear messages about risk. We do so by providing empirical examples of how high levels of trust make a partner's acceptance seem more likely given the objective risks, whereas low levels of trust make a partner's rejection seem more likely given the objective risks. In the third part of this chapter we describe how subjective appraisals of risk function as "emotion tags" that cue appropriate action plans through the if–then *goal orientation* rules. These rules resolve the goal conflict inherent to conflicts of interest by linking the partner's anticipated acceptance (i.e., a positive tag for risk) to the goal to connect and the partner's anticipated rejection (i.e., a negative tag for risk) to the goal to self-protect.

THE OBJECTIVE RISKS IN THE SITUATION

Relationships are composed of a series of interdependent situations (Braiker & Kelley, 1979; Kelley, 1979). Interdependent situations are ones where one's own outcomes depend in part on the partner's actions. The situations partners sample span from the most mundane to the most unfamiliar. They also span from the most benign to the most contentious. Situations vary in objective risk because situations vary on three structural dimensions (see Kelley et al., 2003):

1. Situation content
2. Situation type
3. Situation features

Situations vary in *content* because conflicts can arise in the coordination of life tasks, personality, or relationship goals. Situations vary in *type* because some conflicts of interest compel cooperation and others compel competition. Situations further vary in *features*. For instance, situations where conflicting interests are hidden give the partner greater license to be selfish than situations where conflicting interests are easily discerned. Conflicts of interest that involve long-term sacrifices also give the partner more reason to be selfish than ones that require short-term kindnesses. These three parameters—content, type, and features—mark objective risk by quantifying the partner's temptation to be selfish and the coincident urge to self-protect against exploitation. We now explain the implications of each of these parameters for the state of objective risk in turn.

Situation Content

Interdependent life requires constant efforts at social coordination because partners are interdependent in multiple ways (see Chapter 2, p. 29). First, life together as a couple creates particular tasks and problems. In Harry and Sally's marriage, laundry needs to be done, bills need to be paid, their son's ADHD diagnosis needs to be managed, and domestic responsibilities need to be shifted when Sally is ill. Second, living together necessitates merging discrepant personal preferences, attitudes, and personalities. On those occasions when Harry and Sally have the rare luxury to go to a movie alone together, they must decide whether to favor Sally's yen for drama or Harry's affinity for action. Each weekend they also have to negotiate whether to take their family to church (Sally's preference) or to the zoo (the children's preference) on Sunday morning. Across these situations, they must also work to ensure fairness because Sally's bossy and controlling nature could easily trump Harry's more easygoing personality. Third, living together necessitates negotiating shared goals for their marriage. The incident with the ice trays is so salient to Sally in part because it symbolizes a greater concern. Harry wants his ailing mother to live in their already overcrowded house. Sally worries about this compounding of their marital roles. She can't be a full-time caretaker to Harry's mother and their children and still continue to manage her job and their household without help from Harry. Although Harry seems blissfully content with his role as the provider and her role as the caretaker, when Sally imagined what it would be like to be married, this isn't what she expected.

The gains and losses possible in life-task conflicts are typically concrete and finite (e.g., ice, meals, unwashed clothes, unpaid bills). The gains and losses possible in personality and relationship goal conflicts tend to be more abstract and expansive. Such broad conflicts insinuate themselves into a wider variety of concrete domains. They also come with more substantive symbolic outcomes. Sally is considerably more gregarious than Harry. This dispositional difference creates multiple opportunities for conflicting interests in specific situations because Sally often wants to chat when Harry wants silence, Sally wants to go to a crowded bar when Harry would rather go to a movie, and Sally would rather invite friends over when Harry would rather go to bed early. Moreover, when Sally ends up going to bed early rather than having friends over, she is likely to feel like she just can't "be herself" with Harry, an issue of relationship goals. Because the potential for loss increases with each level of interdependence, each partner's motivation to be selfish and to protect against the other's exploitation also increases proportionately. Therefore, objective risk typically escalates as conflicts shift from life tasks to personality to relationship goals.[1]

But there's an important caveat to this principle. Even life-task conflicts that seem minor on the surface have the potential to involve substantial risk if the "minor" conflict is symbolic of an issue at a broader level of interdependence (Braiker & Kelley, 1979). That's the case with Sally and the ice tray, and it's the reason why she hesitates at the fridge door. Asking Harry for help holds the potential for huge gain and huge loss precisely Sally sees this situation as a test. To her, his helping reveals his respect for her contributions and his willingness to adopt more flexible marital roles. His intransigence instead reveals his disdain for her needs and his unwillingness to even try to be fair and communal. So there's a lot at stake. Unfortunately, this might not be all that apparent to Harry because he isn't likely to construe the implications of his choice to help or to loaf at the same level of abstraction as Sally does. All he might see is an empty ice tray—a lower-level construal that might not impress him with the importance of making a transformation in this instance and therefore makes the situation all the riskier for Sally!

Situation Type

The situations that Harry and Sally encounter at the levels of life tasks, personality, and relationship goals afford mixed motives. These situations offer both the potential for gain and the potential for loss because partner interests are not perfectly correspondent in each situation encountered. The ease of negotiating such situations depends on what specific type of conflict of interest partners face. We refer to situations by type to capture an idea basic to interdependence theory. Any given situation has a "deep structure" that goes beyond its surface content (Kelley et al., 2003). Take the example of the empty ice tray. At its surface, this situation involves the allocation of a specific domestic responsibility. At its core, this situation involves social loafing or freeriding. In deciding to do nothing, Harry has more control over Sally's outcomes than Sally can enact over her own outcomes.

Interdependence theorists carve social life into approximately 20 prototypic types of situations that differ in their deep structure. Kelley and his colleagues (2003) dedicated a book to this topic. Obviously, we cannot recapitulate the entire volume here. Instead, we focus on three types of mixed-motive situations that have great utility for understanding how partners perceive risk within adult romantic relationships. These situations involve: (1) coordination dilemmas, (2) exchange dilemmas, and (3) zero-sum conflicts. These three situation prototypes differ in a deep-structure feature central to objective risk. Namely, they differ in how readily the personal preferences of each partner converge on a common goal (Kelley et al., 2003).

Let us explain. In "coordination situations," partners prefer the same outcome in a given situation, but they can only obtain this outcome by coordinating their behavior. Figure 5.3 illustrates such a dilemma. In this situation, Harry and Sally have a rare Saturday night free and they want to see a movie. Sally has two choices—she can go to the drama she prefers or to the action film Harry prefers. Harry also has two choices—he can go to his action film or her drama. The numbers on top of the diagonal within the cells represent Sally's outcomes from each combination of choices. The numbers below the diagonal represent Harry's outcomes. As these values illustrate, Sally and Harry both gain more by going to the same movie together than either of them gains by seeing their preferred movie alone. This coordination situation poses little objective risk because selfishly pursuing one's own movie choice results in an outcome neither partner desires. As Harry has little incentive to insist on his own movie, Sally has little need to protect against his exploitation; consequently, behaving responsively is straightforward.

In "exchange situations," partners prefer different outcomes, but each partner can only obtain his or her own personal preferences by doing something for the other. Figure 5.4 illustrates such a dilemma. In this situation, Sally wants a Saturday morning to herself to read and relax, something she has no hope of achieving unless Harry takes their children to the mall, something he loathes to do. Harry wants to spend a weekend

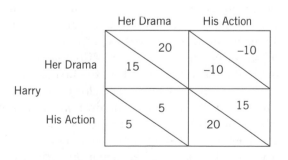

FIGURE 5.3. A coordination dilemma.

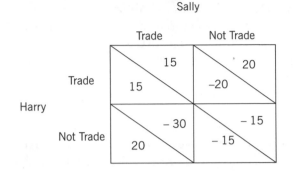

FIGURE 5.4. An exchange dilemma.

camping and fishing with some old high school friends, an expense they might not be able to afford unless Sally picks up a few extra hours of work. Each partner again has two choices, except this time the choice for each partner involves the choice to trade or not to trade. The numbers on top of the diagonal represent Sally's outcomes; the numbers below the diagonal represent Harry's outcomes. They obtain the best joint outcome if they broker a trade or a deal wherein Sally works a few extra hours during the week and Harry then takes the children to the mall (i.e., gain through trade). But each of them stands to gain more personally by receiving, but not providing, a trade. For instance, Harry most prefers to get his money for a fishing weekend without taking the children to the mall (i.e., gain without trade). Harry's temptation not to live up to his end of the bargain gives Sally reason to protect against such exploitation, making behavior coordination more difficult.

In "zero-sum conflict situations," partners prefer different outcomes and no amount of cooperation can result in both partners getting their personal or selfish preference. Instead, one partner's gain requires the other partner's loss. Figure 5.5 illustrates such a dilemma. In this situation, Harry and Sally have one weekend left to prepare their tax returns. Neither of them relishes this onerous and stressful task. Each of them again has a choice—to make the sacrifice and do the taxes or to wait and hope the other one caves and does the taxes. The clock is ticking. The numbers on top of the diagonal within the cells again represent Sally's outcomes from each combination of choices. The numbers below the diagonal represent Harry's outcomes. The values within the matrix indicate that doing the taxes together is not appealing because it only invites bickering over the state of the household's finances. Also Harry and Sally would both

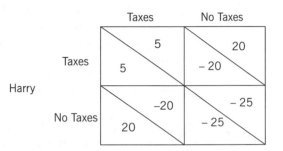

FIGURE 5.5. A zero-sum conflict.

rather escape than shoulder the burden, motivating them each to be self-ish. The goal of completed tax forms is in jeopardy because each of them hates the idea of being the one to suffer while the other one gets off scot-free. If the taxes are to be done, one of them will have to make a major sacrifice. The asymmetrical gains and losses in such situations make coordinating behavior toward a mutually desired goal (e.g., a completed tax return) exceedingly difficult.

Although the matrices focus on situations evoked by life tasks, relationship partners also encounter these types of situations at the levels of personality and relationship goals. For instance, Sally's greater gregariousness means that she likes to chat and fills up silences with a running commentary on her daily activities. Harry craves silence and he is happiest alone with his thoughts. Such divergent interaction styles created multiple situations that force an "exchange." Sally could only satisfy her need to chat if Harry conversed, and Harry could only satisfy his need for silence if Sally ceased and desisted. Over multiple such situations, they brokered a trade where Harry gets 20 minutes to read the paper in silence when he gets home before Sally gets to pepper him with questions about his day and the news of her own day. Unfortunately, divergent philosophies about their marital roles have forced more zero-sum conflicts. These conflicts have persisted. Sally simply does not want to be as traditional a wife as Harry wants her to be. Making Harry happy by tending to cooking, cleaning, meals, children, and empty ice trays too often leaves her feeling like she has gotten the raw end of the deal.

The example matrices make one point clear: Being responsive to the partner's needs is objectively easier when one's own personal outcomes are more closely aligned with the partner's outcomes (Kelley, 1979). Consider the task of coordinating the movie choice (Figure 5.3). The situation itself compels responsive behavior because Sally gains the most when Harry gains the most (and vice versa). Such situations are low in objective risk. Exchange and zero-sum conflicts situations are not nearly as powerful in compelling responsiveness because Sally gains less when Harry gains relatively more (and vice versa). Such situations are higher in objective risk because behaving responsively requires added incentive (Kelley, 1979).

Namely, behaving responsively requires that the situation be transformed. Interdependence theorists define the "transformation of motivation" as the tendency to consider the partner's outcomes as part of one's own outcomes (Kelley, 1979). Figure 5.6 illustrates how Harry might transform the tax conflict. In this transformed situation, Harry might choose to do the taxes because sparing Sally the pain of this task makes doing the taxes less onerous for Harry. In particular, caring about Sally's welfare might motivate him to volunteer to do the federal taxes (which they both hated) if she did the state taxes (which she didn't find nearly as loathsome). Through such a transformation, Harry changes the zero-sum conflict into a more tractable exchange dilemma.

Transformations ultimately require expected reciprocity in commitment. To take on the greater tax burden, Harry needs to care enough about Sally to want to sacrifice for her. That is, he needs to be committed. To make Harry's sacrifice possible, Sally also needs to put her outcomes in Harry's hands. That is, Sally needs to trust in Harry's commitment as well. The necessity of transformation brings the fourth level of interdependence into our discussion. Couples are also interdependent in trust and commitment motivations (see Chapter 2, p. 40). This fourth level of inter-

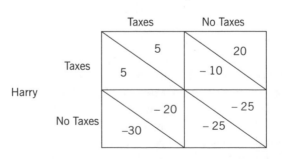

FIGURE 5.6. Harry's transformation of the zero-sum conflict.

dependence shapes the objective risks in conflicts of interest because it determines whether partners are equally likely to set aside self-interested concerns. Imagine that Harry is more committed to Sally than Sally is committed to Harry. Such an asymmetry increases Harry's objective risk of loss over the longer term because Sally is not likely to meet his sacrifices (like doing the federal taxes) with equivalent sacrifices of her own. The interdependent mind works to coordinate the interpersonal goals Harry and Sally pursue in specific conflicts of interest to avoid such destabilizing asymmetries in commitment. We return to this coordination process when we discuss the action plans for eliciting reciprocity in partner commitment in Chapters 6 and 7.

Situation Features

As we reviewed above, coordination situations generally pose less risk than exchange situations, and exchange situations generally pose less risk than zero-sum conflicts. Nonetheless, some coordination situations are riskier than other coordination situations; some exchange situations are riskier than other exchange situations; and some zero-sum conflicts are riskier than other zero-sum conflicts. The situation features that determine risk involve:

1. Dependence and control (unilateral or bilateral)
2. Divergence of preferences
3. Transparency of partner interests
4. Time span (see Holmes, 2002; Kelly et al., 2003)

Within each situation, greater dependence on the partner heightens risk because it lessens one's power over one's own outcomes. For instance, Sally can reserve her left-wing political banter for her friends if Harry is a true-blue conservative. However, Sally cannot achieve her goal of relying on him for support without his cooperation, making the latter negotiations riskier than the former ones. Within each situation type, less-correspondent partner preferences heighten risk because coordination requires that one partner sacrifices more while the other partner gains more. Within each situation type, less-transparent partner preferences similarly heighten risk. If Sally knows that Harry loathes the dishes, she can anticipate what benefits and costs she might incur if she presses him to do his share. Such risks are harder to foresee if Harry conceals which domestic tasks he loathes the most. Within each situation type, conflicts further vary in time span; they vary in the degree to which coordination necessitates short- or long-term sacrifice and realizes short- or long-term gain. Giving up the immediate benefit of going on a vacation to save for a house might offer the greatest long-term gain for the couple, but making such a personal sacrifice underlines the risks of counting on the relationship's future. Each of these structural features of situations control the level of objective risk because each feature puts greater or lesser onus on the partner's goodwill and responsiveness in the face of costs.

Objective Risk Parameters: A Summary

Table 5.2 summarizes the different parameters that mark specific situations as objectively low or high in risk (Holmes, 2002; Kelley, 1979). Situations that are objectively low in risk possess one or more of the parameters in the left-hand column. In lower-risk situations, the benefits to be obtained are clear and the costs are minimal. Partner interests are also largely correspondent, and each partner knows what the other partner wants (i.e., high transparency). In such situations, partners often possess equal power, long-term investment is minimal, and the benefits of personal sacrifice are immediate (Holmes, 2002). Such is the case in Sally and Harry's movie negotiations (see Figure 5.3). In such situations, pursuing his own outcomes is not that pressing for Harry, and consequently, Sally can afford to be vulnerable to him. Situations like the movie dilemma are objectively lower in risk for Sally because Harry does *not* need to transform the situation to behave responsively. The personal gains to be had are already sufficient to motivate him to be responsive (without consideration of Sally's needs).

Situations that are objectively high in risk possess one or more of the parameters in the right-hand column. In higher-risk situations, the potential costs are more prohibitive relative to what might be gained. Partner interests are also largely divergent, and at least one partner might wonder what the other partner really wants (i.e., low transparency). In such situ-

TABLE 5.2. Prototypical Characteristics of Low- and High-Risk Situations

Low-risk situation	High-risk situation
Correspondent interests	Divergent interests
Transparent interests	Concealed interests
Equal power	Unequal power
Minimal long-term investment	Substantial long-term investment
Immediate benefits to be had	Immediate costs to be had

ations, partners often possess asymmetrical power, long-term investment is onerous, and the benefits of personal sacrifice require time to be realized (Holmes, 2002). Such is the case with the ice-tray dilemma. Harry holds power through the status quo, and the long-term benefits he might gain from having a happier wife are not apparent to him in the short term (see Figure 5.1). This situation structure tempts Harry to consider only his own outcomes and tempts Sally to protect herself from vulnerability to Harry's whims. To behave responsively, Harry must somehow transform the situation in a way that takes Sally's needs into account. The necessity of his transformation makes such situations high in risk for Sally because such a transformation is not guaranteed.

Before proceeding to discuss how partners perceive risk, two qualifications merit mention. First, coordination, exchange and zero-sum conflict situations represent pure types. Many situations partners encounter involve mixtures of these elements. For instance, solving the zero-sum tax conflict might involve negotiating a trade such that Sally agrees to prepare the state tax return if Harry agrees to do the federal tax return. Second, the situations we have described do not exist in isolation. Instead, situations are part of the ongoing stream of interactions. The outcome of one situation provides the choices to be made in the next situation partners face (Kelley & Thibaut, 1978). Imagine that Sally did end up asking Harry to fill the ice trays, and he refused. His rejection has created a new situation. It has created a situation in which Sally must choose between forgiving Harry's intransigence and retaliating against it. Harry must choose between being repentant and indignant. In this situation, the combination of Harry's repentance and Sally's forgiveness exacts the best joint outcome, but Sally's strong desire to retaliate makes hoping for her forgiveness a risky choice for Harry, motivating his indignation. We return to the issue of how situations compound themselves in Chapters 6 through 8.

THE SUBJECTIVE APPRAISAL OF RISK

The gains and losses to be had in conflicts of interest can leave people stuck in indecision, torn between seeking connection and avoiding rejection. Because goal conflict is antithetical to action (Cacioppo et al., 1999), the interpersonal mind has a mechanism for resolving such situated approach–avoidance conflicts. It has this mechanism in the capacity to assess and calibrate risk. The interpersonal mind tracks subjective risk by anticipating the partner's actions. The subjective perception of risk is a statement about the partner's likely motivation to be accepting or rejecting of one's needs in a specific conflict of interest.

Classic models of social perception assume that interpersonal judgment is a function of the person and the situation (Griffin & Ross, 1991; Mischel & Shoda, 1995; Monson et al., 1982). The risk assessment made in anticipating a partner's actions is also a property of person and situation factors. These factors include (individually or in combination): (1) the partner's objective temptation to be self-interested (i.e., the situation); (2) the perceiver's chronic level of trust in the partner's responsiveness (i.e., the person); and (3) incidental cues in the situation that signal state shifts in the partner's willingness to be responsive to the perceiver (i.e., the person in the situation). In this calculus, Sally's subjective appraisal of risk resembles an expected utility function. This function weighs the gains and losses of asking (vs. not asking) by the subjective probability she attaches to Harry being acquiescent versus recalcitrant. Expecting his recalcitrance makes the losses attendant on asking for his help more likely to capture her attention and motivate her avoidance (i.e., not asking for his help). Expecting his acquiescence makes the gains attendant in asking more likely to captivate her attention and motivate her approach (i.e., asking for his help).

In the subjective appraisal of risk, reality anchors perception (Kunda, 1990). In zero-sum conflicts over household chores in which Harry gains much and loses little by being lazy, the danger of asking him to be more responsible should be evident to Sally regardless of the incidental cues to trust or her chronic level of trust in his commitment. In coordination situations in which Harry stands to gain the same benefits as Sally, the wisdom of asking him to cooperate should also be evident to Sally regardless of either chronic or situated feelings of trust. In such clear situations, Sally's subjective perception of risk generally mirrors the objective state of risk.

A daily diary study conducted by Overall and Sibley (2008) illustrates how clear signals of risk affect perceptions of one's partner's motivations. In this study, participants completed interaction diaries whenever they had a social interaction lasting 10 minutes or longer. The researchers then singled out interactions with romantic partners for analysis. Participants quantified objective risk in each interaction by rating how much personal influence or control they had in the interaction. They also rated how accepted they felt by the partner in each interaction. Feeling relatively powerless strongly signaled risk: Participants perceived their partner as more rejecting in those situations where they personally felt relatively powerless.

Disambiguating Risk: Incidental Cues and Chronic Expectancies

Not all conflicts of interest immediately reveal the partner's likely motives. In such situations, people need supplemental sources of information. In demystifying the partner's motives, the interpersonal mind attends to more than just the features of the choice itself. Any specific conflict of interest occurs as part of an ongoing and dynamic stream of events (Kelley & Thibaut, 1978). Sally did not just magically appear in front of her fridge. Rather, she came home after a frustrating day of work at the bank, where she got reprimanded for cashing a check without taking proper identification. She then walked in the door to find Harry happily helping their middle son through his math homework. Then, as she started the preparations for dinner, she found the empty ice tray. As she stands there, she sees Harry smiling and making a sheepish and apologetic face. Events from this ongoing stream likely shape and inform her expectations of Harry's likelihood of behaving in an acquiescent and accepting or recalcitrant and rejecting manner should she ask him to take responsibility.

The incidental cues that most capture her attention correspond to the if–then vigilance rules that signal her value to Harry (see Chapter 3). The five vigilance rules dictating that Harry is more likely to accommodate her needs when he would be hard-pressed to replace her. As she stands, ice tray in hand, Sally is more likely to anticipate Harry's responsiveness and acquiescence when the incidental cues give her some reason to think that Harry is either: (1) willing to sacrifice, (2) valuing of her personal qualities, (3) not superior in worth to her, (4) unlikely to be poached, or (5) stuck in the marriage through his dedication to their children.

The balance of these cues in the surrounding situations informs her state or situated level of trust in Harry's responsiveness. As she stands at the fridge, Sally might think back to early that morning when she asked Harry to take more responsibility and he "forgot" to put the wet laundry in the dryer (Holmes & Rempel, 1989). She might also note Harry's happy and relaxed mood as he works through his son's math homework and think he might be in an accommodating frame of mind now (Bellavia & Murray, 2003). She might also remember how Harry complimented her new haircut that morning before she went to work. But she might also reflexively consider whether she herself really deserves his help. Having just had her hours at work cut because of mishandling one too many bank transactions, she might conclude she should do more herself at home (Murray, Aloni, et al., 2009). In many circumstances, the relative strength of such incidental cues might be enough to disambiguate the situation and direct her goals. For instance, if Sally only noted Harry's sheepish grin, the losses to be had in asking for his help might seem too remote to trouble her. If she focused instead on the wet laundry and her feelings of inferiority, these same losses might loom large enough to be prohibitive. Unfortunately, Sally is not so clearly directed. The localized cues send mixed messages, leaving her conflicted still.

Sally's chronic level of trust in Harry functions as a final barometer of risk in ambiguous conflicts of interest (Murray, Holmes, & Collins, 2006). Sally's overall conscious feelings of trust in Harry captures her meta-perspective on the strength of his commitment to her; trust therefore gives her a heuristic means of deciding when to approach and when to be vigilant. Relatively high levels of trust generally signal that it is safe for Sally to approach (i.e., ask for help). Relatively low levels of trust instead signal it is safer for Sally to avoid (i.e., not ask for help).

Chronic trust functions as a heuristic guide to risk by shaping Sally's conscious expectancies for specific outcomes in conflicts of interest and the value she attaches to the outcomes she expects. In shaping expectancies, Sally's level of trust in Harry's commitment forecasts his likely behavior in a conflict of interest. In shaping valuation, Sally's level of trust in Harry's commitment controls how she feels about each action Harry might take. A daily diary study of established married couples aptly illustrates how trust changes how it feels to be disappointed by one's partner (Murray, Griffin, et al., 2003). In this study, both partners completed measures of the partner's perceived rejection and state self-esteem each day for 3 weeks. For people who trusted less in their partner's responsiveness, feeling rejected and exploited by the partner was especially painful. They felt worse about themselves on days after they perceived their partner to be more rejecting. Being rejected had no appreciable effect on the self-esteem of people who were more trusting because highs did not treat isolated events as relevant to the broader issue of their partner's caring (see Chapter 3 discussion of hypothesis testing). Sally is pretty distrusting overall because Harry has let her down in the domestic domain so many times in the past. Her chronic suspicions thus give her all too much reason to expect or bet that Harry will prove to be rejecting once again (i.e., deciding to loaf). To compound matters, Sally's distrust makes the possibility of being exploited again especially painful to her because his recalcitrance would reinforce her fear that their marital roles will never change. For these reasons, being less trusting disposes Sally to perceive the ice-tray situation as high in risk. In her mind, asking for Harry's help only sets her up for a negative outcome (his refusal) that she fears.

Risk Amplification and Minimization: Empirical Examples

Because the interpersonal mind gives avoiding rejection greater motivational priority than seeking connection, generally being less trusting leaves people both vigilant for the possibility of loss in conflicts of interest and readily hurt (Holmes & Rempel, 1989; Murray, Holmes, & Collins, 2006). Why should people be primed to see what they fear? For people who are less trusting, being vigilant to rejection is probably the best means of avoiding hurt (MacDonald & Leary, 2005). Sally's vigilance to situation features that signal Harry's reason to be selfish motivates her to take the appropriate preemptive action (such as filling the ice trays herself rather than asking for help).[2] This general line of reasoning is echoed in discussions of rejection sensitivity and anxiety disorders. Downey and Feldman (1996) argue that chronic differences in the tendency to expect and perceive rejection reflect the operation of the defensive motivational system (Pietrzak, Downey, & Ayduk, 2005). This system serves the goal of avoiding dangerous situations by increasing people's tendency to perceive threat (Lang, Bradley, & Cuthbert, 1990). Similarly, Mineka and Sutton (1992) argue that high levels of chronic anxiety automatically direct people's attention toward threatening stimuli so that they might avoid such situations. For instance, threatening words, such as *injury* or *criticized*, automatically capture attention for people high in generalized anxiety (MacLeod, Mathews, & Tata, 1986). However, with high levels of trust, there is little need to amplify the potential for loss in ambiguous situations because rejection is not that likely or that hurtful. A trusting Gayle can afford to miss or overlook certain cues to risk because the odd occasion when Ron disappoints her does not hurt that much.

The evidence we review next suggests that people who are less trusting actually fill in the informational gaps in situations in ways that amplify the partner's reasons to be selfish. Imagine that Sally comes home exhausted and needing to talk to Harry about her day. Instead of listening, Harry starts complaining about the lack of food in the fridge and demanding she find him something to eat. Because Sally is not terribly trusting, attributing his insensitivity to fatigue and hunger may never occur to her. Instead, she may attribute such grumbling to an interpersonal disposition—his broader displeasure with her. Something quite different typically unfolds in Ron and Gayle's household because Gayle generally trusts in Ron's commitment. When Gayle comes home to find Ron the picture of domestic discontent, she usually excuses his self-involved rant, chastises him gently, and suggests dinner out. For Gayle, knowing that Ron is committed to her affords such motivated interpretations of the evidence at hand by making it easy for her to counter Ron's current complaints with selective recall of his better behavior (Kunda, 1990). We now turn to the evidence that reveals exactly how trust affects the perception of risk. In reviewing this evidence, we report research that utilized both direct measures of trust in the partner's commitment and dispositional proxies for trust (e.g., attachment security).

Direct Measures of Trust

In the first experiment to examine how trust shapes the perception of risk in a specific situation, Holmes and Rempel (1989) asked couples to discuss a major and unresolved problem in their marriage. Before this discussion ensued, they activated situational risk for half of the participants. They either reminded Sally of a time when Harry had disappointed her or they reminded Sally of a time when Harry had sacrificed and really met her needs. Couples then discussed the problem on videotape. Then each member of the couple privately viewed the videotape and rated their partner's behavior and motivations. The results revealed exactly how being less trusting amplifies the meaning of ambiguously selfish behaviors. People who were less trusting reacted to reminders of the past transgression by interpreting their partner's current behavior more negatively. In contrast, people who were more trusting actually reacted to reminders of a past transgression by seeing their partner's current motivations more positively than control participants (Holmes & Rempel, 1989). A daily diary study later conducted by Murray, Bellavia, et al. (2003) provided a conceptual replication of such dynamics. In this study, married intimates who generally questioned their partner's regard for them felt all the more rejected on days after their partner criticized or disappointed them or was in a bad mood (Murray, Bellavia, et al., 2003). This ready sensitivity to perceive risk was not at all characteristic of people who generally felt more positively regarded. Instead, they actually compensated. They reconstrued their partner's behavior in a way that allowed them to feel more loved on days after their partner provoked conflicts and transgressed more.

Indirect Proxies for Trust

Simpson, Rholes, and Philips (1996) found similarly persuasive evidence for risk amplification in a groundbreaking experiment examining the effects of attachment anxiety on the perception of risk. In this study, they asked dating couples to discuss either a minor or a major problem in their relationship. Couples were videotaped during these conversations. After this discussion ended, participants then described how much their feelings of trust and security in their relationship had changed as a result of the discussion. They also rated how much anger and hostility they felt at the end of the discussion. Long after couples left the laboratory, trained observers then coded the interactions for the amount of warmth and supportiveness conveyed during the discussion and how effectively the couple resolved the conflict. These observer ratings provided an index of what actually happened.

Discussing a major problem is riskier and more stressful than discussing a minor problem because major problems raise the issue of whether the partner will make sacrifices to respond to one's needs. Consequently, discussing a major problem should be more likely to activate concerns about risk than discussing a minor problem. However, these investigators reasoned that only people high on attachment anxiety would be likely to question their partner's trustworthiness and value in such taxing circumstances. Why? Because being uncertain of their partner's commitment to them amplifies the meaning of ongoing events. Figure 5.7 illustrates the nature of the results they found for women. The results for men were parallel. As expected, women high in anxious ambivalence evidenced stronger concerns about their relationship when discussing a major than minor problem. Less-anxious women actually showed the opposite effect. They actually felt more secure when discussing a major than minor problem.

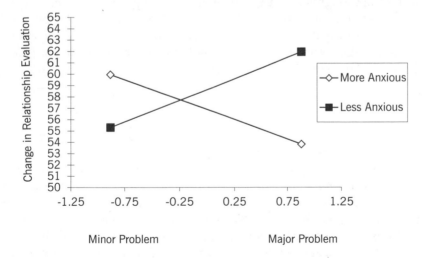

FIGURE 5.7. How attachment anxiety amplifies the perception of risk (as reflected in more negative relationship evaluations). Adapted from Simpson, Rholes, and Phillips (1996). Copyright 1996 by the American Psychological Association. Adapted by permission.

Importantly the reasons for concern that highly anxious men and women perceived in the "major conflict" interactions were not apparent to observers. Simply being suspicious of the partner's motives was enough to use these objectively ambiguous interactions as grounds for being distrustful.

In interdependent situations, people who have some dispositional reason to be less trusting of their partner also see evidence of risk in seemingly neutral events. People who trust more in their partner's commitment evidence no such signal amplification bias. For instance, married intimates who are high in the dispositional need to avoid negative outcomes set a lower threshold for identifying partner misdeeds, seeing misdeeds that the partner did not report (Gable, 2007). Similarly, people high on attachment-related anxiety interpret a partner's clumsy attempts to be supportive as intentionally hurtful (Collins & Feeney, 2004). People high on anxiety also interpret daily conflicts as a sign of their partner's waning commitment (Campbell, Simpson, Boldry, & Kashy, 2005). Dating intimates who are high on anxiety about acceptance also interpret a partner's hypothetical (Collins, 1996) and actual misdeeds in suspicious ways that are likely to exacerbate hurt feelings (Mikulincer, 1998). When gauging their dating partner's thoughts about attractive opposite-sex others, intimates high on attachment-related anxiety are also more empathically accurate. They know whom their partner finds attractive, discerning threatening thoughts that are conveniently and optimistically misunderstood by secure intimates (Simpson, Ickes, & Grich, 1999). People who chronically anticipate interpersonal rejection are so sensitive to violations of trust that they attribute negative intent to a new partner's hypothetical behaviors (Downey & Feldman, 1996).

Impulsive Trust

In the research just cited, trust (or its dispositional proxy) was conceptualized (and assessed) in terms of conscious or deliberative expectations. As we introduced in Chapter 3, the interdependent mind also keeps a supplementary barometer of the safety of approach. Unlike explicitly trusting expectations, this barometer primarily emerges through the experience of interacting with one's partner. Namely, a history of positive interactions conditions more positive automatic evaluative associations to the partner; a history of negative interactions conditions more negative automatic evaluative associations to the partner (Murray, Holmes, et al., 2010). Such automatic evaluative associations to the partner also play a central role in disambiguating risk. Generally speaking, being more impulsively trusting makes it easier and more natural to overlook situational cues to risk. Because feeling safe in Ron's presence is so reflexive for Gayle, his negative behaviors are automatically discounted. Her strong conditioned and positive association to Ron simply overwhelms any more minor negative associations his transgressions elicit. We return to this point in Chapters 8 and 10.

DIRECTING INTERPERSONAL GOAL PURSUIT: IF–THEN GOAL ORIENTATION RULES

The interpersonal mind works so hard to disambiguate the partner's motives because Sally and Harry can only reap the best possible joint outcomes from mixed-motive situations by pursuing compatible goals. In the zero-sum conflict over taxes, Harry's offering to do the federal tax return could reap benefits for both partners provided Sally agrees to do the state return in a trade. Harry's assessment of risk—his expectation that Sally will prove to be cooperative or recalcitrant—resolves his approach–avoidance conflict between offering to do the federal return and keeping silent. Anticipating her cooperation makes the gains to be had in the situation more appealing and motivates him to voice his conciliatory offer (i.e., approach). Anticipating her intransigence instead makes the losses more prohibitive and motivates his silence (i.e., avoid).

How does the interpersonal mind use the subjective appraisal of risk to orient one's interpersonal goals in a specific situation? Risk perceptions orient goals by functioning as an emotion "tag." Situational cues that rejection might be forthcoming—like Harry's irritated glance—remind Sally how bad it feels to be disappointed by Harry because such risk cues are "tagged" in memory to past associated hurts. Indeed, for Sally, simply seeing Harry looking annoyed in the general vicinity of the kitchen sink is enough to make her anxious and dissuade her from asking him for his help because she's been burned so many times in the past. Harry has a similarly strong affective association to the thought of being vulnerable to Sally in zero-sum conflicts. Offering to do the federal taxes makes Harry feel uneasy and guarded because making similar overtures in the past only resulted in Sally accusing him of having ulterior motives.

As these examples illustrate, current situational cues to risk, such as an opportunity for Harry to be lazy or an opportunity for Sally to be ungrateful, are "tagged" to the emotions experienced in past situations that contained these risk features. The affective associations to specific risk cues that result (whether positive or negative) then motivate congruent interpersonal goal pursuits. This analysis of the motivating property of risk appraisals has its roots in a provocative dual-process model of emotion proposed by Baumiester, Vohs, DeWall, et al. (2007). This model describes the distinct roles that automatic affect and conscious emotion play in regulating behavior. In developing this model, these researchers started with a paradox. In human evolutionary history, the situations that posed the greatest threat to human survival (e.g., an approaching bear) required quick action, but the conscious experience of emotion (e.g., fear) arises too slowly to expeditiously direct behavior. To resolve this paradox, they argued that conscious emotion acts as a mechanism for after-the-fact reflection that reinforces behavior met with positive consequences and extinguishes behavior met with negative consequences. In so doing, conscious emotion motivates more adaptive future behavior by attaching affective "tags" to situations after the behavioral fact that can then motivate quick action before the behavioral fact in the future. Once in place, such automatic affective associations to situations motivate quick action to approach "good" and avoid "bad" situations.

According to this theory of emotion, seeing a bear makes people run. Once a safe distance from the bear is gained, the conscious experience of fear at being at risk (and relief at being safe) then motivates people to avoid situations where bears might prowl in the future. How so? Feeling afraid "tags" bear-dwelling locations with negative affective associations after the behavioral fact of encountering the bear. Feeling relief instead "tags" non-bear-dwelling locations with positive affective associations. These affective risk tags are then in place to automatically motivate adaptive and quick bear-avoiding action the next time one takes a walk in the forest. These affective tags evoke an immediate affective tinge that something is good and to be approached or bad and to be avoided before the behavioral fact of encountering the bear.

The subjective appraisal of risk functions similarly. In the past, giving Harry the opportunity to help in domestic matters made Sally feel bad because he rejected her entreaties more often than not. Feeling bad then motivated Sally to avoid situations that had similar high-risk features because contemplating her vulnerability tagged domestic situations with negative affect. However, giving Harry the opportunity to do instrumental things, like fixing her car, made Sally feel good because he accepted her entreaties more often than not. Feeling good then motivated Sally to approach situations that had similar low-risk features because contemplating her comfort tagged nondomestic situations with positive affect. The next time Sally (or Harry) perceives similar risks, these "emotion tags" are in place to automatically elicit appropriate behavior. Imagine that Harry volunteers to do the federal tax return to spare Sally the job. Sally's reciprocated completion of the state tax return reinforces his expression of commitment, and his conscious experience of gratitude and pride "tags" situations with similar risk profiles with positive affective associations. But her recalcitrant refusal to complete the state return punishes his expression of commitment and his conscious experience of hurt and anger tags situations with similar risk profiles with negative affective associations.

Baldwin's (1992) analysis of relational schemas echoes the assumption that affective associations to risk are central in orienting interpersonal goals. He argued that working models of relationships contain if–then behavior outcome expectancies. These representations orient one's interpersonal goals by linking anticipated behavior to its past outcomes (e.g., "If I depend on my partner, then I will get hurt"). In the initial work on such contingencies, Baldwin and colleagues (Baldwin, Fehr, Keelian, Seidel, & Thompson, 1993) reasoned that repeated experience results in people coming to associate certain types of situations (e.g., depending on a partner) with their most common outcome (e.g., getting hurt). That is, people tag a particular type of situation with its most frequent affective consequence. If that is the case, priming the situation of trusting or depending on a partner should activate more positive associations for people who have more positive interpersonal histories (i.e., those secure in attachment style) than for people who have more negative interpersonal histories (Baldwin et al., 1993). This proved to be the case in a lexical decision experiment. When the context of trusting the partner was primed, secure people were quicker to identify words conveying positive than negative outcomes in a lexical decision task. Insecure people were quicker to identify words conveying negative than positive outcomes when the context of trusting the partner was primed. According to Baldwin (1992), such associative tags exist in memory to orient future action, directing people to approach good situations and avoid bad ones. In our terms, risk tags flag prior experiences in good versus bad situations and orient current interpersonal goals appropriately.

Linking Risk to Action: If–Then Goal Orientation Rules

By tagging specific situational cues to risk with strong affective associations, the interdependent mind resolves the approach–avoidance goal conflict inherent to conflicts of interest. It does so through two if–then goal orientation rules. These rules turn an affective association to risk (i.e., "if") into the correspondent goal to connect or self-protect (i.e., "then"). The "if partner accepting, then connect" rule links situation features associated with past experiences of the partner's acceptance (i.e., situation features signaling low risk) to the strengthened goal to approach the partner. The "if partner rejecting, then self-protect" rule links situation features associated with past experiences of the partner's rejection (i.e., situation features signaling high risk) to the strengthened goal to avoid the possibility of rejection. Each of these rules is reflexive in nature, motivating people to want to avoid bad situations and approach good ones upon perceiving the relevant situational cue to risk (or its absence).

In this sense, the assessment of risk functions as an attitude that automatically steers behavior (Cacioppo et al., 1999; Olson & Fazio, 2008). In a dramatic demonstration of the motivating power of evaluative associations, Chen and Bargh (1999) exposed participants to the name of a positively or negatively evaluated attitude object on the computer screen. On half of the trials, participants pulled a lever toward them as soon as the target appeared (i.e., approach). On the other half, participants pushed a lever away from them as soon as the target appeared (i.e., avoid). The results revealed that participants responded more quickly when their evaluation of the object matched the required motor response. They were quicker to "pull toward" for positive objects and "push away" for negative ones than they were to "pull toward" for negative objects and "push away" for positive ones. Simply seeing stimuli that are tagged with emotion is sufficient to automatically elicit the tendency to approach good objects and avoid bad ones.

A similar principle holds in relationships (as we see in Chapters 6 and 7). Namely, simply perceiving more or less risk is sufficient to motivate relationship partners to automatically avoid bad situations and approach good ones. Think again about Sally, empty ice tray in hand. Asking Harry to fill the tray is likely to evoke a stronger and more motivating rejection expectancy the more often he has refused such entreaties in the past. The stronger her rejection expectancy, the stronger is her goal to avoid the loss by making herself safe from yet another refusal. The stronger the acceptance expectancy, the stronger is her goal to secure gains by motivating yet another of his concessions. This logic echoes the "thinking is for doing" motto that underlies the modern study of social cognition (Fiske, 1992). Social cognition scholars assume that perception is linked to behavior in memory because neural connections between perceptual and behavioral systems facilitate quick, adaptive responses to the social environment (Bargh, 2007). For instance, priming a group stereotype (e.g., elderly) automatically elicits the motor propensity to behave (e.g., walking slowly) in a way that facilitates easy interactions with members of the group (Bargh et al., 1996; Cesario et al., 2006).

Our contention that risk expectancies are inextricably linked to goals in memory resonates with a growing body of research on the nature of significant other representations. Collins and Read (1994) spearheaded this work. In a groundbreaking chapter, they argued that working models are organized in memory in ways that link interpersonal expectations of acceptance or rejection to complementary goals and behavioral strategies for achieving such goals (see Mikulincer & Shaver, 2003, for a review). Mikulincer (1998) provides suggestive evidence that trust-related expectancies may well be linked to complementary goals in memory.

In one experiment, Mikulincer (1998) primed trust-related expectancies (e.g., "I count on my partner to be concerned with things that are important to me") or non-trust-related expectancies. He then measured goal activation by examining how quickly people identified trust-related words (e.g., *intimacy, security, control*). Anticipating the partner's acceptance (i.e., the trust-context prime) generally activated the goal to connect. People were quicker to identify *intimacy* as a word in the trust than in the neutral context. But priming the context of being trusted also activated goals linked to people's general expectations about others. For people who anticipate acceptance (i.e., those secure in attachment style), expecting to trust only evoked the goal to be "intimate." For people who instead anticipated rejection (i.e., those anxious-ambivalent or avoidant in attachment style), expecting to trust also evoked the goal to be secure (among anxious participants) and the goal to control (among avoidant participants).

The idea that the interpersonal mind links risk expectancies to goals finds further support in the evidence for automatic goal pursuit in relationships. Fitzsimons and Bargh (2003) reasoned that thinking about a relationship with one's mother, friend, or spouse could have automatic effects on behavior. Why? Because representations of significant others contain the goals one pursues in their presence (e.g., making one's mother proud, helping a friend, making a spouse feel loved). Consequently, priming one's mother activates the goals one holds most often in interacting with one's mother. Mother-induced goal activation in turn compels goal-congruent behavior in an automatic fashion. For people who want to make their mother proud, simply priming the mother's face and physical features elicits more fervent efforts to achieve on an anagram task (Fitzsimons & Bargh, 2003). Such effects speak to a risk expectations-to-goals link in memory because the affective quality of significant other representations reflects one's experiences of risk (Baldwin, 1992). To return to Sally and Harry, the goal to avoid being exploited is likely integral to Sally's representation of Harry, given her chronic distress over the allocation of domestic responsibilities in their home. Simply thinking about Harry in this context might then be enough to strengthen her goal to self-protect.

As we see in later chapters, domestic chores became a "hot issue" for Sally and Harry, one that evoked such a negative risk tag that simply being in such domains was sufficient to motivate avoidance.

SUMMARY AND NOTES FOR FUTURE CHAPTERS

This chapter described how the interdependent mind appraises risk and orients each partner's interpersonal goals in specific conflicts of interest. We made three main points. In the first part of this chapter we described the objective parameters that make some situations relatively high in risk and others relatively low in risk. These parameters include situation content (i.e., life tasks, personality, or relationship goals), type (i.e., coordination, exchange, or zero-sum conflict), and features (e.g., correspondence of interests, transparency of interests, time span for sacrifice). In the second part we described exactly how the interdependent mind appraises risk in specific conflicts of interest. We argued that Sally's perceptions of the risks of putting her outcomes in Harry's hands depends on: (1) his incentive to be selfish (a property of the situation); (2) her chronic trust in his commitment (a property of the person); and (3) incidental if–then cues to vigilance in the ongoing behavioral stream that make Harry seem more or less likely to be responsive (a property of the person in the situation). We also reviewed substantial evidence that people who generally trust less in their partner's commitment amplify the potential for risk in ambiguous conflicts of interest. In the third part of this chapter we described how the subjective perception of risk acts as an "emotion tag" that resolves approach–avoidance goal conflicts in specific conflicts of interest. Risk motivates action through two if–then goal orientation rules. One of these rules links situational cues to the partner's likely rejection to the goal to self-protect; the other rule links situational cues to the partner's likely acceptance to the goal to connect.

Two points of housekeeping bear mention before we proceed. First, in earlier chapters we described how the if–then rules are efficient and flexible. Efficiency implies that the inference, goal-orientation, and implementation rules operate automatically. Flexibility implies that these if–then rules need not compel behavior if people are both motivated and able to override them. We return to these themes in Chapters 6 and 7 when we discuss the action plans the interdependent mind employs to pursue the goals to connect and self-protect, respectively. Second, in this chapter we provided several examples of how being less trusting can sensitize people to risk. The existence of this signal amplification bias means that subjective risk may not be true to the objective risks. Consequently, the goals people pursue in specific situations may not always lend themselves to the objective gains and losses possible. Being overly sensitive to rejection could result in Sally behaving in ways that subvert real opportunities for gains in conflicts of interest. We return to the destabilizing effects such biases can have on relationships in Chapter 8 when we discuss how risk exposure and rule accessibility combine to create the relationship's emerging personality.

Now we turn to the question of how the interpersonal mind marshals the goal to connect (or self-protect) once it is activated into an action plan for promoting reciprocity in commitment. We start on an upbeat note— that is, with the interdependent mind's action plan for connection.

NOTES

1. We conceptualize the progression from life tasks to personality to relationship goals as a hierarchy of influence (Braiker & Kelley, 1979). With each step in the hierarchy, conflicts of interest have more pervasive effects on the relationship as a whole. For this reason, we place personality at a lower level in the hierarchy than relationship goals. Relationship goal conflicts, such as differing desires for closeness versus distance, or differing marital role preferences, control interaction across multiple domains in the relationship. This "pervasiveness" criterion is not always met for personality conflicts. For instance, personality differences in conscientiousness might only affect interactions involving work and household tasks. However, personality differences in attachment style might have broad effects on the relationship as a whole by affecting the goals (e.g., closeness vs. distance) partners pursue across multiple interaction domains (e.g., shared leisure vs. independent leisure pursuits, sharing chores vs. doing chores independently, treating one another as sole confidants vs. confiding to other friends).

2. This logic holds best in situations where Sally is appropriately distrusting of Harry—that is, in situations where Harry is, in fact, not all that motivated to be responsive to her needs. As we discussed in Chapter 3, distrust can also result from people's own insecurities (e.g., low self-esteem, anxious-ambivalent attachment style). In such circumstances, being overly sensitive to risk may lose its functionality as a mechanism for avoiding rejection. We return to this issue in our discussion of relationship personality in Chapter 8.

CHAPTER 6

The Rules for Seeking Connection

Increase and Justify Own Dependence

When we last left Sally, she was standing in front of her fridge, empty ice tray in hand. As she steps back from the fridge, will she turn to Harry or to the kitchen sink? The step she ultimately takes begins with the goals the situation elicits. An uneasy fear of Harry's rejection that arises as she watches him grimacing over her credit card bill might set her feet on track for the sink. But taking comfort in his laughter might put the ice tray squarely into his hands. Locating the impetus for Sally's choices in the goals the situation affords might seem curious. Surely she has a will of her own? As we see in this chapter, the answer is a decided sometimes.

Bargh and his colleagues coined the phrase "the automated will" to capture their hypothesis that goals can elicit behavior without the imposition of conscious will (Bargh, Gollwitzer, Lee-Chai, Barndollar, & Trotschel, 2001). How so? Once people come to associate a given situation with a particular goal pursuit, being in the situation is sufficient to elicit goal-congruent behavior. Will is automated in the sense that it is supplied by the context. To illustrate the power of such effects, Bargh et al. (2001) primed the goal to be cooperative outside conscious awareness. To do this, the researchers asked participants to form four-word sentences from five-word sentence fragments. In the experimental or goal-priming condition, the sentence fragments contained words related to cooperativeness (e.g., *dependable, helpful, honest, cooperative, tolerant,* and *share*). In the control condition, the sentence fragments contained neutral words. For experimental participants, completing the sentences thus primed the goal to be cooperative without making participants consciously aware of the goal (because they were focused on the task of making sentences, not the idea of cooperativeness). Then participants played a fishing game in which they had the opportunity to overfish and squander the resource for all. Relative to control participants, those primed with the goal to be cooperative preserved more fish for future generations of fishermen. Further experiments revealed that participants primed with the goal to achieve (through exposure to words such as *win, compete, succeed, strive, master*) found more hidden words in word puzzles. Such unconsciously willed behaviors had all the characteristics of behaviors consciously undertaken to pursue one's goals. Those engaged in the pursuit of unconsciously willed goals persisted in their effort despite obstacles. They also re-initiated interrupted efforts to achieve their goal (Bargh et al., 2001).

The interpersonal mind is similarly automated. It turns Sally's perception of risk into correspondent goals and such goals into strategies for action. It does so automatically through the if–then goal orientation and goal implementation rules. Imagine Sally standing in front of the fridge, seeing Harry's sheepish grin and hearing his embarrassed laughter. In this scenario, affect-tagged expectancies of acceptance elicit her goal to connect (i.e., "if partner accepting, then connect"). This goal then activates the intention to express her commitment by asking Harry to take responsibility for the ice, while jokingly asking him whether he thinks the tray will fill itself (i.e., "if connect goal, then escalate own dependence"). Seeing her laughter activates Harry's goal to connect. This goal state then prompts him to justify any costs he incurs by going out of his way to fill the ice tray for Sally (i.e., "if connect goal, then justify own commitment"). In this way, the goal orientation and implementation rules foster automatic extensions of commitment. The perception of low-risk situation features (e.g., laughter) is sufficient to compel each partner to behave in ways that maximize opportunities to be responsive.

Now instead imagine Sally standing in front of the fridge, watching Harry grimace over her overdue credit card bill. In this scenario, affect-tagged expectancies of rejection elicit her goal to self-protect (i.e., "if partner rejecting, then self-protect"). Her goal to self-protect then activates the intention not to depend on Harry (i.e., "if self-protect goal, then withdraw own dependence") until she's taken remedial steps to ensure he owes her (i.e., "if self-protect goal, then promote partner dependence"). In this scenario, Sally might fill the ice tray herself, while grumpily reminding Harry that she spent the better part of her morning taking his mother to the grocery store and a doctor's appointment. Hearing annoyance in Sally's voice activates Harry's goal to self-protect. He then takes out the garbage, one of Sally's chores, in his effort to appease her enough to ensure that she will drive his mother to the bank. In this way, the goal orientation and implementation rules promote automatic limitations on commitment. The perception of high-risk situation features (e.g., annoyance) is sufficient to compel each partner to behave in ways that minimize the other's opportunities to be nonresponsive.

In this chapter, we begin our exploration of how the interdependent mind uses the implementation rules to motivate reciprocated expressions of commitment.[1] The demands of this social coordination task are varied, complex, and shifting (Baldwin, 1992; Dijksterhuis & Nordgren, 2006; Forster, Liberman, & Friedman, 2007). No two situations are alike and partners encounter myriad familiar and novel situations at the levels of life tasks, personality, and relationship goals. Automating Sally's "will" to extend or limit commitment to match Harry's anticipated expressions simplifies the demands of social coordination and frees the mind for other pursuits (Dijksterhuis & Nordgren, 2006). As we will see, in automating action the interdependent mind adjusts its plans for action to match the perceived situational risks. It has two action plans at the ready, one for implementing the goal to connect (i.e., match commitment to trust and keep commitment from being derailed) and the other for implementing the goal to self-protect (i.e., match commitment to trust and keep trust from being misplaced).

Gollwitzer describes implementation intentions as set plans to enact a specific goal when a specific "triggering" situation arises (Achtziger, Gollwitzer, & Sheeran, 2008; Gollwitzer, 1999). Sally's plan to stick to her diet and eat fruit when her children bring home cookies constitutes an implementation intention (i.e., "if cookies, then fruit"). Implementation intentions automatically link goal-relevant situations (i.e., "if") to behavioral strategies for achieving one's goals (i.e., "then") in memory. These procedural intentions promote goal attainment because the situational trigger itself provides all the impetus needed for goal-relevant behavior. For Sally, having the intention to "eat fruit" when the "cookie" tempts means that she does not need to consciously self-regulate to forego the cookie. Her implementation intention automatically regulates her behavior for her. The if–then goal implementation rules operate similarly. These rules are set plans to enact particular behavior when a goal-relevant situation arises. One set of rules links the situation-triggered goal to connect (i.e., "if") to intentions to extend commitment by escalating one's own dependence (i.e., "then") and justifying one's commitment (i.e., "then"). The other set of rules links the situation-triggered goal to self-protect (i.e., "if") to intentions to control or somehow limit expressions of commitment by withdrawing one's own dependence (i.e., "then") and promoting the partner's dependence (i.e., "then").[2]

This chapter describes the dual-pronged action plan for implementing the goal to connect. Turning this goal into action involves supplying Sally with the automated will to put her outcomes in Harry's hands, take Harry's outcomes into her own hands, and justify any costs she incurs through either of these expressions of greater commitment. In strategic terms, implementing the goal to connect involves escalating one's own dependence on the partner by soliciting and providing care (Path B_1 in Figure 2.1) and justifying any costs one incurs as a result of these greater commitments (Paths B_2 in Figure 2.1). For instance, to benefit from those occasions when Harry is in a good mood in the kitchen, Sally must ask for his help. To extract the gains possible in a coordination dilemma over a movie choice, she also needs to sacrifice her preference for drama to accede to his preference for action. To maintain such expressions of commitment, Sally needs to come to value Harry more on occasions when his attempts to help in the kitchen only create more work for her or his movie preferences bore her to tears. Harry also needs to come to value Sally more when agreeing to help in the kitchen costs him TV time. Without a plan for managing costs, commitment would flag just when partners need it the most.

This chapter unpacks the action plan for implementing the goal to connect in three parts. Table 6.1 summarizes these arguments, addressed in sequence in the chapter. In part one we explain why the action plan for implementing the goal to connect is a necessary building block for coordinating fluid and mutually responsive interactions. We also explain how the implementation rules for connection operate both efficiently and flexibility. Efficiency involves automated action: The goal to connect activates the propensity to escalate and justify dependence without conscious intent. Efficiency implies that the goal to connect automatically activates Sally's impulse to put her outcomes (and the ice tray) in Harry's hands. Flexibility involves willed action: People can overturn or correct automatically activated impulses when they have the motivation and opportunity to do so. Flexibility implies that Sally can stop the automatic impulse to give the ice tray to a sheepish Harry when chronic distrust gives her reason to self-protect. In part two we delineate the empirical evidence for our

TABLE 6.1. The Main Arguments

1. State goal to connect strengthens intentions to increase commitment and justify any costs to autonomy incurred as a result of getting closer.
2. Empirical evidence for efficiency and flexibility of the if–then rules.
3. Implementing the goal to connect elicits reciprocated expressions of commitment at progressively higher levels of interdependence.

assertions. We detail a variety of different experiments and field studies attesting to the efficient and flexible operation of the "escalate own dependence" and "justify own commitment" implementation rules. In part three we describe exactly how implementing the action plan for connection elicits reciprocated extensions of commitment and thereby promotes fluid and mutually responsive interactions.

IMPLEMENTING THE GOAL TO CONNECT: EFFICIENCY AND FLEXIBILITY

Implementing the goal to connect involves applying a ready plan for capitalizing on the opportunities for responsiveness that low-risk situations afford. The "escalate own dependence" and "justify own commitment" implementation rules together provide this action plan. The state goal to connect strengthens the intentions to increase commitment (i.e., "if connect goal, then escalate own dependence) and to justify the costs that greater commitment creates (i.e., "if connect goal, then justify own commitment"). In applying these rules, the interdependent mind affords Harry and Sally with greater opportunity and willingness to make bolder displays of responsiveness. These rules motivate Harry to come to Sally when he needs support in dealing with a personal crisis and they similarly motivate Sally to provide such support.

How does this happen? The if–then rules for implementing the goal to connect automatically will Sally to extend her commitment in two ways. These rules motivate her to put her outcomes in Harry's hands (i.e., solicit care) and they also motivate her to take Harry's outcomes into her own hands (i.e., provide care). They do so by shaping what situations Sally intends to enter (Snyder & Stukas, 1999) and by shaping how she intends to behave in situations that Harry thrusts upon her (Kelley, 1979). In governing situation entry, the "escalate own dependence" rule motivates Sally to reveal her need for support by disclosing something embarrassing to Harry. It also gives her the will to forego buying herself a new winter jacket so that Harry can buy tickets for his coveted basketball playoffs. In governing situation response, the "justify own commitment" rule motivates Sally to value Harry more on the occasions when he asks her to work extra hours so he could fit a fishing trip into the budget. This rule also gives Harry the will to value Sally's attentiveness to their children when she interrupts his basketball game to remind him to take his turn bathing their youngest child.

Why would the interpersonal mind rely on these rules in particular to maximize the chance of responsiveness in low-risk situations? Even in reasonably safe situations, the potential for loss still exists. Consider the coordination dilemma posed by Harry and Sally's movie choice (see Figure 5.2). Even though both are happier going to a movie together, the momentary inclination to be petty could result in Sally insisting on going to a drama even if doing so costs her Harry's company. To reap the greater joint benefit of seeing a movie together, Harry needs to put his outcomes in Sally's hands by volunteering to forego his own movie in the hopes of soliciting similar sacrifices on her part. Therefore, the goal to connect heightens Harry's willingness to put his outcomes into Sally's hands because partners can generally only behave responsively if they are given the opportunity to do so (Murray, Derrick, et al., 2008; Murray, Holmes, & Collins, 2006). Indeed, situations that make people feel most connected to a partner, such as self-disclosing (Reis & Shaver, 1988), being physically intimate (Gillath & Schachner, 2006), and sharing interests and recreational pursuits (Aron, Norman, Aron, McKenna, & Heyman, 2000), have two things in common. They all involve putting one's outcomes in the partner's hands and taking the partner's outcomes into one's own hands (Collins & Feeney, 2010). To extract the greatest gains from such situations, the interpersonal mind must capitalize on opportunities where the partner is most likely to be receptive to such overtures. Sally needs to match her need for a particular kind of caring to match Harry's willingness to provide such caring (Collins & Feeney, 2010). That is, the interdependent mind needs a rule in place to make escalating one's own dependence on the partner contingent on the anticipation of the partner's accepting and caring response. The "escalate own dependence" rule does just that.

Implementing the goal to connect also requires a means for ensuring one's commitment even, indeed especially, when things go right. In becoming objectively more dependent on the partner, people inevitably incur costs. When Harry draws closer to her, Sally gains the benefits of his responsiveness. But she also loses something important. She loses the autonomy to pursue her own goals without interference from Harry. For instance, she loses some of her personal autonomy to pursue alternate friends or even solitude because Harry wants her to spend as much time at home with the children as possible together. She also has to suffer through his fallibility and unintentional interference with her goals. Being connected to him means that she has to tolerate his seasonal obsessions with basketball, his disparate musical tastes, and his snoring. Even Harry's efforts to be responsive in household chore negotiations have some hidden costs for Sally because his version of "folded" clothes, "swept" floors, and "bathed" children does not meet her standards. Because drawing closer to Harry (and Harry drawing closer to her) can have such unintended consequences, the interpersonal mind needs a mechanism for deflecting one's attention from costs. Otherwise, Harry's increased dependence on Sally could undermine her motivation to be responsive to his needs (Clark & Grote, 1998).

The "justify own commitment" implementation rule keeps commitment on track in the face of autonomy costs. This rule maintains Sally's resolve in her commitment by making Harry more valuable precisely when he is more costly (Murray, Holmes, et al., 2009). By turning adversity into statements of the partner's inherent value (Higgins, 2006), such an impulse sustains one's motivation to be responsive by protecting the newly exercised state of commitment. The inherently reciprocal nature of relationships makes this rule an eminently wise one: Meeting a partner's needs elicits that partner's willingness to meet one's own needs (Clark & Grote, 1998; Holmes, 2002; Kelley, 1979; Reis et al., 2004). Maintaining one's commitment to meeting the partner's needs thereby functions as a safety check to ensure the partner's reciprocal motivation to be responsive. We elaborate on this point later in this chapter.

Automated and Conscious Will: Efficiency and Flexibility

To turn goals into action efficiently, the interpersonal mind has the if–then rules for implementing the goal to connect at the ready. These rules operate automatically (Murray & Holmes, 2009). Situations that afford connectedness goals activate the behavioral strategies that fulfill such goals without requiring the intervention of conscious will. For such automated action to occur, the if–then rules must (and do) exist in memory as implicit procedural features in people's general working models of relationships (Baldwin, 1992; Holmes & Murray, 2007; Murray, Aloni, et al., 2009; Murray, Derrick, et al., 2008; Murray, Holmes, et al., 2009). We detail the evidence for the efficiency of the rules in the next section of the chapter.

Although if–then rule activation is automatic, the interdependent mind can nonetheless impose some judiciousness and flexibility when the intention to escalate dependence or justify commitment results in correspondent behavior. Think back to the arguments about correction we advanced in Chapter 2. The "escalate own dependence" and "justify own commitment" rules satisfy the state goal to connect primed by the risks evident in the immediate situation. But this state goal may or may not be consistent with broader goal pursuits. That's the case for Sally. Harry's sheepish, self-deprecating laugh automatically pushes her to put the ice tray in his hands. Ultimately, she decides to proceed to the sink and fill the tray herself. Why? For Sally, the short-term goal to connect to a sheepish Harry conflicts with her broader and more chronic goal to avoid being hurt by the lazy Harry (yet again). The adaptive quality of automatic behavior rests in this sensitivity to circumstance. Goals that are automatically activated are more likely to result in goal-congruent behavior when the broader situation supports the execution of the goal (Kunda & Spencer, 2003). For instance, people primed with the goal to help are more likely to help pick up dropped pens—but only when the dropped pens are not covered in ink. In that case, they instead pursue the competing goal of clean hands (Macrae & Johnston, 1998).

The MODE model of the attitude–behavior relation states that automatically activated attitudes or goals elicit congruent behavior unless people have the motivation and the opportunity to correct (Fazio & Towles-Schwen, 1999; Olson & Fazio, 2008). In the case of the soiled pens, the desire for clean hands provides the motivation to correct the impulse to help; having the attention resources to notice the risk of soiled hands provides the opportunity. Applied to the interdependent mind, such flexibility means that the automated will to connect results in congruent overt behavior unless people are both motivated and able to correct (Fiske & Neuberg, 1990; Gilbert & Malone, 1995; Hofmann, Gschwendner, Friese, Wiers, & Schmitt, 2008; Kunda & Spencer, 2003; Murray, Aloni, et al., 2009; Murray, Derrick, et al., 2008; Murray, Holmes, et al., 2009; Olson & Fazio, 2008). The motivation by opportunity logic of correction implies that a distrusting Sally will act on the automated intent to put the ice tray in the hands of a sheepish Harry unless she is acutely motivated and able to decide to fill the ice tray herself.

Affording Motivation

Overall levels of trust in the partner's commitment supply the motivation to correct state goals that conflict with broader goal pursuits (see Chapters 1 and 2). For Sally, generally being less trusting heightens the risks attached to pursuing connection in even those situations she perceives to be low in risk (see Chapter 3). She just cannot easily afford to pursue the gains that even reasonably safe mixed-motive situations offer because rejection, no matter how improbable, is still hurtful enough to elicit caution (Holmes & Rempel, 1989; Murray, Bellavia, et al., 2003; Murray, Griffin, et al., 2003). For this reason, Sally's broader and chronic goal to self-protect can motivate her to curb the state goal to connect to Harry when it arises. Such a goal conflict never really arises for Gayle. For her, generally trusting in Ron's responsiveness gives her reason to expect the gains the situation offers and no reason to fear being hurt (Murray, Griffin, et al., 2003). Gayle's chronic goal to connect thus gives her added incentive to act on the state inclination to connect to Ron (Mikulincer & Shaver, 2003; Murray, Holmes, & Collins, 2006).

For these reasons, once the situation activates the behavioral strategies for connection, being less trusting supplies the motivation to curb the automated will to escalate dependence and justify commitment. It does so because Sally's chronic goal pursuits change the broader psychological consequences of pursuing the state goal to connect. Trust essentially changes the subjective utility of acting on the short-term impulse to connect (Murray, Aloni, et al., 2009; Murray, Holmes, et al., 2009). In the domain of household chores, Sally is highly suspicious of Harry's motives. Asking him to help in the current situation could provide the short-term benefit of a filled ice tray, but increasing her dependence on him sets her up for a much greater hurt when his laziness wins out the next time a domestic chore comes up (Murray, Griffin, et al., 2003). Therefore, asking for Harry to help in this instance ultimately has questionable utility for Sally because relying on him counters her more general goal not to be vulnerable to his laziness (Murray, Derrick, et al., 2008; Murray, Holmes, et al., 2009). Trust similarly changes the utility of acting out the "justify commitment" implementation rule. Valuing a costly partner more has the short-term benefit of distracting attention from costs. But it also has the long-term cost of making rejection more painful because losing a valued partner hurts more than losing a less valued one. Therefore, being less trusting also motivates Sally to overturn the state impulse to make light of Harry's lame dishwashing efforts when he does try to be helpful.[3]

Affording Opportunity

The MODE model stipulates that correction also requires the opportunity—or cognitive capacity—to correct. This means that even when Sally is motivated to self-protect, she is still likely to go ahead and put the ice tray into the hands of a sheepish Harry unless she has the executive or conscious control available to stop herself (Gilbert & Malone, 1995; Muraven & Baumeister, 2000; Murray, Derrick, et al., 2008). Indeed, people who are higher in the capacity to allocate and control attention have a much easier time overturning the leanings of their unconscious will. For instance, people high in working memory capacity overturn their automatic impulse to eat the chocolate M&M's they crave and instead eat only as few chocolates as their explicit intention to diet dictates (Hofmann et al., 2008). Because Sally is chronically stressed and tired, she is not always going to be able to curb her automated will to connect every time (or even most times) it arises. Fresh from a nap today, she can and does curb her will to connect to a sheepish Harry, and she proceeds to the sink herself.

IMPLEMENTING THE GOAL TO CONNECT: EMPIRICAL ILLUSTRATIONS

We now turn to the empirical evidence for the "escalate own dependence" and "justify own commitment" implementation rules. To foreshadow, this evidence reveals both efficiency and flexibility in rule application. The evidence for efficiency: Situations that prime the goal to connect automatically elicit the intention to escalate dependence and justify commitment regardless of trust. These "main effects" suggest that the implementation rules are part of the interdependent mind's procedural knowledge for relationships. The evidence for flexibility: People who are less trusting overturn the automated will to connect when they are motivated and able to do so. As we will see, the capacity to correct the activation of the implementation rules makes it possible for Sally to be of two minds about her relationship. In low-risk situations, Sally's unconscious will prompts her to do something different than her conscious will tells her to do. Therefore, on the occasions when Sally has the requisite cognitive resources available to heed her conscious will, she is going to appear behaviorally ambivalent. Imagine that Harry thwarts her goal of going out with friends (through no fault of his own). Her automatic response is to value him more, perhaps thinking of his patience with children, but ultimately she overturns this inclination and chastises him nonetheless. No such ambivalence should be evident for a more trusting Gayle. When her unconscious will motivates her to connect to Ron, her conscious will should go along quite happily and motivate behavior that satisfies this state goal.[4]

Any research strategy for comparing Sally's immediate and reflective reactions to the activation of the goal to connect necessitates a means of distinguishing the unconscious (i.e., automated) from the conscious (i.e., controlled) will. Social cognition scholars distinguish automatic and controlled processes by employing manipulations and measures that differ in the level of circumspection they afford (Bargh, 1994). Consider the distinction between automatic and controlled measures of prejudice. The Implicit Associations Test (IAT) examines how quickly people make "congruent" (i.e., white = good, African American = bad) versus "incongruent" (i.e., white = bad, African American = good) responses (Greenwald, McGhee, & Schwartz, 1998). The IAT captures a relatively automatic form of racial prejudice because people cannot decide to speed up their reactions to incongruent trials to mask their prejudices. In contrast, the Feeling Thermometer asks people to rate how positively they feel toward different racial groups (Haddock, Zanna, & Esses, 1993). It captures a relatively controlled form of racial prejudice because people can decide not to evaluate a minority group member negatively when they rate how positively they feel toward the group on a thermometer scale from 0 to 100.

We use similar logic to distinguish the automatic and controlled pursuit of connectedness goals. Manipulations and measures that limit the opportunity to be circumspect should reveal the automated will. For instance, the reactions of Gayle and Sally (who are more and less trusting, respectively) should be hard to distinguish on reaction time measures. Both should be quicker to "escalate dependence" and "justify commitment" when the goal to connect is activated. But their responses should diverge on manipulations and measures that afford the conscious will the opportunity to correct. For instance, Sally might actually distance herself from Harry on explicit self-report measures because she has the chronic motivation (and now the acute opportunity) to correct her automated will. We discuss the empirical evidence for the efficient and flexible operation of the "escalate dependence" and "justify commitment" rules in turn.

The "Escalate Dependence" Implementation Rule

Basic research in social cognition reveals that active goals increase the cognitive accessibility of goal-relevant information in memory (Aarts, Dijksterhuis, & DeVries, 2001; Shah, Friedman, & Kruglanski, 2002). This implies that activating the goal to connect (i.e., "if") should activate associated behavioral strategies for escalating dependence (i.e., "then") if this hypothesized implementation rule is part of the mind's procedural store of knowledge for relationships (Baldwin, 1992; Baldwin et al., 1993). We begin by reviewing the indirect evidence. Then we turn to experiments conducted specifically to examine how the "escalate dependence" rule operates in adult romantic relationships.

We start with the reasonably indirect evidence. First, priming the general desire to approach automatically activates the behavioral tendency to draw closer. Participants subliminally primed with approach-oriented emotion words (e.g., *happy*) are quicker to draw objects toward them (i.e., arm flexion) than participants exposed to avoidance-oriented emotion words (Alexopoulos & Ric, 2007). Second, priming general feelings of security in relationships activates the general behavioral tendency to draw the social world closer. Participants subliminally primed with security words (e.g., *secure, safe*) are more empathic and helpful (Mikulincer et al., 2001), more accepting of out-groups (Mikulincer & Shaver, 2001), and more likely to seek support from others in dealing with a personal crisis (Pierce & Lydon, 1998). Third, priming connection to a romantic partner activates behavioral representations for escalating one's dependence on others. Participants subliminally primed with the name of an accepting other are more willing to self-disclose (Gillath et al., 2006) and forgive another's serious and personally hurtful transgressions (Karremans & Aarts, 2007). Fourth, priming expectations of acceptance (through the receipt of a supportive note) increases one's own willingness to sacrifice for the partner (Guichard & Collins, 2008). Even people who are chronically distrusting of others "know" this implementation rule (Holmes & Murray, 2007). Priming connectedness goals activates the behavioral representations for greater dependence regardless of trust (or its dispositional proxies, such as self-esteem and attachment anxiety).

We now turn to the more direct evidence. To examine the "escalate dependence" rule in the laboratory, we first had to devise a method for priming connectedness goals. We turned to attachment research for inspiration. Attachment theory assumes that stress automatically activates the goal to seek proximity to others (Bowlby, 1969). For instance, people primed with stress-related words such (e.g., *failure, death*) are quicker to identify proximity-related words in a lexical decision task (Mikulincer, Birnbaum, Woddis, & Nachmias, 2000). Stress-primed participants are also quicker to identify a romantic partner's name in a lexical decision task (Mikulincer, Gillath, & Shaver, 2002). Because these effects emerged regardless of dispositional attachment style, we decided to use stress to "bottle" the "escalate dependence" implementation rule in a series of laboratory experiments (Murray, Derrick, et al., 2008).

We designed our first experiment to show that stress does indeed activate connectedness goals. Participants who were currently involved in dating relationships participated in a study of autobiographical memory and close relationships. Participants in the experimental condition first wrote a vivid story about a time when a significant other, such as a friend, parent, or romantic partner, had seriously disappointed them. Participants in the control condition described their commute to school (a commute that might have been stressful in its own right, but should not activate expectancies about the benefits to be had in social connection). We then measured how quickly participants identified connectedness words (e.g., *vow, join, want, rely*) in a lexical decision task that tapped uncontrolled processes (Murray, Derrick, et al., 2008, Experiment 1). Figure 6.1 presents the results. Relative to control participants, participants reminded of a time when a significant other had seriously disappointed them were actually quicker to identify connectedness words. This effect emerged regardless of trust (as captured by self-esteem).[5]

Did the automated will to connect actually elicit dependence-escalating behaviors? We conducted four more experiments to see whether activating the state goal to connect automatically elicits behavioral strategies for escalating one's dependence on others. The interdependent mind's efficiency and flexibility means that wanting to connect automatically compels the goal-congruent behavior to escalate dependence—unless people are both motivated and able to correct such impulses. The participants in our experiments came with different chronic motivations to

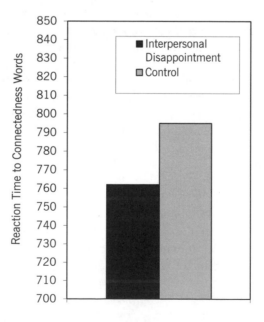

FIGURE 6.1. Reaction time to connectedness words as a function of interpersonal disappointment threat.

correct. Some were high in self-esteem and highly trusting of their dating partner; others were low in self-esteem and less trusting. We expected people low in self-esteem to resist the situated urge to connect, but only when they had the opportunity. Otherwise, we expected low self-esteem people to act just like high self-esteem people and automatically escalate dependence in response to the state activation of connectedness goals.

We varied the opportunity to correct in four experiments by utilizing different tricks of the social cognition trade (Bargh, 2007). In the two "automated will" experiments, we limited the opportunity to correct by taxing executive strength. We exhausted the cognitive resources people need to overturn the automated will (Hofmann et al., 2008) with manipulations of cognitive busyness (Gilbert, 1989) and self-regulatory depletion (Muraven & Baumeister, 2000). In the two "conscious will" experiments, we afforded the opportunity to correct by giving untaxed participants the unhurried luxury to contemplate self-report measures of dependence escalation. In completing such explicit questions, less trusting people can consciously deliberate escalating dependence as they answer each question, and they can decide not to connect.

Let's look first at the experiments in which we made it hard to correct by depleting executive strength. In these experiments, we expected to observe the work of the automated will. People primed with the goal to connect should increase their dependence on their partner regardless of trust. In both experiments, we manipulated connectedness goal activation by manipulating external stress. Participants in the connect goal condition described a time when a significant other seriously disappointed them (as we described earlier). Participants in the control goal condition described their commute to school. (Given the results of our lexical decision experiment, we expected priming such a disappointment to automatically heighten the goal to connect.) We then crossed the goal to connect with a manipulation of executive strength. In the cognitive business version of this design, taxed participants rehearsed and recalled a nine-digit alphanumeric string while they completed the dependent measures (Gilbert, 1989). In the self-regulatory depletion version of this design, taxed participants watched a videotape of an interview while they ignored words flashing at the bottom of the screen (Baumeister, Bratslavsky, Muraven, & Tice, 1998). All participants then completed pseudo-behavioral measures tapping dependence escalation. For instance, they described how willing they were to seek their partner's support (e.g., "distract me from worries when I'm under stress"; "give me advice about problems"), accede decision-making power to the partner (e.g., "make choices for me"; "make decisions about things that affect me"; "consider my needs when he/she

makes decisions about his/her life"), and solicit sacrifices from their partner (e.g., "put me before his/her friends"; "make my needs as important
as his/her needs").

Figure 6.2 presents the results for the cognitive busyness experiment
(Murray, Derrick, et al., 2008, Experiment 6). The motivation by opportunity logic of correction suggests that the automated will prevails when
people do not have sufficient executive strength available to correct (i.e.,
cognitively taxed). In such circumstances, participants primed with the
state goal to connect should escalate dependence regardless of their chronic
motivations to overturn this impulse. We found this exact effect. Look at
the cognitively taxed participants. These participants lacked the executive
or cognitive resources to correct, and they followed the dictates of their
automated will. Those primed with a time when a significant other disappointed them reported engaging in more dependence-escalating behaviors (compared with taxed participants who wrote about their commute).
This tendency was just as strong for low as high self-esteem people. This
suggests that the "if connect, then escalate dependence" rule is part of
the interpersonal mind's store of procedural knowledge for relationships.
Something quite different happened for the non-cognitively taxed partici-

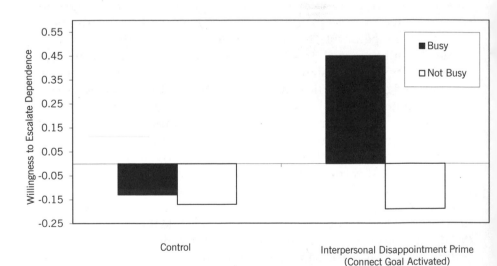

FIGURE 6.2. Willingness to escalate dependence as a function of connectedness goal strength and cognitive busyness. Adapted from Murray, Derrick, Leder,
and Holmes (2008). Copyright 2008 by the American Psychological Association.
Adapted by permission.

pants. Priming the interpersonal disappointment had no significant effect on their willingness to escalate dependence.

The motivation by opportunity logic of correction helps explain why this null effect emerged. The logic of correction implies that conscious will prevails when motivated people have sufficient executive strength available to correct (i.e., when they are not cognitively taxed). In such circumstances, high self-esteem participants should enact primed connectedness goals, whereas low self-esteem people should correct or overturn primed connectedness goals. In the non-cognitively taxed condition (see clear bars in Figure 6.2), high self-esteem people likely increased their dependence-escalating behaviors in response to the interpersonal disappointment prime and low self-esteem people likely decreased such behaviors. These opposite reactions to external stress then cancelled one another other out and yielded a null effect for connectedness goal activation. We found just such opposing reactions for low and high self-esteem people in the second set of experiments in which we made it easy to correct. In the first of these experiments (Murray, Derrick, et al., 2008, Experiment 2), we primed people with a time when a friend, parent, or past partner seriously disappointed them, an external stress. (Given the results of our lexical decision experiment, we again expected priming such a disappointment to automatically heighten the goal to connect.) We then measured reported tendencies to escalate dependence with self-report measures tapping the willingness to seek the partner's support, accede decision-making power, and ask the partner to sacrifice on one's behalf. Figure 6.3 presents the results. Connect-primed high self-esteem people implemented the state goal to connect. They reported greater willingness to escalate dependence relative to high self-esteem control participants. Connect-primed low self-esteem people resisted this impulse. They were not any more likely to escalate dependence when primed with disappointment than not primed.

A further experiment provided a still more dramatic illustration of this dynamic. In this experiment, we utilized a word categorization task to implicitly prime goal states (Murray, Derrick, et al., 2008, Experiment 4). Participants in the connect-goal condition sorted words that fell into the categories of approaching a desired state (e.g., *strive, win, strengthen, accomplish, thrive, achieve, pursue, pledge*), cooking (e.g., *roast, aromatic, sauté*), and childcare (e.g., *baby, bottle, infant, cradle*). Participants in the control condition sorted words into three neutral categories.[6] We then gave the automated will the opportunity to express itself by measuring how quickly people associated their dating partner with positive traits in a person/object categorization task. We gave the conscious will the opportunity

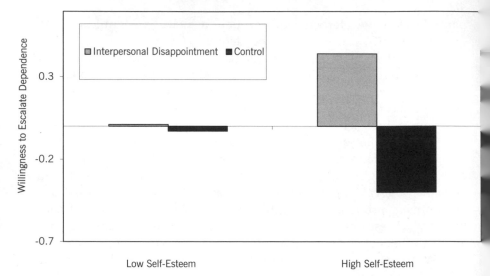

FIGURE 6.3. Willingness to escalate dependence as a function of connectedness goal strength (interpersonal disappointment) and self-esteem.

to express itself by examining self-reported feelings of closeness to the partner. Figure 6.4 presents the results for the implicit (i.e., reaction time) and explicit (i.e., self-report) measures. Connect-primed high self-esteem participants followed the automated will. They were quicker to identify connectedness words on the lexical decision task and they acted on this goal. They expressed greater feelings of closeness to their partner on the explicit measure. Connect-primed low self-esteem participants overrode the automated will. Although they were quicker to identify connectedness words on the lexical decision task, they thwarted this will when they could. Connect-primed lows actually expressed less feelings of closeness to their partner on the explicit measure that afforded the opportunity to correct. This suggests that even unconscious feelings of connection are sufficiently threatening for low self-esteem people to motivate reactive efforts to withhold dependence. We return to the paradoxical effects of connectedness goals on people who are less trusting when we discuss how the personality of the relationship develops in Chapter 8.

What implications does the motivation by opportunity logic have for correcting the "escalate dependence" rule in daily life in relationships? Daily life routinely imposes its own brand of the arcane cognitive busyness and self-depletion tasks researchers employ (Muraven & Baumeister, 2000). The sounds of her children arguing in a nearby room might occupy

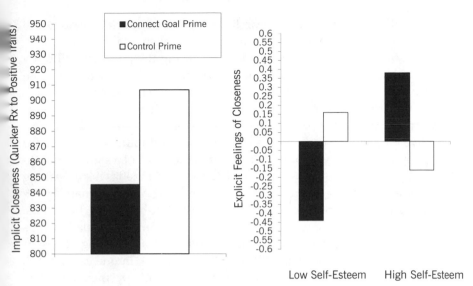

FIGURE 6.4. Implicit and explicit closeness to the partner as a function of connectedness goals and self-esteem.

enough of Sally's attention that she lacks the cognitive capacity to overrule her impulse to ask Harry to fill the ice tray. Being fatigued after a long and stressful day at work might have the same effect. Having spent the past hour resisting the urge to eat the last brownie might similarly leave her without the force of will to correct the impulse to rely on Harry when it arises. Because the vicissitudes of living tax executive strength in so many different ways, even a less trusting Sally might succumb to the automated will to escalate dependence more often than not.

The "Justify Commitment" Implementation Rule

Implementing the goal to connect has a decided downside. Commitment comes with autonomy costs: The more partners rely on each other for need fulfillment, the more opportunity each partner has to inadvertently trample the other's goal pursuits. Exercising commitment in a way that supports mutual responsiveness requires a mechanism for inoculating the interpersonal mind against costs. The "justify commitment" rule sustains the continued motivation to extend commitment by making one's partner more valuable precisely when he or she is more personally costly (Murray, Holmes, et al., 2009). We begin by reviewing indirect evidence for this rule. We then turn to research we conducted specifically to examine the efficient and flexible operation of this implementation rule.

We start with the indirect evidence. Making the partner's fallibility salient automatically elicits behavioral intentions to protect the relationship bond. For instance, imagining that a close other forgot to mail one's application for a coveted job opportunity immediately brings thoughts of forgiving the errant partner to mind (Karremans & Aarts, 2007). This reflexive tendency to compensate for a partner's fallibility is so powerful that people respond with positive facial affect to signs of a significant other's faults in a novel other (Andersen, Reznik, & Manzella, 1996). Making the opportunity costs that come from foregoing attractive alternative partners salient also automatically elicits commitment-bolstering behaviors. Lydon and his colleagues argue that women in committed relationships possess a built-in if–then implementation intention for staving off temptation (Lydon, Menzies-Toman, Burton, & Bell, 2008). In one experiment, they primed feelings of connection to one's romantic partners and then measured how close participants allowed themselves to be to a tempting alternative partner in a virtual reality environment. When primed with connection, women, but not men, actually moved farther away from virtual temptation! Women's implementation intention to shut their eyes to alternatives proved to be so ingrained that simply chatting with an attractive alternative partner increased their willingness to tolerate their own partner's transgressions. Even men evidenced such defenses when the circumstances were right. Men trained in the implemental intention to distract themselves from costs turned away from a tempting virtual alternative partner.

Although suggestive, these findings leave a central prediction of the "justify commitment" rule untested: Do autonomy costs elicit an automatic tendency to view the partner more positively? To examine this question, we created laboratory ruses for making the autonomy costs of commitment salient to our dating participants (Murray, Holmes, et al., 2009). We then measured the automated and the conscious will to deflect such costs by evaluating the partner all the more positively. In our first experiment, we primed the costs of connection indirectly. We asked participants in the autonomy costs priming condition to think back to a time when they complained about their relationship to a friend. Once they had this conversation in mind, we then asked participants to describe the two biggest costs their friend pointed out in their dating relationship (e.g., partner's too jealous, too controlling, too lazy). Participants in the normative costs control condition described two costs their friend perceived in most relationships. Baseline control participants did not describe any costs. We then measured the automated and the conscious will to justify commitment by evaluating the partner all the more positively. We tapped the automated will to compensate by examining how quickly people associated their dating partner with positive traits in a person–object categorization task. We tapped the conscious will to compensate by examining how people decided to describe their relationship on explicit measures tapping perceptions of the partner's traits, perceptions of control over relationship conflicts, and optimism about the future (Murray & Holmes, 1997).

In a second experiment, we primed autonomy costs directly. We had participants in the autonomy costs priming condition complete an electronic survey (which we had biased to suit our purposes). This purportedly diagnostic instrument took participants through a grocery list of the common ways in which the partner could thwart one's personal goals. The caption at the top instructed participants to indicate whether any of the events had happened to them because of their relationship with their partner (e.g., "I couldn't watch something I wanted to watch on TV"; "I had to go out with friends of my partner that I didn't like"; "I had my sleep disrupted"). Participants uniformly indicated that many if not most of these wretched events had happened to them. Then they received "diagnostic" feedback that their involvement in the relationship had caused them to make so many changes that they no longer had much personal control over their life. Participants in the thwarted outcome control condition completed a survey that simply asked them to indicate whether specific events in which they could not meet their goals had ever happened to them (e.g., "I couldn't watch something I wanted to watch on TV"; "I had my sleep disrupted"). Participants in the baseline control condition did not complete a survey. We then administered the measures of the automated and conscious will to compensate.

Figure 6.5 presents the results for the implicit measure of partner evaluations for each experiment. On the implicit measures, the automated will prevailed. Participants primed with autonomy costs justified their commitments in both experiments. Despite conscious ruminations about the costs being connected to their partner had imposed on them, they were actually quicker to associate their partner with positive traits than control participants. Being primed with costs automatically caused them to value their partner more. The automatic tendency to compensate for costs by reflexively associating the partner with positive traits emerged regardless of self-esteem (a dispositional proxy for trust). Such normative effects suggest that the "justify commitment" rule is part of the mind's working store of procedural knowledge for relationships. These results also suggest that the interdependent mind is inclined to justify the costs

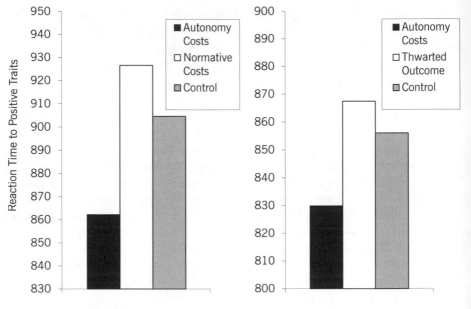

FIGURE 6.5. Implicit evaluations of the partner as a function of autonomy costs (quicker reaction times to positive traits indicate more positive implicit evaluations). Adapted from Murray, Holmes, et al. (2009). Copyright 2009 by the American Psychological Association. Adapted by permission.

the partner imposes in particular. Participants in the control conditions that simply primed negativity (i.e., normative costs and thwarted-outcome condition) did not differ from baseline controls.

The motivation by opportunity logic of correction anticipates a different pattern of results on the explicit measures. On these measures, the conscious will prevailed. By drawing people's conscious attention to their partner, these self-report scales afforded less trusting people the opportunity to be circumspect and to correct the unchecked impulse to value a costly partner. Low self-esteem people jumped at this chance. Figure 6.6 presents these results. In both studies, cost-primed lows countered their automatic impulse to justify by expressing less positive evaluations of their partner, less efficacy, and less optimism on the explicit measures. No evidence of such contrary conscious will emerged for high self-esteem people. Instead, for highs, the automated will to compensate surfaced in explicitly justified commitment.

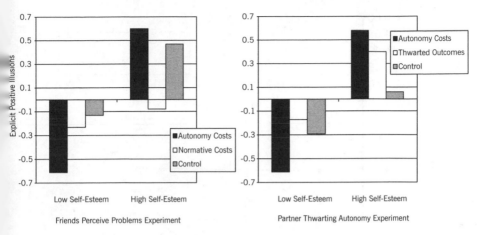

FIGURE 6.6. Explicit positive illusions as a function of autonomy costs and self-esteem. Adapted from Murray, Holmes, et al. (2009). Copyright 2009 by the American Psychological Association. Adapted by permission.

The capacity to act on the leanings of automated will and compensate for costs has important real-world consequences. Recall the daily diary study of newlyweds we discussed in Chapter 4. In this study, newlyweds completed an electronic diary for 14 consecutive days. Each day they indicated how often their partner's actions interfered with their personal goals each day (e.g., Harry doing something he wanted to do rather than what Sally wanted to do, Harry using the last of something Sally needed, or refusing to talk about something Sally wanted to discuss). They also reported on how much they valued their partner each day. When we analyzed the data without taking the motivation to correct into consideration, we found a main effect of autonomy costs. These newlyweds generally compensated for one day's costs by valuing their partner more on the next day. But this picture changed dramatically once we took the conscious will to correct into consideration. Figure 6.7 presents the results. High self-esteem people valued their partner more on days after their partner thwarted more of their goals. Low self-esteem people did not; they effectively curbed this relationship-protective impulse.[7]

If compensating for costs is the interpersonal mind's mechanism for keeping commitment on track, the relationships of low self-esteem people should be more readily derailed. They were. People with lower self-esteem reported significantly greater declines in satisfaction over the first year of marriage (Murray, Holmes, et al., 2009). This happened in part because

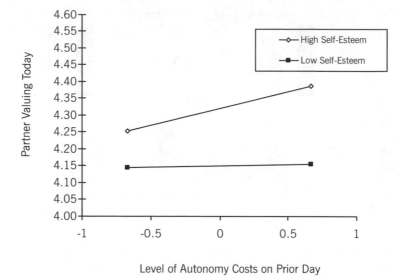

FIGURE 6.7. Compensating for daily autonomy costs as a function of self-esteem. From Murray, Holmes, et al. (2009). Copyright 2009 by the American Psychological Association. Reprinted by permission.

low self-esteem people failed to compensate for the costs their partner could not help but impose. The daily data allowed us to derive an index of cost compensation for each person. This measure can be thought of as a kind of correlation (i.e., a within-person residual slope) that indexes how much (or how little) each participant values the partner more in response to costs. We then used this cost-compensation index in a mediation model. We predicted changes in satisfaction over the year of marriage from initial levels of self-esteem and cost compensation. This analysis revealed evidence of mediation. Newlyweds who compensated less for costs reported relatively greater declines in satisfaction over the first year of marriage, and those people were disproportionately those who were low in self-esteem. Simply put, low self-esteem people reported less satisfaction over the first year of marriage in part because they could not or would not compensate for costs.

When Correction Becomes Automatic

At this point a caveat is in order. Many of the situations that interdependent life samples recur—and recur often. This is not the first time Sally has had the impulse to ask Harry to help with a domestic chore and it probably will not be the last (given Harry's history of leaving a trail of empty ice trays, dirty dishes, and cluttered floors behind him). With repeated experience, checking her impulse to reach out to Harry in such situations might no longer require much conscious control at all. Instead, Sally might become so practiced at suppressing the goal to connect that implementing a self-protective behavioral strategy becomes relatively automatic (Kunda & Spencer, 2003). We return to this issue in Chapters 8, 10, and 11.

COORDINATING MUTUALITY IN RESPONSIVENESS

To implement the goal to connect, the interdependent mind must capitalize on those opportunities in which the partner is most motivated to be responsive. The mind also needs to compensate for the personal costs that depending on the partner ultimately creates. It appears to do both. Situations that afford the goal to connect automatically elicit behavioral intentions to put one's outcomes in the partner's hands, take the partner's outcomes into one's own hands, and justify any costs one incurs as a result of such dependence. We now turn to the last question we posed for this chapter: How might this action plan for implementing the goal to connect help foster the kinds of reciprocated commitments that ease mutually responsive interactions?

Before we describe how this happens, we need to make something clear. The arguments advanced below assume that automatic impulses are carried through to actual overt behavior. That's not always going to be the case. Indeed, if Sally corrects the automatic impulses to connect and instead actually distances herself from Harry, it would short-circuit the adaptive processes outlined below. So, in the ideal case in which the automated will results in congruent behavior, how exactly does the action plan for connection foster reciprocated commitment?

In low-risk situations, coordinating mutuality in responsiveness involves meeting one partner's expression of commitment with the other partner's reciprocated expression of commitment. The rules for implementing the goal to connect provide the behavioral grist for this coordination process (Wieselquist et al., 1999). They do so through the intermediary supplied by trust. Trust—in both its conscious (reflective) and unconscious (impulsive) forms—is partly a reflection of the partner's past behavior in conflicts of interest (see Chapter 3). Witnessing Harry's willingness to meet her needs bolsters Sally's trust in him. But Harry cannot behave responsively if Sally does not let him. The "escalate own dependence" rule automatically motivates Sally to put her outcomes in Harry's hands and take his outcomes into her hands in precisely those low-risk situations where he is most likely to reward her for doing so. The gains she incurs through trusting Harry in turn solidify Sally's own commitment to being responsive to Harry's needs the next time he puts his outcomes in her hands.

However, the unexpected costs that come with Sally's new state of dependence on Harry could undermine Harry's motivation to express his commitment through responsiveness. The if–then rule for justifying commitment ensures that Harry is not so easily distracted or dissuaded. By valuing Sally more precisely when she inflicts greater restrictions on his autonomy, Harry strengthens his resolve. Compensating for costs essentially makes the partner intrinsically valuable and worthy of the sacrifices one might need to make. Indeed, this day-to-day process of value creation motivated newlyweds in the diary study to behave more responsively toward their partner (Murray, Holmes, et al., 2009). When Harry compensated for the ways in which Sally thwarted his goals by valuing her more, Sally actually perceived him as behaving all the more responsively toward her the next day. Compensating for costs thus cements resolve in ways that can reinforce cycles of increasingly responsive behavior. Namely, witnessing Harry's responsiveness strengthens Sally's trust in him. Being more trusting then relaxes her vigilance for signs of risk in the next conflict of interest they encounter. Her greater trust allows her to put her outcomes in Harry's hands in objectively riskier situations. Such situations give Harry a better or more diagnostic opportunity to demonstrate how much he is willing to sacrifice to meet her needs. Her greater trust also increases her commitment and willingness to take Harry's outcomes into her hands the next time Harry finds himself in need. Through such cycles of positive reinforcement, escalating dependence and justifying commitment can slowly and imperceptibly steer partners to reciprocate higher levels of commitment.

SUMMARY AND THINKING AHEAD

This chapter described how the interdependent mind uses the if–then rules for implementing the goal to connect to motivate reciprocated expressions of commitment. This chapter had three main points. First, we explained why the "escalate own dependence" and "justify commitment" rules are necessary building blocks for reciprocated expressions of commitment. We described how the automated will to connect heightens Sally's intention to put her outcomes into Harry's hands, take his outcomes into her own, and justify the costs she incurs in doing so. We also described the motivation by opportunity logic of correction. Being less trusting (i.e., motivated) and having the requisite cognitive capacity (i.e., opportunity) allows Sally to correct and overturn the automated will to connect on occasion. Second, we reviewed the empirical evidence for the efficient and flexible operation of the "escalate own dependence" and "justify commitment" implementation rules. Activating the goal to connect automatically heightens Sally's (and Gayle's) commitment intentions. For instance, priming the costs of being close automatically activates the tendency to value one's partner more. However, people who question their partner's commitment (i.e., low in self-esteem) counter this state impulse when they have the opportunity to do so. Third, we described exactly how implementing the "escalate own dependence" and "justify commitment" rules ultimately help wed one partner's expression of commitment to the other partner's reciprocated expression of commitment.

At several points in this chapter, we saw a less trusting Sally correct the leanings of her automated will. Rather than approach connection, she decided to avoid it. The interdependent mind's flexibility means that there is not a one-to-one correspondence between the goal a specific situation automatically activates (i.e., connect) and the behavior that results (i.e., distance). In those low-risk situations where Harry signals his sincere interest, a less trusting Sally might correct the impulse to confide to him and talk to a friend instead. When Harry's domestic ineptitudes become hard to ignore, she might also curb any impulse she has to laugh and decide to chastise him for his incompetence. Indeed, the goal to connect is itself sufficient to motivate a less trusting Sally to self-protect. For instance, implicit approach goal primes make low self-esteem people distance from their partner (Murray, Derrick, et al., 2008). The potential problem with correction is that sometimes the unconscious mind might know something worth paying attention to. Had Sally gone ahead and confided to Harry, she might have discovered he can be responsive. Because connectedness goals are activated in situations that offer some real potential for gain, correcting can cause Sally to miss out. She might actually foreclose real opportunities for strengthening her commitment to Harry (and his commitment to her) by not connecting in situations where she really should. For this reason, correction plays a critical role in shaping the relationship's personality. We take this issue up again in Chapter 8.

Next we turn to the question of how the interdependent mind marshals the goal to self-protect against rejection and nonresponsiveness into a plan for action that nonetheless coordinates reciprocity in commitment and ultimately eases mutually responsive interactions.

NOTES

1. A reminder of the meaning of reciprocity is perhaps instructive here. We use the term *reciprocated expressions of commitment* to refer to reciprocity across situations and time (see Chapters 1 and 2). With a reciprocated commitment, Sally's expressions of commitment generally match Harry's expressions of commitment across time and situations within the relationship. In any given situation, Sally might be more dependent than Harry (or vice versa). Indeed, such situational variations are central to risk as we saw in Chapter 5.
2. As we introduced in Chapter 2, the term *commitment intention* refers to the concrete and symbolic ways in which partners can both put their outcomes in each other's hands *and* tend to each other's outcomes. For instance, Sally expresses her commitment to Harry when she relies on him to take out the garbage or fix her car. She also expresses her commitment to Harry when she takes his mother on errands. He similarly expresses his commitment to her when he relies on her to cook his meals and mother their children.
3. Although low levels of trust generally motivate people to curb the situated goal to connect, this motivation will not reveal itself in every instance. Whether being chronically less trusting motivates people to correct the state goal to connect depends on the strength of the goal itself. Goal strength is a direct property of the strength of one's affective association to risk (see Chapter 5). In situations that strongly signal connection (e.g., a partner's expression of love), the state goal to connect may overwhelm competing chronic goals. Reveling in the glow of such a situation, even a less trusting partner might lose the motivation to correct.
4. As we illustrate in Chapter 10, such dynamics are critical to understanding how Sally might develop an automatic evaluative association to Harry that conflicts with her more general deliberative expectations.
5. People who are lower in global self-esteem generally report less trust in their romantic partner's positive regard and commitment to them (Murray, Holmes, & Griffin, 2000, 2001), though of course, this correlation is not a perfect one. Some low self-esteem people can be quite trusting (and some high self-esteem people can be quite distrusting) as we show in Chapter 10.
6. Such procedures activate goal states with limited conscious awareness

because participants are exposed to the goal words incidental to the task of categorization (Bargh, 2007).

7. The fact that low self-esteem people failed to compensate for autonomy costs in the diary study raises an interesting question. How did they do it? We suspect the time that elapsed between the events of the day and their later reflections on these events provided the catalyst. Had we caught participants at the moment of goal-thwarting we probably would have been able to catch the automatic propensity to value the partner more. But we caught them at the end of the day when the day's cumulative frustrations had likely corrected such sentiments.

CHAPTER 7

The Rules for Avoiding Rejection

Withhold Own and Promote Partner Dependence

When we last left a sheepish Harry, he was standing in the kitchen, watching Sally, slightly mystified. He had just been about to take the ice tray out of Sally's hands when she, consumed by thoughts about the unfairness in her marriage, slammed the fridge door and moved to the sink, empty ice tray in hand. Just as he was about to utter, "Let me get that for you," Sally lashed out at him, angrily saying, "Do you ever think about anyone but yourself? Why can't you ever take care of your own mother? I spend all of my time doing things for you. Can't you ever think to do anything for me?" As Harry stands there, wondering what he did, will he manage to be conciliatory or apologetic? The impetus for Harry's choice rests in the situation itself. Feeling hurt and unfairly maligned, the situation he finds himself in automatically activates his goal to self-protect. He just wants to escape from the kitchen. Whether considered judgments prevail depends on his motivation and opportunity to overcome his automated will.

This chapter describes how the interdependent mind applies the if–then rules for self-protection in ways that elicit reciprocated, but limited, expressions of commitment. Even though the ice tray dilemma started off as a low-risk situation (with Harry looking sheepish), Sally's decision not to connect turned it into a high-risk situation. In throwing out accusations, Sally withdrew her commitment. Now that she's angry, she's not going to be at all disposed to be responsive toward Harry should he take this inopportune moment to ask her to bathe the children so he can watch the basketball game. For Harry to avoid rejection, discretion now needs to be the better part of valor. In high-risk situations, discretion dictates being careful *not* to ask too much of Sally until she owes him enough to have little choice but to be responsive. Harry exercises such prudence by limiting his own willingness to put his outcomes in Sally's hands until he's managed to limit Sally's capacity not to be responsive. In short, he doesn't ask for too much until he's sure that Sally owes him. In this situation in particular, Harry first might try to gain control over Sally and effectively turn the tables on her by putting Sally on the defensive, perhaps by quickly moving to take out the garbage or by reminding her that he spent 5 hours at the mechanic having her car serviced just the week before. If she cannot be appeased, he might try to cut Sally's tirade short by leaving the room, quite literally taking his outcomes out of her hands (because she can't hurt him if he can't hear her). The artful evasion of house and Sally provided by a weekend game of basketball has served that purpose on more than one occasion. Should Sally only follow him to the basement to continue her diatribe, he might ultimately inoculate himself against hurt by leveling his own accusations. In telling her she's an unreasonable "nag," he blunts the pain of her criticisms, gives himself license to be selfish with her, and steers himself clear of any future situations in which Sally might reject his need to escape mundane household chores again.

As these examples illustrate, turning self-protection goals into action involves supplying Harry with the automated will to hold his own expressions of commitment back until he has taken steps to get the upper hand and control how Sally can express her commitment. In strategic terms, Harry minimizes how much he allows himself to depend on Sally and how much he allows himself to do for her until Sally is sufficiently indebted to him to have little choice but to be responsive. Putting this plan for avoiding rejection into action involves the "if self-protect goal, then withhold own dependence" (Path C_2 in Figure 2.1) and "if self-protect goal, then promote partner dependence" (Path C_2 in Figure 2.1) implementation rules. For instance, Harry might generally increase Sally's tolerance for his slips around the ice trays by showcasing his greater computer skills, mechanical expertise, and easy roughhousing with their sons (Murray, Aloni, et al., 2009). In making Sally depend on him in these domains, Harry gains the power he needs to ensure that Sally has little choice but to tolerate his lapses because she owes him. He might further limit his exposure to loss by distancing himself from Sally in domains where she has been rejecting in the past. For instance, Harry might steer clear of confessing his job worries to Sally if she has always been unsympathetic to such concerns. In situations where she behaves nonresponsively, such as is the case with the escalating ice tray conflict, he might be proactive with criticisms himself to ward off hurt. This latter response highlights a paradox we explore in this chapter. Behaving somewhat badly can serve the goal of mutuality in responsiveness because negative interactions can motivate partners to avoid domains where responsiveness has not been forthcoming. Having learned early on that bringing his job stresses to Sally only started arguments, Harry now sees her as unsympathetic on this front and avoids relying on her for emotional support. He instead confines his self-disclosures to weight and sleeping problems, domains in which she consistently provides more helpful and practical instrumental advice. In this way, Harry reduces his commitment to match the evident limits on Sally's commitment.

This chapter unpacks the action plan for implementing the goal to self-protect in three parts. Table 7.1 summarizes these arguments, addressed in sequence in the chapter. In part one we explain why the "withhold own dependence" and "promote partner dependence" rules are necessary building blocks for coordinating fluid and mutually responsive interactions. We argue that the goal of avoiding rejection automatically activates Harry's tendency to reduce his commitment while taking steps to make Sally more committed to him. Such a coordinated strategy limits Harry's losses in conflicts of interest by limiting Sally's power to be hurtful. Harry basically takes away her license to be rejecting by making sure that he only asks for the type of favors that she is already sufficiently indebted to repay. Such a tactic has resulted in the rigid exchange of car maintenance (Harry's purview) for mother-in-law chauffeuring (Sally's purview) duties in his marriage. As we will see, the utility of imposing such limits on commitment shifts when people are highly trusting of their partner's responsiveness. Being highly trusting, Gayle has little general need to self-protect against Ron's rejection. When Ron chastises her for

---

TABLE 7.1. The Main Arguments

1. State goal to self-protect strengthens intentions to restrict one's own commitment while promoting the partner's commitment.
2. Empirical evidence for efficiency and flexibility of the if–then rules.
3. Implementing the goal to self-protect elicits reciprocated expressions at lower and more limited levels of interdependence.

leaving dirty dishes in the sink, she might correct her automated will to self-protectively chastise him in return. Instead, she might choose to apologize. In part two we detail the empirical evidence for the efficient and flexible operation of the "withhold own dependence" and "promote partner dependence" implementation rules. We show that activating the goal to protect automatically elicits intentions to withhold one's own and/ or promote the partner's dependence. However, people who trust more in their partner's commitment correct and overturn such controlling intentions when they have the opportunity to do so. In part three we describe exactly how implementing the plan for self-protection automatically controls expressions of commitment in ways that nonetheless promote mutually responsive (albeit cautious) interaction patterns. As will become evident, heeding the automated will to self-protect steers Harry and Sally's interactions away from risky domains and toward ones at lower levels of interdependence that afford easier, and thus safer, opportunities to be responsive.

IMPLEMENTING THE GOAL TO SELF-PROTECT

Implementing the goal to self-protect involves applying a ready plan for minimizing the opportunities for nonresponsiveness that high-risk situations afford. The "withhold own" and "promote partner dependence" rules together provide this action plan. These if–then rules link the activation of self-protection goals to two behavioral strategies for avoiding loss in conflicts of interest. First, Harry can limit his own commitment by taking his outcomes out of Sally's hands in situations where she might prove to be rejecting (i.e., "if self-protect goal, then withhold own dependence"). When he's had a bad day at work, Harry can avoid talking to Sally and distract himself with a baseball game on TV instead. When Sally's had a tough day at home with the children, he can also bury himself in the newspaper rather than trying to comfort Sally and risk saying something that might direct Sally's frustrations at him. Second, Harry can also leverage Sally's commitment to meeting his needs by making sure that she depends on him in some respect (i.e., "if self-protect goal, then promote partner dependence"). By keeping secret how to program the VCR, hook the computer up to the Internet, and change the oil in the car, Harry gains control over Sally. He can better meet his goal to loaf in future negotiations over dishes and laundry because Sally cannot afford to lose the contributions he makes in his domains of strategic expertise. In applying these rules, the interdependent mind thereby affords Harry and Sally with greater opportunity and willingness to make cautious displays of responsiveness. These rules motivate Harry to come to Sally when he (or his mother) need something tangible and concrete, and these rules motivate Sally to provide such instrumental support.

How does this happen? The implementation rules for self-protection automatically cause Harry to limit his commitment and control Sally's commitment in predictable ways. These rules govern what situations he chooses to enter and what situations he chooses to avoid (Snyder & Stukas, 1999). They also shape how he behaves in situations that Sally imposes on him (Kelley, 1979). These rules generally make Harry hesitant to solicit or provide care to Sally (i.e., "if self-protect goal, then withhold own dependence") unless Sally's reciprocated commitment is already guaranteed (i.e., "if self-protect goal, then promote partner dependence). As we will see, the risk parameters of the situation at hand determine whose commitment the interpersonal mind first tries to control. Imagine a situation in which Harry must confess that he did not get the pay raise he expected. As he contemplates entering this situation, his automatic impulse is to do something in advance to motivate Sally to be forgiving. Bringing home a take-out dinner so she does not have to cook might be his way of averting her criticism. Instead imagine a situation, like the ice tray conflict, in which Harry must respond to a situation Sally created. In this case, escaping from Sally might be his first tactic for self-protection. Making Sally more dependent on him might only become a focus of his energies once he has avoided the immediate danger of being further criticized. Let's now consider each implementation rule in turn.

Limiting One's Own Commitment Intentions

The "withhold own dependence" rule automatically motivates Harry to take his outcomes out of Sally's hands while limiting how far he goes to sacrifice on Sally's behalf. In limiting his willingness to solicit care, this rule motivates Harry to avoid entering into conversations in which Sally might have the chance to belittle his job concerns. In fact, he has a well-rehearsed list of perfunctory answers at hand should the topic of his activities at work happen to come up. In limiting his willingness to extend care, this rule also motivates Harry to turn a deaf ear to Sally's entreaty for him to change his disciplinary tactics with their children.

Harry's options in the ice tray dilemma aptly illustrate how avoidance can minimize his losses in high-risk situations. Figure 7.1 captures the situation he faces. Harry can respond to Sally's accusations by escaping to the basement or he can apologize. The top values in each cell cor-

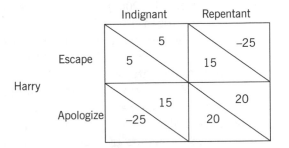

FIGURE 7.1. The zero-sum conflict over the ice tray.

respond to Sally's outcomes; the bottom values correspond to Harry's outcomes. In this situation, his automatic inclination is to take his outcomes out of Sally's hands and escape to the basement. Limiting his commitment in this way provides his best means of avoiding hurt because Sally's actions (i.e., indignant vs. apologize) have little practical consequence for him once he's in the basement. Extending his commitment by apologizing only sets him up for large losses because feeling unfairly treated gives Sally a strong temptation not to accept his apologies. For it to be safe for him to apologize, Harry needs assurance that Sally would transform the situation in a way that sets aside her strong desire to be indignant—but there's nothing in the situation that gives him such assurance. So his best bet is to reflexively retreat to the basement because retreat at least protects him from the worst possible outcome (i.e., having his apology met by Sally's indignation). With this evasive tactic, he removes himself physically and psychologically from Sally, much as he might reflexively withdraw his hand from a hot stove.

The general functionality of such avoidance is evident in other social domains as well. MacDonald and Leary (2005) argue that social loss elicits a social pain akin to a physical pain as an evolved mechanism for removing oneself from hurtful situations. Building on this logic, Ford and Collins (2010) argue that experiences with rejection trigger a biological stress response (i.e., cortisol release) that motivates self-protective social behavior. In particular, social loss seems to decrease the willingness to put one's personal outcomes in another's hands. Experiences with social loss, such as being ostracized by strangers or anticipating a future bereft of social connection, both decrease people's willingness to sacrifice their own self-interest to benefit others (Twenge, Baumeister, DeWall, Ciarocco, & Bartels, 2007) and increase their willingness to aggress against hurtful others (Twenge, Baumeister, Tice, & Stucke, 2001). Attachment theorists similarly argue that finding that a significant other is not available or responsive in times of crisis is sufficiently self-threatening that such experiences can effectively deactivate proximity-seeking behaviors (Mikulincer & Shaver, 2003). For instance, when infants' attempts to elicit care go unmet, they develop avoidant behavioral patterns in stressful situations, actively diverting attention away from their caregivers (Ainsworth et al., 1978). Such defensive avoidance is also evident in adult relationships. People who suffer hurt feelings at the hands of specific others report that the incident caused them to limit or sever the nature of their relationship with the transgressor (Leary, Springer, Negel, Ansell, & Evans, 1998).

Increasing the Partner's Commitment Intentions

While retreating to the basement does provide Harry with short-term relief from Sally's criticisms, it does little to solve his long-term problems. Sooner or later, Harry is going to have to come out of the basement, and when he does, he needs a point of leverage to motivate Sally to be more committed to meeting at least some of his needs. For this reason, implementing the action plan to self-protect also involves a complementary if–then rule for controlling the partner's commitment. By making sure Sally owes him, Harry forecloses her options. If he comes back upstairs with a bicycle he just built for their son (which Sally had tried to build and failed), he's now gained some short-term power or leverage that he might be able to use to get her to accede to his wish to watch the basketball game while she bathes the children (Huston, 1983). Once he has Sally in his debt, she loses her power not to do things for him because she needs or depends him to do things for her (Murray, Aloni, et al., 2009). She is committed.

Because commitment is rooted in the structural state of dependence (Rusbult et al., 1998), Harry can unilaterally increase Sally's commitment by behaving in ways that make her more dependent on him. He can satisfy more of her needs, elicit her greater investment, and reduce the quality of her alternatives (Murray, Aloni, et al., 2009). To create such indebtedness on Sally's part, Harry took over the finances and became the resident expert on all things mechanical. He also befriended her friends and enlisted his mother-in-law as his ally in their domestic conflicts. In escalating the practical and instrumental benefits Sally gains from the relationship and limiting her freedom to find such benefits elsewhere, he effectively curtailed her options. She now finds herself cooking his meals and doing his laundry without comment more often that not. The "promote partner dependence" rule thus motivates Harry to ensure that Sally needs him for certain practical considerations. In fact, pointing out how his mechanical acumen spared Sally a car repair bill that she could not afford to pay on her own silenced her complaints about his household contributions more than once in the past. Harry effectively leveraged Sally's motivation to transform (and eventually apologize) in situations like the ice tray dilemma by making sure Sally "owed" him certain sacrifices in those domains.

Automated and Conscious Will: Efficiency and Flexibility

The MODE model stipulates that automatically activated attitudes control behavior unless people have the motivation and opportunity to correct (Olson & Fazio, 2008). Applied to high-risk situations, such logic implies that the automated intention to self-protect will be carried out through congruent overt behaviors unless people are both trusting and capable of correcting. The logic we outline below conceptually parallels our Chapter 6 analysis. In that chapter, we argued that being less trusting motivates Sally to correct the state goal to connect because this state goal conflicts with the greater chronic priority she puts on avoiding rejection. In this case, being more trusting motivates Gayle to correct the state goal to self-protect because this state goal conflicts with the greater chronic priority she puts on seeking connection.

As we have seen, high-risk situations automatically elicit the behavioral strategies for implementing the state goal to self-protect. However, the necessity of reflexively limiting one's own and increasing the partner's commitment intentions shifts depending on one's chronic level of trust in the partner's commitment. High levels of trust render the possibility of loss less likely and less hurtful (Holmes & Rempel, 1989; Murray, Griffin, et al., 2003; Murray, Holmes, & Collins, 2006). This means that people who are more trusting do not necessarily need to be so quick to control commitment at the first sign of risk. Indeed, for them, mindlessly acting on the automated will to self-protect might prematurely foreclose real opportunities for closeness.

Consider the "withhold own dependence" rule. Let's start by transplanting a trusting Gayle into the ice tray dilemma. When faced with the fastidious Ron's diatribe about empty ice trays (and her lackadaisical approach to kitchen tasks), Gayle can afford to take the risk of being apologetic. She should correct or rethink her automatic impulse to escape to the basement because she doesn't expect Ron to stay indignant. Instead, she knows that if she apologizes, Ron is likely to be embarrassed and contrite. For Gayle, mindlessly acting on her impulse to escape and withhold her own dependence robs her of the likely and greater gains to be had through their joint apologies (Murray, Bellavia, et al., 2003). Mindlessly acting on the impulse to avoid Ron could also prematurely weaken Gayle's commitment before his behavior is nonresponsive enough to truly warrant her disfavor. Acting on the "promote partner dependence" rule has costs as well. For instance, soliciting Ron's indulgence of her sloppy kitchen habits by going out of her way to buy him his favorite wine each week involves substantial time and effort for Gayle. Such actions might also introduce an unsettling fear. Normally Gayle takes Ron's willingness to indulge her football obsession as a sign of his genuine caring for her. But acting on the "promote partner dependence" rule and heading to the wine store could leave her wondering whether Ron only granted her football dispensation because she bought him wine. Such a fear could leave Gayle wondering whether Ron's responsive behavior in general has to be "bought." Believing he was motivated by such tit-for-tat considerations would then threaten her trust in him (Holmes, 1981; Seligman et al., 1980). Because mindlessly acting on the state impulse to self-protect can have such undesirable consequences, being more trusting should motivate Gayle to correct the automated will to limit commitment provided she has the executive strength needed to do so.[1]

IMPLEMENTING THE GOAL TO SELF-PROTECT: EMPIRICAL ILLUSTRATIONS

We now turn to the empirical evidence for the "withhold own dependence" and "promote partner dependence" implementation rules. To foreshadow, this evidence reveals both efficiency and flexibility in rule application. The evidence for efficiency: Situations that prime the goal to self-protect automatically elicit the intention to withhold one's own and promote the partner's commitment regardless of trust. The evidence for flexibility: People who are more trusting overturn the automated will to self-protect when they are motivated and able to do so. As we will see, the capacity to correct the activation of the implementation rules makes it possible for a highly trusting Gayle to be of two minds about her relationship. In high-risk situations, Gayle's unconscious prompts her to limit commitment, but her conscious will prompts her to expand it. Therefore, on the occasions when Gayle has the requisite executive strength, she is going to appear behaviorally ambivalent. Ron's criticisms of her competitiveness and ambition might elicit her automatic impulse to lash back at him (thinking about how unmotivated he can be). But ultimately she overturns this inclination and draws closer to him. No such ambivalence should be evident for a less trusting Harry. When his unconscious will motivates him to reduce or limit commitment, he should do just that.

As we did in Chapter 6, we distinguish automatic (i.e., efficient) and controlled (i.e., flexible) processes by utilizing manipulations and measures that differ in the level of conscious circumspection they afford (Bargh, 1994). The reactions of Gayle and Harry (who are more and less trusting, respectively) should be hard to distinguish when their capacity for conscious deliberation is limited. In such situations, we should see the effects of the automated will. Both should withhold their own dependence and promote their partner's dependence when the goal to self-protect is activated. But their responses should diverge in response to manipulations and measures that afford the conscious will the opportunity to correct. For instance, Gayle might automatically distance herself from Ron on reaction-time measures but not on self-report measures that give her the opportunity to correct. We discuss the evidence for the "withhold own dependence" and "promote partner dependence" implementation rules in turn.

The "Withhold Own Dependence" Implementation Rule

Do self-protection goals call the behavioral strategies for withholding one's own dependence to mind? And do such strategies compel correspondent behavior unless people are both motivated and able to impose the conscious will to correct? A variety of empirical findings point to this conclusion. We begin with some indirect evidence. Activating the general goal of avoidance automatically compels cautious efforts to avoid loss. For instance, subliminally priming avoidance-oriented words, such as *sadness* or *fear*, activates the behavioral tendency (i.e., arm extension) to push away (Alexopoulos & Ric, 2007). Priming the color red, a conditioned cue to risk, also activates the behavioral tendency to avoid loss in achievement settings by choosing only moderately difficult test items (Elliot & Maier, 2007; Elliot, Maier, Moller, Friedman, & Meinhardt, 2007). Of course, such findings do not suggest that the goal to self-protect automatically elicits behavioral efforts to take one's outcomes out of the partner's hands. We now turn to experiments that directly examined the "withhold own dependence" rule.

Efficiency

The motivation by opportunity logic of correction implies that the goal to self-protect automatically elicits the intention to control commitment, unless people are both motivated and able to correct. This logic implies that measures that limit the opportunity to correct should reveal the workings of one's automated will. For instance, a highly trusting Gayle and a less trusting Harry should both "withhold dependence" in response to the activation of self-protection goals, provided that the measure of withholding is one that limits Gayle's opportunity to correct, such as a reaction-time measure. A number of studies point to this conclusion.

As one example, Gillath and colleagues primed self-protection goals outside conscious awareness by subliminally priming the name of a rejecting attachment figure (Gillath et al., 2006). They then measured the spontaneous activation of the associated behavioral strategy for withholding dependence. They did so by measuring how quickly participants identified words such as *distance, dismiss, withdraw,* and *detach* in a lexical decision task. Their results pointed to the existence of an automated will to withhold or limit dependence in response to rejection risk. Participants subliminally primed with the name of someone who had consistently hurt them in the past were quicker to identify distancing words as words (as compared with control participants).

We found a conceptually parallel effect using a supraliminal means of priming self-protection goals (Murray, Derrick, et al., 2008). In this experiment, we activated rejection expectancies, and thus primed the goal to self-protect, by asking experimental participants to vividly describe a time when their dating partner had seriously hurt or disappointed them. We then measured the automatic activation of the "withhold dependence" strategy by examining how quickly participants identified words such as *oppose, condemn, angry, blame, hate, annoy,* and *accuse* in a lexical decision task. Control participants completed the lexical decision task before they described a time when their partner had hurt them. Figure 7.2 presents the results. Participants primed with the goal to self-protect automatically activated the strategy for suspending dependence. Rejection-primed participants were quicker to identify words imposing distance between themselves and others as compared with control participants. In both this experiment and the Gillath et al. (2006) experiment, the automated will to distance from others emerged regardless of trust (or at least its dispositional proxies). Rejection expectancies elicited associated behavioral strategies for withholding dependence even among people secure in attachment style (Gillath et al., 2006) and high in self-esteem (Murray, Derrick, et al., 2008).

Finkel and Campbell (2001) employed a different trick of the social cognition trade to reveal Gayle's automated will to self-protect in high-risk conflicts of interest: Deplete self-regulatory strength. The logic they

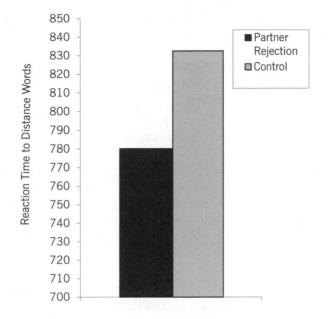

FIGURE 7.2. Reaction time to distance words as a function of recalling a serious partner transgression versus commute. (Quicker reactions indicate greater accessibility of distancing goals.)

advanced built on classic interdependence theory assumptions about the transformation of motivation (Kelley, 1979). In fact, their logic fully anticipated our arguments about the "withhold own dependence" rule's efficiency. They argued that the automatic reaction to a partner's rejecting behaviors is to distance oneself from the source of the hurt. But people can curb such impulses if they have conscious will (i.e., commitment) and the cognitive fortitude (i.e., executive strength) needed to do so (Rusbult et al., 1991). In one such experiment, they limited the capacity to correct by depleting self-regulatory strength (Muraven & Baumeister, 2000). They instructed participants in the taxed condition to watch an emotionally evocative movie clip while working to quash any glimmer of emotion. Participants in the nontaxed condition watched the same clip, emoting as much or as little as they wished. All participants then imagined ways in which their dating partner might be rejecting (e.g., showing up late for a date) and described how they would respond. Taxed participants heeded their automated will. They reduced commitment in reaction to a rejecting partner. Taxed participants were significantly less positive, forgiving, and loyal (i.e., accommodative) in the face of a partner's rejecting behavior than nontaxed controls.

Still further evidence for the efficient and flexible operation of the "withhold dependence" rule comes from an inventive series of experiments conducted by Cavallo and colleagues (Cavallo et al., 2009; Cavallo, Fitzsimons, & Holmes, 2010). These researchers based their research on a broader assumption than we have made to this point. They reasoned that withholding dependence is such a fundamental response to risk that risk automatically enlists the general motivational system for avoidance (Elliot, 2008). This led to a far-reaching assumption about the power of the automated will to protect. Implementing the goal to self-protect against a romantic partner's rejection should "spill over" into other domains. The goal to self-protect should not only elicit efforts to keep one's outcomes out of the partner's hands, but it should also elicit automatic efforts to avoid loss in nonromantic domains.

How did they test for such a spillover effect? The principle of regulatory fit states that people are more effective in pursuing goals when the goals required by the situation fit or match chronic goals (Higgins, 2000). This means that people primed to self-protect will perform better on any kind of task framed in terms of avoiding loss if the goal to self-protect does indeed activate a general behavioral strategy to avoid negative outcomes. Cavallo et al. (2010) primed self-protection goals by activating rejection expectancies. They focused experimental participants on the dark, seamy sides of themselves they wanted to keep from their partner. Control participants had no such preoccupation. Participants then created words from anagrams under the gain-framed instruction to "find 90% or more of the available words" or under the loss-framed instruction to "avoid missing any more than 10% of the words." Priming the goal to protect against the partner discovering one's darker sides automatically elicited efforts to avoid loss. Participants primed with rejection solved more anagrams when they were instructed not to fail than when they were instructed to succeed.

Flexibility

The motivation by opportunity logic of correction also implies that measures that give a more trusting Gayle a clear and obvious warning that she might be withdrawing too rashly should enable her motivation to correct. For Gayle, mindlessly and routinely reducing her own commitment in response to the state goal to self-protect counters her chronic goal to connect to Ron. For this reason, people who are more trusting, such as those high in self-esteem, should counter the automated will to self-protect when they can. The results of a further experiment conducted by Cavallo et al. (2009) suggest that high self-esteem people might over-compensate for the goal to self-protect and willfully approach instead. In this study, participants in the self-protect goal condition described a time when their dating partner seriously disappointed them. Participants then chose between a safe investment strategy that offered a high probability of low returns and a risky investment strategy that offered a low probability of high returns. Low self-esteem people heeded the automated will to self-protect. Rejection-primed lows were more likely to choose the safe investment strategy than controls. But high self-esteem people actually overturned the automated will to self-protect. Rejection-primed highs were even more likely to choose the risky investment strategy than control participants. Of course, this study does not address whether a highly trusting Gayle is more likely to overturn the "withhold dependence" rule when she's in the midst of a conflict with Ron. Evidence that we review in Chapter 8 suggests that a more trusting Gayle is more likely to correct the automatic impulse to distance from a rejecting partner than is a less trusting Harry.

The "Promote Partner Dependence" Implementation Rule

Satisfying the goal to self-protect by taking one's outcomes out of the partner's hands has two downsides. The first is short-term: Harry cannot stay in the basement forever. The second is long-term: Taking his outcomes out of Sally's hands limits her capacity to be responsive. By retreating to the basement, Harry limits Sally's power to hurt him, but he also takes away her opportunity to be apologetic. Because Harry has no choice but to depend on Sally in at least some basic respects, minimizing the losses to be had in high-risk situations also requires a mechanism for increasing Sally's commitment to him. The "promote partner dependence" implementation rule does just that. In making Sally more dependent on him, Harry gains the power or leverage he needs to ensure that she must be responsive when he puts his outcomes in her hands again (Murray, Aloni, et al., 2009). Being "beholden" to Harry essentially constrains Sally's commitment to him in a way that limits her power to choose not to be responsive.

To re-create the "promote partner dependence" rule in the lab, we first had to decide on the best means of inducing the goal to self-protect. Usually we activate self-protection goals by making the partner's rejection unavoidable, perhaps by asking Harry to think of a time when Sally disappointed him. We decided against this tactic in this case. As we reasoned earlier, promoting the partner's dependence is a better strategy for avoiding loss in situations where rejection is a possibility, not an actuality. In our experiments, we decided to make rejection a possibility by activating the "exchange script." This cultural script specifies that partners need to make matched or equitable contributions to the relationship to avoid being replaced (Thibaut & Kelley, 1959). In daily life, commercials advertising dating websites, magazines touting new ways to be sexy, televised snippets of divorce court, and watching a beautiful young woman dining with an older, stodgy, but wealthy man all serve as not-so-subtle reminders that partners are up for equitable trades. Because the exchange script is part of the collective unconscious, priming this script gave us a great means of raising rejection fears in the laboratory (Murray, Aloni, et al., 2009).

The interpersonal mind's efficiency and flexibility implies that priming the goal to self-protect (through the exchange script) automatically elicits the tendency to promote the partner's dependence, unless people are both motivated and able to correct such impulses. To bottle efficiency and flexibility in the lab, we then had to decide how to discriminate between the automatic and controlled operation of the rule. We quantified motivation by using global self-esteem as a proxy for trust in the partner's commitment. High self-esteem people are more trusting and more likely to pursue the chronic goal to connect (Murray, Rose, et al., 2002). So we expected a high self-esteem (and highly trusting Gayle) to correct her state goal to self-protect and limit Ron's commitment when she had the opportunity to do so. We manipulated opportunity by varying how much conscious thought participants put into deliberating the exchange script. In two experiments, we activated the exchange script while participants were preoccupied with a different task (and thus unable to correct). In these studies, we expected a highly trusting Gayle to promote Ron's dependence automatically, just like a less trusting Harry. In two other experiments, we had participants consciously use the exchange script. In these studies, we expected a highly trusting Gayle to correct her automatic inclination to promote Ron's dependence in response to the state goal to self-protect and instead insist that he take care of his own needs for clean clothes, cooked meals, or purchased wine.

Efficiency

In the two "automated will" experiments, we limited people's opportunity to correct by utilizing implicit reminders of the exchange script. We brought the exchange script to mind as participants were busily engaged in another task and thus had little cognitive wherewithal to suppress or dispute the script. In one experiment, we activated the exchange script incidental to the "real" task of evaluating how appealing a set of personal ads would be to other people (Murray, Aloni, et al., 2009, Experiment 2). In the self-protect goal condition, these ads happened to emphasize the romantic hopefuls' expectations of making an equitable or matched trade. As an example, one of the ads in the exchange condition conveyed a highly desirable romantic hopeful's high expectations for a match. This ad read: "Accomplished man seeking attractive woman for a meaningful relationship. I am looking for someone who is a good fit for me and can live up to the qualities I bring to the relationship in her own way. My hobbies include sailing, tennis, and going out to restaurants." Another ad, one from someone less enthralled with herself, read: "Twenty-ish female seeking male for a serious relationship. My friends describe me as attractive in my own way, and as being a great conversationalist, intelligent, and as having a great sense of humor. I'm not interested in aiming too high, but I'm looking for a partner who would bring similarly desirable qualities to the relationship." In the control condition, the personal ads that participants evaluated conveyed no exchange stipulations. In the second experiment, we invoked the exchange script by using money to prime the economic metaphor that quantities are bought and sold (Vohs, Mead, & Good, 2006). In the self-protect goal condition, we superimposed pictures of U.S. coins on the computer screen. In the control condition, we superimposed pictures of circles (Murray, Aloni, et al., 2009, Experiment 3).

In both experiments, we then measured the activation of self-protection goals and the associated enactment of behavioral strategies for promoting the partner's dependence. We indexed self-protection goals through rejection expectancies. To do this, we tapped both feelings of inferiority to the partner (e.g., "My partner has a more interesting personality than I have"; "I feel inferior to my partner") and concerns about being replaced (e.g., "I worry about somebody taking my partner away from me"). We created a general measure of self-protection goal strength in each experiment by averaging responses to both of these scales.

Our measures of intentions to promote the partner's dependence tapped a constellation of behavioral strategies for putting the partner in a state of debt. These strategies centered on two main ways in which people can make their partner need or owe them: (1) fulfilling more of the partner's practical or instrumental needs and (2) limiting their partner's capacity to fulfill such needs in alternate relationships. To tap need fulfillment, we measured the desire to specialize roles within the relationship in ways that heightened one's general responsibility for the partner (e.g., "It bothers me when my partner does things for him/herself that I could do for him/her"; "I want my partner to feel like there are some things that he/she needs me to do for him/her"). To further tap need fulfillment, we also measured how often people took specific responsibility for mundane, instrumental aspects of the partner's life (e.g., "cooking for my partner," "keeping track of my partner's school schedule," "remembering my partner's important appointments," "making sure my partner's bills get paid on time"). To tap limiting alternatives, we measured people's efforts to center their partner's social worlds on themselves (e.g., "I do the things my partner likes to do so he/she won't need to do those things with other people"; "I make a lot of effort to make sure my partner's friends like me"). To further tap limiting alternatives, we also measured how much people thought their partner stood to lose by ending the relationship (e.g., "My partner would lose friends we share"; "My partner would have trouble finding a partner who did as much for him/her as I do"). We then created a general and reliable measure of dependence promotion in each experiment by averaging responses to all four of these scales because all of these scales tap different means to the same end of partner dependence promotion.

Figures 7.3 and 7.4 present the results of these experiments. As Figure 7.3 illustrates, implicit reminders of the exchange script activated self-protection goals regardless of self-esteem. Participants who simply read exchange-oriented personal ads reported greater feelings of being inferior to their partner and greater worries about being replaced relative to controls. So did participants primed with the mere metaphor of an economic exchange that the coins imparted. As Figure 7.4 illustrates, these implicit reminders of the exchange script elicited the automated will to make the partner more dependent. Participants incidentally exposed to personal ads that conveyed expectations of an even trade made greater efforts to put their partners in a state of need or debt (relative to controls). Even the simple image of U.S. coins was enough to auto-motivate people to promote their partner's dependence. Because we had limited people's capacity to correct by using such subtle priming procedures, we expected these automated effects to be just as strong for high as for low self-esteem people. They were.

Any set of laboratory experiments could produce results that have no parallel in the real world. As we described in Chapter 3, we also found real-world evidence of the automated will to promote dependence in a daily diary study of newlyweds. In this study, we used daily feelings

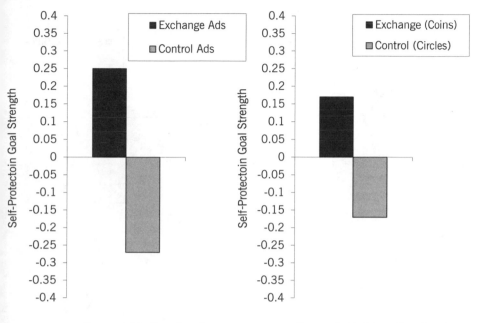

FIGURE 7.3. The effects of implicit exchange-script priming on self-protection goal strength.

of inferiority to the partner as a state measure of rejection expectancies (and the goal to self-protect). We measured daily efforts at dependence promotion through the number of times Harry did something "nice" for Sally that she could just as easily do for herself. The newlyweds in this study responded to feeling inferior one day by doing practical things to draw their partner closer the next day, such as searching for keys, packing lunches, picking up the partner's clothes, and running the partner's errands (Murray, Aloni, et al., 2009). This remedial response appeared to be automatic: On the days these newlyweds worked to put their partner in their debt, they were no longer conscious of the inferiority concerns that drove them! That is, the effect of Monday's feelings of inferiority in eliciting Tuesday's dependence-promoting behavior emerged in analyses that controlled for Tuesday's feelings of inferiority. More impressive still, this remedial response also worked. Working to put the partner in one's debt did indeed escalate the partner's commitment the next day. We return to this point about functionality later in the chapter.

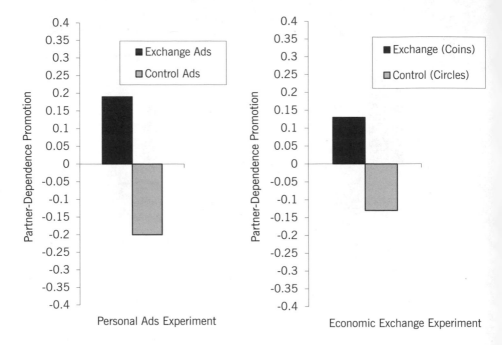

FIGURE 7.4. The effects of implicit exchange-script priming on partner-dependence promotion.

Flexibility

Although eliciting the partner's dependence does work to promote the partner's greater commitment, this strategy for securing the partner's responsiveness has a potential cost. Seeing Ron as dependent on her for buying his wine and reading his legal briefs might make Gayle wonder whether he really cares about her or just cannot afford to lose her. Because perceiving a partner as *merely* dependent can threaten trust, people who are already highly trusting have reason to correct the automated will to control the partner's commitment.

We examined the potential for flexibility in the application of the "promote dependence" rule in two further studies. In these "conscious will" experiments, we increased the opportunity to correct by inviting experimental participants to consciously use and debate the exchange script (Murray, Aloni, et al., 2009, Experiments 4 and 5). In our first experiment, we primed the exchange script by having people play matchmaker within a dating service simulation. Experimental participants received laminated cards containing profiles of potential dates to match. Each profile contained a self-description and numerical ratings of the profiled person on four communal qualities, such as emotional stability. The experimental participants then selected a "good" match for each date. Control participants picked magazine articles for others to read. In our second experiment, we invoked the exchange script by having experimental participants divine the fate of marriages based on how well participants matched on social commodities. The computer feedback reinforced such exchange deliberations by responding "correct" when participants designated a mismatched couple as divorced or a matched couple as together, and "incorrect" when they designated a mismatched couple as together or a matched couple as divorced. Control participants completed a neutral matching task.

We then measured dependence promotion in each of these studies as we did in the unconscious will experiments. Figure 7.5 presents the results. Low self-esteem people heeded their automated will to self-protect. Even when they consciously deliberated the exchange script, they doubled their behavioral efforts to put their partner in their debt. Once low self-esteem people become preoccupied with exchange they may have little choice but to promote their partner's instrumental dependence on them. Why? Because a low self-esteem Harry might doubt that he has much more than that to offer Sally (Baumeister, 1993). However, high self-esteem people curbed the automated will to self-protect. When they had the opportunity to consciously debate the script, they overrode it. In the marital divination experiment, high self-esteem people actually downplayed their partner's dependence on them (relative to controls).

Making the Rules Fit the Circumstance

At this point a caveat is in order. Although self-protection goals elicit the will to limit both one's own and the partner's expressions of commitment, the automatic means to this end is inherently flexible. In a situation where Harry is confronted with an immediate hurt, such as with Sally's ice tray–inspired accusation of incompetence, promoting her dependence may have little immediate functionality. Such a situation is much more likely to elicit the automated will to escape. But escape is not an option in every high-risk situation of dependence. Sometimes Harry must confess a problem at work and sometimes Harry must rely on Sally to make a sacrifice she is not all that inclined to make. In such situations, the goal to self-protect may instead elicit the automated will to promote her dependence

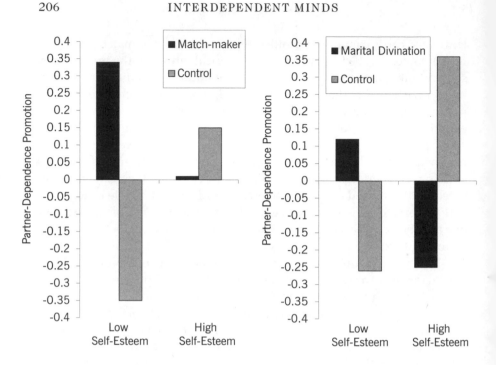

FIGURE 7.5. The effects of explicit exchange-script priming on partner-dependence promotion.

and thus "right the balance" in the relationship. But the ways in which he enacts this behavioral strategy may be further sensitive to context. In his traditional marriage, his most obvious means of making Sally indebted comes through upping his responsibility for "male" tasks, such as car and computer repair. In a less traditional marriage, like Ron and Gayle's, Gayle might instead elicit Ron's greater dependence on her by making sure he comes to her rather than his friends when he needs support. The ways in which the "promote dependence" rule gets instantiated also may differ across cultures. For instance, people in more interdependent cultures might more often limit the partner's freedom through limiting alternatives, perhaps through the intercession of in-laws (MacDonald & Jessica, 2006). People in more independent cultures might instead more often limit the partner's freedom by fulfilling more of their personal needs. We return to this issue in later chapters.

COORDINATING MUTUALITY IN RESPONSIVENESS

To implement the goal to self-protect, the interdependent mind limits the partner's power to be selfish and nonresponsive. Situations that activate the goal to self-protect automatically elicit behavioral strategies for both withholding one's dependence and promoting the partner's dependence. How does this strategy for increasing the partner's commitment while putting limits on one's own commitment actually foster mutually responsive interaction patterns?

Before we describe this logic, we need to make one point clear. The arguments advanced next assume that automatic impulses are carried through to overt behavior. That's not always going to be the case. A highly trusting Gayle is going to correct at least some of the leanings of her automated will to self-protect. Doing so would set the interaction cycle described below on a different course. We return to this point in our Chapter 8 discussion of relationship personality.

In high-risk situations, coordinating mutuality in responsiveness involves meeting one partner's limited expression of commitment with the other partner's reciprocated extension of commitment. The rules for implementing self-protection goals smooth this coordination process from one situation to the next (Wieselquist et al., 1999). They do so through the intermediary supplied by trust. When Harry promotes Sally's dependence on him for mechanical matters, he delimits one domain in which Sally depends on him. Because commitment motivates responsiveness (Van Lange et al., 1997), a more dependent Sally is likely to be more committed and behave more responsively toward Harry. But her willingness to take his outcomes in her hands is likely to be constrained to similar types of favors. In fact, the more dependent Sally becomes on Harry for the simple satisfaction of her instrumental needs, the more she may feel trapped or resigned rather than resolved in her commitment (see Chapter 4). Feeling resigned, but not resolved, Sally is willing to make small sacrifices (like taking Harry's mother to the doctor), but not big ones (like letting Harry's mother move in). Witnessing the limited ways in which Sally expresses her commitment to him then gives Harry reason to trust Sally in some domains, but not in others. His circumscribed level of trust in her then limits how he expresses his commitment the next time Sally needs something from him. He might willingly make the instrumental sacrifice of fixing her computer, but hesitate to listen to her unhappiness about working only part-time. Through such cycles of positive reinforcement, matching what he asks of Sally to what she is already indebted to provide steers their interactions toward less risky, lower levels of interdependence that afford each of them objectively easier opportunities to be responsive.

When Harry instead responds to the activation of self-protection goals by opting to take his outcomes out of Sally's hands, he cuts short her opportunity to make costly sacrifices. He also reduces his own such motivation in the process. Think again about the ice tray dilemma. Ensconced in the basement, preoccupied by the thought that Sally is little more than a compulsive nag, Harry loses whatever motivation he had to apologize. Witnessing his recalcitrant refusal to apologize when he comes out of the basement then further limits Sally's trust in him in this domain. Her newly heightened reason to distrust his motivations then motivates her to avoid putting her outcomes in his hands the next time they encounter a conflict of interest in domestic matters. Through such cycles of negative reinforcement, taking his outcomes out of Sally's hands when she is inclined to be rejecting steers their interactions away from risky domains and toward ones affording easier opportunities to be responsive.

SUMMARY AND LOOKING FORWARD

This chapter described how the interdependent mind uses the if–then rules for implementing the goal to self-protect to motivate reciprocated expressions of commitment. The chapter had three main points. First, we explained why the "withhold own dependence" and "promote partner dependence" rules are necessary building blocks for reciprocated expressions of commitment. We described how the automated will to self-protect both heightens Harry's intention to take his outcomes out of Sally's hands and limits which of her outcomes he chooses to take into his own hands. We also described the motivation by opportunity logic of correction. Being more trusting (i.e., motivated) and having the requisite cognitive capacity (i.e., opportunity) allows for the occasional correction of the automated will to self-protect. Second, we reviewed the empirical evidence for efficiency and flexibility in the application of the "withhold own dependence" and "promote partner dependence" implementation rules. Activating the goal to self-protect automatically heightens Harry's (and Gayle's) intentions to limit or control commitment. For instance, priming thoughts of being rejected automatically activates the tendency to stop and limit one's own dependence. However, people who trust in their partner's commitment, like Gayle, counter this state impulse when they have the opportunity to do so. Third, we described exactly how implementing these if–then rules automatically limits Harry's commitment to match the evident constraints on Sally's commitment and thereby ensures that Harry asks no more of Sally than she is already indebted to provide to him.

As we have seen in this chapter, there is flexibility in whether (and how) the interdependent mind implements the goal to self-protect. This means that partners can sometimes consciously decide to seek rather than reflexively avoid risk. Think back to how a highly trusting Gayle behaved in the ice tray conflict. Even though there was a chance that Ron would succumb to his fastidious nature and reject her apology, she nonetheless took the risk of apologizing. Ron then rewarded her risky overture with his repentance. Gayle then gained the short-term pleasure of being forgiven and vindicated. More important, she also gained greater reason to trust in Ron's commitment. In this conflict, Ron's willingness to forego any personal gratification he takes in asserting his own fastidious indignation at her comparatively sloppy kitchen habits reveals how much he cares for her. In deciding to approach rather than reflexively avoid such high-risk situations, Gayle gives Ron more diagnostic opportunities to demonstrate his commitment. As we saw in Chapter 3, witnessing such sacrifices provides a direct and diagnostic basis for increased trust in the partner's commitment (Holmes, 2002; Simpson, 2007; Wieselquist et al., 1999). This brings us to a crucial consideration that we continue to explore in the next chapter. Being able to curb the automated will to self-protect—at least sometimes—can provide diagnostic opportunities for the growth of trust in the partner's commitment. Because trust grows by approaching risk, trust stagnates when people routinely bend to the automated will to self-protect. As we will see, partners who are preoccupied with self-protection limit themselves to more cautious forms of mutuality, such as those involved in the exchange of car maintenance for mother-in-law chauffeuring activities. Such partners include those exposed to multiple high-risk situations, those with dispositional reasons to be distrusting, and those unlucky enough to be both distrusting in disposition and exposed to excessive situational risk.

We turn to this issue of relationship personality in our next chapter. There we describe how experience in less risky relationship circumstances (e.g., compatible partner interests, being highly trusting) makes seeking connection a stronger if–then rule habit, whereas experience in riskier relationship circumstances (e.g., incompatible partner interests, being less trusting) makes avoiding rejection a stronger if–then rule habit. As we will also see, such rule habits control the general constitution of the automated will. By providing an automatic guide to action, these rule habits set the limits (or lack thereof) on each partner's commitment and motivation to be responsive. In so doing, they define the relationship's emerging personality.

NOTE

1. Although high levels of trust generally motivate people to curb the situated goal to self-protect, this motivation will not reveal itself in every instance. Whether or not being chronically trusting motivates people to correct the state goal to self-protect likely depends on the strength of the goal itself. Goal strength is a direct property of the strength of one's affective association to risk (see Chapter 5). In situations that strongly signal rejection (e.g., a partner's infidelity), the state goal to self-protect may overwhelm competing chronic goals. Recoiling from such a situation, even the most trusting of partners might succumb to the automated will to self-protect.

CHAPTER 8

Relationship Personality

Making Certain Rules a Habit

After the first couple of months, she and Charlie didn't see much of each other except at breakfast. It was a marriage just like any other marriage.
— JEDEDIAH LELAND, character in *Citizen Kane* (1941),
 speaking of Charles Foster Kane and his first wife, Emily

Marriage accustomed one to the good things, so one came to take them for granted, but magnified the bad things, so they came to feel as painful as a grain in one's eyes. An open window, a forgotten quart of milk, a TV set left blaring, socks on the bathroom floor could become occasions for incredible rage. . . .
— MARILYN FRENCH, *In the Women's Room* (1977)

Chains do not hold a marriage together. It is threads, hundreds of tiny threads which sew people together through the years. That is what makes a marriage last—more than passion or even sex!
— SIMONE SIGNORET, French film actor. (*Daily Mail*, London, July 4, 1978)

There was a time when you couldn't make me happy. Now the time has come when you can't make me unhappy.
— IRVING LAYTON, "Aphs," *The Whole Bloody Bird* (1969)

It is a lovely thing to have a husband and a wife developing together and having the feeling of falling in love again. That is what marriage really means: helping one another to reach the full status of being persons, responsible and autonomous beings who do not run away from life.
— PAUL TOURNIER, *The Meaning of Persons* (1957)

Each of these quotes paints a different picture of marriage. Each is just as apt a reflection. In some marriages, partners move in complementary streams, joining for breakfast and separating to fulfill mutually agreed-on roles. In others, partners are locked in conflict, the most minor slights symbolizing the most serious offenses. In some marriages, partners delight in sharing recreational activities and supporting each other in fulfilling personal goals. In others, partners grow emotionally and then behaviorally detached and lead largely separate lives. In still other marriages, interactions are so fluid and satisfying that the relationship becomes a central thread creating meaning, purpose, and happiness in the lives of both partners.

This chapter examines how such variations in the "personality" of the relationship develop. We directly tackle perhaps the most challenging aspects of our analysis: How can common sets of if–then rules produce variability in the observable character of relationships? How can the interdependent mind lock Harry and Sally in domestic conflicts while Ron and Gayle more happily coordinate their domestic stresses? Why does Gunter fear and sometimes resent the time Lastri wants to spend furthering her education while Ron makes multiple personal sacrifices to help Gayle better her career? Why do Hector and Helena enjoy spending time together hiking and watching movies while Harry and Sally work as parallel cogs in the instrumental roles of breadwinner, homemaker, and parent? Why will some of these marriages ultimately prove to be satisfying and resilient over time while others eventually fail?

We start answering this question with a telling observation from the German philosopher Nietschze. He described marriage as "the will that moves two to create the one which is more than those who created it".[1] Stated less elegantly, the relationship "whole" is more than the sum of its "partner" parts. In interdependence terms, partners come together to create unique dyadic situations. The "relationship personality" we describe in this chapter takes its roots in this situational foundation. Two partners with separate life experiences, personalities, and individual goals join to face the problems of forging common life experiences, complementary personalities, and convergent relationship goals. This coordination process creates complex and challenging situations to negotiate in even the best of circumstances. But the forces that draw partners together seldom create such amenable conditions. More often than not, these forces draw partners with at least some incompatible interests together. Although partners who are similar in age, ethnicity, and religion do tend to flock together (Berscheid & Regan, 2005), existing research also reveals that some of the forces that draw partners together are at best adventitious and at worst malicious. In fact, when it comes to the personality and relationship goals that are hardest for partners to coordinate, human mate selection is nearly random. Partners in real marriages were no more similar in personality than partners in the pseudomarriages Lykken and Tellegen (1993) created through the luck of a draw!

The capricious aspects of pairing means that some partners are luckier than others as the couple profiles in Table 8.1 reveal. In joining together, some partners encounter a wealth of situations where coordination is easy. Their interests are largely compatible, and as a result Gayle often finds herself putting her outcomes in the hands of Ron and Ron often finds himself sacrificing on her behalf. Other partners encounter a wealth of situations in which coordination is difficult. Their interests are largely incompatible, and as a result Sally often doubts Harry's motives and avoids relying on him for anything but the most minor favors. Still other partners find themselves in a mixture of easy and difficult situations. In joining together, Gunter and Lastri found they had compatible preferences when it came to dishwashing and laundry responsibilities, but less

TABLE 8.1. Updating Our Couple Profiles

Couple	Basic demographics	Life task preferences	Personality preferences	Relationship goal preferences
Ron and Gayle	African American Lawyers Two young children	Ron likes cooking; Gayle likes washing dishes. Both enjoy child care.	Gayle: More gregarious. Ron and Gayle: Secure.	Both value Gayle's working.
Harry and Sally	White Mechanic/customer service officer Three children, eldest 17	Harry dislikes all things domestic.	Sally: More gregarious. Sally: More fastidious. Harry: More reserved. Harry: Avoidant. Sally: Preoccupied.	Sally wanted to work; Harry wanted her at home.
Hector and Helena	Hispanic Factory worker/ homemaker Three young children Catholic Economically stressed	Stay tuned . . .	Stay tuned . . .	Stay tuned . . .
Gunter and Lastri	Indonesian PhD student/ homemaker One toddler	Gunter likes doing laundry; Lastri likes gardening.	Gunter: Enjoys outside social activities.	Gunter wants another baby; Lastri wants to return to school.

compatible ones when it came to deciding how frugally and socially they should live.

Through the successes and failures in coordinating responsiveness that partners experience in specific situations, the personality of the relationship emerges. We use the term personality in a dual sense. Namely, personality has both a genotype (i.e., a deep causal structure) and a phenotype (i.e., an observable manifestation of this deep causal structure). At the level of the relationship's inside-of-the-mind genotype, the term *personality* captures if–then habits of rule use. This process aspect of personality tunes the ease with which the if–then rules for vigilance, goal orientation, and goal implementation are activated and corrected to meet the situational risks. For Sally, the too-often victim of a freeloading Harry, the if–then rule for withholding her dependence on Harry is highly accessible in memory because she so often faces zero-sum conflicts over household chores. She also is quick to correct the if–then rule for justifying costs because she so rarely trusts in any potential opportunity for coordination.

At the level of the relationship's outside-of-the-mind or observable phenotype, the term *personality* captures exactly what behavioral expressions of responsiveness entail. Do partners rely on each other for inconsequential favors, instrumental tasks, socioemotional support, everything, or nothing? The relationship's personality phenotype emerges as each partner's if–then rule habits shape reciprocated expressions of commitment—that is, what each is willing to ask of the other and what each partner is willing to do for the other. As we saw in the last chapter, Harry came to rely on Sally for advice about weight management, but not for relief from his work troubles, because her behavior rewarded the former solicitations and punished the latter ones. By controlling how partners express commitment, if–then rule habits elicit the type of mutuality in responsiveness that is best suited to the relationship's perceived risks. In relationships composed mostly of high-risk situations, partners might comfortably rely on each other for the exchange of small favors. In moderately risky relationships, partners might expand interaction to circumscribed role responsibilities. In relationships mostly composed of low-risk situations, partners might willingly support each other in the pursuit of personal goals.

Consider how such dynamics enfolded in Harry and Sally's marriage once they had their first child and realized they had a major conflict over marital roles. Although Harry had talked a good game about equality when they were dating, once their first child was born, he insisted Sally quit work to be a stay-at-home mom. She acquiesced, but reluctantly. With time, Sally's efforts to leverage greater power (by making Harry's dentist appointments, meeting his sexual appetites, and chauffeuring his mother) got Harry to concede she could at least work part-time. Nonetheless, gaining some control over her outcomes by promoting Harry's dependence has left Sally less trusting and highly vigilant—fearful that his commitment to being responsive might waver if she let up her extra efforts. For Harry, knowing that he's unable to manage responsibilities himself or care for his ailing mother has left him feeling resigned in his commitment. As situations continued to accumulate, Sally's self-protective if–then rule habits limited her to asking small favors of Harry and performing small favors for him. Witnessing such limited expressions of Sally's commitment circumscribed Harry's trust in her and similarly constrained his expressions of commitment. Ultimately, the if–then rules that became their habit created a shared experience of the marriage as one in which relying on each other to fulfill circumscribed roles (i.e., caretaker, provider) provided the best guarantee of responsiveness.

In positing a procedural basis for relationship personality, we echo Mischel and Shoda (1995). These scholars define individual "personality" in terms of situation-specific patterns of behavior (Mischel & Morf, 2003). Viewing individual personality as "situated" means that deeming a child "aggressive" reveals little about the child because it takes the child out of the situation. More useful depictions of this child's personality come in knowing when aggression is likely—in responding to a peer's taunts, reacting to a teacher's demand, or rejecting a parent's affection. Individual personality is a system that adapts affect, cognition, and behavior to match the characteristics of interaction partners in specific situations. In our analysis, relationship personality is a similar system. This dyadic system captures how two partners tailor the generic if–then rules for vigilance, goal orientation, and goal implementation that the interpersonal mind supplies to match the character of the risks posed by the unique situations they repeatedly face.

This chapter presents a picture of relationship personality that bridges the micro to the macro level of analysis. We describe how situations elicit particular habits of thought that compel both micro-level behaviors and macro-level sentiments of trust and commitment. This chapter deconstructs the emergence of the relationship's personality into five parts. These parts generally correspond to the model of relationship personality re-depicted in Figure 8.1. Table 8.2 summarizes our arguments, addressed in sequence in the chapter.

In part one we describe the foundation of situations that constrain what type of relationship personality can develop. Relationships differ

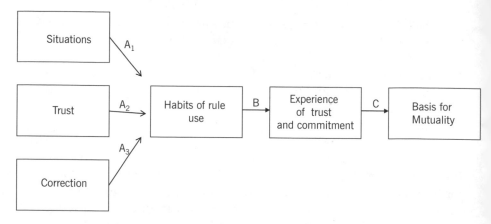

FIGURE 8.1. The development of relationship personality.

at their situational foundation because partners are more or less interdependent and more or less compatible at the levels of life tasks, personality,
and relationship goals. In part two we describe the three sources of variability in if–then rule habits (i.e., variability in personality genotype) this
foundation provides: (1) the risk profile, that is, the nature and extent of
the objective risks partners face; (2) trust, that is, the nature and the extent
of the risks partners who are more or less vigilant perceive; and (3) correction, that is, when and how often partners override the inclinations of
the automated will. In part three we delineate how the resulting if–then
rule habits control observable behavior in conflicts of interest. We do so
by describing empirical examples of how the accessibility and power of
the vigilance, goal orientation, and goal implementation rules vary across
situations and relationships with predictable consequences for behavior.

TABLE 8.2. The Main Arguments

1. Couples vary in the nature of the objective situational risks they routinely
   face in their relationship.
2. The objective risks, trust, and correction provide three bases for
   variability in the if–then rules that become a habit in a given relationship.
3. The if–then rules that become a habit control observable behavior in
   conflicts of interest, shaping how partners perceive and treat each other.
4. The if–then rules that become a habit elicit particular kinds of mutually
   responsive behaviors over others.
5. The mind can fail to elicit mutuality if there is too much risk, too little
   trust, or both too much risk and too little trust.

In part four we detail how idiosyncratic habits of rule use elicit particular kinds of mutually responsive behaviors over others (i.e., variability in personality phenotype). We argue that Sally's tendency to be "self-protective" in her rule habits elicits cautious displays of responsiveness (e.g., exchanging roles) because: (1) Harry tends to reciprocate her behavior (i.e., behavioral reciprocity); and (2) the instrumental attributions they make for each other's commitment limit how they themselves express commitment (i.e., motivational interdependence). This discussion provides a platform for explaining why Sally's conservative if–then rule habits have left her feeling committed but relatively dissatisfied in her marriage. In the final section of the chapter, we delineate why the interdependent mind can fail to elicit mutually responsive interactions. We do so by showing how excessive exposure to situational risk, chronic difficulty trusting, or the unlucky combination of excessive exposure to high-risk situations and chronic vigilance slant interactions in ways that make it difficult for partners to find any consistent way of being mutually responsive.

THE SITUATIONAL FOUNDATION

Situations provide the foundation for the relationship's emerging personality by constraining the types of attitudes and dispositions partners can most readily express (Holmes, 2002). Imagine a utopian relationship in which Lastri and Gunter encountered only coordination dilemmas. Each time they went out socially, they wanted to go to a movie together, and they wanted to see a comedy. Each time they discussed household finances, Lastri happily acceded to Gunter's greater expertise. Each time they had to discipline their children, they discovered still greater convergence in their parenting philosophies. The situations encountered by such a blissfully compatible pair of partners offer few opportunities to be selfish and little reason to protect against the remote possibility of being exploited. To optimize mutuality in responsiveness, the interdependent mind would have little to do but motivate partners to approach each other. Now imagine a less-than-utopian relationship in which Harry and Sally encountered only zero-sum conflicts. Each time they had a night free from parenting duties, Harry wanted to stay in when Sally wanted to go out. Each time they discussed household finances, Sally wanted to save when Harry wanted to spend. Each time Sally disciplined the children, Harry contradicted her efforts. The situations encountered by such a woefully incompatible pair of partners offer frequent opportunities to be selfish and great impetus to protect against the very real possibility of being exploited. To optimize mutuality in responsiveness, the interdependent mind would have little to do but avoid rejection.

Of course, neither of these depictions is a realistic one. We draw these extremes to make the point that the situational foundation of the relationship constrains if–then habits of thought. In a marriage composed of only coordination dilemmas, the interdependent mind might spend little if any time concerned with trust issues and the bulk of its energies implementing the goal to connect. However, in a marriage composed of only zero-sum conflicts, the interdependent mind might spend the bulk of its energies gauging the partner's trustworthiness and implementing the goal to self-protect. The if–then rules that become a habit differ across relationships because situations different across relationships.

Interdependence and Risk Profile

Situations differ across relationships because interdependence varies across relationships. Some partners have a lot of life responsibilities to coordinate; others have just a few. For some partners, child care tasks present coordination dilemmas, whereas getting the housework done presents repeated zero-sum conflicts. For other partners, getting diapers changed, soccer games chauffeured, and homework done present a series of exchange dilemmas, whereas getting the laundry, cooking, and dishes done present a series of coordination dilemmas. Some partners spend their free time together; others spend free time with friends. For some partners, being happy together requires that the extravert not trample on the predilections of the introvert; for others, it requires capitalizing on partners' shared desires to socialize. Some partners have shared goals for the relationship, both reveling in defying social convention; others have divergent goals, one desperately seeking greater closeness while the other craves greater autonomy.

In a structural sense, partners are interdependent at the levels of life tasks, personality, and relationship goals because partners typically must coordinate activities in each of these respects (see Chapter 1, p. 2). In a lived sense, the nature of interdependence varies substantially across relationships because partners are interdependent in different ways and with different results. Interdependence varies in two respects: (1) *influence*, that is, how often partners control each other's outcomes at each level of interdependence; and (2) *compatibility*, that is, how easy it is for partners to reconcile their preferences in the situations in which they are most interdependent. As we describe next, these sources of variability in interdependence determine the character or risk profile of the situations that provide the foundation for the relationship's personality. This *risk profile* captures the content and tractability of the conflicts of interest partners routinely encounter (see Chapter 5). In relationships with a low risk profile, partners have largely compatible preferences in the domains in which they influence each other the most. Partners in such relationships encounter more conflicts of interest offering much to be gained through cooperation and little to be lost through dependence. In relationships with a high risk profile, partners have largely incompatible preferences in the domains in which they influence each other the most. Partners in such relationships encounter more conflicts of interest with much to be gained through cooperation, but much to be lost through exploitation.[2]

Variability in Influence

Variability in the degree to which partners influence each other's outcomes at the levels of life tasks, personality, and relationship goals determines the predominant content of conflicts of interest. Consider life tasks. Parents have more to do together at the level of life tasks than childless couples. Parents not only negotiate cleaning, laundry, and dishwashing responsibilities, but they also negotiate diapering, play-date, and homework responsibilities. Because most parents are more interdependent in life tasks than most nonparents, parents are likely to encounter more conflicts of interest in this domain than nonparents. Similarly, childless couples without the financial resources to pay someone else to cook and clean are likely to encounter more conflicts of interest over the allocation of life tasks than childless couples with the financial freedom to outsource such responsibilities.

Now consider personality and relationship goals. Ron and Gayle each have to be at least somewhat selfless to successfully coordinate how much time to spend socializing because Gayle is extraverted and Ron is introverted. If they were both gregarious by nature, no such sacrifices would be needed. As another example, parents who aspire to be each other's best friends and confidants also have greater opportunities for conflicts over relationship goals than partners who aspire only to be parents. Being confidants first and parents second requires finding ways to mesh Gayle's penchant for football with Ron's affinity for fine wine and foreign films. It also requires ensuring that Gayle's career ambitions do not exact too great a toll on Ron's aspirations for time together as a couple and an idyllic family life. For Sally and Harry, however, being parents first and friends a remote second limits the bulk of their potential conflicts of interest to ones directly involving the coordination of household and parenting tasks.

Variability in Compatibility

Variability in the degree to which partner interests are compatible determines the tractability of the predominant conflicts of interest. For instance, in daily life Gunter and Lastri and Harry and Sally similarly influence one another's outcomes at the level of practical tasks. But Gunter and Lastri's conflicts in this domain are less risky overall because each happened to bring compatible attitudes and preferences toward life tasks to the relationship. Gunter takes pleasure in the laundry and dishes that Lastri loathes, and Lastri delights in the gardening that Gunter dreads. These complementary interests made household chore negotiations easy exchanges. Harry and Sally were not so lucky because their shared disdain for housework and gardening turned these same negotiations into zero-sum conflicts.

Because partners do not selectively assort on personality (Lykken & Tellegen, 1993), this element of chance also ensures that some couples encounter objectively more tractable personality and relationship goal conflicts. For instance, people with different attachment styles possess different goals within relationships (Mikulincer & Shaver, 2003). Those who are secure are comfortable relying on others and comfortable having others rely on them. Those who are avoidant value autonomy and independent pursuits and prefer that their partner not rely on them too much for support. Those who are anxious-ambivalent want to merge completely with their partner and perceive solitary pursuits as a rejection of the relationship. The pairing of an avoidant and an anxious-ambivalent partner will likely sample more situations involving power asymmetries than the pairing of two secure partners. In the former case, the partner who desires less closeness can control interactions simply by moving away (Christensen & Heavey, 1990). The pairing of such insecure types creates more intractable conflicts than the pairing of two secures because the avoidant partner possesses disproportionate power to be selfish.

The element of chance in personality matching also means that couples vary in the degree to which they perceive tractable conflicts at each level of interdependence. In relationships where both partners are neurotic or low in self-esteem, preoccupation with rejection disposes both to magnify the losses to be had in even relatively safe conflicts of interest (Murray, Rose, et al., 2002). In contrast, partners who are both agreeable and high in self-esteem are likely to perceive greater commonality in such situations. They are also more likely to trust enough in the other to make their personal preferences in such situations clear (Perunovic & Holmes, 2008). In contrast, the pairing of a more neurotic and a more agreeable partner might create more frequent exposure to situations in which personal goals are discordant and unclear to each partner.

Summary

Through various combinations of choice and random luck, some couples build their relationship on situation foundations that offer great potential for gain, some build on situation foundations that offer great potential for loss, and some build on situation foundations that offer a good mixture of both possibilities. The profile of the risks contained in these situations sets the seeds for the relationship's emerging personality. In lower-risk relationships, partners face fewer conflicts of interest, and the conflicts they do face are relatively easy to coordinate. In higher-risk relationships, partners face more frequent and more serious conflicts of interest at each level of interdependence, and the conflicts they face are comparatively difficult to coordinate.

At this point a caveat is in order. Partners are not forever "good" fits or "bad" fits. The risk profile of the relationship is dynamic rather than static. Preferences, personalities, and relationship goals can change as the relationship progresses. With time, Gayle's greater extraversion may increase how much Ron enjoys socializing with friends, lessening this potential source of conflict within the marriage. New and more serious conflicts may also arise with points of transition, such as moving in together or having a first child. Such events create new situations to be negotiated (e.g., 3 A.M. chauffeur), in which partners can discover entirely new compatibilities and incompatibilities. We return to this point in Chapter 10.

GENOTYPIC VARIABILITY IN PERSONALITY: SITUATIONS, TRUST, AND CORRECTION

How do the situations partners routinely encounter create genotypic variability in the relationship's personality? That is, how do the situations partners routinely encounter determine which particular if–then rules become a stronger mental habit? We use the term *habit* to capture the accessibility of the if–then rules for vigilance, goal orientation, and goal implementation in memory (Higgins, 1996; Wood & Neal, 2007). Figures

8.2 and 8.3 take us inside the mind of Sally and Gayle. These figures capture their if–then rule habits through two associative network models. The circles correspond to the "if" and "then" components of each rule. Thicker paths connecting "if" to "then" reflect stronger habits. That is, thicker paths reflect more accessible if–then rules. Plus signs reflect positive associative links between rule components; minus signs reflect negative associative links between rule components.

Let's look at Sally's rule habits (Figure 8.2). Frequently encountering high-risk situations with Harry in the kitchen gave her lots of practice applying the if–then rules for vigilance, orienting avoidance, and restricting commitment. Because these rules for self-protection are so accessible within her relationship representations, Sally cannot help but assiduously monitor Harry's responsiveness and respond quickly and vigorously to any perceived infraction. A closer look at Figure 8.2 also reveals specialization in Sally's if–then rule habits. She has now had so much practice correcting the goal to connect that wanting to be closer to Harry now automatically primes her goal to self-protect (and its associated strategies

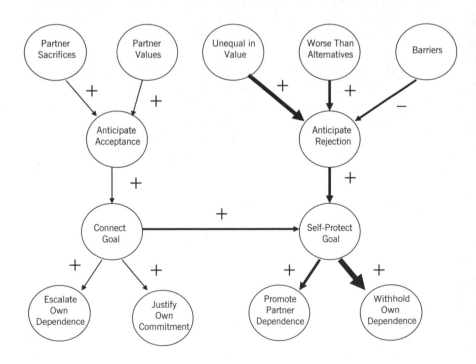

FIGURE 8.2. Mental habits of rule use in Sally's high-risk relationship.

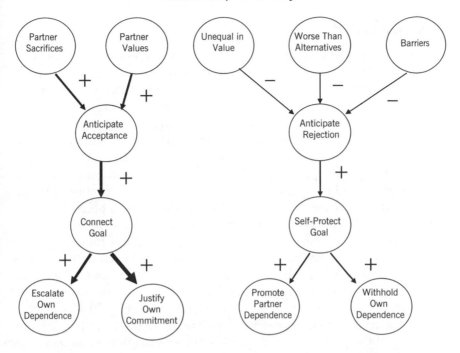

FIGURE 8.3. Mental habits of rule use in Gail's low-risk relationship.

for promoting the partner's and withholding her own dependence). Now let's look at Gayle's rule habits (Figure 8.3). Frequently encountering low-risk situations with Ron gave her lots of practice applying the if–then rules for orienting approach by escalating her own dependence and justifying her commitment. Because these rules for seeking connection are so accessible, Gayle rarely questions her value to Ron and easily compensates the costs she incurs when she puts her outcomes in Ron's hands and takes his outcomes into her own hands.

We turn now to the question of exactly how some of the if–then rules the interdependent mind supplies become a stronger if–then habit. That is, we describe exactly how the if–then rules for self-protection became more accessible for Sally, whereas the if–then rules for seeking connection became more accessible for Gayle. We also describe how Sally developed the idiosyncratic habit to self-protect when she wants to connect. That is, we describe how specialized if–then rules develop. We describe the three factors that create such variability in Sally and Gayle's if–then rule habits in turn: objective risk, trust, and correction.

Objective Risk

The objective risks in the situations partners encounter most often provide one source of variability in if–then rule accessibility. Sally gets more practiced in applying the if–then rules for self-protection the more often she finds herself in high-risk situations where Harry has a strong temptation to be selfish. That is, objective situation exposure promotes some mental habits of rule use over other habits of rule use. Habits are situation bound (Wood & Neal, 2007). Passing by the newsstand triggers the purchase of the morning paper, passing by the café triggers the consumption of a favorite snack, and the clock striking 11 P.M. triggers preparations for bed. If–then rule habits are no different. For specific rules to become a habit, the situations that provoke the rule need to occur with some frequency.

In the process of making rules a habit, objective situations matter because objective situations partly control how often each if–then rule is activated. In low-risk relationships, partners are more compatible. They face fewer conflicts of interest at each interdependence level, and the conflicts they do face are easier to coordinate. The situations partners encounter most often in such relationships therefore highlight the potential gains to be had at the partner's hands. Such situations disproportionately activate the if–then rules for orienting the goal to connect (i.e., "if partner accepting, then connect"), and implementing the goal to connect (i.e., "if connect goal, then escalate own dependence," "if connect goal, then justify own commitment").

In high-risk relationships, partners are less compatible. They face more conflicts of interest at each level of interdependence, and the conflicts they face are harder to coordinate. The situations partners encounter most often in such relationships therefore highlight the potential costs to be had at the partner's hands. Such situations disproportionately activate the if–then rules for vigilance, orienting the goal to self-protect (i.e., "if partner rejecting, then self-protect"), and implementing the goal to self-protect (i.e., "if self-protect goal, then escalate partner dependence," "if self-protect goal, then withhold own dependence").

Models of attitudes, habit, and stereotyping assume that frequent associations between cues and responses compel stronger behavioral leanings (Fazio, 1986; Kunda & Spencer, 2003; Wood & Neal, 2007). This supposition suggests that repeated exposure to low-risk situations increases the accessibility of the rules for orienting and implementing connectedness goals in memory by strengthening the association between signals (i.e., "if") and responses (i.e., "then"). Because Gayle often finds herself in situations that highlight gains, such exposure repeatedly activates the goal orientation rules linking acceptance expectancies to connect goals and the associated propensities to escalate dependence and justify costs. Because Sally often finds herself in situations that highlight losses, such exposure repeatedly activates the if–then rules linking rejection expectancies to self-protection goals and the associated propensities to promote Harry's dependence and withhold her own dependence on him.

Trust

The subjective risks partners perceive in the situations they encounter most often provide a second source of variability in rule accessibility. In the process of making rules a habit, chronic trust in a partner's commitment matters because the level of situational risk partners perceive most often also determines how much practice they get in applying each if–then rule. Being less trusting motivates people to assiduously monitor cues that signal their value to their partner, making the if–then vigilance rules more accessible (Holmes & Rempel, 1989; Murray, Holmes, & Collins, 2006). Being less trusting also disposes people to perceive greater risk in ambiguous conflicts of interest (Holmes & Rempel, 1989; Murray, Bellavia, et al., 2003). Sally's perceptual bias to perceive greater risk disproportionately activates the if–then rules for escalating Harry's dependence on her and limiting her own dependence on him. Being more trusting, Gayle amplifies the gains to be had in such situations, a perceptual bias that disproportionately activates the if–then rules for escalating dependence and justifying its costs.

Correction

The motivation and opportunity to correct poorly fitting if–then rules provides a third source of variability in rule accessibility. It also provides a mechanism for the development of specialized or idiosyncratic rules. As we saw in Chapters 6 and 7, trust in the partner's commitment motivates people to correct if–then rules for pursuing state goals to connect or self-protect that conflict with chronic goal pursuits (Murray, Aloni, et al., 2009; Murray, Derrick, et al., 2008; Murray, Holmes, et al., 2009). When Sally was staring at the empty ice tray, being less trusting motivated her to correct her automatic inclination to approach the sheepish Harry. In that situation, she also had the executive strength needed to correct this impulse, and as a result, Harry ended up on the receiving end of a rebuke rather than an ice tray.

Practice in correcting specific if–then rules has two interrelated effects on Sally's (and Gayle's) rule habits. First, repeatedly correcting a specific rule decreases its motivating power in memory. Correction essentially dissociates the "if" from the preset "then." The more often Sally curbs her impulse to justify her commitment to Harry, the less likely she is to be tempted to do so in the future. The stereotyping literature makes a similar point. Curbing stereotypes whenever they come to mind is thought to be critical in undoing one's automatic or unconscious prejudices (Monteith, 1993). Second, greater practice in correction can eventually impose a new or specialized "then," one that might become automatic with practice and no longer require the intervention of conscious will to be deployed. That has happened for Sally. She is now so suspicious of Harry in the domain of household chores that her slightest impulse to depend on him again now automatically activates her goal to self-protect. The stereotyping literature again makes a similar point. People flexibly activate and suppress even highly accessible stereotypes to meet the goals that are most salient in the moment (Kunda & Spencer, 2003). For instance, when people want to embrace the personal praise offered by a black doctor, they automatically suppress the negative stereotype of African Americans as incompetent and activate the positive stereotypes of doctors as competent. When people instead want to dispute that black doctor's criticisms, they activate the negative stereotype of African Americans and suppress the positive stereotype of doctors (Sinclair & Kunda, 1999).

But there is a very practical limit on the capacity to develop specialized or substitute if–then rules for negotiating conflicts of interest. Correction requires opportunity. Some relationships may simply afford more opportunities for correction than others. Some partners might simply have less capacity to correct because they are low in dispositional self-control (Muraven & Baumeister, 2000) or chronically short of the working memory capacity needed to correct for the influence of automatic impulses on behavior (Hofmann et al., 2008). The contexts in which some partners live might also afford fewer opportunities to correct because partners face more objectively stressful life circumstances. Having a colicky infant, a dissatisfying job, too many bills, or a house in a crumbling state of disrepair might be so demanding of one's executive resources that stressed partners have little capacity for conscious reflection left to correct the automatic activation of the if–then rules. In fact, in stressful times that tax cognitive resources, newlyweds are less equipped to overturn destructive habits of thought. In periods of greater stress, newlyweds let their partner's bad behaviors taint daily relationship satisfaction; in periods of lesser stress, they check or curb such relationship-threatening impulses

(Neff & Karney, 2009). Therefore, the chronic inability to correct, whether due to personal deficiency or chronic stress, could make learning new habits (or unlearning old ones) unlikely.

Summary

So how did these three sources of variability combine to produce Sally's resulting habits of rule use (Figure 8.2)? Being exposed to more objectively high-risk situations and perceiving greater risk in ambiguous situations gave Sally more practice applying the if–then rules for vigilance and self-protection than the if–then rules for connection. This differential practice increased the accessibility of the rules for vigilance and self-protection relative to the rules for connection in memory. Being less trusting also gave Sally more practice correcting the rules for escalating her own dependence and justifying her commitment than she had correcting the rules for restricting her own and Harry's commitment. Such practice eventually made it easier for her to suppress the automatic will to connect. It also supplied the opportunity to learn a new procedural rule. Repeatedly curbing her impulse to put her domestic outcomes in Harry's hands when his good humor or accepting smile tempted her to connect eventually created a new procedural or if–then association between wanting help and acting to self-protect.

HABITS OF RULE USE IN CONTEXT:
EMPIRICAL EXAMPLES

The particular if–then rules that become a habit impart a unique constitution to the automated will. They also impart a unique flavor to behavior. With a stronger (i.e., more accessible) if–then rule habit, a smaller provocation is sufficient to activate the "if" component of the rule. Because Sally has been burned so often by Harry's domestic slights, leaving one dish in the sink is now all it takes to make him seem worth avoiding (i.e., "if partner rejecting, then self-protect goal"). With a stronger habit, activating the "if" component of the rule also more quickly and uniformly provokes the contingent "then" component of the rule. Because Sally is so reactive to domestic slights, being in the kitchen almost always compels her to take herself out of Harry's hands (i.e., "if self-protect goal, then withhold own dependence").

Such different constitutions to the automated will also impart different constitutions to behavior (Fiske, 1992). In our way of thinking, Sally criticizes Harry more often than she praises him because the "withhold own dependence" rule is more accessible in memory than the "justify commitment" rule. She also runs Harry's errands more often than she asks him to run errands for her because she has a harder time correcting the "promote partner dependence" rule than the "escalate own dependence" rule. This logic implies that the if–then rule habits we attributed to Sally (Figure 8.2) and Gayle (Figure 8.3) should be evident in their behavior.

We now turn to the empirical literature to see if that is the case. So what exactly are we expecting to see? Stronger or more accessible if–then rules are more likely to govern perception and behavior than weaker or less accessible if–then rules (Higgins, 1996). As a result, Sally should be more likely to withdraw from Harry in a situation where she perceives him to be rejecting than Gayle is to withdraw from Ron. Why? Sally's greater history of high-risk kitchen encounters made the "withhold own dependence" rule more accessible in her memory and more likely to compel her behavior. In contrast, Gayle should be more likely than Sally to actually draw closer to Ron in a situation where she perceives him to be rejecting. Why? Being more trusting gave Gayle greater practice in correcting the automated impulse to self-protect. In reviewing the evidence, we compare the behavioral imprint of the if–then rules in more versus less risky relationships. We focus on trust (and its dispositional correlates) as a barometer of relationship risk for two reasons. First, trust controls the subjective appraisal of risk, and so trust plays a large role in controlling how much practice people get applying the if–then rules that are appropriate to low- and high-risk situations, respectively. Second, trust also controls how much practice people get correcting if–then rules that provide poor fits to chronic relationship goals. We start by looking for the behavioral imprint that the vigilance rules leave in more or less risky relationship circumstances, then we look for the imprint of the goal orientation rules, and finally, we look for the imprint of the goal implementation rules.[3]

If–Then Vigilance Rules

The if–then vigilance rules link salient cues to one's value to the partner to shifts in trust. Table 8.3 recapitulates these rules. These if–then rules dictate that being replaced is less likely (and trust more warranted) when the partner is willing to sacrifice self-interest, valuing of one's personal qualities, not superior in worth, unlikely to be poached by alternatives, or fettered to the relationship largely by constraints and obligations. As we saw in Chapter 3, the vigilance rules are more accessible and more likely to provoke correspondent revisions in inferences about the state of the

TABLE 8.3. The If–Then Rules for Controlling Vigilance

If partner sacrifices, then trust.

If partner values traits, then trust.

If equal in worth to partner, then trust.

If better than alternatives, then trust.

If barriers, then trust.

partner's commitment in less trusting (i.e., riskier) relationship circumstances.

A daily diary study of married couples aptly illustrates this point (Murray, Bellavia, et al., 2003; Murray, Griffin, et al., 2006). In this study, both members of long-term married couples completed a diary for 21 days. Each day they indicated what events had occurred inside (e.g., conflict) and outside the relationships (e.g., criticized at work), and they also indicated how accepted and how rejected they felt by their partner (i.e., state barometers of trust). People who were generally less trusting made cautious inferences that matched the dictates of the if–then rule for vigilance. Specifically, people who generally felt less valued by their partner expected their partner to be more rejecting on days after their partner failed to behave well, such as days after conflicts or on days after their partner had simply been in a bad mood. On the flip side, a low self-esteem Sally expected Harry to be more accepting of her on days when she outperformed him by succeeding at work. These inferences reveal the ready accessibility and application of the if–then rules for vigilance in less trusting relationship circumstances.

Very different appraisal processes are evident in more trusting relationship circumstances. In fact, people who generally trust in their partner's responsiveness seem practiced in the art of correcting the if-then" rules for vigilance. They did not anticipate their partner's rejection in the face of conflicts or evidence of their own personal deficiencies. Instead, they actually felt more accepted and loved by their partner on days after conflicts (Murray, Bellavia, et al., 2003) and on days after they had failed at work (Murray, Griffin, et al., 2006). Through such practice in correcting, they seemed to develop a specialized rule to offset or augment the vigilance rules. This specialized rule linked reasons to fear the partner's rejection to reasons to anticipate the partner's acceptance (i.e., "if partner selfish, then trust"; "if unequal in worth to partner, then trust"). How might such a compensatory rule develop for people who are more trusting? According to our MODE logic (Olson & Fazio, 2008), the acute prospect of rejection motivates more trusting people to decide to preserve their connection (provided the opportunity to do so is available). But, once the state goal to self-protect is activated, instead pursuing the chronic goal to connect likely requires added motivational incentive. Defensively exaggerating the reasons to anticipate the partner's acceptance could provide just this incentive (Brickman, 1987; Murray & Holmes, 1993). For instance, witnessing Ron's selfishness in a recent conflict over dishes might motivate a more trusting Gayle to remind herself of all the times Ron proved to be especially supportive in the past (Kunda, 1990).

If–Then Goal Orientation Rules

The if–then goal orientation rules link expectancies of partner acceptance (i.e., low risk) and expectancies of rejection (i.e., high risk) to the goals to approach gains and avoid losses, respectively (see Chapter 5). The accessibility and ease of correcting these rules again vary according to the general climate of risk in the relationship. In less trusting relationships, the if–then rule linking rejection expectancies to self-protection goals is more accessible and plays a more powerful role in orienting one's interpersonal goals. The rule linking acceptance expectancies to connectedness goals is more readily corrected or suppressed. In more trusting relationships, the if–then rule linking acceptance expectancies to connectedness goals is more accessible and plays a more powerful role in orienting action. The rule linking rejection expectancies to self-protection goals is more readily corrected or suppressed.

The behavioral evidence for such divergent rule habits is limited, but encouraging. Consider an experiment we conducted examining automated goal regulation (Murray, Derrick, et al., 2008, Experiment 7). We asked our experimental participants to think of a time when their partner had seriously disappointed them. We also asked them to indicate whether they had forgiven their partner. We asked this question to find out what "risk tag" participants attached to the transgression. We reasoned that forgiving a transgression tags this event as low risk in memory and not forgiving tags this event as high risk. Therefore, priming such transgressions gave us a means to prime different goal orientation rules. Namely, priming a forgiven transgression "tags" expectancies of partner acceptance in memory—the "if" component of the connect goal orientation rule. Priming an unforgiven transgression "tags" expectancies of partner rejection in memory—the "if" component of the self-protect goal orientation rule.

We then assessed the automatic activation of the "then" component of the goal orientation rule. We did this by looking at how quickly participants identified words associated with connectedness and self-protection goals. People who are more trusting, such as those high in self-esteem, perceive less risk (as we just saw). Such a bias toward perceiving the partner's acceptance gives them more practice applying the "if partner accepting, then connect" goal orientation rule. For them, this rule should be more readily activated (i.e., more accessible) and less readily suppressed. However, people who are less trusting, such as those low in self-esteem, perceive more risk. Such a bias toward perceiving the partner's rejection gives them more practice applying the "if partner rejecting, then self-protect" goal orientation rule. For them, this rule should be more readily activated and less readily suppressed.

So what did we find? Figure 8.4 presents the reaction times to self-protection words. Lower scores on this measure (i.e., faster reaction times to self-protection words) reflect the stronger activation of self-protection over connection goals. Higher scores on this measure (i.e., slower reaction

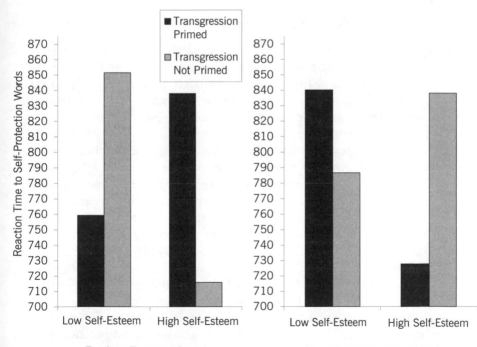

FIGURE 8.4. Reaction times to self-protection words as a function of transgression salience, forgiveness and self-esteem.

times to self-protection words) reflect the stronger activation of connection over self-protection goals. All of the experimental action centers around how low and high self-esteem people respond to forgiven transgressions (the results on the left-hand side of the figure). Because being more trusting increases the accessibility of the connect goal orientation rules in memory, we expected high self-esteem people to automatically connect (and not self-protect) in response to the activation of acceptance expectancies. They did. When high self-esteem people recalled a forgiven transgression, they were slower to identify self-protection words like *retreat*, *defense*, and *caution* as words (relative to controls). But being less trusting gives people more practice correcting or suppressing the goal-orientation rules for connection. So we expected low self-esteem people to suppress the goal to connect when we primed their expectancies of acceptance. They did. When low self-esteem people recalled a transgression they had forgiven, they were actually quicker to identify self-protection words. Rather than connect in response to acceptance, they self-protected.

If–Then Goal Implementation Rules

The if–then goal implementation rules regulate expressions of commitment. Two rules link the goal to connect to the automated will to escalate one's dependence and justify any costs incurred, respectively. The other two rules link the goal to self-protect to the automated will to withhold one's own and promote the partner's dependence, respectively. The accessibility and ease of correcting these if–then rules again vary with relationship risk. In more trusting relationships, the if–then rules for implementing the goal to connect are more accessible and more likely to result in heightened expressions of commitment. The rules for implementing self-protection are more readily corrected or suppressed. In less trusting relationships, the if–then rules for implementing the goal to self-protect are more accessible and more likely to result in restrictions on commitment. The rules for implementing connection are more readily corrected.

In looking for the behavioral imprint of such divergent rule habits, we focus on the "escalating" and "withholding" rules that govern expressions of commitment. We reviewed evidence for the behavioral effects of the "justify commitment" and "promote partner dependence" rules in Chapters 6 and 7, respectively. Sally can extend her commitment practically or symbolically. She can put her outcomes in Harry's hands by seeking his support or she can take his outcomes into her hands by sacrificing her time with friends so he can go see a basketball game. She can also invest herself more in the relationship by coming to value his qualities, such as his easy way playing with the children. Sally can also limit her commitment practically or symbolically. She can reject Harry's needs for support on days when he comes home frazzled after work or separate psychologically from him by focusing and dwelling on his faults. The bipolar nature of the escalating and withholding dependence rules raises an immediate practical problem. In any specific situation, extending her commitment to Harry also means that Sally is not restricting her commitment (and vice versa). Because moving away from the partner means that one is not moving toward the partner, the behavioral traces for the escalate and withhold dependence rules cannot be easily parsed.

For this reason, we focus on situations that clearly activated the goal to self-protect in reviewing the empirical literature. Because people in less trusting relationship circumstances are more likely to anticipate rejection (Murray, Holmes, & Collins, 2006), they are also more likely to experience the state activation of the goal to self-protect. As a result, they should get more practice applying the "withhold dependence" rule in specific situations. Making this rule a habit means that less trusting people should be more likely to predicate their willingness to approach their partner on the situation being low in risk. But people who are more trusting are likely to get more practice correcting this rule because withdrawing at the first sign of risk contradicts their chronic goal to connect. As this logic anticipates, the "withhold dependence" rule leaves a stronger behavioral imprint among people who are less trusting. This imprint appears in a variety of different forms in the literature. We review our favorite empirical examples of these dynamics next. We start by reviewing research that focused on trust itself as a proxy for relationship risk. We then turn to evidence that examined dispositional proxies for trust. Each of these lines of research reveal that experiencing greater rejection anxiety in a given situation puts stronger limits on commitment for people who are less trusting (relative to people who are more trusting).

Direct Measures of Trust

One of the more telling examples comes from a daily diary study involving married couples (Murray, Bellavia, et al., 2003). In this study, people who generally felt less valued by their partner responded to feeling acutely rejected by their partner one day by treating their partner in colder and more critical ways the next day. Feeling rejected essentially elicited the contingent response to withhold dependence and restrict commitment by divesting oneself from the partner. However, people who generally felt more valued by their partner effectively corrected or overturned this rule. They also seemed to possess a more specialized compensatory rule. Indeed, they overcorrected; they drew closer to their partner on days after they felt most rejected! Such findings suggest that people who are more trusting might learn a new rule as they gain experience in correction, a substitute rule that can make escalating dependence contingent on the presence of risk. Such effects might emerge precisely because countering the state goal to self-protect involves overjustifying the case for commitment. We return to this point in Chapters 10 and 11.

Dispositional Proxies for Trust

A diary study conducted by Overall and Sibley (2009) provides a great exemplar of this approach. In this study, participants completed a standardized diary describing each interaction they had with their romantic partner over a 2-week period. The researchers gauged the risks inherent to each interaction by asking participants to rate how much personal control they had over their own outcomes (low control = high risk). They gauged commitment expressions by asking participants to describe how negatively they behaved toward their partner (e.g., "I was critical and unpleasant toward my partner"). People high in attachment anxiety were more likely to react to risky (i.e., less controllable) situations by distancing themselves from their partner, suggesting the greater accessibility of the withhold rule.

Other findings within the attachment literature echo these findings. They also go further in pointing to rule correction for people who are less anxious. For instance, people high on attachment-related anxiety report feeling less close to their partner on high- than low-conflict days (Campbell et al., 2005). After discussing a serious relationship problem, people high in attachment anxiety also reported greater anger and hostility (as compared with controls, who discussed a minor problem). They also downplayed their feelings of commitment. In response to the same threat posed by discussing a major conflict, people low on attachment-related anxiety actually came to value their partner more (Simpson, Rholes, & Phillips, 1996). In a situation where they accurately inferred their partner's attraction to opposite-sex others, anxious people reported feeling less close to their partner (Simpson et al., 1999). But less anxious people felt even closer the better they discerned their *partner's* attraction to these tempting alternatives.[4]

Parallel behavioral traces of the "withhold dependence" rule are also evident in research utilizing global self-esteem as a dispositional proxy for trust. People with low self-esteem respond to induced anxieties about their partner's possible rejection by depending less on their partner as a source of self-esteem and comfort (Murray et al., 1998). They also evaluate their partner's qualities more negatively (Murray et al., 1998; Murray, Holmes, & Collins, 2002). However, high self-esteem people seem to decide to correct the "withhold dependence" rule. They respond to the experimental induction of self-doubts by reporting greater dependence on their partner as a resource for self-esteem (Murray et al., 1998) and by reporting greater feelings of closeness to that same partner (Murray, Rose, et al., 2002).

Specialized Rules: When Correction Becomes Automatic

The evidence that people who are more trusting sometimes draw closer to their partner in situations posing greater perceived risk of rejection raises an obvious question. Do such behavioral traces imply that making dependence contingent on the absence of risk is not a basic procedural or if–then feature of the interdependent mind? Given the evidence for the automatic activation of these rules we reviewed in Chapters 6 and 7, we do not think so. In our view, these differential behavioral imprints reveal the flexibility with which the interpersonal mind employs its if–then rules to motivate mutuality in responsiveness (see Chapters 6 and 7). Because less risky relationships lessen the need for vigilance, people who are more trusting correct the automated response to distance in response to risk when they have the force of will available to do so. With repeated corrections, drawing closer in response to rejection might itself gain the status of an automated but specialized rule. Indeed, drawing closer in response to risk might reflect such a highly rehearsed curbing of the automated will in more trusting relationships.

This brings us to a further caveat. The expression of the if–then rules is in a constant state of flux. The accessibility of the vigilance, goal orientation, and goal implementation rules changes as situations change within the relationship (see Chapters 10 and 11). The relative power of these rules also changes as people adopt new habits of thought that are better attuned to the climate of risk within their relationship. With time, Sally learned that Harry let her down domestically even when he was at his most cooperative and accepting. Through sheer force of corrective habit, she learned not to trust his smiles and laughs as a sign he might actually accede to a request to pick up his clothes. She supplied herself with a new and specialized rule in the "hot" domain of household chores, one that disputed the positive inferential cues to trust.

But learning a "new" rule does not necessarily supplant the "old" rule. The if–then rules the interpersonal mind supplies represent general solutions to the general problem of motivating responsiveness. Because these rules operate across situations, they have a long history of activation in memory (Collins & Read, 1994). Any propensities that develop as Sally (or Gayle) corrects these rules to fit their unique relationship circumstances solve new and specialized problems. Because these new rules build on the correction of the default rules, these specialized rules necessarily have a shorter history of activation in memory (Collins & Read, 1994). The differential accessibility of old (i.e., default) and new (i.e., specialized) rules raises an important limitation to the interpersonal mind's capacity to adjust to its risk circumstances. Because the default rules have a longer history of activation in memory, they may compete with the corrected ones even when they have outlived their utility. This logic builds on social cognitive reasoning about the structure of new and old attitudes and new and old attachment representations. Attitude theorists argue that new and old attitudes exist independently in memory, exerting distinct effects on judgment (Petty et al., 2006; Wilson et al., 2000). Attachment theorists also argue that working models include both generalized expectations (based on one's experience across relationship partners) and specific expectations about particular partners (Baldwin, 1992; Collins & Read, 1994; Rholes et al., 2001). Under stress, more negative general expectations can trump the influence of a more positive specific expectation because stress elicits more familiar and rehearsed behavioral patterns (Mikulincer & Shaver, 2003). So when she's stressed, Gayle might revert to the old habit to criticize Ron when he criticizes her in the kitchen because she isn't yet practiced enough in using her new rule to respond to such taunts with forgiveness. We return to this point in later chapters.

PHENOTYPIC VARIABILITY: MOTIVATIONAL INTERDEPENDENCE, RESPONSIVENESS, AND SATISFACTION

As we have seen, the if–then rule habits we have attributed to low- and high-risk relationships (see Figures 8.2 and 8.3) produce predictable behavioral imprints. Vigilant to rejection, a less trusting Sally sees her broken diet and burnt meatloaf as an omen of Harry's rejection. With rejection imminent, she reduces her dependence on Harry. Not wanting to be hurt, she distracts his attention from her weight (and her meatloaf) by criticizing his failure to cut the grass and take the car to the mechanic. Not nearly as vigilant to rejection, a more trusting Gayle perceives Ron's offhand comment about her diet as a sign of Ron's support and acceptance. With rejection remote, she resists pulling away from Ron in risky situations and instead seeks out those opportunities to draw closer. In fact, she typically finds all the more to value in him on those occasions when drawing closer imposes costs on her own goal pursuits. Given such divergent interaction styles, it's perhaps not surprising that Gayle is considerably more satisfied in her marriage to Ron than Sally is in her marriage to Harry.

As these examples illustrate, relationships have different phenotypes. They look different to outsiders and they feel different to the insiders within the relationship. Some couples are happy together; others are miserable. Some partners take joy in each other as best friends; others take comfort in each other as necessary cogs in the machinery of domestic life. Some couples rarely emote; other couples cannot stifle their attraction to each other; other couples cannot stop fighting. If–then rule habits create such visible differences in relationship satisfaction and quality by determining the type of mutuality in responsiveness partners practice. In formal terms, the if–then rules that are applied most often direct whether behavioral coordination involves partners relying on each other for the exchange of small favors, assigning each other circumscribed role obligations, or seeking shared identities and personal goals. In so doing, the if–then rules that become a habit control how satisfied each partner comes to be in the marriage. Varying habits of rule use create and reinforce variability in the type of mutuality in responsiveness partners practice through two sources: (1) behavioral reciprocity and (2) motivational interdependence. We explain each in turn. We then explain how the variable expressions of responsiveness that result can shape each partner's experience of satisfaction.

Behavioral Reciprocity

The role that behavioral reciprocity plays in reinforcing variability in the type of mutuality partners practice is straightforward. By controlling expressions of commitment, the if–then rules that are more accessible and the if–then rules that are more readily corrected control what type of responsive behavior each partner is likely to solicit and provide. In Sally's case, her frequent concerns about Harry's rejection constantly goad her to do something to increase his practical or instrumental dependence on her, from making his mother's doctor's appointment, to running his errands, to making his lunch. Because social behavior elicits a pull to reciprocate (Cialdini & Trost, 1998; Collins & Miller, 1994; Kenny, 1994), Harry reflexively does similar favors for Sally, routinely taking her car to the mechanic and doing her share of the gardening. Through reciprocation, they developed a mutually responsive behavior pattern in which they comfortably respond to each other's very practical needs. In Gayle's case, frequently anticipating Ron's acceptance often motivates her to solicit his support when she has work-related anxieties. Because such emotional self-disclosures elicit a pull to disclose in kind (Collins & Miller, 1994), Ron reflexively makes similarly revealing self-disclosures. Through reciprocation, they develop a mutually responsive behavior pattern wherein they routinely make the necessary sacrifices to be each other's main sources of support. In each relationship, the if–then rules that are most routinely applied elicit the kind of mutuality that is commensurate with the perceived risks each partner perceives in conflicts of interest.

Motivational Interdependence: Making Sense of Commitment

The role that motivational interdependence plays in reinforcing variability in the type of mutuality partners practice requires more explanation. Trust and commitment are motivated but reasoned sentiments (Kunda, 1990). In the process of interaction, partners construct reasons or stories to make sense of their relationship (Harvey & Omarzu, 1997; Murray & Holmes, 2009). Each partner's if–then rule habits constrain the composition of the stories he or she tells by delimiting the contents of the behavioral interaction base that is available to explain commitment. Motivated to protect herself against Harry's exploitation, Sally works assiduously to secure Harry's dependence on her, but she resists depending on him for any more than the easiest of favors. In behaving in this way, she gives herself reason to attribute Harry's commitment to what she does for him and Harry more than enough reason to explain his own commitment in the same way. By making some explanations for commitment more plausible than others, the if–then rules constrain and reinforce the type of mutuality in responsiveness partners practice. We break this dynamic down into its three component parts. First, we explain how Sally's if–then rule habits compel unique expressions of responsiveness (i.e., commitment) that inform her and Harry's attributions. Second, we describe how the attributions Harry and Sally then reach in explaining the meaning of their marriage make them motivationally interdependent. Third, we describe how the stories Harry and Sally tell limits (or frees) commitment in ways that reinforce behavioral expressions of responsiveness that are best suited to a relationship's risks. As we will see, mutuality in responsiveness depends on partners explaining their commitments in similar ways. Without such a shared sense of the meaning of their commitment, power imbalances develop and make it difficult to sustain fluid and mutually responsive interactions at any level of interdependence.

Rule Use Informs Attributions

Classic models of attribution point to three varying ways in which people can explain their relationships to themselves (e.g., Kelley, 1967). People can attribute commitment to intrinsic factors, such as the value placed on the partner's inherent qualities (e.g., sense of humor, intelligence, athleticism). They can attribute commitment to instrumental factors, such as the value put on the tangible benefits the partner provides (e.g., cooking, child rearing, social support). They can also attribute commitment to extrinsic factors, such as the barriers to dissolving the relationship imposed by pressures from family or religious prohibitions against divorce. Sally's if–then rule habits shape the attributions she makes for her own commitment and Harry's commitment by shaping the constitution of the behavioral interaction or evidence base that informs such sentiments (Murray & Holmes, 2009).

In most Western marriages, being intrinsically motivated and perceiving such motivation in the partner sets a qualitatively distinct relationship tone. Such attributions provide an unequivocal and promotive guide for behavior (Rempel et al., 1985). Experiencing her commitment as motivated by Ron's intrinsic value gives Gayle the resolve she needs to sacrifice on his behalf. Experiencing Ron's commitment as motivated by her intrinsic value to him also gives Gayle reason to expect similar sacrifices from him. By contrast, attributions to instrumental motivations provide a more tentative and preventive guide for behavior because commitment is perceived to be contingent on one's continued provision of tangible benefits. In making such attributions, Sally might refrain from asking Harry to sacrifice his plans for her unless she could think of a way to compensate him. She might also hesitate to benefit Harry unless she could be guaranteed a later benefit herself. Attributions to extrinsic motivations provide an unequivocal and avoidant guide for behavior. In making such attributions, Sally might only expect Harry to do the favors she compelled him to do and she might be similarly grudging in her willingness to sacrifice for Harry.

Think about Harry and Sally's relatively high-risk relationship. Unhappily for them, Harry is avoidant in attachment style and Sally is preoccupied in attachment style. This personality incompatibility means that they encounter many situations that highlight the potential for loss because Harry wants his autonomy and Sally wants to cling. In fact, a good number of domestic conflicts arise because Harry interprets Sally's requests for his help with the dishes or laundry as an affront to his independence. Sally interprets his loafing as evidence that he does not want to be with her. For both, frequent exposure to high-risk situations makes the if–then rules linked to self-protection goals highly accessible. Being chronically less trusting also makes it easier for both to correct the if–then rules linked to connectedness goals. Such shared habits of rule use constrain how Sally (and Harry) can explain their commitment to each other.

For Sally, preoccupation with keeping Harry committed compels her to do things for him, from packing his lunch to chauffeuring his mother, in an effort to make him "owe" her. While extracting some measure of responsiveness, these efforts have made the instrumental reasons and constraints governing Harry's commitment very salient to Sally. She hesitates to trust him, vigilant that Harry's dependence on her might disappear if she let up her efforts to keep him contained. Her well-rehearsed tendency to correct her impulses to compensate for Harry's faults also distances Sally from any intrinsic reasons she might have for her commitment. Harry's limited responsiveness makes Sally still more resigned to her commitment by making the barriers keeping her in the marriage (e.g., children) more salient. For Harry, preoccupation with keeping his outcomes out of Sally's hands compels him to behave in ways—like keeping his work-related worries to himself—that limit Sally's opportunities to demonstrate responsiveness. Through his avoidance, Harry constrains her role to the instrumental housekeeper role that she has come to resent so much. By checking any impulse he has to value Sally more when she invariably thwarts his goals, he also stays unhappily resigned in his commitment.

Now consider Ron and Gayle's relatively low-risk relationship. They are both reasonably secure in attachment style. They are also each highly trusting. They encounter many situations that highlight the potential for gain because they would both prefer to do things together rather than apart. Cooking the meals and doing the dishes represents something more to them than a series of onerous tasks to be divided. It represents an opportunity for togetherness. Frequent exposure to low risk-situations makes the if–then rules for connection highly accessible. Anticipating acceptance allows Gayle to ask for Ron's support even when he truly seems preoccupied. This gives him multiple opportunities to demonstrate the value he puts on meeting her needs. Anticipating acceptance also motivates Ron to value Gayle all the more because she interfered with his own goal pursuits. Gayle's trust in Ron motivates her to correct any impulse she has to respond with anger if he breaks a promise to do his share of the household chores. Such shared if–then rule habits flag the great value each puts upon meeting the other's needs and on the intrinsic or inherent value of the marriage itself.[5]

Attributions Inform Motivational Interdependence

Because partners can develop different if–then habits of rule use, they can also compose more or less similar stories to explain their commitments to each other. The similarities and differences in the reasons Sally has for trusting in Harry, the reasons Harry has for trusting in Sally, and the reasons Sally and Harry each have for his or her own commitment brings us back to the fourth level of interdependence we introduced in Chapter 2. Partners are interdependent in trust and commitment. Because Harry explains his commitment to Sally and her commitment to him in ways, they are motivationally interdependent. There are three facets of motivational interdependence that are crucial in understanding how mutuality in responsiveness results (or not). First, partners can be more or less similar in their reasons for trusting in the other's commitment (i.e., similarity in trust motivations). Second, partners can be more or less similar in their reasons for being more or less committed (i.e., similarity in commitment motivations). Third, the reasons underlying each partner's level of trust can correspond to the other's reasons for commitment to a greater or lesser extent (i.e., understanding of commitment motivations).

Motivational Interdependence Reinforces Responsiveness

So how does similarity in trust and commitment motivations reinforce particular types of mutual expressions of responsiveness over others (e.g., exchanging household tasks vs. exchanging childhood hopes and dreams)? Similarity in trust motivations governs the degree to which partners ask similar things of each other. That is, similarity in trust motivations governs the degree to which partners solicit similar expressions of commitment. For instance, when Sally believes that Harry's commitment is motivated by instrumental factors and Harry believes that Sally's commitment is similarly motivated, each is only likely to ask one another for practical and easily met favors (e.g., taking Harry's mother to the dentist, fixing Sally's car, giving Harry advice about his diet). Similarity in commitment motivations governs the degree to which partners do similar things for each other. That is, similarity in commitment motivations governs the degree to which partners make similar expressions of commitment. For instance, when Ron's commitment is motivated by Gayle's intrinsic value to him and Gayle's commitment is motivated by Ron's intrinsic value to her, each is likely make career sacrifices to better the other's career. Understanding the basis of the partner's commitment governs the degree to which people make what they ask contingent on what the partner is actually willing to provide given the basis of the partner's commitment.

Ron and Gayle have congruent motivations in each of these respects. They each correctly assume the other's commitment is intrinsically motivated. Given reciprocity in their experience of commitment, their interactions naturally gravitate toward situations that involve higher levels of risk and high levels of reward (e.g., revealing important career goals for a partner's approval). Harry and Sally also have congruent expectations in each of these respects. However, they each correctly assume the other is committed to the relationship largely because they could not otherwise fulfill their role as parents. Given reciprocity in their experience of commitment, their interactions naturally gravitate toward coordinating household roles, such as mother-in-law chauffeur and mechanical expert, because they can at least count on each other in this respect (Berscheid & Regan, 2005).

By contrast, dissimilarity in trust and commitment motivations creates power asymmetries that make coordinating fluid and mutually responsive interactions much less likely (Murray & Holmes, 2009). Imagine Sally perceived Harry as largely extrinsically motivated (because she is inclined to self-protective rule habits), but he perceives her as more intrinsically motivated (because he is not inclined to such self-protective rule habits). Such dissimilarity in their reasons for trusting is likely to make behavioral coordination difficult. Being more suspicious of Harry's motivations, Sally is likely to avoid asking Harry for the sacrifices he more readily solicits. Harry is also likely to press Sally to make the kinds of disclosures he feels safe revealing to her but she fears revealing to him. Over time, the violations of basic requirements for commitment reciprocity that such divergent expectations create may foretell conflict. Indeed, such violations may result in Harry coming to see his trust in Sally as more extrinsically based precisely because his initial expressions of trust are not met by her equal expression.

Something altogether different might happen if one partner's commitment is intrinsically motivated, whereas the other partner's commitment is more extrinsically motivated. Imagine that Ron is more willing to sacrifice for Gayle than vice versa. As time goes on, partner interactions would grow more negative because Ron makes disproportionate sacri-

fices. As the more giving partner's actions go unreciprocated, the resulting fears of being taken for granted might amplify broader concerns about
equity and justice. Such concerns might in turn erode the more intrinsic
partner's commitment to being responsive, thereby increasing the objective risk inherent in conflicts of interest (Clark & Grote, 1998). In such
ways, the power imbalances that come with dissimilarity in commitment
motivations make mutually responsive interactions impossible (Sprecher
et al., 2006). We return to the issues raised here in Chapters 11 and 12.

Responsiveness Shapes Relationship Satisfaction

The personality of Ron and Gayle's marriage differs markedly from the
personality of Harry and Sally's marriage. Ron and Gayle take relatively
risky opportunities to express their commitment to each other. Ron not
only takes over Gayle's grocery-shopping duties on occasion (responsiveness at the level of life-task conflicts), but he sympathetically responds
to Gayle's complaints about his mother's interference in their conflicts
(responsiveness at the level of relationship goal conflicts). For her part,
Gayle often gives up her desire for more social outings to accommodate
to Ron's desire for solitude (responsiveness at the level of personality
conflicts). Harry and Sally tread much more cautiously and limit their
reliance on each other to those life tasks that can be most easily traded
(e.g., mother chauffeuring for car maintenance). Our model of the interdependent mind assumes that Ron and Gayle's greater satisfaction in their
marriage is an outcome of the unique expression of their relationship's
personality (in both if–then rule habits and the resulting type of mutual
responsiveness they practice). Let us explain.

From a classic perspective on interdependence, satisfaction is a function of the rewards partners experience in interacting (Kelley, 1979).
But the value of the rewards to be gained increases as interdependence
increases from life tasks, to personality, to relationship goals. Gayle gains
more when Ron tempers his introversion to accommodate her gregariousness than she gains when he takes her turn washing the dishes. This
means that the behavioral expression of the relationship's personality
through the type of mutuality partners practice puts an upper limit on the
rewards to be gained. In this way, if–then habits of rule use put an upper
bound on satisfaction. Having restricted interactions to limited, lower levels of interdependent situations (i.e., life tasks), Harry and Sally are stably together, but only as satisfied as the rewards afforded by adhering to
meshed instrumental roles allow them to be. Having placed no such limits on their interdependence, Ron and Gayle by contrast are much more

satisfied. We return to the issue of how if–then rule use affects satisfaction in Chapters 10 and 11.

Directing Mental Habits: Approach and Avoidance Goals

As we have seen, if–then rule habits elicit risk-appropriate expressions of commitment, and thereby elicit phenotypic variability in how personality is expressed. Self-protective habits tend to restrict expressions of responsiveness (i.e., commitment) to lower levels of interdependence (e.g., life tasks, exchanging laundry for dishwashing). Connectedness-promoting habits tend to broaden responsiveness to higher levels of interdependence (e.g., providing support for life goals). No research to date has provided a direct test of the effects of if–then habits on mutual expressions of responsiveness per se. However, indirect evidence suggests that the chronic goal orientations that consume the mind do create qualitatively different relationship experiences. A fascinating program of research conducted by Shelly Gable and her colleagues provides a case in point (Gable, 2005; Gable & Poore, 2008; Impett, Gable, & Peplau, 2005; Impett, Strachman, Finkel, & Gable, 2008).

These researchers examine how approach and avoidance motivations influence affect, cognition, and behavior in romantic relationships. Approach motives involve a preoccupation with obtaining positive outcomes, such as enhanced intimacy; avoidance motives involve a preoccupation with avoiding negative outcomes, such as conflict (Gable, 2005). In terms of our analysis, approach motives map onto habits of rule use linked to connectedness goals; avoidance motives map onto habits of rule use linked to self-protection goals. As our logic anticipates, approach and avoidance motives create qualitatively different types of relationship experiences, from shaping the meaning of daily events to keeping time from squelching sexual desire. For people strongly motivated by approach, daily feelings of relationship satisfaction are a comment on what went right that day. People strongly motivated by approach are more satisfied on days when they feel more passionately toward the partner. For people strongly motivated by avoidance goals, daily relationship satisfaction is a comment on what did not go wrong. People strongly motivated by avoidance are more satisfied on days when they feel less anxious and insecure (Gable & Poore, 2008). Making daily sacrifices for the partner to obtain positive outcomes, such as the partner's happiness, predicts greater daily satisfaction; making daily sacrifice to avoid negative outcomes, such as the partner's anger, predicts less relationship daily satisfaction (Impett et al., 2005). Finally, being motivated by approach goals even protects people from suffering the declines in sexual desire that come as the relationship progresses from the initial throes of infatuation to deeper levels of interdependence (Impett et al., 2008).

WHEN THE INTERDEPENDENT MIND FAILS

The differential effects of if–then rule habits that serve self-protection and connectedness goals offer a partial answer to the last question we posed for this chapter. Why do some relationships fail? Relationships can fail when partners are disproportionately self-protective in their rule habits. Elaborating this point occupies us for the rest of this book.

We only foreshadow our arguments here. Let's return to the trust paradox introduced in Chapter 3. To gain objective reason to trust, people first need to take the risk of trusting. Those mixed-motive situations that offer the partner the most temptation to be selfish offer diagnostic opportunities to learn about the partner's trustworthiness. To learn about Ron's commitment in these types of situations, Gayle needs to leap before she looks. She must first take the risk of putting her outcomes in Ron's hands before she can find out whether he is truly committed to her (Kelley, 1979; Holmes & Rempel, 1989; Simpson, 2007). The interdependent mind is generally averse to taking such risks. As we have seen, such high-risk situations provoke the automated goal to self-protect and keep one's outcomes out of the partner's hands until it is safe.

For the permanent foundation of trust (and commitment) to develop, something needs to happen to nudge or trick the mind into perceiving high-risk situations as low in risk. Experience can nudge. Experiencing the benefits of the partner's responsiveness in low-risk situations can provide fledgling feelings of trust sufficient to anticipate responsiveness in higher risk situations. In fact, the initial stages of relationship development naturally nudge the mind to ignore risk. As we discuss in Chapter 9, partners are not only awash in the neurochemistry of attraction and sex, but they selectively focus interactions around shared interests and activities (Holmes & Rempel, 1989). As we discuss in Chapters 10 and 11, personal dispositions can also nudge. Being higher in self-esteem or secure in attachment style can foster fledgling feelings of trust in the partner sufficient to overanticipate responsiveness (Mikulincer & Shaver, 2003; Murray et al., 2001).

The paradoxical aspect of trust suggests that the interdependent mind can fail to elicit satisfying interactions when it cannot be readily nudged. Namely, relationship instability can result when partners cannot gratify each other's needs because they experience excessive exposure to high-risk situations, because they have chronic difficulty establishing trust, or both. Sally got pregnant within months after she and Harry first started dating. This abrupt life transition—one that required her to quit college—created excess exposure to high-risk situations early on in their marriage. These situations stalled the growth of trust. Sally's attachment anxiety and Harry's avoidance only compounded their difficulties. They each got locked into self-protective rule habits. Because Sally once aspired to a professional life outside the home, she now largely resents Harry for the instrumental roles they each fill. Harry is simply tired of being a constant disappointment to her. Yet they have little hope of breaking out of these roles because they so rarely perceive any opportunity for gain in the situations they encounter.

SUMMARY, CAVEAT, OMISSION, AND LOOKING FORWARD

This chapter described how the interdependent mind creates each relationship's distinct personality. This relationship personality has both a genotype and a phenotype. At the level of its genotype, relationships differ in personality because partners make different if–then rules a habit. At the level of its phenotype, relationships differ in personality because partners are mutually responsive in different ways and with different consequences.

This chapter had five main points. First, relationships are built on different situational foundations that constrain what kinds of dispositions partners can express. The nature of the situational risks partners encounter varies across relationships for two reasons. Couples differ in how much they influence each other's outcomes at each level of interdependence, and they differ in how compatible their preferences are in their main domains of interdependence. In high-risk relationships, partners encounter many domains in which it is difficult to reconcile their interests; in low-risk relationships, they encounter few such domains of conflict. Second, the if–then rules that become a habit vary across relationships for three reasons. Partners differ in the objective risks they face, they differ in their perception of risk, and they differ in the motivation and opportunity to correct the automated will. Because it takes practice to make if–then rules a habit, partners who perceive more risk are more likely to develop the habit to be vigilant, avoid rejection, and restrict commitment. They are also more likely to develop the habit of correcting the if–then rules for connection.

In contrast, partners who perceive less risk are more likely to develop the habit to approach and extend commitment. They are also more likely to develop the habit of correcting the if–then rules for self-protection.

Third, the if–then rules partners make a regular practice or habit have a behavioral imprint. As we reviewed, partners in higher risk (i.e., less trusting) relationships are more likely to use ongoing events to gauge each other's commitment (using the vigilance rules), and they are also more likely to limit and restrict commitment at the first sign of rejection (using the goal orientation and goal implementation rules for self-protection). In contrast, partners in lower risk (i.e., more trusting) relationships are more likely to dispute the relevance of ongoing events to their partner's commitment (correcting the vigilance rules). They are also more likely to draw closer and seek stronger connections at the first sign of risk (correcting the goal orientation and goal implementation rules for self-protection). Fourth, the specific if–then rules that become a habit control behavioral expressions of responsiveness by controlling how partners explain their commitments to themselves. Because Sally so often applies the rule to promote Harry's dependence, she now sees his commitment as driven by the favors she provides. This limits her to soliciting the same types of instrumental favors from him that she provides to him. It also limits how much reason to be happy she can find in her marriage. Finally, the interdependent mind can fail to elicit any type of mutuality in responsiveness when it cannot be nudged into perceiving high-risk situations as low in risk (at least some of the time).

We should note one caveat before we proceed. More trusting couples do not uniformly experience low-risk situations and less trusting couples do not uniformly experience high-risk situations, our examples notwithstanding. Despite being compatible in most respects, Ron and Gayle do have some risky or "hot-button" issues in their marriage. Both lawyers, they can get more than a little competitive with each other professionally. Although Gayle hates to admit it, she envies Ron's successes in the courtroom. Especially when she's tired, her envy has been the source of all-too-pointed derisions of Ron's accomplishments. For another, Ron gets jealous of Gayle's male colleagues too readily, and his insecurity has spurred conflicts on more than one occasion. In these risky situations, Gayle and Ron both typically succumb to the automated will to self-protect. Despite experiencing near-constant strife over domestic chores, Harry and Sally also enjoy some safe or "cool-button" issues in their marriage. They both enjoy recreational time together with their children immensely, and their sexual goals and energies have stayed compatible (despite their conflicts). In these safe situations, Harry and Sally both typically succumb to the automated will to connect. Such texturing to the risk profile of each couple's marriage provides the situational foundation for both the erosion of trust (should Gayle's professional pettiness or Ron's jealousy get the best of them) and the growth of trust (should enjoyable times together ease Sally's domestic demands on Harry while increasing his motivation to be helpful). We return to these issues in Chapters 9 through 11.

Now that we have had the chance to fully develop our model of the interdependent mind, we turn to questions of application. In the next three chapters, we describe how relationships develop and change over time. As we will see, the situations that sow the seeds for the emergence of the relationship's personality also sow the seeds for its change. These situations change throughout the life cycle of the relationship (Kelley et al., 2003). In the throes of infatuation, partners may do little more than coordinate needs for sex, fun, and companionship. In such circumstances, the if–then rules for connectedness goals may dominate the relationship's personality. In the midst of diapers and colic, partners may do little more than coordinate the more onerous of childcare tasks. In such circumstance, the if–then rules for self-protection goals may dominate the relationship's personality. Throughout such varied life situations, partners who differ in their typical habits of rule use are likely to have disproportionate difficulty settling into mutually responsive and satisfying interactions patterns. We return to all of these issues in the chapters that follow. We begin with the initial stages of the relationship's development—that is, with lust and limerence!

NOTES

1. Friedrich Nietzsche, *Thus Spoke Zarathustra* (1883).
2. As we described in Chapter 5, situations vary in *content* because conflicts can arise in the coordination of life tasks, personality, or relationship goals. Situations vary in *type* because some conflicts of interest compel cooperation and others compel competition. Situations further vary in *features* because situations in which conflicting interests are hidden give the partner greater license to be selfish than situations in which conflicting interests are easily discerned. Conflicts of interest that require long-term sacrifices also give the partner more reason to be selfish than ones that require short-term kindnesses. These three parameters—content, type, and features—mark objective risk inherent in any particular situation by quantifying the partner's temptation to be selfish and the coincident urge to self-protect against exploitation. The relationship's risk profile presents a kind of statistical summary or

average of the content, type, and features of the situations that partners most often encounter in living together.

3. A relationship is generally higher in risk when one or both partners are less trusting.

4. Conceptually similar findings emerge using the dispositional tendency to anxiously expect rejection as a dispositional proxy for trust (Downey & Feldman, 1996). Women chronically high on rejection sensitivity respond to a potential partner's disinterest by evaluating that partner more negatively. Rejection-sensitive women are also more likely to initiate conflicts on days after they felt more rejected by their romantic partner, and simply priming rejection-related words automatically activates hostility-related thoughts for these women (Ayduk, Downey, Testa, Yen, & Shoda, 1999).

5. The attributions partners make for trust and commitment are not "pure" types, our examples notwithstanding. Ron and Gayle and Harry and Sally perceive both a mixture of intrinsic, instrumental, and extrinsic reasons governing their commitments. What sets these couples apart is the predominant strength of these motivations.

CHAPTER 9

Being Swept Away

How Passionate Love Makes It Natural to Connect

Who ever loved that loved not at first sight?
—CHRISTOPHER MARLOWE,
Hero and Leander (1598)

Christopher Marlowe's poem about a forbidden love captures a universal human condition – the experience of falling rapidly, tumultuously, hopelessly, and passionately in love (Fisher, 1998; Fisher, Aron, Mashek, Haifang, & Brown, 2002). In this besotted condition, the beloved's every word is wise, every touch is tingling, and every absence is agonizing (Aron, Fisher, Mashek, Strong, Haifang, & Brown, 2005; Tennov, 1979). Why is such a state of obsessive preoccupation the starting point for the majority of adult romantic relationships?

The risks inherent in initiating a romance certainly warrant trepidation. Think back to Harry and Sally's first date at a high school dance. As Harry led Sally onto the dance floor, he wiped his palms on his pants, wondering whether she might find him too tall and left-footed a partner. Days later, Sally sat by the phone, wondering whether Harry would call, fearing her joke about his two left feet had hurt his feelings. When he did finally call and suggest a movie date, she fretted for hours about what film to suggest, worried her choice might not match his cinematic sensibilities. After he hung up, Harry then spent the next several days questioning how prolonged a kiss he might risk at the evening's end. Such rejection anxiet-ies are endemic in fledgling relationships because one knows little about the partner's preferences, dispositions, and goals (Baumeister et al., 1993; Holmes & Rempel, 1989). To make matters worse, people actually fuel their own rejection anxieties because they overestimate the transparency of their behavior. In new interactions, that is, people can think they are making crystal, even painfully, clear expressions of their romantic inten-tions when the intended recipient of such heartfelt overtures does not pick up on a thing (Vorauer, Cameron, Holmes, & Pearce, 2003).

To return to the relationship personality analysis we advanced in the previous chapter, the beginning of any relationship consists of a series of situations that are objectively high in risk. In such situations, anticipating rejection normally activates the goal to self-protect and behavioral strat-egies for reducing one's dependence until the partner's trustworthiness seems certain (Murray & Holmes, 2009). But such self-protective tactics could stymie the development of any budding romance (Holmes & Rem-pel, 1989). If Harry and Sally both surrendered to the urge to self-protect, they would be stuck, waiting for the other to make the first (and second) move. For relationships to begin, the interpersonal mind needs a means of inoculating itself against rejection anxiety. That is, it needs a mechanism for allowing people to risk closeness and commitment without the secu-rity afforded by solid and long-standing reasons to trust in the partner's responsiveness. We suspect the interpersonal mind has just this mecha-nism for decoupling trust from commitment in the directive and motivat-ing experience of passionate love.

In this chapter we detail how passionate love functions as a trust substitute early in relationships. We argue that feeling head over heels in love temporarily suspends the if–then rules for trust appraisal and self-protection in a way that can naturally foster initial expressions of commitment. Such early behavioral experiences in turn provide a grow-ing basis for developing actual trust in the partner's responsiveness. We develop these arguments in four parts. Table 9.1 summarizes our argu-ments, addressed in sequence in this chapter. In part one we describe why one partner becomes the focus of one's amorous interests and not others. Here we focus on the dynamics of mate selection and argue that partners are not so much chosen as happened upon. In part two we describe how feeling passionately in love with one's new soul mate prioritizes approach over avoidance motivations. In this section we localize passionate love in the reward centers of the brain and describe how being in this state effectively decouples trust from expressions of commitment. Indeed, a defining feature of infatuation comes in approaching despite consider-

TABLE 9.1. The Main Arguments

1. Partner selection is governed in part by the happenstance of finding someone desirable who seems likely to accept oneself.
2. Being passionately in love prioritizes approach over avoidance motivations: Anxiety about rejection fuels approach.
3. Being passionately in love creates a myopic behavioral focus on rewarding situations, an initial but incomplete basis for trust.
4. Selectively focused positive interactions can mask real incompatibilities.

able apprehension about rejection. In part three, we describe how being passionately in love creates a behavioral myopia—a selective focus on rewarding situations that provides an initial, if incomplete, basis for trust. Here we describe how situations involving sexuality, self-disclosure, and mutual support foster initial feelings of trust by creating mental associations between the partner and the experience of relationship rewards. At the height of passionate love, trust is akin to a conditioned reflex—an impulsive inclination to approach based on limited but highly rewarding, experiences with one's partner.

We conclude by foreshadowing the downside of passionate love. This downside comes because the rewarding experiences that passionate love selects are more representative of continuing interactions for some couples than others (Acevedo & Aron, 2009). Think about Harry and Sally. In the initial heady days of their romance, they were lost in the experience of discovering each other. They had little reason to suspect that they had fundamentally different philosophies about marital roles and outside friendships. But now Sally spends many a waking moment wishing that she had not been so blind to how often Harry asked his mother to clean his apartment and do his shopping and to how often Harry refused to go out with her friends and stayed home alone instead. The myopic effects of passionate love can leave partners open to the experience of such situational sleeper effects once burgeoning feelings of trust create sufficient interdependence to reveal incompatibilities that always existed beneath the surface.

THE DYNAMICS OF PARTNER SELECTION

What ignites that first flicker of romantic attraction? Evolutionary and exchange theorists assume that people possess ideal standards for the characteristics they desire in a mate and that such ideals govern choice

(Buss, 1989; Fletcher, Simpson, & Thomas, 2000). Guided by sexual strategies theory (Buss & Schmitt, 1993), evolutionary theorists assume that men and women face different adaptive dilemmas and consequently maximize reproductive success by seeking different characteristics in potential mates. Because women invest considerably more in offspring (i.e., pregnancy and lactation) than men (i.e., sperm), women are more judicious in sexual choice. Men can maximize their reproductive success by having sexual relationships with as many fertile women as possible. However, women cannot have an unlimited number of offspring; they can only maximize their reproductive success by ensuring resources for their offspring. Accordingly, sexual strategies theory anticipates sex-differentiated standards for the ideal partner: Men should pursue young and attractive women (who are likely to be fertile) and women should pursue high-status men (who are likely to provide more resources to offspring).

When researchers ask men and women to describe the qualities they seek prefer in a romantic partner, sex-differentiated standards emerge (Sprecher, Sullivan, & Hatfield, 1994). In a study of 37 cultures, men ranked physical attractiveness as more important and women ranked status and resources as more important (Buss, 1989).[1] Yet such sex-differentiated preferences do not always translate into sex-differentiated choice. A speed-dating study conducted by Eastwick and Finkel (2008a) provides an apt illustration of this dynamic. In this study, participants first described their ideal romantic partner's attractiveness (i.e., "physically attractive," "sexy/hot"), earning prospects (e.g., "good career prospects," "ambitious/driven"), and general personality (e.g., "fun/exciting," "responsive," "dependable/trustworthy," "friendly/nice"). Then participants went on to the actual speed-dating event where each had a series of 4-minute dates with up to 13 potential suitors. At the conclusion of each date, participants rated each suitor on attractiveness, earning prospects, and general personality and indicated their interest in romantically pursuing each one.

The findings revealed that standards for an ideal romantic partner differed by sex. As sexual strategies theory anticipates, men rated physical attractiveness as more important (as compared with women); women rated earning prospects as more important (as compared with men). But such sex-differentiated standards did not turn into sex-differentiated choices. Both men and women were more interested in dating more attractive and resource-heavy suitors. Moreover, the idiosyncratic importance each participant put on a partner being attractive, high in status, and personable did not predict his or her choices either. For instance, participants with higher ideal standards for earning potential were just as likely to end up pursuing someone with little financial means as someone with lower ideal standards. Similar findings emerged in a speed dating study conducted in Germany (Todd, Penke, Fasolo, & Lenton, 2007). In this study, people who made more positive assessments of their own physical attractiveness and financial status set higher standards for the level of attractiveness and financial status they wanted in a mate. However, people who were more attractive (or financially well off) were no more likely to pick people who were more attractive (or well off) as dates. The findings from both speed-dating studies suggest that ideal standards have little bearing on people's romantic choices.

What governs romantic attraction, then? People are not free to choose any partner they desire; the partner one aspires to possess must also want to be caught. Because romantic choice is reciprocal, it would not be adaptive for people to possess rigid standards for the partner they might accept (Gangestad & Simpson, 2000; Hazan & Diamond, 2000). People who would not compromise would risk being left out in the reproductive cold. For this reason, evolutionary scholars working from an attachment-theoretic perspective argue that the initial spark of romantic attraction evolved to be adventitious in nature (Diamond, 2003; Hazan & Diamond, 2000; Lykken & Tellegen, 2003; Gangestad & Simpson, 2000). Rather than being driven by one's internal ideal standards, this romantic spark is calibrated to real-world cues that suggest a nearby person might be both desirable and responsive to one's romantic advances.

Cues to desirability and responsiveness are varied in nature; they range from subtle cues that likely escape conscious notice to cues that directly capture it. Consider the cues at the less conscious end of the spectrum. Men are more attracted to women whose facial features (i.e., high eyebrows, large pupils, large smile) signal friendliness and expressiveness (Cunningham, 1986). Men are also more attracted to women photographed on red (than neutral) backgrounds because the color red, such as the blush of flirtation on the face and neck, provides a biological marker of sexual receptivity (Elliot & Niesta, 2008). Men and women are also more attracted (and even more likely to marry) people who share the letters in their names, perhaps because such familiarity signals partner responsiveness (Jones, Pelham, Cavallo, & Mirenberg, 2004).

Such findings suggest that romantic choice may be governed by the happenstance of finding a person nearby who matches a generic template for being a "good and responsive" prospect. Further evidence that attraction and even choice can be influenced by factors well outside of conscious awareness buttresses this conclusion. For instance, the qualities that women find most attractive in men vary across the menstrual cycle

(Pillsworth & Haselton, 2006). When women are ovulating, they are more attracted to the scent of men with symmetrical facial features (Gangestad & Thornhill, 1998; Thornhill & Gangestad, 1999) and to men who display masculinity, social assertiveness, and dominance (Gangestad, Simpson, Cousins, Garver-Apgar, & Christensen, 2004). Both men and women also gravitate toward partners whose genes provide a reproductive complement to their own. That is, established partners are more dissimilar in genes underlying immune function (i.e., major histocompatibility complex) than would be expected from chance pairings (Garver-Apgar, Gangestad, Thornhill, Miller, & Olp, 2006; Ober & Adrich, 1997).

Even the cues at the more conscious end of the spectrum still may take much of romantic "choice" out of one's hands. An early study examining the origins of romantic love conducted by Aron and his colleagues is telling in this regard. These researchers asked people to provide detailed descriptions of their most recent falling-in-love experience (Aron, Dutton, Aron, & Iverson, 1989). In their stories, people uniformly described the realization that someone else liked them as the most central factor in crystallizing their own feelings of love. Even the abundant evidence that the perception of similarity triggers attraction puts partner "choice" largely within the province of happenstance. Berscheid and Reis (1998) reviewed a wealth of evidence suggesting that people are more likely to date and marry those who are similar to them in terms of basic preferences, attitudes, and values (e.g., political, religious). But such an affinity need not imply that people are making choices on this basis. Instead, people may be drawn to similar others because they are more likely to meet similar others (Lykken & Tellegen, 1993) and then assume that such similar others are more likely to like them (Condon & Crano, 1988).

These various findings suggest that the spark of romantic attraction can ignite when people happen upon someone who seems both desirable and reassuringly familiar—someone who seems ready and willing to like them. Consistent with this logic, Hazan and Diamond (2000) argue that the capacity for romantic love is relatively innate. Such an automatic capacity to fall precipitously in love naturally and easily attaches itself to those who are nearby and signal a willingness to be responsive (whether it be through baby-faced and expressive features, a symmetrical face, or a pleasingly familiar name). Once the spark of attraction is lit, only then might one's hopes for an ideal partner come into play. Rather than functioning as a harsh standard, such hopes instead might function as a vehicle for justifying one's infatuation.

A longitudinal study of developing dating relationships conducted by Fletcher and his colleagues supports this later possibility (Fletcher et al., 2000). The researchers asked individuals in new (i.e., 3-week-old) dating relationships to describe their ideal partner and their current dating partner on different clusters of traits (i.e., warmth/trustworthiness, vitality/attractiveness, and status/resources). Participants provided these descriptions at several time points over the course of a year. This methodology allowed the authors to contrast two different functions for relationship ideals. If ideals function as a standard, people with higher ideals should come to see their dating partner less positively over time (because most partners fell short of such lofty standards). But if ideals provide a means of preserving infatuated feelings, people should actually change their ideals to match the qualities they perceive in their less-than-perfect partners. The findings were clear. People's initial ideal standards did not predict changes in their impressions of their partner over time. Instead, people changed their ideals in a way that allowed them to preserve infatuated feelings. For instance, someone who perceived their partner as more curmudgeonly than charming came to desire less charm in their ideal partner. Similarly, someone who perceived their partner as more couch potato than athlete came to value a certain amount of sloth in their ideal partner. The capacity to flexibly redefine one's ideals in the partner's image strengthened these fledgling romances: People who created greater consistency between their ideals and perceptions of their partner were less likely to break up (see Murray et al., 1996b, for conceptually similar findings).

HOW BEING PASSIONATELY IN LOVE
MOTIVATES APPROACH GOALS

For someone immersed in the experience of romantic love, the partner becomes the very embodiment of his or her hopes and ideals (Brehm, 1988; Brickman, 1987; Murray et al., 1996b). Caught up in this idealized image, people cannot help but dote on their partner's every word and touch. According to Fisher (1998), such an energizing and obsessive quality to romantic love solves the adaptive problem posed by mate choice. Dedicating one's energies and focus to the chosen partner distracts one's attention away from competing alternative partners until feelings of attachment to the chosen partner have time to form (Fisher et al., 2002; Fisher, Aron, & Brown, 2005). Indeed, Fisher et al. argue that the experience of passionate love is a cross-cultural universal one.[2] According to our theory of the interdependent mind, such singlemindedness also has a concrete behavioral effect in managing each partner's motivations. It allows people literally to be carried away by the motivation to connect and ignore reasons to be inferentially cautious and self-protect against rejection until an incipient attachment to the partner has time to form.

The metaphors most often used to describe passionate love—falling in love, being swept off one's feet, being caught in a rush of feelings—all capture the idea that passionate love compels people forward. That is, passionate love motivates people to approach the partner and the imagined rewards the relationship offers (Reis & Aron, 2008). Recent neuropsychological evidence supports such a conclusion (Diamond, 2004). It suggests that feeling passionately in love activates subcortical areas of the brain that control reward sensitivity (Aron et al., 2005; Bartels & Zeki, 2000; Fisher et al., 2005).

In one study, Aron and his colleagues (2005) invited participants who had recently fallen passionately in love to participate in a study utilizing functional magnetic resonance imaging (fMRI). While lying in the fMRI machine, participants viewed a photograph of their beloved and a photograph of a neutral acquaintance. The researchers then compared the areas of the brain activated in these two conditions to index the brain regions associated with the experience of romantic love. Thinking about one's beloved activated the areas of the brain implicated in reward sensitivity and goal-directed behavior (Fisher et al., 2005). Similar findings emerged in a study conducted by Bartels and Zeki (2000). These researchers compared the brain regions activated when participants viewed pictures of their beloved versus a friend. Viewing pictures of one's beloved was associated with increased activity in areas implicated in reward sensitivity and decreased activity in areas implicated in fear and sensitivity to punishment. These fMRI findings suggest that passionate love affects the brain much like cocaine addiction (Aron et al., 2005). Just as addicts can think only about the next fix (while ignoring the pitfalls of their addiction), someone passionately in love can only think about the reasons to connect (while ignoring the vulnerability and pain that can come with connection).

Carried Away by Approach Goals

Because passionate love sensitizes people to reward, this heady experience can function as a much-needed substitute for trust early on in relationships. Let us digress. In Chapter 2, we argued that satisfying vigilance (i.e., avoidance) motivations comes before satisfying connectedness (i.e., approach) motivations in adult romantic relationships. That is, people generally only risk stronger expressions of closeness and commitment (i.e., satisfying approach motivations) when they are confident their partner's love and commitment is secure (i.e., satisfying avoidance motivations). A wealth of data from already established relationships supports this general risk-regulation principle (see Murray, Holmes, & Collins, 2006, for a review).

However, there is a paradox to trust that complicates the application of this principle at the start of a relationship. People cannot test the limits of their partner's responsiveness without first taking the risk of putting their outcomes in their partner's hands (Holmes & Rempel, 1989; Simpson, 2007). Think back to Harry, anxious as he approaches Sally at the dance. He cannot find out whether she will be responsive to his need to feel suave and sophisticated despite his two left feet, without first taking the risk of exposing Sally to his less-than-adept dancing ability. Because trust in the partner can only develop when people first risk some expression of commitment (see Chapter 3), establishing a relationship bond requires temporary immunity from the tendency to self-protectively regulate risk (Holmes & Rempel, 1989; Murray, Holmes, & Collins, 2006). It basically requires immunity from the "withhold own dependence" rule.

Being awash in the dopamine-induced throes of passionate love might supply this immunity. The possibility of decoupling rejection anxiety from distancing first emerged in theoretical writing on love (Brehm, 1988; Brickman, 1987; Tennov, 1979). In a thought piece on the origins of romantic love, Brehm (1988) argued that uncertainty about an intended's affections motivates people to love their intended more (rather than extinguishing the spark of romance). In a treatise on commitment, Brickman (1987) similarly argued that uncertainty about a lover's intentions motivates people to see their beloved as the image of their ideals. Early research on two-factor theories of emotion suggests that simply needing a label for diffuse and undifferentiated feelings of arousal can induce feelings of romantic love. A classic study conducted by Dutton and Aron (1974) provides a case in point. In this study, men who had just crossed a vast and rickety suspension bridge 230 feet above a canyon floor misattributed their anxious and fearful state as the pangs of passion. They were more likely to make romantic overtures toward an attractive female research assistant than men who had crossed a stable bridge (see Cantor, Zillman, & Bryant, 1975, for an experimental replication).

More recent empirical research examining relationship initiation also suggests that passionate love can mask and transform apprehension and distrust, turning anxieties about rejection into reasons to approach rather than avoid the partner. Consider a series of studies conducted by Eastwick and Finkel (2008b). In an experimental study, single participants first generated the name of someone with whom they hoped to have a roman-tic relationship. Participants in the "anxiety" condition then described a time when their intended was reluctant to get as close to them as they would like. Control participants described what their intended did on a typical day. All participants then completed dependent measures tapping feelings of passionate love toward the intended (e.g., "I am in love with *X*") and willingness to approach the intended (e.g., "*X* is the first per-son I would turn to if I had a problem"). Participants primed with rea-son to be *un*certain and distrusting reported being more passionately in love then control participants. They also reported greater willingness to seek their intended out for connection. This suggests that passionate love has a self-regulatory or compensatory function in promoting attachment. Uncertainty actually motivates the interdependent mind to overstate the reasons to connect.

The authors replicated these basic dynamics in two correlational studies of fledgling relationships. In the first of these studies, the research-ers asked participants to nominate up to three people with whom they wanted to pursue a romantic relationship. For each intended partner, par-ticipants then completed measures tapping anxiety about the partner's responsiveness (e.g., "I feel uncertain about *X*'s feelings about me"), items tapping their willingness to approach the partner as a safe haven for sup-port (e.g., "*X* is the first person I would turn to if I had a problem"), and items tapping feelings of passionate love toward the intended (e.g., "I am in love with person *X*"; "I think person *X* is my soul mate"). Anxiety about an intended partner's responsiveness seemed to spur passionate love and approach. The greater their anxiety about the intended's affections, the more passionate the love people professed and the more effort they devoted to seeking the intended out for support and connection.

In the second of these studies, participants had a series of 4-minute dates with up to 13 potential suitors. At the end of these speed dates, par-ticipants then indicated which of the potential suitors they wanted to pur-sue (and they found out which of those suitors were interested in pursu-ing them). The researchers then tracked how participants' feelings about their desired matches changed over the ensuing month. Every few days, participants visited a study website where they completed items tapping uncertainty about a desired match's responsiveness (e.g., "I worry that *X* does not care about me as much as I care about him"), items tapping their own feelings of passionate love (e.g., "*X* always seems to be on my mind"), and items tapping their desire to pursue a serious relationship with the desired match (i.e., "I would like to have a serious relationship with *X*). Anxiety about the partner's responsiveness again seemed to spark passionate love and approach: The greater the anxiety about the match's affections, the more love people professed and the more likely they were to have e-mailed or called the match.

The data reported by Eastwick and Finkel (2008b) raise the possibility that passionate love can function as a substitute for trust in fledgling relationships.[3] Research on the projection of communal responsiveness in new relationships further supports this possibility (Lemay & Clark, 2008; Lemay, Clark, & Feeney, 2007). These authors reasoned that people might quell early uncertainties about their partner's responsiveness by projecting their own communal motivations onto the partner. They demonstrated this possibility in both experimental and field studies. In an experimental study, previously unacquainted participants reported in pairs to the laboratory for a study of social interaction (Lemay & Clark, 2008). In the experimental (i.e., projection) condition, the target participant was instructed to behave in a positive and responsive way to the other participant. In the control condition, the target participant was instructed to behave neutrally. The participant pairs then interacted. Experimental participants projected their own responsiveness onto the partner; they perceived their partner as behaving more responsively toward them (as compared with control participants). Experimental participants also reported greater attraction to their interaction partner than control participants. Therefore, the projection of their own responsiveness seemed to provide a substitute basis for trust, which in turn strengthened their own motivation to connect to their partner.

A study of soon-to-be married couples (likely in the throes of passionate love) replicated these general dynamics (Lemay & Clark, 2008). In this study, both members of the couple completed a measure of their own motivation to be responsive to their partner (e.g., "How far would you be willing to go to help your spouse?") and a measure of their partner's motivation to be responsive to them (e.g., "How far would your spouse be willing to go to help you?") a few weeks prior to marrying and then again 2 years after marrying. Longitudinal analyses suggested that projecting one's own responsiveness (a likely concomitant of feeling passionately in love) functioned as a trust substitute. That is, people who were more likely to assume their partner shared their own desire to be responsive became even more motivated to be responsive to their partner over time. As in the experimental study, projecting one's own responsiveness onto the partner provided a projected or substitute basis for trusting in the partner's responsiveness. Such emboldened trust further strengthened the motivation to be responsive toward the partner.

HOW BEING APPROACH MOTIVATED
FOSTERS SITUATIONAL MYOPIA

As these diverse findings illustrate, perceptions of a partner's responsiveness are central to the experience of passionate love. Initial signs that an intended's romantic interest might be forthcoming first ignite the spark of romantic attraction (Aron et al., 1989). Fear and uncertainty that one's growing attraction might not be fully reciprocated then fan the flame of passionate love. According to Diamond (2003), the capacity to experience such a strong emotional pull in response to uncertainty provided a critical mechanism for the evolution of pair bonds in adult relationships (see also Fisher et al., 2005; Hazan & Diamond, 2000; Hazan & Zeifman, 1994).

Let us explain. For an attachment or pair bond to develop, interaction partners must spend considerable time alone in each other's presence. The time spent must also be experienced as rewarding and nurturing of one's needs (Diamond, 2003). By decoupling trust from commitment, the experience of passionate love provides partners the motivation to seek out another's exclusive company (Fisher et al., 2005; Hazan & Diamond, 2000). By focusing partners on the rewards such interaction offers, the experience of passionate love also helps ensure that the time partners spend together stimulates the development of a more enduring attachment by making interactions with the partner feel responsive and rewarding.

The nature of the time those passionately in love spend in each other's presence is qualitatively different than the time partners spend together as part of an established couple. First, when passionate love is at its peak, partners spend more time in sexual contact than they spend later in the relationship (Impett et al., 2008; James, 1981; Klusmann, 2002). Such skin-to-skin contact is critical in fostering attachment bonds because sexual contact and orgasm stimulate the release of oxytocin, an endogenous hormone critical in the formation of bonds between infants and mothers (Diamond, 2003; Hazan & Diamond, 2000).

Second, when passionate love is at its peak, partners become immersed in new and exciting activities together as they explore each other's unique interests. When they first started dating, Sally started going on Harry's early-morning runs and came to love running herself. Harry delighted in meeting Sally's extended family (who were more close and involved in one another's lives than his own family). Such new and self-expanding experiences strengthened their growing attachment because each experienced greater self-esteem and self-efficacy in each other's presence. Aron and Aron (1986) formalized such dynamics in the self-expansion model.

This model conceptualizes relationship development as a process that involves literally including the partner in one's self-concept (Aron et al., 2000; Aron, Paris, & Aron, 1995). For instance, in taking on Harry's love of jogging, Sally "includes" his athletic self-concept as part of her own. In coming to adopt Sally's friends and family, Harry "includes" her interdependent and relational self-definition as part of his own.

Self-expansion is most rapid in the throes of passionate love because partners have so much new to learn about each other's interests, values, and personality. In an illustrative longitudinal study, Aron and colleagues (1995) tracked how people's self-concepts changed as a consequence of having just fallen passionately in love. Every 2 to 3 weeks, participants provided a written description of "who they were today." They also indicated whether they had recently fallen in love. This methodology allowed the researchers to compare the qualities people included in their self-concept descriptions before and after they fell. The results revealed that falling in love expanded the self. Merely days after falling in love, people included more domains and more identifiably diverse domains in their self-descriptions. They also likely experienced such self-expansion as intrinsically satisfying. A second study revealed that falling in love produced increases in self-esteem and self-efficacy over the days that people went from simply aspiring to actually being in love (Aron et al., 1995).

As is the case with sexual contact, such self-expanding activities likely strengthen trust and the developing attachment bond because people implicitly associate the partner with the rewards they experience in interacting. If that is the case, self-expanding activities should have an immediate beneficial effect on the evaluative associations made to one's partner. A series of experimental studies in which Aron et al. (2000) linked the partner to a self-expanding opportunity speaks to this possibility. In these studies, experimental couples had their wrists and ankles Velcroed together (as if they were participating in a three-legged race). Bound together, they had to traverse a series of obstacles across a gym mat to beat the clock and receive a prize. Control couples simply engaged in the much more mundane task of rolling a ball back and forth. The researchers then measured feelings of satisfaction in the relationship and passionate love (in one study) and observed how couples behaved (accepting vs. hostile) in a marital interaction. For experimental couples, participating in this self-expanding activity reignited the spark of passionate love and increased relationship satisfaction (relative to control couples). With the spark of passion relit, experimental couples also interacted in a more accepting (and less hostile) manner as they made hypothetical home improvement plans.

Finally, when passionate love is at is peak, partners also engage in accelerated but selective self-disclosure (Altman & Taylor, 1973). People generally strive to present the most positive aspects of their traits and behavior at the start of any relationship (Brickman, 1987). Such selectively positive self-disclosures can strengthen the developing attachment bond by providing partners with frequent opportunities to delight in each other's good news and good fortune. Research conducted by Gable and colleagues suggests that those passionately in love are awash in such capitalization experiences. That is, people who report being more passionately in love describe their partner as responding more warmly, supportively, and excitedly to their own good news and good fortune (Gable, Gonzaga, & Strachman, 2006). Over time, such "capitalization experiences" also play a critical role in fostering greater chronic levels of trust in the partner's responsiveness (Gable et al., 2006; Gable, Reis, Impett, & Asher, 2004).

THE UNCONSCIOUS BAROMETER: TRUST AS A CONDITIONED OR REFLEXIVE RESPONSE

Because the rewards partners experience in initial interactions are so high, passionate love largely immerses partners in coordination dilemmas. In such situations, partners prefer the same outcome and they can easily obtain this outcome by coordinating their behavior (see Chapter 5). Consider how easy it was for Sally and Harry to resolve dilemmas over the choice of leisure activities when they started dating (see Figure 9.1). In this situation, an infatuated Sally has two choices. She can go to a movie alone with Harry or she can go to a movie with friends (and have

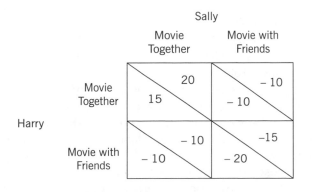

FIGURE 9.1. A coordination dilemma.

Harry tag along). An infatuated Harry also has two choices. He can go to a movie alone with Sally or he can go to a movie with friends (and have Sally tag along). They can also forego each other's company and simply go to movies with their respective friends. The numbers on top of the diagonal within the cells refer to Sally's outcomes from each combination of choices. The numbers below the diagonal refer to Harry's outcomes. These values reveal how natural it was for Harry and Sally to behave responsively in this type of coordination dilemma. Because they both so valued spending time together alone, they easily made the decision to forego the company of friends to be alone together.

Situations involving sexual contact, self-expansion, and self-disclosure are all similar in this regard. Partners have little incentive to be selfish because the greatest rewards the situation offers come through joint interaction and cooperative choices (Kelley, 1979). Sex provides an obvious example of such a dynamic (Hazan & Diamond, 2000). Immersed in the throes of passionate love, Harry and Sally each gained greater personal pleasure by coordinating their sexual overtures than either could gain by playing hard to get. At the height of passionate love, the personal rewards that each partner anticipates simply from the prospect of being together (whether in bed, leisure, or conversation) are sufficient to compel cooperation. With each new interaction, the rewards that come from behaving cooperatively (like enjoying a movie together) then become attached to the partner through simple processes of associative learning. Sally came to trust Harry early on because she felt safe, happy, and valued in his presence.

At this stage in the relationship, trust is little more than an automatic reflex. At the height of passionate love, we suspect that trust is represented largely as associative knowledge, an impulsive and conditioned inclination to approach the partner (Holmes & Rempel, 1989; Murray, Pinkus, Holmes, et al., 2010). The high level of rewards one has experienced in the partner's presence make the inclination to approach automatic and relatively uniform (Murray, Holmes, et al., 2010). Such impulsive inclinations likely play a critical role in fostering pair bonds. Namely, they motivate the kinds of expressions of commitment (e.g., commitments to exclusivity, combining households, having children) that provide the platform for the broadening and deepening of interdependence (Braiker & Kelley, 1979). Once established, greater interdependence then reveals the conflicts of interest that provide the testing ground for refining both the impulsive and the reflective trust barometer (see Chapter 3). In refining the strength of Sally's unconscious motivation to approach, greater interdependence (and conflict) reconditions uniformly positive automatic evaluative responses to match the evaluative totality of the new situations being experienced. In refining the strength of one's conscious motivation to approach, greater interdependence also establishes more deliberative or considered expectations about the actual limits of the partner's trustworthiness. We discuss the interplay between these relatively unconscious (i.e., impulsive) and relatively conscious (i.e., reflective) barometers of trust in Chapter 10.

The Situational Suppression of Personality

Before proceeding, we need to revisit an issue we left in the previous chapter. In Chapter 8, we argued that each relationship possesses a unique personality. Figure 8.1 illustrates its origins. Relationships possess different personalities because partners encounter situations that differ in objective risk, because partners differ in trust, and because partners differ in their motivation to correct the leanings of the automated will. Consequently, partners develop different if–then rule habits for motivating responsiveness (paths A_1 through A_3 in Figure 8.1). Such idiosyncratic rule use in turn compels different experiences of trust and commitment (path B in Figure 8.1) and correspondent behavioral differences in the way partners in different relationships solicit and provide responsiveness (path C in Figure 8.1).

Few of the interactions Sally and Harry had in the days and months following their first date at that school dance forecast the cautious, role-regimented, and conflict-habituated personality their marriage eventually came to inhabit. Early on, they loved to spend time alone together, they loved to talk, and no topic was off limits. Harry loved that Sally kept her apartment so spotlessly clean; Sally appreciated Harry's insistence that he pay for their dinner and movie dates. Indeed, she took pleasure in tidying his bedroom and bath (on those rare nights she spent at his less-than-neat abode). Limiting interactions to situations that made it easy to be responsive helped to mask their real differences in gregariousness, traditionalism, and standards for household cleanliness. Because being passionately in love uniformly directs partners toward such low-risk situations, the initial months of Harry and Sally's romance looked much like the initial months of Ron and Gayle's ultimately more satisfying marriage. In each relationship, being passionately in love strongly motivated both partners to connect. In each, the activation of this goal routinely elicited efforts to increase dependence (e.g., disclosing yet another secret) and justify any costs incurred through such dependence (e.g., seeing Harry (or Ron) as all the more lovable when he forgot to put the toilet seat down). To return to our "personality" logic, the experience of passionate love draws partners into a narrow range of similar and highly rewarding situations.

By standardizing situation exposure and goal activation in this way, passionate love also standardizes and constrains if–then rule habits. Because the rewards to be had are great (and the costs few), the interdependent mind generally only has to apply the if–then rules for connection to motivate responsiveness. As a result, passionate love makes each relationship's personality relatively nondescript. Increased interdependence makes it unique.

SLEEPER EFFECTS: WILL REALITY EVENTUALLY BE OUT?

Even though the connectedness-promoting situations that passionate love samples are highly select, besotted lovers rarely recognize them as such. Instead, partners at the point of marriage generally assume that the future will mirror the past. They imagine a future where conflicts are seldom, partners rarely criticize, conversations hardly ever ebb, and sex and support flow freely (McNulty & Karney, 2004). When the occasional conflict intrudes to disrupt such rosy imaginings, partners caught up in the rush of love typically explain such incidents away. In fact, love and conflict peaceably coexist at the point of marriage; greater conflict neither detracts nor ads to feelings of love (Braiker & Kelley, 1979). Similarly, more negative behavior, such as showing anger or impatience or criticizing or complaining about one's partner, neither detracts nor adds to feelings of satisfaction (Huston, McHale, & Crouter, 1986).

As interdependence increases, this peaceable coexistence becomes strained. Consider the transition Harry and Sally experienced from dancing together, to dating exclusively, to getting pregnant and then married, and to having more children. With each transition, they became more interdependent. With each transition, the number of domains in which their interests could mismatch increased. They discovered conflicts that had always existed beneath the surface, but biased sampling of situations had masked. For instance, once they moved in together Sally realized that the criteria Harry used to declare a floor or a dish "clean" fell annoyingly short of her own. As the rush of infatuation faded, Sally's greater gregariousness resulted in her wanting to spend more time with friends (rather than spending all her time going on leisure outings alone with Harry). They also encountered new conflicts that developed only as a result of evolving life events. Before having children, Sally and Harry easily agreed that they would preserve a special date night each week. Only after having children did Sally realize that family time was now more precious to her. Time and greater interdependence thus revealed incompatibilities that made it difficult for them to be responsive to one another's needs. In so doing, time interjected the potential for considerable negative emotion into their interactions (Berscheid, 1983).

Their story is a common one. With increased interdependence, more conflicts of interest begin to populate the situational landscape (Huston, Caughlin, Houts, Smith, & George, 2001; Huston et al., 1986; Huston & Vangelisti, 1991). These conflicts also become harder to ignore because sex, self-expanding activities, and new domains of self-disclosure plateau (and sometimes drop precipitously). In a longitudinal study of newlywed marriages, Huston and Vangelisti (1991) reported that both sexual activity and affectionate expressions (e.g., complimenting spouse, making spouse laugh, talking about the day, sharing emotions) declined significantly over the first 2 years of marriage. Moreover, negative behavior remained relatively constant (e.g., showing anger or impatience, criticizing or complaining about the spouse). Coincident with this overall negative shift in the situational landscape, one's feelings of love also become less obsessive and less preoccupying, freeing the mind to mull such reasons to be vigilant and cautious (Reis & Aron, 2008). In this new situational landscape, evaluative associations to the partner are reconditioned and sometimes even shift in evaluative tone. This happened for Harry and Sally. They experienced so many intractable zero-sum conflicts so quickly that they soon developed predominantly negative evaluative associations to being in the other's presence. In this new situational landscape, trust also develops into articulate and contingent expectations about the limits of the partner's responsiveness. At this point, the five if–then evidential cues that constrain appraisals of the partner's trustworthiness (see Chapter 3) come fully into play. This also happened for Harry and Sally. We turn to this issue in our next two chapters, where we describe how the relationship's personality emerges when the full force of situational realities eventually is out and trust becomes evaluative in nature.

SUMMARY AND LOOKING FORWARD

This chapter described how the experience of passionate love makes the relationship's personality relatively nondescript. We argued that passionate love functions as a substitute for trust early in relationships, one that allows even ill-suited lovers to suspend the if–then rules for controlling vigilance and exercising self-protection. In so doing, passionate love "tricks" the interdependent mind into pursuing connection despite the risks. This chapter had four parts.

In part one we described how one partner and not another becomes the focus of one's romantic interest. Here we argued that romantic choice is not so much purposeful as it is adventitious. The ideals for a romantic partner that people articulate in conversation, in personal ads, or in the lab have little impact on the partner they actually choose. Instead, the spark of romantic attraction is ignited when people discover that someone desirable and nearby seems to like them. People then redefine their ideals to match the partner they "chose." In part two we described how feeling passionately in love prioritizes approach over avoidance motivations by activating the reward centers of the brain. This obsessive and driven quality to passionate love effectively decouples trust from commitment. Besotted lovers ignore the if–then rule for withholding one's own dependence: Swept away in a dopamine rush, they commit despite anxiety about rejection. Indeed, at the height of passionate love, greater anxiety about rejection actually motivates greater willingness to approach one's partner and express commitment.

In part three we described how being passionately in love narrows the situational field in ways that provide an initial, albeit incomplete, basis for trust. Caught up in the exhilaration of being together, Harry and Sally selectively focused their interactions on positive domains. They could not get enough of each other in bed, expanded their self-concepts by taking on each other's interests, and disclosed to each other about everything and anything under the sun. Through positive experiences in such coordination dilemmas, Harry and Sally felt they could trust each other. Each had an automatic positive evaluative response to being in the other's presence. Unfortunately, the dramatic increase in interdependence that came with Sally's unexpected pregnancy reconditioned this reflexive inclination to approach. In part four we foreshadowed what happens when reality is eventually out. Once interdependence increases, negative interactions and conflicts begin to populate the situational landscape. Unfortunately, this shift happens just as the dopamine-induced high of romantic love starts to fade and frees partners to consider the real risks of rejection. As conflicts surface, automatic evaluative responses can then be reconditioned as partners learn when and how seriously they can disappoint each other. With this shift in the situational landscape, trust becomes a decision to make. That is, trust takes on its explicitly evaluative and deliberative tone and the unique personality of the relationship begins to define itself more clearly. We turn to this process in the next chapter.

NOTES

1. It's important to note that men and women both rate qualities like intelligent, honest, and trustworthy as being most desirable in a potential mate (Buss, 1989).
2. Although passionate love may be a universal experience, committing to a partner solely on the basis of such feelings may be largely a Western phenomenon (Berscheid & Regan, 2005; Henrich, Heine, & Norenzayan, 2010).
3. Our logic suggests that passionate love should at least partially mediate the association between anxiety about the partner's responsiveness and willingness to approach the partner. Unfortunately, the authors did not present such meditational analyses, which renders our conclusions more speculative in this case.

CHAPTER 10

Being Mowed Over

How Real Life Makes It Natural to Self-Protect

> Love is . . . seeing something as ideal that is not ideal.
> The primal dissonance that accompanies romantic
> passion is . . . the placing upon a partner of hopes
> and dreams and fantasies that cannot possibly be
> fulfilled. The partner that would be required to
> fulfill them would have to be ideal and unchanging,
> and real partners . . . change, they grow old. . . .
> The objects of love are not permanent, but romantic
> passion commits itself to permanence.
> —PHILIP BRICKMAN (1987, p. 80)

Something few couples expect happens as the heady months of infatuation blend into greater interdependence and a more lasting commitment. Partners change; fun, frivolousness, and fantasy fade. To use Brickman's turn of phrase, "the objects of love are not permanent." Think back to our introduction to Ron and Gayle in Chapter 2.

When they first started dating, they only had occasion to see the best in each other. On the Friday and Saturday nights they spent together, the most intractable conflicts they had concerned the choice of take-out restaurants; Ron preferred Italian; Gayle, Thai. On the odd occasion, Gayle wanted to go a hockey game when Ron wanted to go to the local wine shop, but they easily resolved such disputes through good humor and compromise (opting to watch the hockey game on television while they sipped a new Bordeaux). Then something happened. They each passed the bar exam, got jobs at prestigious law firms, and decided it was time to buy a condo and move in together. Now somebody had to cook, clean, and take out the garbage even though both of them juggled long days at work. Despite increased interdependence in drudgery, they still managed to laugh off most of their differences (even though Gayle's obsession with televised sports had become harder for Ron to ignore). Then something else happened. Seven years into marriage, Gayle got pregnant. Their initial excitement soon gave way to the reality of greater responsibility. They still had the cooking, the cleaning, and the garbage to manage, but now they also had the countless activities involved in caring for a new baby. Not quite as content as they once were, they eventually found a way to negotiate new roles and responsibilities. (Using Gayle's raise to hire a full-time nanny helped in this regard.) Two years later they welcomed their daughter's birth. Now they laugh at their dating selves—wondering at how they had once been so naïve—and they delight in how they have grown up together. Even though the occasional argument about their careers gets heated now, they are truly happy.

Unlike Ron and Gayle, Harry and Sally's transition out of the haze of infatuation was abrupt. Six months after that high school dance, Sally discovered she was pregnant. They got married 2 months later. Sally gave up on her plans to attend college and Harry started working as a junior mechanic at the local automotive shop. They went from dancing to diapers in the blink of an eye. Even though they loved each other deeply at the start, they were not prepared for the conflicts they faced once their daughter was born. Sally adored being a mother to her new baby, but she resented having to mother Harry as well. She could not begin to understand why his socks and underwear could not find the hamper (no matter how conspicuously she placed it). She also could not fathom why Harry seldom noticed when their daughter's diaper needed changing. Her resentment over the imbalance in their domestic responsibilities only grew as they had a second and then a third child. Now she dreads the thought of becoming the primary caretaker to her ailing mother-in-law—the new living arrangement Harry is pushing. For his part, Harry has never understood why Sally can't just be happy with what they have. He's always had the uneasy suspicion that Sally is not happy with him being "just" a mechanic. Now he even takes her wistful comments about missing out on college as a slight against him. He's always thought he did a good job providing for his family and he doesn't understand why she can't see that. Over the years, her growing complaints about his contributions to household chores have only made him feel more misunderstood. They once reveled in talking about everything and kept no secrets. Now they tread cautiously, guard their words, and talk mostly about their children. They are committed, but they take little pleasure in each other's company—except for the occasion when they make the effort to have sex.

Hector and Helena's trajectory followed a more conventional route. Not quite as happy as Ron and Gayle, they are not nearly as disgruntled as Harry and Sally, either. Their relationship is comfortable for the most part. It used to be exhilarating. When they first started dating, they could not bear to be away from each other. Everything they did together was exciting. They still enjoy each other's company, but the stress of raising three young children on a limited income means that they have less time for each other. The things they used to delight in doing together (e.g., taking a walk in the park, playing cards with friends, going to the movies) are a distant memory. Now they spend their walks in the park chasing three wandering preschoolers rather than sharing their hopes and dreams. In recent weeks, things have gotten tense at home. The most recent round of layoffs at Hector's factory has left him much more sensitive than usual to Helena's concerns and occasional criticism of him. Knowing that Hector can be touchy when his masculinity is threatened, Helena has tried hard to be forgiving (although she hasn't always succeeded). When she gets frustrated and angry with Hector, it helps her to remember the promise she made to her family, friends, and God to love and honor him for better or worse.

Introduced through the matchmaking skills of their parents, Lastri and Gunter followed a different trajectory altogether. They got married in Indonesia, moved to the United States so that Gunter might pursue his PhD. Shortly after they immigrated, they had their first child. Isolated from family and friends and bewitched by their new daughter, they slowly fell in love with each other. Much like Harry and Sally when they first met, they now find it hard to stop thinking about each other. Gunter feels like he has to literally tear himself away from his wife and his daughter to go to school or work. Recently something has happened to challenge the bliss and tranquility of their domestic existence. Gunter wants to have another baby, but Lastri wants to start university. Gunter will soon face the unsettling question of whether his wife is the traditionalist he always wanted her to be. Their future happiness is a question mark hanging in the balance of how they negotiate the conflict between Gunter's family-mindedness and Lastri's educational aspirations.

Figure 10.1 depicts the trajectories of each of these marriages graphically. These trajectories capture changes in trust and commitment across time within each relationship. As the figure makes evident, the relationships of Ron and Gayle, Harry and Sally, and Hector and Helena were hard to distinguish 3 months in. They were passionately in love and highly responsive to one another's readily met needs. Then things changed, sometimes gradually, sometimes precipitously. For Ron and Gayle, early

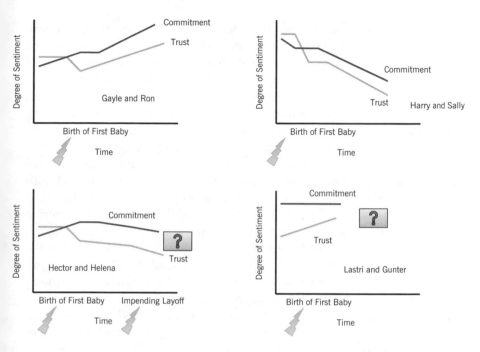

FIGURE 10.1. The relationship fates of each couple.

trusting sentiments led to the gradual expression of their commitment, first living together and then marrying. For Harry and Sally, the impending birth of their first child forced the quick escalation of their commitment. Unlike the other couples, Gunter and Lastri professed commitment first, only then coming to fall in love and trust in the other's responsiveness. Events, like the birth of the first and subsequent children, economic stress, and new personal ambitions and goals, intervened for all of these couples. These conflicts of interest tested each relationship. To this point, Ron and Gayle have passed these tests. Despite ebbing commitment after their son was born, working through their conflicts established a strong sense of trust in each other's responsiveness and such faith strengthened and reaffirmed their commitment. They turn first to each other for socioemotional support, and Ron has willingly sacrificed some of his own career ambitions to take Gayle's needs into account. Sally and Harry faltered in the face of these tests. The birth of their first child revealed incompatibilities that raised persistent doubts and dashed trust. They now hesitate to rely on each other for anything but superficial favors and they restrict most of their one-on-other interactions to the sexual domain (because they can never seem to say the right thing to each other outside the bedroom). The relationships of Hector and Helena and Gunter and Lastri are both at turning points. In each, continued trust in the other's responsiveness hinges on how each partner responds to the conflicts they now face.

In this chapter, we explore how the interdependent mind creates such unique relationship personalities, and ultimately such distinct relationship trajectories. Table 10.1 summarizes the main arguments we make, addressed in sequence in the chapter. Table 10.2 updates our couple profiles with information revealed in this chapter. Because situations provide the seeds for relationship personality (see Chapter 8), we start with the new situational landscape that develops as partners emerge from the myopia of passionate love. In the first part of this chapter we describe the declines in satisfaction that typically come with increased interdependence (Huston et al., 1986). Here we describe how the risk profile of situations normatively shifts with greater interdependence. Such shifts are all the more dramatic for couples that make the transition to parenthood (Doss, Rhoades, Stanley, & Markman, 2009). Partners who once encountered largely approach–approach situations at lower levels of interdependence (e.g., "Your place or mine?") now encounter myriad conflicts of interest (e.g., "Your baby to feed at 3 A.M. or mine?"). This new situational landscape routinely puts the goal to connect to the partner in conflict with the goal to self-protect against rejection. This newly experienced goal conflict makes the disambiguation of the partner's motives a new and ongoing concern. In this more textured situational landscape, trust becomes a decision to be made. That is, it develops as a contingent expectation about the limits of the partner's responsiveness. In this risk-laden climate, partners grow more tuned to the evidential cues that signal each other's trustworthiness (see Table 3.1). In fact, Sally never hesitated to trust Harry until they had their daughter. Once they faced the dilemma of coordinating

TABLE 10.1. The Main Arguments

1. With greater interdependence (e.g., parenthood), more frequent conflicts of interest populate the situation landscape. Satisfaction declines. Trust becomes a decision to make.

2. More frequent exposure to conflicts of interest makes the if–then rules for self-protection more central to interaction. Increases vigilance in appraisal and caution in goal orientation and implementation.

3. Situations differ across relationships and compel different if–then rule habits.

4. Impulsive and reflective trust jointly control how partners express commitment.

5. If–then rules that become a habit and the associated expressions of commitment control the nature of mutuality that results.

TABLE 10.2. Updating Our Couple Profiles

Couple	Basic demographics	Life task preferences	Personality preferences	Relationship goal preferences
Ron and Gayle	African American Lawyers Two young children	Ron likes cooking; Gayle likes washing dishes. Both enjoy child care. Gayle loves sports. Ron loves wine.	Gayle: More gregarious. Gayle: More competitive. Ron and Gayle: Secure.	Both value Gayle's working.
Harry and Sally	White Mechanic/customer service officer Three children, eldest 17	Harry dislikes all things domestic.	Sally: More gregarious. Sally: More fastidious. Harry: More reserved. Harry: Avoidant. Sally: Preoccupied.	Sally wanted to work; Harry wanted her at home.
Hector and Helena	Hispanic Factory worker/ homemaker Three young children Catholic Economically stressed	Largely compatible preferences.	Helena: Lower self-esteem; fearful in attachment style.	Stay tuned . . .
Gunter and Lastri	Indonesian PhD student/ homemaker One toddler	Gunter likes doing laundry; Lastri likes gardening. Gunter: Enjoys outside social activities.	Gunter wants another baby; Lastri wants to return to school.	

onerous child care responsibilities, she discovered that his mood was a reliable barometer of his receptiveness to her requests for help.

In the second part of this chapter we describe how the emerging conflicts of interest partners now face control exactly how the interpersonal mind coordinates expressions of commitment across partners. Here we review how varying appraisals of risk compel different if–then rule habits (i.e., the personality genotype we introduced in Chapter 8). Over the transition to parenthood, Ron and Gayle discovered a happy alignment of their preferences. Most of the time, Gayle preferred waking to feed their son in the wee hours of the night; Ron liked the early morning hours. Such correspondent preferences facilitated an easy exchange of sleep and infant care. Harry and Sally were not so lucky; Harry insisted he needed his sleep every night because he had to get up to go to work in the morning. Such divergent preferences turned every time Sally needed extra sleep for herself into a zero-sum conflict. Because these couples faced situations that varied systematically in risk, the interpersonal goals they pursued in their interactions diverged systematically as well. For Ron and Gayle, satisfying the goal to connect occupied most of their mental energies, making the if–then rules for escalating dependence and justifying commitment stronger if–then rule habits. For Harry and Sally, satisfying the goal to self-protect preoccupied the mind, making the if–then rules for withdrawing one's own dependence while promoting the partner's dependence stronger habits.

In the third part of this chapter we detail how such divergent if–then rule habits might create the relationship trajectories evident in Figure 10.1. We do so by describing in detail how the interpersonal mind keeps two barometers of the safety of approach (and, conversely, the necessity of avoidance). As we introduced in Chapter 3, one of these barometers is impulsive and relatively unconscious; it captures Helena's automatic evaluative associations to Hector. This form of trust develops through associative learning (i.e., conditioning). It captures the cumulative history of Helena's concrete behavioral experiences with Hector, interactions that emerged through their if–then habits of rule use (Murray, Holmes, et al., 2010). In her case, a history of rewarding experiences conditioned a highly positive evaluative association—a sense of safety in his presence that automatically pulls her to approach connection. In Sally's case, a history of more punishing experiences conditioned her more negative evaluative association—an automatic sense of vulnerability in Harry's presence that automatically pushed her to avoid connection. The other trust barometer is reflective and relatively conscious; it captures deliberative expectations about the benefits and costs of approaching or avoiding the partner. This form of trust develops as conflicts of interest prompt more circumspect appraisal of the partner's motives on the basis of the five evidential cues to trust described in Chapter 3 (see Table 3.1).

To explain how these two barometers of the safety of approach can shape different relationship trajectories, we return to the principles of efficiency and flexibility. Efficiency means that situations automatically activate the associated if–then rules; flexibility means that people can correct automatic inclinations and judgments if they are both motivated and able to do so. Practically speaking, these principles mean that unconscious (i.e., automatic) inclinations and judgments are not always corroborated by conscious (i.e., deliberative) judgment and behavior. Consider Sally's response to tripping over the shoes Harry mislaid on the kitchen floor. Tripping automatically wills her to laugh at his forgetfulness, but she often substitutes that charitable inclination with annoyance. The potential for one's automatic and controlled reactions to the partner to diverge raises a fascinating possibility that we explore in the third section of this chapter. Namely, it suggests that impulsive trust (i.e., unconscious or automatic inclinations to approach) might moderate the effect of reflective trust (i.e., conscious inclinations to avoid). The different relationship trajectories of Hector and Helena and Harry and Sally are instructive in this regard. Both faced serious conflicts in the early years of their marriage— strife over domestic chores for Harry and Sally and economic stress for Hector and Helena. Yet Hector and Helena do not yet tiptoe around each other in the vigilant and cautious fashion Harry and Sally do. When they have the time available, Hector and Helena still enjoy being each other's sole confidants. We argue that unconscious sentiments—in particular, her level of impulsive trust—differentiated their fates. Once interdependence increased, Helena sustained her positive evaluative association to Hector while Sally's automatic association to Harry gradually became more negative. Rooted in a history of continued rewarding experiences with Hector, Helena's more positive automatic evaluative response left her less reactive to rejection. Being more impulsively trusting essentially functioned as a built-in buffer against risk that allowed Helena to approach Hector in even high-risk situations and strengthened her commitment.

We conclude this chapter by describing how the unconscious and conscious residue of if–then rule use helps create different behavioral expressions of responsiveness (i.e., the personality phenotype we introduced in Chapter 8). Here we explain why Ron and Gayle comfortably rely on each other for major sacrifices, whereas Harry and Sally cautiously rely on each other only for minor favors. We argue that the if–then rule habits control how partners experience the meaning of their commitment to each other. Such explanations then facilitate some types of behavioral expressions of responsiveness over others. The nature of the responsiveness that is exchanged creates a behavioral foundation for continued satisfaction, growing dissatisfaction, or the dissolution of the relationship.[1] In the final pages of the chapter we transition to Chapter 11 by suggesting how the preferences and personalities partners bring to the relationship may set the course for one trajectory over another. Had Sally not had the misfortune of meeting a Harry who was just as neurotic as she, her marriage might not have taken quite as destructive a turn. Had Ron adhered to his traditional values and insisted that Gayle stay at home after their son was born rather than supporting her decision to return to work, well, their marriage might not have taken quite as blissful a turn. Indeed, they might now look a lot more like the distrusting and dissatisfied Harry and Sally.

RESTRUCTURING THE SITUATIONAL LANDSCAPE: FROM APPROACH–APPROACH TO APPROACH–AVOIDANCE

Let's return to Brickman's (1987) turn of phrase: "The objects of love are not permanent." What this means practically is that one's experience of the relationship changes over time. This experiential change is perhaps most evident in satisfaction. Almost inevitably, satisfaction declines as the time partners spend in each other's company increases (Huston et al., 1986; Karney & Bradbury, 1997; Kurdek, 1999, 2002). A 10-year longitudinal study of marriage conducted by Kurdek (1999) reveals an ominous portrait of this decline. In this study, satisfaction declined linearly over the first 4 years of marriage, had a brief lull of stability for the next 4 years, and then declined linearly again over the next 2 years. This erosion was just as evident for husbands as it was for wives (suggesting that neither sex escapes unscathed). Such declines are also just as evident for people who are high on neuroticism as those who are low on neuroticism (Karney & Bradbury, 1997). Not surprisingly, couples that divorced reported less satisfaction initially and their satisfaction in the marriage declined more precipitously over time (Kurdek, 1999). It seems that the only thing about love that is permanent is the decline in satisfaction that comes with the passage of time.

In his writing on the "accommodation" stage of relationship development, Eidelson (1980) argued that such declines serve "as a warning to the individual that caution and careful evaluation are preferable to blind pursuit or premature commitment" (p. 460). Indeed, as interdependence increases, the situational landscape shifts in ways that make "caution and careful evaluation" a prerequisite. A longitudinal study of newlywed marriage conducted by Ted Huston and his colleagues (Processes of Adaption in Intimate Relationships [PAIR]) illustrates this situational shift (Huston & Vangelisti, 1991; Huston et al., 1986, 2001). In this study Huston and colleagues had newlyweds provide behavioral interaction records (over the telephone) just after they were married and 1 year into their marriage.

Inspection of these interaction records at each time point revealed that the time newlyweds spent in each other's presence shifted substantially in the first year of marriage. By the end of this year, partners spent more of their time together doing instrumental rather than leisure tasks. When first married, they went to movies, concerts, plays, and socialized with friends; a year later, they went on errands to the grocery store, cleaned the house, gardened, and paid the bills. Their activities shifted from mutually desirable and pleasing ones (i.e., coordination dilemmas) to mutually taxing and displeasing ones (i.e., exchange dilemmas, zero-sum conflicts). The incidence of overt conflict also increased. In this more difficult situational landscape, the number of positive and responsive behaviors partners emitted (e.g., being complimentary, talking together, having sex, saying "I love you") dropped 40%. It essentially became harder for partners to be responsive to one another. In fact, Kurdek (2002) reported that overall feelings of trust in the partner's responsiveness decline significantly over the initial 4 years of marriage.

Such changes in the situational landscape are all the more dramatic for partners who make the transition to parenthood. Anyone who has had made this transition can appreciate this immediately; having a child is like detonating a bomb (a sweet, intoxicating, and exhilarating bomb, but a bomb nonetheless). No aspect of the relationship escapes the collateral damage. Both wives and husbands experience persistent declines in satisfaction after the birth of their first child (Doss et al., 2009; Kluwer & Johnson, 2007; Kurdek, 1999; Lawrence, Nylen, & Cobb, 2007; Lawrence, Rothman, Cobb, Rothman, & Bradbury, 2008). This downswing in satisfaction occurs coincident with an upswing in drudgery. In fact, the shift from leisure to instrumental activities is even starker for partners who become parents (Belsky, Spanier, & Rovine, 1983; Huston et al., 1986). For Harry and Sally, marriage plus one not only brought the onerous life tasks that come with living together (e.g., dishes, laundry, vacuuming), but it also brought the unending tasks that come with nurturing a new baby (e.g., diapers, bottles, baths, and more laundry, vacuuming, and dishes). In most relationships, the exponential elevation in the responsibilities to be allocated precipitates more frequent disagreements and poorly negotiated conflicts involving finances, housework, child care, in-laws, and life goals (Cox, Paley, Burchinal, & Payne, 1999; Doss et al., 2009; Kluwer & Johnson, 2007). The heightened burdens that come with new parenthood also erode supportive and responsive behaviors. Over the first 6 months of parenthood, wives suddenly come to see their husband as less than fully supportive, and their husbands agree with these jaded assessments (Simpson & Rholes, 2002).

Although time generally marches toward greater negativity in the relationship, some couples do fare better than others. Consistent with our theme that relationships possess unique personalities, there is considerable variability in the trajectories couples take (Karney & Bradbury, 1997). The average satisfaction trajectory is one of decline, but some couples experience a precipitous drop (like Harry and Sally), some couples stay reasonably steady (like Hector and Helena), and some couples actually get happier (like Ron and Gayle). In fact, Karney and Bradbury (1997) reported that satisfaction improved linearly over the first 4 years of marriage for 10% of couples in their study. After the birth of a first child, some couples buck the trend toward greater distress and become more satisfied in their marriage despite the greater stress (Doss et al., 2009). The average relationship trajectory that longitudinal research reveals thus conceals a multitude of sins (as well as virtues).

Making Trust and Commitment Relevant

Why do some couples respond to the conflicts of interest that come with greater interdependence with only a small dip in satisfaction while others experience a precipitous drop? Answering this question takes the rest of this chapter and the subsequent one. We start by considering how greater exposure to conflicts of interest normatively changes the balance of the if–then rules the interdependent mind applies. As it turns out, the interdependent mind needs to do something more than connect to coordinate expressions of responsiveness once the mundane drudgeries of interdependence replace the rush of infatuation.

Consider interactions before and after a marked escalation of interdependence (as comes with partners moving in together, marrying, or having a child). Here's the "before" shot. Newly in love partners are caught up in the thrill of sex, joint leisure, and scintillating self-disclosure. In such situations, it is easy to be responsive because behaving responsively generally only requires acting in one's own self-interest. For instance, when Harry and Sally were dating, they both enjoyed being together so much that they always wanted to talk. Then this meant that Harry could meet Sally's needs to chat simply by acting on the basis of his own self-interested desire. The gains or rewards the situation offered to him were sufficient to motivate his responsiveness even without his consideration of Sally's needs. Because the situations that populate early interactions offer strong potential for mutual gain, there is little incentive to be selfish and little need to protect against the possibility of exploitation. In such low-risk situations, the if–then rules for connection are sufficient to motivate mutually responsive interaction patterns.

Here's the "after" shot. Once interdependence increases, slowly, and sometimes suddenly, life intervenes and partners discover that interactions are anything but bliss (McNulty & Karney, 2004). The situational landscape shifts from one that offers much more potential for gain than loss to one that offers at least as much potential for loss as gain. When partners are trapped in the drudgery of dishes, diapers, and bills, behaving responsively is no longer likely to be one's immediate inclination. Why? The potential for loss in such situations creates a strong motivational incentive to be selfish and act in one's own self-interest. In this situational landscape, trust and commitment become indispensible to responsiveness. For instance, early in his marriage, Harry learned that if he simply ignored Sally's pleas, Sally eventually would do the dishes. Behaving selfishly gave him both clean dishes and freedom from doing the dishes. To behave responsively, he needed to be committed enough to transform this situation to take Sally's desire for more egalitarian norms into account. In this new situational landscape, his commitment to Sally becomes an indispensable motivator of his behavior because his greater commitment motivates making caring and selfless transformations. Sally's vulnerability to Harry's actions in such contexts also gives her greater objective reason to self-protect against the possibility of his household exploitation. In this new situational landscape, her trust in Harry is inextricably intertwined with her appraisal of risk and willingness to be dependent on him.

Therefore, the shift in the situational landscape from approach–approach to approach–avoidance situations inserts much stronger self-interested temptations into ongoing interactions. In so doing, it makes applying the if–then rules for self-protection central to ongoing interactions. Once Harry and Sally moved in together and began to coordinate domestic responsibilities, Harry faced the temptation to be selfish and leave the chores to the woman, just like his father did with his mother, and Sally faced the temptation to protect against his exploitation. The insertion of such self-interests into ongoing interactions necessarily makes the interdependent mind more conservative in how it applies the if–then rules.

The first consequence of moving into more situations that tempt self-interest is greater vigilance. Because one's outcomes more often hinge on the partner's willingness to transform, disambiguating the partner's motives becomes a central preoccupation. Rather than being extended as a passionate expression of love, trust becomes a decision to be made. Expectations about the partner's commitment become much more explicitly evaluative and conditional. At this point people start to rely more heavily on the if–then vigilance cues to discern their partner's commitment (Holmes & Rempel, 1989). Once living together revealed that Harry did not share Sally's passion for cleanliness, she started to actively gauge the strength of his commitment to meet her needs rather than simply assuming his better nature. Behavior she had once explained away (e.g., his sloppy dishwashing) she now also saw as telling of his commitment to her. Such appraisal shifts are common as interdependence increases. Findings reported by Huston et al. (1986) are revealing in this regard. In this study, a spouse's negative behaviors had no bearing on satisfaction at the point of marriage. The picture changed several months into marriage. By that point, those same criticisms and annoyances predicted diminished satisfaction because partners had started using such behavioral lapses to measure each other's responsiveness—that is, these criticisms and annoyances now took on a deeper meaning.

The second consequence of moving to more situations that tempt self-interest is greater caution in goal orientation and implementation. This situational shift brings the if–then rules for orienting the goal to self-protect online. In this new and risky situational terrain, partners are essentially primed to tag some situations as "good" and to be approached and others as "bad" and to be avoided (Chapter 5). After a few experiences of trusting Harry to do the dishes (only to end up doing them herself), simply spying dirty dishes in the sink was enough to make Sally anticipate rejection and hurt. The same thing happened to Ron when he spotted Gayle engrossed in a football game. This situational shift also brings the if–then rules for implementing the goal to self-protect online. Tagging specific situations as high in risk heightens the accessibility of the if–then implementation rules for avoiding the losses to be had in such situations (i.e., "if self-protect goal, then withdrawn own dependence and/or promote partner dependence"). This conservative shift in goal implementation became evident soon after Gayle and Ron moved in together. Once Ron realized that Gayle would happily spend all of her free hours glued to televised sports, he learned to tread cautiously in this domain and suppress any attempt to enlist her in conversation when "her" team was losing and she was not inclined to be responsive.

THE EMERGING RELATIONSHIP PERSONALITY: DEVELOPING HABITS OF RULE USE

Each of the couples we described at the beginning of this chapter experienced different trajectories because they experienced more or less serious self-interested temptations and because they responded to these temptations in different ways. For Harry and Sally, their abrupt exposure to multiple high-risk situations fundamentally changed how they related to each other. When they were first together, they were so in love and so enamored with the fun they had together that they never hesitated to seek each other out because they just did not expect each other ever to behave badly or selfishly. Then they did just that. They treated each other badly and they are now vigilant and self-protective. In fact, couples like Harry and Sally, who were once blissfully happy and ebullient about the future, often experience the sharpest increases in conflicts and problems with the birth of a first child (Doss et al., 2009). Ron and Gayle, pessimists by nature, never expected life to be perfect. When conflicts of interest came after they moved in together, they expected them. When they had their son, they were pleasantly surprised that parenthood was not the hell that they had anticipated (Lawrence et al., 2007). For them, expecting the worst actually lessened their sensitivity to each other's occasional selfishness in a way that allowed them to protect and preserve their motivation to connect. Gunter and Lastri are just now experiencing their first major conflict of interest. Their marriage's fate now hangs in the balance.

Our model assumes that some couples fare better than other couples over time because situations differ across relationships. Because situations differ, relationships compel different if–then rule habits. These if–then rule habits in turn have different consequences for trust and, consequently, for the trajectories partners' commitments take. Let us explain.

Situations differ across relationships because interdependence varies across relationships (see Chapter 8). As we discussed earlier, interdependence varies in two respects: (1) influence; that is, how often partners control one another's outcomes at each level of interdependence; and (2) compatibility; that is, how easy it is for partners to reconcile their preferences. These sources of variability determine the character or risk profile of the situations partners face. In relationships with a low risk profile, partners more often encounter conflicts of interest that offer much to be gained through cooperation and little to be lost through dependence. In such a relationship, partners seldom face strong temptations to be self-interested. This happened for Ron and Gayle. Because they agreed on role performance (i.e., who should do what in terms of household chores), they largely faced coordination problems in the household domain. Therefore, they had little objective need to be selfish or to protect against each other's exploitation here (Houts, Robins, & Huston, 1996). Because they shared the philosophy that fathers can be just as nurturing as mothers, they also largely encountered coordination problems in the child care domain. They did face some zero-sum conflicts because they had different preferences for leisure activities. Gayle could not satisfy her need to be gregarious and surrounded by friends while meeting Ron's need for solitude. But they had so little free time that this conflict rarely arose. They do continue to face serious zero-sum conflicts in the career domain because Gayle is more competitive than Ron. She expects him to be the one to make the greater career sacrifice, and this makes him feel like she doesn't respect his professional accomplishments (which left him sensitive to her criticism in this domain).

The situations Gayle and Ron faced had two systematic effects on if–then rule habits. First, the limited number of high-risk situations they faced limited or localized the activation of the if–then rules for controlling vigilance to the career domain. In this domain, Ron is inferentially cautious. He only expects Gayle to be accepting of his needs for praise or support when he had a good day in court (and thus felt on more even footing to her). In household and child care domains, they simply expect each other to behave well. Such limited sensitivity to the if–then rules for vigilance had a transformative effect on the trajectory trust took. Namely, such insensitivity allowed trust to stay high despite their occasional problems because they did not generally use ongoing events to diagnose the other's responsiveness (Holmes & Rempel, 1989). Second, the large number of low-risk situations they faced frequently activated the if–then rules for pursuing the goal to connect in the household, child care, and leisure domains. In these domains, each had the strong habit to seek greater connection to the other and to justify any costs incurred in doing so. Such heightened sensitivity to the if–then rules for connection had the effect of creating the steady and reciprocal upswing commitment took for each of them.

In relationships with a high risk profile, partners more often encounter conflicts with something to be gained through cooperation but much to be lost through exploitation. In such a relationship, partners often face the strong temptation to be self-interested. This happened for Harry and Sally. Once they had their first child, they discovered a major incompatibility involving the division of household and child care tasks. This incompatibility turned the myriad chores they had to allocate into frequent zero-sum conflicts because Harry could not enact his traditional values without Sally sacrificing her goal of being egalitarian. This serious incompatibility in their role preferences then magnified conflicts in other domains. Harry generally craved more solitude than Sally, which she had viewed as part of his mystique when they were dating. Once they got locked into conflict over marital roles, she started to take his preference for solitude as a further affront to her. She feels like he just does not care that she cannot be the gregarious person she wants to be around him.

The situations Harry and Sally faced had two systematic effects on their if–then habits of rule use. First, the large number of high-risk situations they faced generalized the activation of the if–then rules for controlling vigilance across multiple domains in the relationship. Each became preoccupied with discerning whether the other could be trusted to concede the next time they had a conflict. This frequent imperative to disambiguate the other's commitment increased the accessibility of the if–then rules for making vigilant inferences. For instance, Harry quickly learned that Sally was not going to accommodate his desire to get out of washing the dishes on those occasions when he had shirked his responsibilities as household disciplinarian. Such greater sensitivity to the if–then rules for vigilance had a transformative effect on the downward trajectory trust took. Once they started actively gauging the other's commitment, they too often found reason to distrust, because they were looking for such violations. Second, the large number of high-risk situations they faced frequently activated the if–then rules for pursuing the goal to self-protect in the household, child care, and leisure domains. Sally developed the strong habit to tread cautiously and not put her outcomes in Harry's hands or take his outcomes into her hands until she had taken some remedial step to make him need her. Such frequent activation of the if–then rules for self-protection had the effect of steadily eroding intrinsic motivations for their commitment on both of their parts.

Ron and Gayle and Harry and Sally got to their current states because each couple managed the self-interested temptations they faced through different if–then rule habits. So what kind of trajectory will trust and commitment take now that Gunter and Lastri are facing their first major conflict of interest (i.e., education for Lastri vs. new baby for Gunter)? To make this prediction, we start with the situation itself. Imagine that Gunter and Lastri perceive this conflict as a situation with the potential for mutual gain. For instance, Lastri might try to convince Gunter that she could have a baby while going to school part-time. Turning this conflict into such a low-risk situation activates the if–then rules for promoting connection. Should applying these rules become their habit, trust and commitment then might take an upward trajectory. Imagine instead that Gunter and Lastri perceive this situation as one imposing asymmetric losses. For instance, Gunter might believe that he cannot ever get what he wants (another baby) if Lastri gets what she wants. Turning this conflict into such a high-risk situation activates the if–then rules for self-protection. Should applying these rules become their habit, trust and commitment then might take a downward trajectory.

Rule Habits and Relationship Trajectories

The research we've conducted to this point has not yet caught up with the arguments we have advanced here. Nonetheless, there is some evidence to suggest that one's if–then rule habits can set relationships on different relationship trajectories. Consider an indirect indicator or symptom of sensitivity to the if–then rules for vigilance: declines in trust. In a longitudinal study of newlyweds, Kurdek (2002) reported that declines in trust precede declines in satisfaction. Those newlyweds who experienced the greatest erosion in trust over the first 4 years of marriage were the least satisfied 8 years into marriage. They were also more likely to separate. Huston et al. (2001) reported similar findings. Those newlyweds who perceive their partner as becoming increasingly less responsive over the first 2 years of marriage (i.e., less forgiving, sincere, and generous) were more likely to divorce by the sixteenth year of their marriage.

Now consider another indirect indicator of sensitivity to the if–then rules for vigilance: attributions made for one partner's transgressions. In a longitudinal study of newlyweds, Karney and Bradbury (2000) asked participants to complete measures of attributions and relationship satisfaction every 6 months over 4 years. The relationship attribution measure is a scenario-based measure that indexes the extent to which people see their partner as the source of relationship problems. For instance, in one such scenario, Sally might imagine that Harry failed to take out the garbage and then rate whether his failure reflected something about him (e.g., his selfishness or laziness) or something about the situation (e.g., his fatigue). In such a scenario, an attribution to his selfishness captures greater vigilance to rejection. Such sensitivity forecast the fate of these marriages: Husbands and wives who were more likely to see each other as the source of relationship problems (i.e., those who made more vigilant attributions) experienced steeper declines in satisfaction over the first 4 years of marriage.

The diary data collected in the Murray lab provides a still more direct means of indexing if–then habits of rule use (Murray, Bellavia, et al., 2003; Murray, Holmes, et al., 2009). Diary data can index the strength of mental habits because such data involve multiple reports of situation "ifs" (e.g., Ron thwarting Gayle's goals) and "then" responses (e.g., Gayle's valuing of Ron). Having such daily data allows us to obtain a kind of correlation (i.e., slope coefficient) for each person in the sample that reflects the strength of the tendency to respond to a triggering "if" with a contingent "then." Consider the connectedness-promoting if–then rule habits evidenced by Gayle and the self-protective if–then rule habits evidenced by Sally (see Figures 8.2 and 8.3). We can index the strength of Gayle's tendency to compensate for costs by examining her reports of autonomy costs and evaluations of Ron across days. Using multilevel modeling, we can calculate a slope coefficient that captures Gayle's tendency to value Ron more on days after he thwarted more of her goals. Similarly, we can index the strength of Sally's tendency to respond to feeling hurt by withdrawing by calculating a slope that captures her tendency to be cold and distant toward Harry on days after he hurt her feelings. We can then use these indices to predict changes in satisfaction (trust or commitment over time). Such analyses suggest that if–then rule habits do matter in determining the trajectory couples take. Newlyweds who compensate more for the autonomy costs their partner imposes on them report more satisfaction over a year (Murray, Holmes, et al., 2009). In contrast, married women who self-protect and respond to feeling hurt by being cold and distant toward their spouse have husbands who grow less satisfied over a year (Murray, Holmes, & Collins, 2006).

TWO BAROMETERS FOR THE SAFETY OF APPROACH: WHICH IS HEEDED?

How exactly do situations and the if–then rule habits they inspire create trajectories for commitment that vary across relationships? Why did Gayle and Ron become progressively more resolved in their commitment to each other (after a blip with their firstborn) while Harry and Sally became progressively more resigned? As should be no surprise to the reader by now, trust—in both its impulsive (i.e., relatively unconscious) and its relative (i.e., relatively conscious) forms—plays a central role in this process.[2]

As we described in Chapter 3, the meta-perspective-taking involved in gauging the partner's commitment is riddled with error. For this reason, the interpersonal mind keeps both impulsive and reflective barometers of trust. Impulsive trust captures Helena's conditioned association toward Hector. It provides an automatic "gut" answer to the question: Is he generally safe to approach (or better to avoid)? Reflective trust provides a deliberate or thoughtful answer to the question: Is the partner generally safe to approach (or better to avoid) given broader considerations? The if–then cues for vigilance, including the social comparison Helena makes to Hector (Is she equal?), the social comparison she makes to Hector's alternatives (Is she better?), Hector's willingness to sacrifice, his perceived regard for her traits, and the constraints that govern his commitment all govern these broader considerations. As we explore next, Helena is of two minds when it comes to trusting Hector. She's always felt reasonably safe and good in his presence, but nonetheless she's never been able to construct a fully satisfactory explanation for why he would want to stay with her. Consequently, in her daily interactions her unconscious impulses push her forward and her conscious reservations sometimes pull her back.

Is the Partner Safe to Approach?: Impulsive and Reflective Trust

Before considering how being of two minds might affect Helena's commitment trajectory and Hector's reciprocal commitment trajectory, we need to take a step back to address an obvious question. How could the interpersonal mind develop conflicting impulsive and reflective answers to the question: Is the partner safe to approach? We turned to the attitudes literature for insights here. This literature suggests that automatic or unconscious evaluations are often formed through concrete experience, whereas deliberative or conscious evaluations are often formed through abstract reasoning (Fazio, 1986; Gregg, Seibt, & Banagi, 2006; Whitfield & Jordon, 2009; Wilson et al., 2000). Applied to trusting sentiments, this literature suggests that automatic evaluative associations to the partner (i.e., impulsive trust) might be formed primarily through the actual behavioral rewards of interacting, whereas deliberative expectations of responsiveness (i.e., reflective trust) might be formed more through processes of abstract reasoning. Namely, Helena's automatic evaluative association to Hector might develop in an unadulterated way through her actual concrete experiences in interacting with Hector. She might simply feel good in Hector's presence because she associates him with the long history of good times they have had together, from early walks in the park alone to the later births of their children. By contrast, her conscious or deliberative expectations about Hector's commitment and responsiveness might develop in a more processed or reasoned way, through the projection of her own low self-esteem (Murray, Holmes, & Griffin, 2000), the projection of her uneasy relationship with her parents (Mikulincer & Shaver, 2003) or through her defensive distortion of ongoing events in her relationship (Murray, 1999).[3] We detail these processes next.

Behavioral Influences

So how, then, does the automatic or unconscious motivation to approach one's partner develop? Why is Helena quick to associate Hector with good things, while Sally is quick to associate Harry with bad things? These divergent evaluative associations are rooted in the situations they faced.[4] As we described in Chapter 5, couples vary in the degree to which they influence each other's outcomes at each level of interdependence and in the degree to which their outcomes are compatible. Situational risk varies across relationships as a result. Some couples are exposed to more low-than high-risk situations; other couples are exposed to more high- than low-risk situations (Kelley, 1979). Because low- and high-risk situations prime correspondent if–then rules, some partners develop the habit to connect; others develop the habit to self-protect (Murray & Holmes, 2009). Moreover, the interpersonal mind is highly efficient in how it applies the if–then rules (as we saw in Chapters 6 and 7). Consider the "justify own commitment" rule. Valuing the partner more is the automatic response to costs even for people with low self-esteem, like Helena. This means that situations can condition evaluative associations toward the partner without requiring the intercession of consciousness (Higgins, 1996). Consequently, Helena's automatic evaluation of Hector might diagnose ongoing behavioral realities that her conscious beliefs about his trustworthiness miss (or intentionally cover up).

Indeed, different situation exposure (and coincident if–then rule habits) played a central role in making Helena's automatic evaluation of Hector more positive than Sally's automatic evaluation of Harry. Even after the rush of infatuation faded, Helena continued to find herself in low-risk situations that automatically activated her goal to connect. These situations strengthened Helena's already positive automatic evaluation of Hector by motivating her to seek Hector out for support (i.e., "if connect goal, then escalate own dependence") and justify any costs she incurred through greater closeness (i.e., "if connect goal, then justify commitment). After the rush of infatuation faded, Sally more often found herself in situations that automatically activated her goal to self-protect. These situations reconditioned Sally's once-positive automatic evaluation of Harry to be more negative. They pushed her to find fault in Harry as a means of protecting herself from his rejection (i.e., "if self-protect goal, then withdraw dependence").

These examples are more than speculation on our part. A longitudinal study of newlyweds gave us a great means of testing our hypotheses about the behavioral origins of impulsive trust; that is, unconscious (i.e., automatic) evaluations of one's partner (Murray, Holmes, & Pinkus, 2010). Within 6 months of marriage, newlyweds completed standardized electronic diaries for 14 days. These diaries provided both indirect and direct indices for if–then habits of rule use. The types of situations partners encountered provided an indirect index of rule use. In our model, situations provide a proxy for rule habits because low-risk situations prime if–then rules for seeking connection; high self-situations prime if–then rules for seeking self-protection. More frequent exposure to low-risk situations thus makes the if–then habit to connect more accessible; more frequent exposure to high-risk situations makes the if–then habit to self-protect more accessible. We indexed low-risk situation exposure by asking participants to report when they behaved in ways that were responsive to their partner's needs (e.g., "I listened to and comforted my partner"; "I did a chore that is normally my partner's responsibility"). We indexed high-risk situation exposure by asking participants to report when their partner behaved in ways that were rejecting or not responsive to their needs (e.g., "My partner put his/her tastes ahead of mine"; "My partner criticized or insulted me"; "My partner rejected my desires for affection/ sex"; "My partner did something I didn't want him/her to do").

The association between one day's feelings and behaviors (i.e., "if") and the next day's feelings and behaviors (i.e., "then") provided a direct index of rule use. Such contingencies directly assess if–then rule habits because feeling, thinking, or doing X in response to Y presupposes a procedural association in memory between X and Y (Bargh, 2007). We indexed connectedness-promoting if–then rule habits through cost compensation. Each day we measured how often Helena perceived Hector to be thwarting her goals and how much she valued Hector. Having these measures for multiple days allowed us to compute a slope coefficient for each person (using multilevel modeling) that captured the strength of Helena's tendency to value Hector more on days after he thwarted more of her goals (i.e., "if connect goal, then justify commitment"). We indexed self-protective rule habits through daily risk regulation. This index (also derived through multilevel modeling) captured the strength of Sally's tendency to behave in a cold and distant way toward Harry on days after she felt more rejected (i.e., "if self-protect goal, then withdraw dependence").

Four years later we went back to these couples to try to capture the later associative residue of such early behavioral experiences in marriage. At this time, we asked a subset of the couples in the original study to come back to the laboratory to complete the Implicit Associations Task (IAT). The IAT captures one's unconscious or automatic evaluative response toward particular social objects, such as a spouse (Greenwald et al., 1998; Zayas & Shoda, 2005). In our version of the IAT, participants categorized words belonging to four categories: (1) pleasant words (e.g., *vacation, pleasure*); (2) unpleasant words (e.g., *bomb, poison*); (3) words associated with the partner; and (4) words not associated with the partner (Zayas & Shoda, 2005). We then contrasted reaction times on two sets of trials to diagnose partners' automatic evaluations of each other. In one set of trials, participants used the same response key to respond to pleasant words and partner words (i.e., compatible pairings). In the other set of trials, participants used the same response key to respond to unpleasant words and partner words (i.e., incompatible pairings). The logic of the IAT says reaction times should be faster when the nature of the task matches immediate associations to the partner. In particular, people who possess more positive automatic evaluative associations (i.e., people who are more impulsive trusting) should be faster when categorizing words using the same motion for *partner* and *pleasant* than when using the same motion for *partner* and *unpleasant*. Thus the IAT captures the strength of people's unconscious or automatic inclination to approach.

We then used our indirect and direct indices of if–then rule use in the first 6 months of marriage to predict automatic evaluative associations to the partner (i.e., impulsive trust) after 4 years. The findings were stunning. Consider the situational proxy for rule use. Those participants who reported more high-risk situation exposure later evidenced less positive automatic evaluations of their partner. That is, the more often Harry behaved in an unresponsive way in a 14-day period early in his marriage, the stronger Sally's automatic inclination to avoid him 4 years later. Now consider the direct behavioral measure of rule use. Self-protective if–then habits of rule use similarly conditioned more negative evaluative associations. The more often Sally responded to feeling hurt by behaving in a cold and distant way toward Harry, the stronger her automatic inclination was to avoid him 4 years later. The impulsive trust levels of participants who evidenced more connectedness-promoting rule habits fared much better. The more often Helena compensated for costs by valuing Hector more, the stronger her automatic inclination was to approach him 4 years later.

These findings suggest that the habits of thought that develop through early experiences with situational risk leave an unconscious imprint, in the form of impulsive trust, that automatically conveys that the partner is safe to approach or better off avoided. However, people's initial conscious expectations about their partner left no such unconscious residue. Feelings of satisfaction, trust, and commitment a few months into marriage (all deliberative sentiments) did not forecast later automatic evaluative associations to the partner. These contrasting findings suggest that impulsive trust (i.e., automatic evaluative associations to the partner) develops as a consequence of concrete behavioral experiences, not necessarily as a consequence of one's deliberative expectations.

Reasoning Influences

Now consider how deliberative or abstract reasoning processes could either complement or contradict such automatic orientations to approach or avoid the partner. In Helena's case, her conscious beliefs about Hector's responsiveness are less positive than her unconscious inclinations. Although she expects Hector to be responsive more often than not, a tumultuous childhood left her low in self-esteem and somewhat hesitant to trust others (Hazan & Shaver, 1987). Because of this checkered history, applying the if–then rules for controlling vigilance has always gotten her in some trouble. She cannot escape the belief that Hector must see her faults or the worry that she isn't as good a person as Hector. She has trouble trusting him as a result. Her more circumspect deliberative conclusions thus compete with the concrete behavioral experiences that generated her positive automatic evaluative association to him. These doubts can also motivate her to counter her automatic inclination to connect to Hector when she is both motivated and able to do so (Olson & Fazio, 2008). On those occasions when she second-guesses herself, she might go to a friend for support rather than risk disclosing her worries about their finances to Hector. In this way, the flexibility inherent within the interdependent mind helps sustain a contradiction between her impulsive reaction to trust Hector and her more circumspect deliberative beliefs.

The longitudinal data in our newlywed study are telling in this regard as well. Although situation exposure and habits of rule use predicted later automatic evaluative associations to the partner (i.e., impulsive trust), such experiential evidence did not predict changes in explicit beliefs about the partner's trustworthiness over the same 4-year period (i.e., reflective trust). These findings echo the broader literature. People's automatic evaluative associations to their partner do not generally predict the nature of their explicit evaluations of their partner's traits or their overall feelings of trust in their partner (Murray, Pinkus, et al., 2010; Scinta & Gable, 2007). In fact, automatic evaluations of the partner seem to capture something "true" about the relationship that deliberate judgments can miss. For instance, more positive automatic evaluations of a dating partner predict greater relationship stability even when deliberative sentiment (i.e., satisfaction) is taken into account (LeBel & Campbell, 2009; Lee, Rogge, & Reis, 2010).

A Typology of Approach Motivations in Relationships

Dual-process models of attitudes generally anticipate some disassociation between the more experiential origins of automatic evaluative associations and the propositional base of explicit ones (Gawronski & Bodenhausen, 2006; Hofmann, Friese, & Strack, 2009; Olson & Fazio, 2008). Because people can possess more or less trusting unconscious and conscious sentiments, dual-process models also anticipate four different types of approach motivations in relationships. Figure 10.2 illustrates this typology. In this typology, we assume that the motivation to approach the partner is guided by

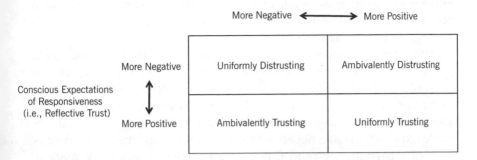

Automatic Evaluative Associations to the Partner (i.e., Impulsive Trust)

More Negative ←————→ More Positive

	More Negative	Uniformly Distrusting	Ambivalently Distrusting
Conscious Expectations of Responsiveness (i.e., Reflective Trust) ↑↓ More Positive		Ambivalently Trusting	Uniformly Trusting

FIGURE 10.2. A typology of partner-specific approach motivations.

both conscious (i.e., reflective trust) and unconscious (i.e., impulsive trust) sentiment. We also assume that impulsive and reflective trust can some-times send conflicting messages about the safety of approach (with behavioral consequences that vary as a function of the person and relationship context, as we will see in this chapter and the next). Unlike typological formulations of adult attachment style (e.g., Griffin & Bartholomew, 1994), this typology captures orientations toward a specific partner, not general orientations toward all partners. Let us explain.[5]

People can be *uniformly trusting*, that is, high on both reflective and impulsive trust. For them, more trusting conscious expectations motivate approach, and their unconscious sentiments reinforce such orientations (e.g., a consciously trusting Gayle who unconsciously associates Ron with more positive outcomes). People can also be *uniformly distrusting*, that is, low on both reflective and impulsive trust. For them, less trusting conscious expectations motivate avoidance, and their unconscious sentiments reinforce such orientations (e.g., a consciously distrusting Sally who unconsciously associates Ron with more negative outcomes). People can also be of two different types of contradictory minds. They can be *ambivalently distrusting*, that is, low on reflective trust but high on impulsive trust. For them, less trusting, conscious expectations of partner responsiveness motivate avoidance, but more positive unconscious sentiments motivate approach (e.g., a consciously distrusting Helena who unconsciously associates Hector with positive outcomes). For such people, being more impulsively trusting has some power to stop them from distancing from their partner. People can also be *ambivalently trusting*, that is, high on reflective trust but low on impulsive trust. For them, more trusting, conscious expectations motivate approach, but more negative unconscious sentiments motivate avoidance (e.g., a consciously trusting Harry who none-theless unconsciously associates Sally with negative outcomes). For such people, being less impulsively trusting has some power to stop them from drawing closer to their partner.[6]

This typology raises a host of fascinating issues that we continue to explore here and the next chapter. But before turning to this discussion we should probably address a couple of issues about the state of being ambivalent in impulsive and reflective trust. The first issue: How could automatic evaluative associations to the partner be positive when delib-erative expectations are negative? Our discussion to this point already provides a partial answer to this question. Helena's automatic associa-tions are more positive because she has encountered so many low-risk situations in which Hector treated her well. But the mind's flexibility is also implicated in this process. Helena is high on impulsive trust because the if–then connect impulses that she corrected nonetheless left a linger-ing positive, but cognitive, associative residue. Imagine that Helena could not go to a friend's party because Hector wanted her at his family reunion. Such an infringement on her freedom automatically prompts her to appre-ciate Hector's strong family values more (e.g., "if self-protect goal, then justify commitment"). This automatic impulse leaves a cognitive residue in the form of her more positive automatic association to Hector. But it does not create as strong a behavioral residue. Because valuing him more conflicts with her chronic goal to self-protect, she corrects such impulses when she has the opportunity to do so. Rather than communicating her appreciation of his family values, she criticizes him for always bowing to his mother, a correction that reinforces her conscious, reflective doubts about his responsiveness.

The second issue: How could deliberative expectations about the partner be positive when automatic associations are negative? Someone can be ambivalently trusting when conscious beliefs somehow defend against or are slow to catch up to unconscious associations. Think about Harry in the initial year of his marriage. He and Sally started to fight more and more about domestic chores; these fights made him feel uneasy and anxious in her presence. Because he was a just-married father to a new baby girl, he was highly motivated to sustain (and implement) the deci-sion he made to commit to Sally (Gagne & Lydon, 2003). Because he loved her, he just did not want to admit to himself that he and Sally might have real problems. He made every excuse and rationalization he could think of to explain away these problems (e.g., Sally is just tired from being up with the new baby; things will get better once I get promoted and money isn't such a stress; she'll be happy once we move into a bigger apartment).

The interpersonal mind's flexibility is implicated in this process as well. Getting criticized by Sally activated an automatic tendency to self-protect (and conditioned his more negative evaluative association to Sally). Being motivated to protect his commitment earlier in his marriage motivated Harry to counter such inclinations with a consciously forgiving response. Such a motivated discounting process is probably a lot more common than one would expect. In fact, Braiker and Kelley (1979) famously reported that feelings of love remain unscathed by more frequent conflicts at the point of marriage (which we mentioned earlier in the chapter).

How Impulsive and Reflective Trust Shape Relationship Trajectories

So what form of trust will eventually win out? Will automatic evaluative associations to the partner determine the trajectory trust and commitment take? Will deliberative judgments prevail? Alternately, might impulsive trust amplify or dampen one's reflective judgments about the partner's responsiveness in ways that set couples on trajectories toward increasing, decreasing, or stable levels of trust and commitment?

Figure 10.3 takes our four-fold typology of partner-specific approach motivations one step further. It presents a dual-process model to antici-pate how impulsive and reflective trust jointly influence the trajectory that trust and commitment take over time (for similar dual-process logic see Gawronski & Bodenhausen, 2006; Hofmann et al., 2009; Strack & Deutsch, 2004; Wilson et al., 2000). This model links both impulsive (i.e., uncon-scious) and reflective (i.e., conscious) trust to specific expressions of com-mitment. Such behaviors, such as soliciting a partner's support, forgiv-ing a partner's transgression, or giving a partner decision-making power, underlie concrete expressions of responsiveness. Such behaviors then shape the trajectories trust and commitment can take across time (Murray, Pinkus, et al., 2010). The multiplicative function in the model implies that impulsive and reflective trust can interact in shaping approach and avoid-ance behaviors as our four-fold typology anticipates (Murray & Holmes, 2009). It also assumes that the relative power of the impulsive and reflec-tive trust in shaping expressions of commitment depends on situational and dispositional factors. Two factors are crucial: (1) factors that govern chronic defensive responses to rejection risk (e.g., self-esteem, attach-ment style) and (2) factors that govern the capacity to correct automatic impulses (e.g., distraction, executive control).

What types of conscious and unconscious influence are possible in different types of situations and relationship circumstances? The predic-

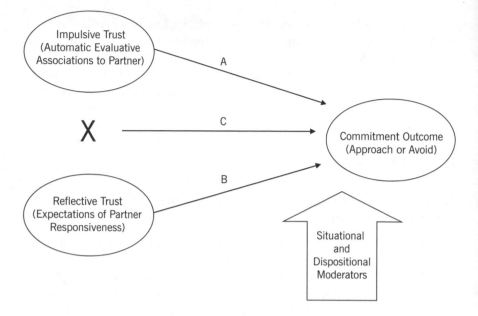

FIGURE 10.3. A dual-process model of how impulsive and reflective trust regulate approach.

tions for people who are uniformly trusting or distrusting are straightforward. People who are uniformly trusting should be highly responsive to the partner and evidence stable and even increasing levels of trust and commitment over time. People who are uniformly distrusting should be much less responsive to the partner and evidence stably low or decreasing levels of trust and commitment over time. We examine these dynamics in Chapter 11. The predictions for people who are ambivalently trusting (i.e., high on reflective trust and low on impulsive trust) or ambivalently distrusting (i.e., low on reflective trust and high on impulsive trust) are more complex. In elaborating on these predictions here, we focus the majority of our discussion on people who are low on reflective trust and high on impulsive trust because the majority of the existing data address the dynamics of this ambivalently distrusting group.

The State of Being Ambivalently Distrusting

Helena is ambivalently distrusting: Her reflective expectations about Hector's responsiveness are relatively negative, but her impulsive associations to Hector are relatively positive. In experiential terms, Helena consciously questions Hector's responsiveness, but she nevertheless associates Hector with feeling good and safe. In our typology, being more impulsively trusting can change the motivational immediacy or heft of her conscious doubts. Essentially, feeling safe in Hector's presence can desensitize her to her conscious concerns in a way that leaves her less likely to react defensively to these doubts. In Helena's case, her automatic evaluative associations to Hector capture feelings of connection that she is afraid to admit to herself (because her self-doubts motivate her to talk herself out of feeling too attached). Therefore, her automatic evaluative associations to Hector might elicit strong expressions of commitment despite her fears of rejection because the behavioral rewards that come from interacting smoothly with Hector imperceptibly function to make her more impulsively trusting (Rusbult & Van Lange, 2003). In social cognitive terms, Helena's unconscious associations function as a "selfish" goal to approach Hector that can override her conscious doubts (Bargh & Huang, 2009).

Now imagine Helena trying to decide whether to ask Hector for help in solving a problem. For an ambivalently distrusting person, the reflective, less trusting mind signals "danger," but the impulsive, more trusting mind signals "safety." In such a conflicted mind state, an automatic sense of safety in the partner's presence might mask or attenuate the signal conveyed by one's conscious doubts. Essentially, it might lessen the motivational impetus attached to these doubts. Therefore, someone in this state of mind might be more likely to solicit a partner's help despite his or her conscious doubts. Whether someone who is ambivalently distrusting actually risks expressing commitment in specific situations depends on the person and the relationship context—namely, the person's chronic defensive reactions to rejection and the person's chronic capacity to correct. Let us explain.

Chronic Rejection Defenses

In Chapter 3, we described how making more positive automatic evaluative associations to the partner (i.e., being high on impulsive trust) automatically takes the motivational immediacy away from conscious concerns about the partner's rejection. For instance, people who are more impulsively trusting resist the impulse to distance themselves from a partner who seems to find an inordinate number of faults in them (Murray, Pinkus, et al., 2010). But taking the motivational sting away from less trusting conscious expectations is not likely to have the same behavioral consequences for all people. We know a lot about low and high self-esteem people's chronic defensive reactions to rejection, so let's work through the consequences of ambivalently distrusting as a function of self-esteem.

Before we do, we need to take a step back to explain ourselves. Throughout this book, we have often treated self-esteem as a proxy for reflective trust in the partner's commitment. We took this tack because people with low self-esteem are generally less trusting than people with high self-esteem (Murray, Holmes, & Griffin, 2000; Murray et al., 2001). But the association between self-esteem and trust is far from a perfect. Indeed, it is rarely more than a middling correlation (.40 or so). So while self-esteem functions like trust more often than not, it is not isomorphic with trust. Because trust is also a property of the relationship (Murray & Holmes, 2009), someone can be low in self-esteem and high in trust. Someone can also be high in self-esteem and low in trust because some property of the relationship warrants being distrusting.

So now let's turn to the consequences of being ambivalently distrusting (i.e., low on reflective trust and high on impulsive trust) for low and high self-esteem people. For low self-esteem people, conscious doubts about the partner's responsiveness typically motivate self-protective defensive tactics. Low self-esteem people are not only likely to blow up the import of their partner's ambiguous behavior, but they are also quick to react to perceived hurts and rejections by withdrawing from their partner (Murray, Holmes, & Collins, 2006). High self-esteem people usually expect their partner to be responsive. Nevertheless, sometimes they can (and do) find themselves in situations that make them question their partner's responsiveness. For highs, such doubts typically motivate relationship-protective defensive tactics. In fact, high self-esteem people draw closer to their partner when their partner seems to be rejecting (Murray, Rose, et al., 2002).

In summary, low and high self-esteem people have different motivational orientations to risk. Risk threatens lows and challenges highs. Basically, low self-esteem people wallow in the possibility of rejection and nonresponsiveness; highs rationalize and deny it. Such motivational differences mean that any force (like a more positive evaluative association) that lessens the motivating signal imparted by doubts about the partner's responsiveness is likely to have very different behavioral consequences for low and high self-esteem people. For a low self-esteem person, automatically feeling safe in the partner's presence might lessen the motivational impetus to self-protect in response to deliberative concerns about the partner's responsiveness. Desensitized to the psychological impetus to defend, a low self-esteem Helena might seek out Hector's support (rather than avoiding him as someone low in self-esteem and uniformly distrusting would do). For a high self-esteem person, automatically feeling safe in the partner's presence might lessen the motivational push to protect the relationship in response to deliberative concerns about the partner's responsiveness. Desensitized to the impetus to defend, a high self-esteem Helena might keep her problems to herself (rather than approaching Hector as someone high in self-esteem and uniformly distrusting would do). We elaborate on this logic below as we describe data bearing on these contrasting (and likely counterintuitive) hypotheses.

A series of studies reported by Murray, Pinkus, et al. (2010) illustrates exactly how self-esteem moderates the relationship effects of being ambivalently distrusting. In one of these studies, we invited people involved in dating relationships into the laboratory to complete measures tapping different aspects of the model illustrated in Figure 10.3. As we described in Chapter 3, we measured impulsive trust using the IAT because it captures automatic evaluative associations. We also measured deliberative or reflective beliefs about the partner's responsiveness through self-report measures of trust (e.g., "I feel I can trust my partner completely"), perceived commitment (e.g., "My partner would be very upset if our relationship were to end in the near future"), perceived closeness (e.g., "My partner is closer to me than any other person in his/her life"), and perceptions of the partner's regard for one's traits. We also measured the strength of the participant's commitment to the partner through measures of closeness (e.g., "I am closer to my partner than any other person in my life and commitment") (e.g., "I would be very upset if our relationship were to end in the near future").

Figure 10.4 depicts the strength of the tendency to self-protect against doubts about the partner's responsiveness for people with low and high self-esteem who were low and high on impulsive trust (i.e., less vs. more positive associations on the IAT). The results for low self-esteem people are on the left; the results for high self-esteem people are on the right. The slopes central to each graph capture the strength of people's tendency to self-protect against risk (i.e., reducing commitment in response to doubts about the partner's responsiveness) as a function of their automatic evaluative associations to the partner. The slope lines ended by circles capture the overall tendency to self-protectively regulate risk among people who are relatively high on impulsive trust. The slope lines ended by triangles capture this tendency for people who are relatively low on impulsive trust.

Let's consider low self-esteem participants first. These are the people for whom being ambivalently distrusting should be more beneficial. For lows, an automatic sense of safety in the partner's presence should lessen the motivational push to distance in response to deliberative concerns

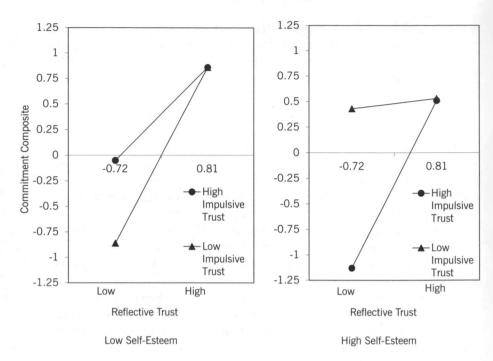

FIGURE 10.4. Closeness to the partner as a function of self-esteem, impulsive trust, and reflective trust.

about the partner's responsiveness (i.e., danger). In such circumstances, doubts about a partner's responsiveness should lose some of their power to compel avoidance because low self-esteem people may not subject these danger signs to the same rumination and magnification (they otherwise would). Bereft of this motivational impetus to self-protect, low self-esteem people who are high on impulsive trust can connect in the face of rejection risk. In contrast, low self-esteem people who are low on impulsive trust should ruminate, magnify risk, and hesitate to commit in the face of doubts about their partner's responsiveness (i.e., danger). The results support these hypotheses. Low self-esteem people who evidenced less positive evaluative associations to the partner (i.e., those low on impulsive trust) heeded danger signs and self-protectively regulated risk. They expressed markedly less closeness the greater their doubts about their partner's responsiveness. But this self-protective tactic was much less evident for low self-esteem people who made more positive associations to their partner (i.e., those high on impulsive trust). They connected and committed to their partner despite the risk.

Now let's look at participants high in self-esteem. These are the people for whom being ambivalently distrusting should be more detrimental. For highs, an automatic sense of safety in the partner's presence should lessen the motivational pull to compensate and draw closer in response to deliberative concerns about the partner's responsiveness (i.e., danger). In such circumstances, doubts about a partner's responsiveness should gain power to compel avoidance because high self-esteem people are not subjecting these doubts to the same rationalizations and minimizations (they otherwise would). Bereft of this motivational impetus to protect the relationship, high self-esteem people who are high on impulsive trust then might reduce closeness in the face of rejection risk.

In contrast, high self-esteem people who are low on impulsive trust should still be compelled to defensively compensate and draw closer in response to risk. The results also supported these predictions. High self-esteem people who evidenced more positive evaluative associations to the partner (i.e., those high on impulsive trust) self-protectively regulated risk. This self-protective tendency was not at all in evidence for high self-esteem people who were low on impulsive trust. These highs ably compensated for doubts about their partner's responsiveness in ways that allowed them to preserve feelings of connection. Although the results depicted in Figure 10.4 are complex, the bottom line is simple. When impulsive and reflective trust send different messages about the safety of approach, both sentiments must be understood to foreshadow the relationship's trajectory.

Chronic Capacity

Now let's consider a capacity factor that might moderate the relationship effects of being ambivalently distrusting. Dual-process models of behavior assume that automatic impulses direct behavior unless people are both motivated and able to correct for the influence of their automatic attitudes (Hofmann et al., 2009; Olson & Fazio, 2008). Imagine Helena is on a diet and she's standing in front of the fridge staring at the last wedge of her favorite chocolate cake. Her automatic impulse is to eat the cake, but her deliberative intention is to diet. Whether she gives in depends on how much self-regulatory capacity she has available. When she's in full control of her self-regulatory powers, newly energized after a good night's sleep, it should be easy for her to resist. At the end of the day, after wrestling three toddlers into bath and bed, she is much more likely to succumb (Muraven & Baumeister, 2000).

This capacity logic implies that automatic evaluative responses to the partner should be more powerful in motivating approach when the opportunity to correct for one's automatic impulses is most limited. Such is the case for people who possess limited ability to shield information in working memory from distraction or interference, such as those low in working memory capacity (Baddeley & Hitch, 1974; Hofmann et al., 2008). People low in working memory capacity have difficulty with cognitive tasks involve dual demands, like remembering the results of a series of algebraic equations (e.g., $2 + 3 = 7, 6 - 4 = 2$) while simultaneously deciding whether each equation is true or false (i.e., a computation span task). This capacity limitation has major consequences for self-regulation in situations where automatic impulses promote behavior X and explicit intentions promote behavior not-X. For instance, people who do poorly on such tasks succumb to the temptation compelled by their automatic evaluative response to M&M's and eat what their impulses dictate, not what their conscious intentions to diet dictate (Hofmann et al., 2008). Such findings suggest that being high on impulsive trust may be more likely to counteract doubts about a partner's responsiveness for people who are low in working memory capacity and thus chronically lack the cognitive capacity or opportunity to override automatic impulses to approach.

We found tantalizing evidence of such dynamics in a correlational study of married couples reported by Murray, Pinkus, et al. (2010). In this study, we again measured impulsive trust using the IAT. We also measured deliberative beliefs about the partner's responsiveness through self-report measures of trust, perceived commitment, perceived closeness, and perceptions of the partner's regard for one's traits. New to this study, we measured working memory capacity using a computation span task utilized by Hofmann et al. (2008). We also measured a different commitment outcome than we measured in our dating couples study: resisting the impulse to be rejecting and nonresponsive. We obtained an objective index of such self-protective distancing behavior by asking Hector how often Helena engaged in cold, hostile, and rejecting behaviors toward him in the previous 2 weeks (e.g., "My partner rejected my desires for physical affection or sex"; "My partner pushed or hit me"; "My partner snapped or yelled at me"; "My partner criticized or insulted me"; "My partner ignored or did not pay attention to me").

We expected the benefits of being ambivalently distrusting to be most evident for people low in working memory capacity. Think about the behaviors that are most characteristic of someone who does not consciously expect their partner to be responsive. Typically, people self-protectively regulate risk and distance themselves from their partner before their partner has the chance to hurt them again. That is certainly the case for Sally (who is uniformly distrusting). In fact, she routinely yells at Harry for not doing the dishes before he's even had enough time not to do them. But Helena (who is high on impulsive trust despite her doubts) should not be nearly this rejecting of Hector. Instead, people (like Helena) who are armed with more positive automatic evaluations should resist the impulse to behave badly in response to rejection concerns. But our capacity logic introduces a further complication. It suggests that such an inoculation effect should be most evident for people who have little self-regulatory capacity available to correct for the automatic impulse to approach—that is, people who are both ambivalently distrusting and low in working memory capacity. Otherwise, Helena could use her powers of self-regulation to counter her positive automatic evaluative associations to Hector and instead remind herself of the risks of closeness (and the wisdom of inflicting a little retaliatory pain on Hector).

Figure 10.5 presents the three-way interaction we obtained. This figure presents the association between reflective trust (i.e., deliberate expectations of partner responsiveness) and distancing as a function of two factors: (1) impulsive trust, as assessed by the IAT, and (2) working memory capacity. The results for people who are low in working memory capacity (the left side of Figure 10.5) are the most telling. These are the people most likely to act on the basis of impulsive trust; therefore, these are the

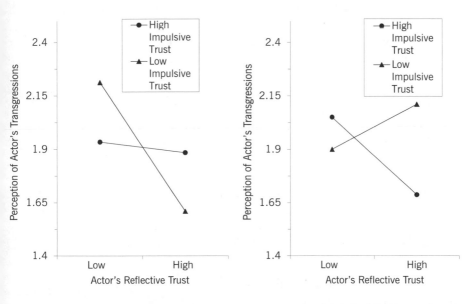

Actors Low in Working Memory Capacity   Actors High in Working Memory Capacity

FIGURE 10.5. Partners' perception of actors' transgressions as a function of actors' impulsive trust, reflective trust, and working memory capacity.

people who should benefit most from being ambivalently distrusting. That's exactly what we found. When people consciously expected their partner to be less responsive, those people who were low on impulsive trust behaved in a more distant, cold, and rejecting way than people who were high on impulsive trust. Making more positive automatic evaluative associations to the partner essentially inoculated people low in working memory capacity against acting out in response to deliberative concerns about rejection. In this case, Helena's deliberative doubts about Hector's responsiveness lost all of their power to compel her to distance and treat him badly (fortunately for Hector). None of the effects of impulsive trust for people high in working memory capacity (the right side of Figure 10.5) were significant.

The State of Being Ambivalently Trusting

For a quick point of contrast, now consider the state of being ambivalently trusting (i.e., high on reflective trust but low on impulsive trust). In this case, automatic evaluative associations to the partner capture something negative about ongoing realities that people can consciously excuse and distort when they are immersed in the task of justifying their commitment to themselves. In our typology, such a heightened conscious motivation to defend one's positive perceptions of the partner's responsiveness might change the motivational immediacy or heft of one's unconscious hesitations. Indeed, being low on impulsive trust might motivate deliberated and positive compensatory sentiments as a defense against new behavioral realities. For instance, people who face greater pressure to justify their commitments because they are highly invested and have few alternatives to staying in the relationship claim to be relatively happy and satisfied even when their automatic reactions to their partner are relatively negative (Scinta & Gable, 2007). In light of such research, it is perhaps not surprising that Harry developed a reasonably strong conditioned aversion to approaching Sally in the kitchen long before he finally gave up trying to make compelling excuses for her nagging and accusations. Given the power of the unconscious, it's also not surprising that Harry's efforts to defend his conscious trust in Sally ultimately fell short.

Applying the Model to Predict Trust
and Commitment Trajectories

So how might we use the tenets of our dual process model to predict what trajectory trust and commitment might take once the situational landscape shifts and partners find themselves in terrain characterized by more frequent conflicts of interest? An upswing in conflicts of interest strengthens the automated will to self-protect—activating the if–then rules for vigilant appraisals, the if–then rules for orienting self-protection goals, and the if–then strategies for withdrawing one's own and promoting the partner's dependence. Such activation allows the interdependent mind to minimize the losses to be had in conflicts of interest. But—and this is an important but—an obsessive preoccupation with self-protection could also foreclose any gains to be had in such situations. Think back to the first time Sally asked Harry to take responsibility for a domestic chore he disliked. She could only experience the gain of his acceptance and responsiveness by taking the risk of asking for his assistance. The paradox of trusting means that Sally must give Harry the opportunity to be nonresponsive to discover how willing he is to be responsive. Essentially, she can best learn about his willingness to be responsive by setting aside the goal to self-protect in conflicts of interest (e.g., bribing him to do a chore by cooking his favorite meal), and instead pursuing the goal to connect (e.g., simply asking him to do a chore without stipulating what he might get in return).

This paradoxical aspect to trust (which we explore further in Chapter 11) anticipates exactly how impulsive trust might shape the trajectory trust and commitment take. Our logic hinges on situations, such as an exchange dilemma or a zero-sum conflict, in which deliberative ruminations about the partner's rejection and nonresponsiveness are acute. Such conscious preoccupations automatically provoke the automated will to self-protect and distance oneself from the partner even for people who are generally trusting (Murray, Derrick, et al., 2008). In such situations, more positive automatic evaluative associations to the partner might provide a crucial counterincentive to approach and not self-protectively distance oneself. Such a mechanism could explain exactly why Sally's trust (and commitment) took such a downswing while Helena's trust and commitment dipped a bit, but did not dive, with the escalation of interdependence.

Both Helena and Sally had reason to suffer serious declines in trust and commitment over time. Both experienced stressful circumstances— an early transition to parenthood for Sally, chronic economic stress for Helena. They both had some dispositional reason to question their partner's responsiveness—low self-esteem for Helena, preoccupied attachment style for Sally. Nonetheless, Helena experienced fewer high-risk situations over the transition to marriage than Sally did because she and Hector largely agreed on their role preferences. The relative ease of coordinating their interactions made her more impulsively trusting (through the mechanisms we detailed earlier). These more positive automatic associations to Hector also lessened her susceptibility to perceiving risk in subsequent situations, turning objectively high-risk situations into ones she perceived as opportunities for connection. Indeed, experimental data suggest that conditioning more positive evaluative associations toward the partner alters risk perceptions. People who are subliminally conditioned to associate their partner's name with positive words (e.g., *good*) actually report less anxiety about their partner's responsiveness (Murray, Pinkus, et al., 2010, Experiment 1). They also resist the impulse to distance themselves from a rejecting partner (Murray, Pinkus, et al., 2010, Experiment 2). Helena's positive automatic associations to Hector thus curbed her motivation to self-protect in ways that sustained behavioral expressions of responsiveness. Simply feeling safe in his presence motivated her to be responsive and allowed her to give Hector the motivation to prove his responsiveness. In so doing, this automatic and unconscious response sustained her feelings of trust and commitment. Sally was not so lucky because her automatic evaluative response to Harry only reinforced her growing conscious doubts about his responsiveness.

THE BASIS OF MUTUALITY IN RESPONSIVENESS

Brickman (1987) argued that the difference between mature and immature forms of love "lies in whether love proceeds by denying the imperfections of the loved one or recognizing them, accepting them, and loving anyhow" (p. 80). The personality of the relationship evolves in a similar sense. When besotted partners are immersed in approach–approach dilemmas (e.g., "Your place or mine?"), little differentiates the character of one relationship from the character of another. This changes dramatically once greater interdependence introduces stronger conflicts of interest and self-interested temptations into the situational landscape. The difference between the mature (i.e., differentiated) and immature (i.e., nondescript) forms of the relationship's personality then rests in whether interactions proceed by prioritizing the goal to self-protect or by recognizing risk, embracing it, and sometimes seeking connection nonetheless.

Each of our couples handled the transition to greater interdependence differently. In so doing, they created the personality that came to define their relationship. Let's consider contrasting examples of these personalities, at both the level of personality genotype (i.e., if–then habits of rule use) and phenotype (i.e., mutuality in behavioral expressions of responsiveness). Ron and Gayle were lucky enough to encounter low-risk situations once they had their first child. Such situation exposure elicited if–then habits of rule use that automatically willed Gayle to put her outcomes in Ron's hands and Ron to justify any costs he incurred in being responsive to Gayle's needs. The rewards Gayle experienced in such situations had two effects on the strength of her general motivation to approach him. They conditioned her automatic and positive evaluative association to Ron; they also took the sting away from any concerns she had about his responsiveness in their new lives as parents. Because impulsive and reflective trust both motivated approach, Gayle easily sustained faith in Ron's responsiveness. Her resolve in her commitment strengthened, and Ron's trust and commitment quickly followed suit. They became each other's best friends. They rely on each other as a primary resource for social support because they know they can count on each other. Despite the occasional conflict, they are very happy in their marriage because the rewards they experience in interacting traverse all three levels of interdependence (i.e., life tasks, personality, and relationship goals).

Helena and Hector also had the relative good fortune of encountering objectively low-risk situations early on in their marriage. They both valued a traditional home in which the mother was the caregiver and the father the provider, so they had few zero-sum conflicts in this domain. But Helena came into the marriage hesitant to trust Hector fully. She couldn't always understand why he would love someone like her. Such personal uncertainties got the better of her on days when her responsibility for three toddlers got overwhelming. Fortunately, being more impulsively trusting counter most of her acute concerns, but when Hector gets irritated and impatient because he's stressed about his job, Helena's hesitations about Hector's responsiveness do get the better of her. Such sensitivity adds a texture to Helena's if–then rule habits that is not evident for Gayle. Helena often finds herself doing things for Hector to make sure he needs her (i.e., "if self-protect goal, then promote partner dependence"). Being less reflectively trusting also motivates her to correct the automatic impulse to connect, and she sometimes stops herself from disclosing her financial fears even when he's in a good mood. Because Helena's impulsive and reflective trusting sentiments toward Hector sometimes send different messages, her commitment, though strong, developed more tentatively. She takes comfort in the constraints, such as their shared religious faith, that cement their marriage. Hector's trust and commitment followed suit. Helena and Hector are a team; they really enjoy spending leisure time together, and most of the time they are good sources of support to each other. But in the highest risk situations, Helena is most comfortable relying on Hector to fulfill his obligations as a husband and a provider.

Sally and Harry had the misfortune of encountering multiple high-risk situations, most of which Sally's accidental pregnancy and their quick marriage precipitated. Harry wanted Sally to be a domestic diva and Sally did not. She very much wanted to be a mom, but she wanted a career outside the home as well. These conflicts proved intractable in part because they came up so early in their relationship. Unlike Gayle and Ron, Harry and Sally had not yet had the chance to develop a solid foundation of rewarding experiences together when they had their first child. Without this learning history, the positive associations they first had to each other were quickly extinguished. Indeed, domestic strife soon conditioned an uneasy discomfort in each other's presence that made even tractable conflicts of interest seem ominous. Their quick sensitivity to risk elicited self-protective if–then habits of rule use that increased their vigilance to signs of each other's selfishness. They hesitated to depend on each other, and instead, spent considerable energy taking steps to promote each other's dependence. Through such tactics, they each came to feel resigned in their commitment. They largely restricted their interactions to their role responsibilities and now trust each other to provide only the most superficial of favors. They are now growing increasingly unhappy because they cannot rely on each other in the ways that they had hoped to. Their story is all too common. Satisfaction is often fleeting in relationships where "events" precipitate the commitment (Surra & Hughes, 1997).

SUMMARY AND CAVEAT

This chapter described how the rapid escalation of interdependence that comes with marriage and children begins to make the relationship's personality distinct. We argued that the nature of the conflicts of interests that come with such transitions provokes the if–then rule habits that come to define the relationship's personality. This chapter had four parts.

In the first part of the chapter we described the shift in situational landscape that comes with marriage and children. Satisfaction typically declines. While partners caught up in the thralls of passionate love encounter mostly coordination dilemmas, partners caught up in the drudgery of dishes and diapers more often encounter exchange dilemmas and zero-sum conflicts. This shift in situational landscape elicits a conservative shift in the if–then rules that preoccupy the interdependent mind. As this point in the relationship, trust becomes a decision to be made. The if–then rules for vigilance become more accessible as partners try to gauge each other's true motivations in conflicts of interest. Commitment also becomes contingent on trust. Indeed, the if–then rules for orienting and implementing self-protection goals come into force now that partners must more often self-protect against exploitation. Although Sally never hesitated to disclose to Harry when they were dating, now she is considerably more circumspect, only putting her outcomes in his hands when she is confident he will prove to be responsive. In the second part of this chapter we described how couples vary in the nature of the risks they encounter with increased interdependence. Because relationships vary in risk, partners come to adopt if–then rule habits. Such risk-congruent rule habits in turn set the relationship on the course for either upswings or downswings in trust and commitment. Being vigilant to rejection (i.e., accessible appraisal rules) and withdrawing in response to rejection forecast declines in satisfaction over time. In contrast, compensating for costs seems to ward off such declines.

In the third part of the chapter we described how the trajectory couples ultimately take depends on the signals supplied by both impulsive and reflective trust. Helena developed her positive evaluative association to Hector through their history of rewarding interactions. Being exposed to many low-risk situations conditioned her to find the best in Hector, an automatic impulse that left her feeling safe in his presence. Nonetheless, when the conflicts that came with financial stress prompted Helena to evaluate Hector's commitment more thoroughly, her deliberations always came up short. She has never been able to construct a fully satisfactory justification for why Hector would want to stay with her. In the end, she's of two minds when it comes to trust. Her automatic impulse is to trust Hector, but reflection pulls her back. Nonetheless, being of two minds actually helped sustain her commitment over time. Low in self-esteem and vulnerable to doubts about Hector's long-term commitment, Helena tends to magnify potential rejections. But more often than not, being more impulsively trusting curbs her tendency to self-protectively regulate risk. As a result, she sometimes approaches Hector in high-risk situations. Taking such risks then provided Hector with behavioral opportunities to prove his commitment to her. In the final part of this chapter we foreshadowed how situations, if–then rule habits, and reflective and impulsive trusting sentiments combine to shape partners' experience of their commitments and how they express (and do not express) responsiveness.

As the stories of each of our couples illustrate, the type of mutuality in responsiveness that develops through the workings of the interdependent mind controls the rewards the relationship offers. In so doing, the responsive behaviors that are enacted (and the ones that are not) place an upper bound on satisfaction (Kelley, 1979). Gayle and Ron ended up much happier than Sally and Harry because the if–then rule habits they practice offer greater rewards. Being each other's best friends, confidants, and sources of support (Ron and Gayle) simply makes interactions more rewarding and fulfilling than being entrenched in an uneasy alliance of instrumental role responsibilities (Harry and Sally). This brings us to an important caveat that we fully explore in the next chapter. The personality of the relationship is a function of the if–then habits of rule use of both partners. Harry and Sally experienced such a dramatic downswing in part because Harry did not have the motivational or wherewithal to counter Sally's self-protective if–then habits with more connectedness-promoting if–then habits of his own. We turn to the issue of the merging of two partners' if–then habits in Chapter 11, where we begin with a thought experiment. What would happen had a more egalitarian Ron married Sally? Would his marriage then be doomed to the same unhappy fate that Harry experienced in his marriage to Sally?

NOTES

1. As we introduced in Chapter 8, we think of satisfaction as an *outcome* of the expression of the relationship's personality genotype (i.e., mental habits of rule use) and phenotype (i.e., level and type of responsiveness enacted). From a classic perspective on interdependence, satisfaction is a function of the rewards partners experience in interacting (Kelley, 1979). But the value of the rewards to be gained increases as interdependence increases from life tasks, to personality, to relationship goals. Gayle gains more when Ron tempers his introversion to accommodate her gregariousness than she gains when he takes her turn at the dishes. This means that the behavioral expression of personality in the type of mutuality enacted puts an upper limit on the rewards to be gained. In this way, mental habits of rule use put an upper bound on satisfaction. We develop these points further in this chapter.

2. Let's be clear in how we are using the terms *unconscious* and *conscious*. We are *not* using the term *unconscious* to say that Helena has no insight into her automatic evaluative response to Hector. At some level, we would expect her to be well aware that she feels good or safe in his presence. Instead, we are using the term *unconscious* to imply that the if–then procedural rules that *create* such evaluative associations are likely to be inaccessible to consciousness (Bargh & Morsella, 2008). We are *not* using the term *conscious* in parallel with the term *deliberative* to argue that trust in the partner's responsiveness only involves conscious, propositional knowledge. Instead, trust should be sensitive to one's more automatic evaluative response toward the partner because

both sentiments provide related, albeit distinct, barometers of the safety of approach (see Gawronksi & Bodenhausen, 2006, for similar arguments).

3. In drawing these contrasts, we are not trying to argue that concrete experience plays no role in shaping deliberative expectations of responsiveness. For instance, witnessing a partner's behavioral sacrifices does bolster trust (Wieselquist et al., 1999). We are simply trying to make the point that abstract reasoning processes play a larger role in shaping deliberative expectations about the partner's commitment and responsiveness than they do in shaping automatic evaluations, and that automatic evaluations of the partner are likely to capture a wider range of behavioral experiences than deliberative expectations about the partner's responsiveness.

4. As we described in Chapter 3, attitude theorists believe that attitudes automatically orient people toward their social worlds, signaling which objects are safe to approach and which objects are better avoided (Chen & Bargh, 1999; Fazio, 1986). For this reason, we use "automatic evaluative association to the partner" and "automatic motivation to approach the partner" interchangeably.

5. This typology makes impulsive and reflective trust independent barometers of approach. This typology does *not* mean that unconscious sentiments do not influence conscious sentiments (and vice versa). Instead, considerable mutual influence is likely as our discussion of relationship trajectories in Chapters 11 and 12 reveals (Gawronski & Bodenhausen, 2006).

6. These conflicted states of mind might be difficult to sustain over time and there may well be a pressure toward more convergent levels of reflective and impulsive trust, as we explore in Chapters 11 and 12.

CHAPTER 11

How the Person, the Pairing, and the Context Make (or Break) Relationships

The whole is more than the sum of its parts.

The basic principle of holism that Aristotle introduced in *Metaphysics* has mind-bending implications for adult romantic relationships. Let's try a simple thought experiment. Imagine that Ron approached Sally at that high school dance instead of Harry. Years into their marriage would Ron now perceive Sally to be the nagging shrew that Harry so often perceives her to be? Imagine now that Gayle and Ron never had children, but devoted themselves steadfastly to their careers? Would Ron's occasional jealousy of Gayle's legal accomplishments still have so little consequence for their relationship? Had Hector married the lawyerly Gayle instead of the homemaking Helena, would his job anxieties now have a much more disruptive effect on his marriage? The principle of holism suggests that the relationship fates of each of these people would have been quite different had each encountered different circumstances.

Applied to relationships, the principle of holism means that the relationship itself (i.e., the whole) determines how partners (i.e., the parts) behave. Bluntly put, Sally might not have turned out to be a "nagging shrew" had she married Ron because Ron would have shared her zest for doing household chores. His preferences could have turned the zero-sum conflicts she experienced with Harry over ice trays, dishwashing, and laundry into coordination dilemmas. In such low-risk situations, Sally would have had no reason to be distrusting and demanding. This thought experiment reveals that Sally's caustic and demanding behavior is not intrinsic to her, but emergent from the whole of her relationship with Harry. In fact, his comparatively slovenly household habits might not have brought her marriage to its breaking point had Sally (or Harry) earned enough money to pay for domestic help. Similarly, Hector's machismo and traditionalism could have had a much more disruptive effect had he married Gayle and routinely compared his earnings as a factory worker to Gayle's earnings as an accomplished lawyer.

This chapter examines how the characteristics of each partner and the context surrounding the relationship combine to shape if–then habits of rule use with either conducive or disruptive consequence for responsiveness, trust, and commitment. In presenting this portrait of the relationship's personality, we depart from the previous two chapters. These chapters pointed out features of the situational landscape that standardize rule use. Chapter 9 argued that passionate love selectively samples low-risk situations. Such situations disproportionately activate the if–then rules for seeking connection, escalating dependence, and justifying commitment. Chapter 10 argued that increased interdependence and transitions, such as the birth of a first child, selectively sample high-risk situations. Such situations disproportionately activate the if–then rules for vigilance, seeking self-protection, withholding one's own dependence, and promoting the partner's dependence. In this chapter, we examine features of the relationship whole that introduce greater individual variability in if–then rule use. This relationship whole is composed of three parts: (1) the person: the preferences, attitudes, personality, and goals each partner brings to the relationship (e.g., Gayle's gregariousness); (2) the pair: the degree of compatibility or fit between the preferences, attitudes, personality, and goals partners together bring to the relationship (e.g., Harry and Sally's divergent role preferences); and (3) the context: the life circumstances that surround the relationship (e.g., economic stress, religion).

To understand how the relationship whole affects situation structure and rule use, consider something about Ron and Gayle we had little reason to mention until this point. They are both reasonably neurotic. Being prone to negative emotional states (i.e., neurotic) often leads to relationship distress and instability (Caughlin, Huston, & Houts, 2000; Kelly & Conley, 1987), but it did not for Ron and Gayle. Why not? Fortunately for them, they were fairly compatible. The conflicts of interest they faced as they moved in together, married, and had children were easily remediable ones. In terms of domestic chores, the things that Gayle most disliked doing were the things that Ron actually liked doing. Even one of their biggest personality differences—Gayle's greater gregariousness—seldom got them into trouble. They had so little time once work and child care were done that they seldom had the occasion to decide whether to go out with friends (Gayle's preference) or stay home and watch a movie (Ron's preference). Because they faced so few high-risk situations, neuroticism had little opportunity to express itself through greater sensitivity and reactivity to rejection. Had they faced a relationship fate in which they encountered more objectively high-risk situations, they might now interact considerably more cautiously, being vigilant to rejection and quick to withdraw from each other.

This chapter has two sections. Table 11.1 summarizes the arguments we make in each section, addressed in sequence in the chapter. Table 11.2 updates the couple profiles. In the first half of this chapter we examine how each component of the relationship whole affects if–then habits of rule use. We link the three pieces of the relationship whole to three paths of influence over rule use: (1) trust and risk appraisal, (2) goal orientation, and (3) correction. We begin with aspects of the person, including neuroticism, self-esteem, and attachment style. Here we explore how such factors predispose some if–then rule habits over others. We generally argue that such individual differences matter in relationships because they capture chronic motivations to approach positive outcomes (i.e., connect) and avoid negative outcomes (i.e., self-protect). For instance, people who are low in self-esteem, insecure in attachment style, and high in neuroticism are generally motivated to avoid negative outcomes (Gable, 2005; Heimpel, Elliot, & Wood, 2006). Such a chronic orientation disposes the possessor to self-protective if–then rule habits.

TABLE 11.1. The Main Arguments

1. The person, the pairing, and the context influence if–then rule habits through trust and risk appraisal, goal orientation, and correction.
2. Developing trust requires expressing trust (i.e., the trust paradox). Capacity to anticipate responsiveness in high-risk situations shapes how interaction unfolds.
3. Three points of leverage in shifting the willingness to approach the partner in high-risk situations: (1) situations, (2) trust, and (3) correction.
4. The if–then rules partners practice freeze or narrow the situational field by controlling how partners express commitment.
5. Expressions of commitment elicit similarity in the reasons partners have for being committed and thereby control the type of mutuality they practice.

TABLE 11.2. Updating Our Couple Profiles

Couple	Basic demographics	Life task preferences	Personality preferences	Relationship goal preferences
Ron and Gayle	African American Lawyers Two young children	Ron likes cooking; Gayle likes washing dishes. Both enjoy child care. Gayle loves sports. Ron loves wine.	Gayle: More gregarious. Gayle: More competitive. Ron and Gayle: Neurotic. Ron and Gayle: Secure.	Both value Gayle's working.
Harry and Sally	White Mechanic/customer service officer Three children, eldest 17	Harry dislikes all things domestic.	Sally: More gregarious. Sally: More fastidious. Harry: More reserved. Harry: Avoidant. Sally: Preoccupied.	Sally wanted to work; Harry wanted her at home.
Hector and Helena	Hispanic Factory worker/ homemaker Three young children Catholic Economically stressed	Largely compatible preferences.	Helena: Lower self-esteem; fearful in attachment style.	Stay tuned . . .
Gunter and Lastri	Indonesian PhD student/ homemaker One toddler	Gunter likes doing laundry; Lastri likes gardening.	Gunter: Enjoys outside social activities.	Gunter wants another baby; Lastri wants to return to school.

Why would that be the case? First, chronic motivations to approach gains (or avoid loss) shape how readily people can develop trust in the partner's responsiveness; therefore, such dispositions can shape if–then habits of procedural rule use by controlling the appraisal of risk. Such chronic motivations might also lower or raise the psychological threshold for activating the state goal to connect or to self-protect. Therefore, such dispositions can shape if–then habits of rule use by controlling one's chronic goal orientations within the relationship. For instance, weaker signs of rejection might be sufficient to "trip" the activation of a self-protect goal for a low self-esteem Helena than a high self-esteem Hector. Third, chronic motivations to approach gains (or avoid loss) might shape which if–then rules are likely to be corrected by controlling the "fit" between the state goal to connect or self-protect, trust in the partner's responsiveness, and these more chronic personality-based motivations, as we explain in more detail later. For instance, a low self-esteem Helena might get more practice correcting her automated will to disclose to Hector than a high self-esteem Hector gets correcting his automated will to disclose.

Next we turn to partner compatibility or fit. Here we explore how particular combinations of partner dispositions might predispose the interdependent mind toward some habits of thought over others. For instance, Helena can blow up Hector's slightest criticism because being low in self-esteem leaves her readily hurt. Such an easy sensitivity to rejection predisposes her toward more self-protective habits. Luckily for Helena, her relationship whole provides an effective counterweight to her insecurities. Despite his machismo issues, Hector is high in self-esteem and capable of suppressing his urge to self-protect when he's feeling hurt by her moodiness. In fact, Hector's steady and generally positive behavior helped sustain Helena's automatic positive evaluation of him. We conclude our discussion of how the relationship whole affects rule use with surrounding life context. Here we explore how particular life circumstances, such as economic stress, selectively sample some risky situations over other situations and consequently favor some if–then rule habits over others.

In the second half of this chapter we extend the relationship whole analysis to anticipate when the interdependent mind is likely to elicit satisfying and mutually responsive interactions and when it is likely to be stymied by circumstance. This is the basic question of why some relationships thrive while others falter. To begin to answer this question, we return to the trust paradox we introduced in Chapter 3. The paradox is that people cannot learn about their partner's trustworthiness without first trusting their partner. That is, people must put their own outcomes in their partner's hands to gain objective reason to trust in the partner's responsiveness (Holmes & Rempel, 1989). Consider the zero-sum conflicts over nighttime feedings Gayle and Ron faced. Overwhelmed at work and home, neither wanted to get up at 3 A.M. to lull their colicky son back to sleep. To test the limits of Ron's responsiveness, Gayle had to risk putting her outcomes in his hands (i.e., asking him to do a nighttime bottle feeding). His willingness to let her sleep gave her greater objective reason to trust in him, which in turn made her more willing to put her outcomes in his hands again and more willing to sacrifice on his behalf herself. Extending trust thus created a self-reinforcing cycle of commitment.

The interdependent mind we described in Chapter 7 generally is averse to taking such steps in high-risk situations. High-risk situations typically provoke the automated goal to self-protect and keep one's outcomes out of the partner's hands until it is safe. For a solid foundation for trust (and ultimately commitment) to develop, the relationship "whole" needs to be one that can nudge the interpersonal mind into perceiving high-risk situations as low in risk (a kind of positive transformation). Such an analysis suggests that the capacity to anticipate responsiveness in high-risk situations is a pivotal counterforce in developing trust and strengthening commitment. Imagine how Harry and Sally might have fared had they not disagreed over marital roles. If Sally had aspired to be a stay-at-home mother, she probably would not have seen Harry's unwillingness to do household chores as a testament to his nonresponsiveness. She might instead have noted his willingness to put aside his own leisure activities to spend time with her. The greater trust in Harry that resulted from such an optimistic appraisal of the strength of his commitment might then have elicited an entirely different form of mutuality. It might have steered their marital interactions toward ones involving mutual self-disclosure, supportiveness, and sacrifice rather than the uneasy distance they now inhabit.

For this reason, we argue that relationship dissatisfaction and instability can result when partners experience excessive exposure to high-risk situations, have chronic difficulty trusting, or both. In such situations, trust and commitment are likely to falter because if–then rules for pursuing self-protection occupy too much of the interdependent mind's energies. In the second section of this chapter we examine the consequences of faltering (and failed) commitment. Here we focus on the behavioral interaction patterns, such as demand–withdraw, that discriminate more and less satisfying and stable relationships. We argue that the state of commitment feeds back into trust by generating new situations that dictate the gains and the losses to be had in interacting. Faltering (or failed) commitment makes partners unwilling to sacrifice, unwilling to forgive, willing to mislead, and willing to betray (Rusbult & Van Lange, 2003). Strong (or resolute) commitment instead makes partners willing to sacrifice, willing to forgive, willing to support, and unlikely to betray. Because satisfaction is a function of the rewards partners experience in interaction (Kelley, 1979), the state of commitment that results from habits of rule use put an upper bound on satisfaction. Once Harry and Sally came to see their commitment as constrained by their children, it sealed their fate. Neither had sufficient conviction in their marriage or faith in each other to create the types of situations in their marriage that could generate greater rewards and potential for gain. Instead, they gravitated toward the types of situations and interactions that further eroded trust. We conclude this chapter by introducing a model of motivational interdependence that emerges from consideration of the relationship whole. This model also reveals points of leverage for intervention, our topic in Chapter 12.

THE PERSON, THE PAIRING, THE CONTEXT

We begin by describing how each aspect of the relationship whole—the person, the pairing, and the context—might shape if–then habits of rule use. Figure 11.1 presents a heuristic guide for our discussion. This template links the person, the pairing, and the context to potential paths of influence over if–then rule use: (1) the appraisal of risk, (2) thresholds for goal activation and orientation, and (3) correction. In illustrating how each aspect of the relationship whole might shape if–then habits of rule use, we do not provide an exhaustive review of the effects of personality or context on relationships. Rather, we hope to reveal how our model of the interdependent mind might be used as a tool to understand when, why, and how personality and context might shape patterns of responsive (and nonresponsive) behavior.

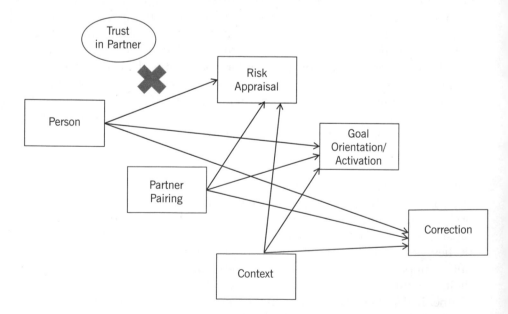

FIGURE 11.1. The relationship "whole" and "if–then" rule use.

The Person

People do not enter their relationships as tabula rasa. Hector and Helena each have unique personalities and goals. Each also had unique relationship experiences prior to their marriage. Helena had a difficult childhood after her parent's divorce and a painful romantic breakup in her teenage years. These experiences left her low in self-esteem and hesitant to trust others. Hector's childhood and young adulthood was comparative bliss. For Helena, the initial months of her relationship with Hector were so exhilarating in part because she felt like she had finally met someone she could really trust. It was only after they moved in together and had children that Helena's low self-esteem sometimes disposed her to be a bit too sensitive and reactive to normal ups and downs in Hector's mood (Bellavia & Murray, 2003).

This example reveals the starting point for our analysis of how individual personality and goals might influence if–then habits of rule use: Greater interdependence makes personal dispositions and goals relevant to ongoing interactions. It essentially reveals personality. In fact, Helena's low self-esteem did not exact any negative effect on her relationship until she and Hector became close and interdependent enough for him to feel comfortable being testy and disagreeable around her. The situations that resulted from their greater interdependence made certain aspects of her personality more relevant to ongoing interactions than others.

In formal terms, Kelley and Holmes (2003) argue that personality is a situational adaptation (see also Mischel & Shoda, 1995). This means that personality dispositions express themselves in situations that possess specific structural features that make the disposition relevant to solving the problems posed by the situation. For Helena, her low self-esteem expresses itself in situations that make the possibility of Hector's rejection salient. For Gayle, her competitiveness reveals itself in situations that make Ron's professional accomplishments and need for the occasional reprieve from his household responsibilities salient. Bowlby (1969) made a similar point in his conceptualization of attachment over the life span. He argued that specific features of the context (situation in our terms) make expectations about one's own worthiness of love and the responsiveness of others relevant. Such situation features then call working models of attachment to the perceptual and behavioral fore.

Consider the transition to parenthood in this regard. The birth of a first child imposes multiple conflicts of interest on the relationship as partners negotiate new responsibilities and roles. In this newly competitive situation, dispositions that signal the possibility of exploitation and loss should suddenly become relevant. Such logic led Steve Rholes and his colleagues (2001) to predict that women's chronic level of attachment anxiety would be more strongly associated with their relationship experiences after the birth of their first child than before. Their longitudinal study of this transition revealed that becoming a parent made attachment anxiety relevant within ongoing interactions. Women's attachment anxiety better diagnosed (i.e., predicted) concerns about the husband's supportiveness and diminished satisfaction in the stressful months after the baby's arrival than in the blissful weeks before the baby's arrival (Rholes et al., 2001).

These data suggest that situational risk makes personal dispositions and goals relevant to ongoing interactions. This brings us to our next point. Which particular chronic personality dispositions and goals should matter most in shaping if–then habits of rule use? Let's start with the structural features of conflicts of interest. Such situations offer both the opportunity for gain by putting one's outcomes in the partner's hands and the opportunity for loss. The structure of these situations puts the state goal to connect to the partner in conflict with the state goal to protect against rejection (see Chapter 5). Therefore, the basic structure of conflicts of interest makes personal dispositions that help direct action in such contexts highly relevant. Namely, it makes dispositions that help disambiguate the partner's motives and likely behavior relevant. It also makes dispositions that help prioritize one's own goal to either approach gains (or avoid losses) relevant (Gable, 2005). In this light, it becomes immediately apparent why the personality dispositions that matter most in relationships—such as self-esteem, neuroticism, attachment style, and expressiveness—have the effects they do.[1]

Let's start with the personality strengths, such as being expressive, secure in attachment style, or high in self-esteem. These dispositions generally map onto the strength of one's chronic goal to approach or seek gain. Certain of these dispositions help disambiguate the partner's motives and goals (Leary & Baumeister, 2000). For instance, people who are higher in self-esteem or secure in attachment style express greater trust in their partner's commitment because they assume their partner sees the same desirable qualities in them that they see in themselves (Mikulincer & Shaver, 2003; Murray, Holmes, & Griffin, 2000). Certain of these dispositions also help disambiguate one's own motivations and goals. For instance, people who are highly expressive possess personal qualities, such as being kind and understanding, that direct them to seek situations involving interpersonal connection (Miller, Caughlin, & Huston, 2003).

Now consider how such dispositions might exert their effects on if–then habits of rule use through risk appraisal, goal orientation, and/or correction (see Figure 11.1). Let's consider self-esteem first. People with high self-esteem trust more in their partner's commitment than people with low self-esteem. Such a disposition might strengthen connectedness-promoting if–then rule habits by controlling the appraisal of risk. High self-esteem people often perceive high-risk situations, such as soliciting a partner's support in the face of personal failure, as low in risk (see Chapter 3; Murray et al., 1998; Murray, Holmes, & Collins, 2006; Murray, Rose, et al., 2002). Such a dispositional insensitivity to risk should selectively activate the if–then rules for implementing the goal to connect over the goal to self-protect. Because Hector's high self-esteem lends itself to perceiving Helena's acceptance, he has become more practiced in escalating than restricting his dependence on Helena. Being high in self-esteem also might weaken self-protective if–then rule habits by controlling his motivation to correct. High self-esteem people typically perceive their partner's commitment as intrinsically motivated, and they resist any impetus to see it otherwise (Murray, Aloni, et al., 2009). On those occasions when Hector finds himself worried about Helena's responsiveness, he actively resists his urge to curry her favor by cooking her favorite meal or making her dentist appointment. Because he has become so practiced at suppressing the urge to promote her dependence, his occasional insecurities are rarely sufficient to provoke self-protective efforts.

Let's consider expressiveness as our second example. It seems reasonable to assume that people who are kinder, gentler, and more understanding experience a stronger chronic motivation to connect to others. Such a chronic motivation should affect how readily someone is oriented to pursue the goal to connect (vs. self-protect) in specific conflicts of interest within the relationship. Ron's high level of expressiveness helped him ride out the initial bumps in his marriage that came with the birth of his son. Like our other couples, Ron and Gayle faced conflicting interests in the allocation of the more onerous child care responsibilities (e.g., diapers, 3 A.M. feedings). Despite desiring sleep and unoffended nostrils, Ron's kind and gentle nature sensitized him to the fact that these tasks were just as onerous for Gayle. It also helped him to prioritize meeting her needs in this context. His disposition made it easier for Gayle to trust him, and their interactions proceeded relatively smoothly. However, Harry's greater instrumentality and traditionalism did him no favors as he and Sally faced the transition to parenthood. Indeed, Harry and Sally got into so many protracted conflicts over the allocation of domestic responsibilities in part because Harry just could not see himself as the type of person who did such "womanly" tasks (e.g., diapering, laundering, singing lullabies).

Longitudinal data from the PAIR project reported by Miller and his colleagues is instructive in this regard (Miller et al., 2003). In this study, both members of newlywed couples described themselves on a measure of trait expressiveness (e.g., kind, gentle, aware of other's feelings, helpful, warm). They also described their partner's level of responsiveness (e.g., pleasant, helpful, cooperative, forgiving, and generous) and completed telephone diaries tapping their level of affectionate behavior toward each other (e.g., expressing physical affection, seeking support, providing support). The results revealed that expressiveness fostered connectedness-promoting behaviors that stabilized the relationship. People, like Ron, who were higher on expressiveness behaved more affectionately toward their partner at each time point. They were more likely to do things like seeking support that put their outcomes in their partner's hands (a manifestation of the "escalate dependence" rule). The partners of expressive people then responded to such positive treatment by behaving more affectionately in return. Through this self-reinforcing cycle, expressive people like Ron ended up perceiving their partner as more responsive. In essence, Ron's expressiveness lent itself to connectedness-promoting rule habits that made Gayle want to be responsive to him—a dynamic that kept highly expressive people in the Miller at al. (2003) study happy over 13 years later in their marriage.

Now let's turn to personality liabilities, such as being neurotic, low in self-esteem, or insecure in attachment style. These dispositions generally map onto the strength of one's chronic goal to avoid or protect against loss. Certain of these dispositions again help disambiguate the partner's motives and goals. For instance, people with low self-esteem often question their partner's responsiveness; they are also quick to perceive reasonably safe situations as high in risk. Chapter 3 provided multiple examples of how the if–then rules for vigilance in appraisal are highly accessible for people low in self-esteem. The hyperaccessibility of these rules has an ironic consequence for people low in self-esteem: No news is better than good news. We once hoped to increase low self-esteem people's confidence in their partner's acceptance by pointing to the particular virtues they possessed. So we conducted experiments where we led low self-esteem people to think of themselves as highly considerate or highly intelligent (Murray et al., 1998). But it backfired: Low self-esteem people who learned they possessed a new strength in their relationship (like being highly considerate) actually reported less confidence in their partner's acceptance than controls did! It seemed that focusing on their strengths made low self-esteem people worry all the more about how they could fall short of their partner's expectations.

Certain of these personality liabilities also help prioritize one's own motives and goals. When it comes to the task of implementing commitment, people who are low in self-esteem or anxious-ambivalent in attachment seem preoccupied with the goal of avoiding loss (Baumeister, Tice, & Hutton, 1989; see Chapter 8). They are especially likely to respond to perceived rejection by distancing from the partner (i.e., "if self-protect goal, then withdraw own dependence"). For instance, people with low self-esteem respond to induced anxieties about their partner's possible rejection by evaluating their partner's qualities more negatively (Murray et al., 1998; Murray et al., 2002). In so doing, they protect themselves against loss because it hurts less to be rejected by a less valuable partner than by a more valuable partner. Women higher in attachment-related anxiety display greater anger toward their partner in a situation in which their partner may not have been as responsive as they hoped (Rholes, Simpson, & Orina, 1999). After discussing a serious relationship problem, more anxiously attached men and women also reported greater anger and hostility (as compared with controls who discussed a minor problem), and they downplayed their feelings of closeness and commitment (Simpson et al., 1996). People high on attachment-related anxiety also reported feeling less close to their partner in a situation in which they accurately inferred the (threatening) content of their partner's thoughts about attractive opposite-sex others (Simpson ct al., 1999). They also react to higher levels of daily conflict by minimizing their feelings of closeness to their partner (Campbell et al., 2005). From our perspective, such dynamics emerge in part because being chronically motivated to avoid loss sets a hair-trigger on the activation of the if–then goal orientation rules for self-protection. Indeed, Sally responds with so much hostility to Harry's domestic intransigence because she is both distrusting of him and neurotic by nature. The very prospect of loss is averse to her, and the slightest indication that it may be forthcoming mobilizes her into action.

Still a Role for Partner-Specific Expectations

As the template set out in Figure 11.1 illustrates, considering individual personality traits in terms of the if–then rule habits they foster explains why approach-oriented qualities like expressiveness forecast continued marital satisfaction (Miller et al., 2003) and avoidance-oriented qualities like neuroticism forecast decreased satisfaction and divorce (Kelly & Conley, 1987). Of course, each partner's personality and goals is only one part of the relationship whole. They do not define it. This brings us to an important caveat about the role individual personality plays in relationships. Being neurotic, low in self-esteem, or insecure in attachment style need not doom relationships, because if–then rule habits are also tied to relationship-specific expectations of responsiveness. Reflective trust is in part a projection of one's own self-esteem and prior attachments, as we have seen. However, impulsive trust and the willingness to approach the partner, is more rooted in behavioral realities within the relationship. We saw this with Helena. Despite her low self-esteem and shaky relationship history, her automatic evaluative association to Hector still motivates approach because his behavior makes her feel safe in his presence (even though she did not always let herself fully believe that she really could trust Hector).

This logic implies that the effects of individual personality dispositions can only be fully understood in the context or "whole" of trusting sentiments (both impulsive and reflective). The moderating effect of trust in a partner's responsiveness also illustrated in Figure 11.1 captures this assumption. The Rholes et al. (2001) transition to parenthood study is instructive in this regard. The transition to parenthood preoccupies partners with reasons to self-protect because they encounter so many new zero-sum conflicts (e.g., who gets to sleep, who gets freedom from laundry, who gets time to read, who gets time spend with friends)..Such transitions should be especially difficult for people, such as those who are anxious-ambivalent in attachment, who are already vigilant to the possibility of exploitation. Nonetheless, Rholes and his colleagues reasoned that trusting in a husband's responsiveness might buffer highly anxious women against self-protective behaviors through this transition. Their results strongly supported this assumption. Women who were both ambivalent and less trusting sought less support from their husbands over this transition. That is, they became more self-protective in their rule habits (i.e., greater accessibility of the "withdraw own dependence" rule). They also reported significant declines in satisfaction. In contrast, women who were ambivalent yet trusting nonetheless sustained their level of support seeking and satisfaction across this transition.

The Pairing

The metaphor of a relationship whole reveals something else important about individual personality: The context of the relationship changes its expression and meaning. Gayle is a different person with Ron than she is with anybody else because being with Ron involves accommodating herself to him. Such accommodations are necessary because partners do not selectively assort on basic dimensions of personality, such as extraversion, agreeableness, neuroticism, or conscientiousness (Feng & Baker, 1994; Lykken & Tellegen, 1993; Robins, Caspi, & Moffitt, 2000). Extraverts sometimes pair with introverts (and sometimes not); neurotics sometimes marry neurotics (and sometimes not); and those who strive to be ahead of deadlines sometimes find themselves attached to partners who take pride in not owning a watch. Such capriciousness to pairing means that some partners are more compatible than others; it also means that some are better equipped to deal with their incompatibilities. Indeed, in satisfying relationships, partners somehow become more similar in personality and emotional experience with time (Gonzaga, Campos, & Bradbury, 2007).

How might partner compatibility or fit affect if–then habits of rule use? To answer this question, we need to tackle an issue seldom broached in the literature: Defining compatibility. In our way of thinking, partners can be more or less compatible in two distinct ways, each of which has different effects on if–then habits of rule use. First, partners can be more or less compatible in terms of the outcomes each partner prefers in a specific situation of interdependence. Such compatibilities help determine the gains and losses to be had in specific situations of interdependence. Second, partners can be more or less compatible in the if–then rule habits that typically occupy their mental energies. Such compatibility helps determine the ease of coordinating Helena's expression of commitment with Hector's reciprocal expression of commitment across situations of interdependence within the relationship. In conjunction, such compatibilities and incompatibilities shape both the nature and tractability of the conflicts of interest partners face (i.e., the relationship's risk profile).

Let's consider compatibility in outcome preferences first. Certain personality dispositions, like extraversion, conscientiousness, openness to experience, and attachment-related avoidance, lend themselves to particular outcome preferences in specific situations. For most people, being high on attachment-related avoidance creates a preference for a late night at the office over an intimate dinner with one's spouse (Hazan & Shaver, 1990). Being low in openness to experience creates a preference for the familiar restaurant over a new one. How might compatibility in such personality-based preferences affect the nature of the if–then rule habits Gayle and Ron and Harry and Sally each gravitate toward? Gayle is considerably more gregarious than Ron. In situations requiring a choice between going out with friends or staying home alone, going on a group tour for a vacation or a solitary camping trip, or going to the office holiday party or making appropriate excuses, she usually prefers the outcome opposite to the one he prefers. Sally is considerably more conscientious than Harry. She always prefers the outcome opposite to his preference when it comes to situations like deciding how neat the house needs to be, whether doing the dishes or watching a movie is a more important priority, and how much self-discipline to expect from each of their children.

Because incompatibility in conscientiousness made Harry and Sally's preferences opposite in multiple domains, they encountered more high-risk situations than Gayle and Ron (who only encountered conflict on the rare occasions when they had free time). For Sally, such situation exposure frequently primed the if–then rules for implementing the goal to self-protect. Such rule use made Sally hesitant to depend on Harry, and Harry resistant to her frequent efforts to control him by making his doctors' appointments and limiting his time with friends. Had Ron married Sally, things might have turned out differently. Ron is fastidious to a point that a reasonably conscientious and perfectionist Gayle sometimes wonders why he cannot leave a dirty dish in the sink. Sally would have found the same quality in Ron a perfect match to herself. Their greater compatibility would have turned the zero-sum domestic conflicts she faced with Harry into coordination dilemmas with Ron. In such low-risk situations, Sally might have developed more connectedness-promoting if–then rule habits. She might have willingly turned to Ron to help her find ways to accommodate her goals for a career and a family (rather than resenting him for her status as a part-time bank teller, as she does Harry). She might also have found Ron's occasional forgetfulness endearing rather than chastising him for neglecting to pick up the dry cleaning or buy milk at the store (as she does Harry).

Now let's consider partner compatibility in if–then rule habits. Let's assume that certain personality dispositions, like being high in self-esteem, secure in attachment, or motivated to approach gains, elicit connectedness-promoting if–then rule habits (Gable, 2005; Murray, Holmes, & Collins, 2006). For people who are high in self-esteem, drawing closer to the partner is such a well-rehearsed habit that highs even approach their partner in situations where they perceive their partner to be rejecting. For instance, people who are high in self-esteem actually feel closer to their partner in the face of experimental feedback that their partner is annoyed with them (Murray et al., 2002)! Other dispositions, like being neurotic, anxious-ambivalent in attachment, or motivated to avoid losses, make self-protective if–then rule habits more likely (Higgins, 1998; Murray, Holmes, & Collins, 2006). For instance, people who are anxious-ambivalent in attachment style are compulsive caregivers; they practice the "promote partner dependence" rule to such a fault that they actively infringe on their partner's freedom and competence (Feeney, 2004; Feeney & Collins, 2003). What happens if someone who is more comfortable seeking connection matches up with someone who is more comfortable avoiding rejection? Can partners in such a pairing coordinate reciprocated expressions of commitment more or less readily than partners who are both motivated to self-protect or partners who are both motivated to connect?

Consider Gunter and Lastri in this regard. Gunter is promotion oriented; it is most natural for him to charge ahead in life and strive for good things to happen. Lastri is prevention oriented; it is most natural for her to be cautious and try to keep bad things from happening (Higgins, 1998). Now consider the conflict of interest they face between Lastri going to university (her preference) and having another baby (Gunter's preference). Even though Lastri has trusted Gunter to this point, the situation she faces now is a new one. So she reverts to her old and comfortable habits; she self-protects. In this unfamiliar terrain Lastri expects a fight, and her mind prepares her to avoid the rejection she fears. She avoids engaging in discussions with Gunter about her preferences (i.e., "if self-protect goal, then withdraw own dependence"). Instead, she drops hints, cooks his favorite meals, and enlists their Western friends as allies in the hope of making him more accommodating (i.e., "if self-protect goal, then promote partner dependence"). Gunter, too, reverts to his old familiar habits—but these habits prompt him to connect to Lastri. He expects Lastri to trust him just as he trusts her. He tries to be honest and forthright with her about what it would mean to him to have another child (i.e., "if connect goal, then escalate own dependence"), and now he cannot understand why she has so much trouble being disclosing with him. He looks at her avoidant behavior (e.g., cooking instead of talking) and worries that she really does not trust him as much as he trusts her. He's hurt. Their divergent if–then rule habits have created a communication impasse that could now threaten Gunter's trust in Lastri and make him question his commitment. Had a promotion-focused state of mind been a more natural one for Lastri, things might have turned out differently. She might have divulged why she wanted to attend school, an expression of trust in Gunter that could have given him a better opportunity to demonstrate his commitment to her.

Now contrast Gayle and Ron to Hector and Helena. Gayle and Ron grew up with parents who loved them, but each set of parents had their share of conflicts. Such experiences left them both reasonably secure in attachment style, albeit somewhat neurotic and easily agitated. Fortunately, being immersed in low-risk situations allowed their secure expectations to assert themselves, disposing both of them to if–then rule habits that promoted connection. Hector had even more security-inducing childhood experiences; his parents not only communicated unconditional love to him, but they rarely fought with each other. But losing her father because of her parent's divorce left Helena somewhat fearful. Such experiences dispose her to more self-protective if–then rule habits than Hector. Despite their diverse backgrounds, these two sets of couples are relatively happy and their interactions relatively indistinguishable in most of the situations they encounter. However, when it comes to negotiating the most difficult issues in their relationships, these couples have different styles (Senchak & Leonard, 1992).

Consider the tendency to "kitchen-sink." This destructive tactic involves drawing unrelated issues (i.e., everything but the kitchen sink) into the current discussion. Partners who make the if–then rules for vigilance a stronger rule habit are likely to make such accusations more naturally because they have greater ammunition for such exchanges at their disposal. Helena's chronic fearfulness makes it hard for her to consciously trust in Hector, a state of uncertainty that makes the if–then rules for gauging his trustworthiness (see Table 3.1) chronically accessible. The accessibility of these rules means that she notices when he forgets to compliment her on a new haircut, makes a snide comment about her overdone meatloaf, or breaks a promise to spend alone time with her to go out with his friends. In the midst of a conflict over Hector's job stresses, these episodes flood back to Helena and she cannot help but regale Hector with the "evidence" of his misdeeds ("if self-protect goal, then withdraw own dependence"). In the face of such accusations, Hector then feels hurt and mistreated precisely because he does not keep track in this way. In response to such unexpected attacks, he automatically withdraws. In such circumstances, he simply loses the motivation he normally has to correct such an impulse and he loses all motivation to be responsive to Helena. Ron and Gayle rarely get locked into such stalemates because neither keeps a running tally of complaints.

As these varying examples illustrate, compatibility in the if–then rule habits each partner more naturally enacts further define the severity and tractability of the conflicts that partners face (i.e., the risk profile). This happens because partners look to each other's behavior to define the meaning of the conflict itself. Think about Hector and Gunter. In each case, witnessing the more self-protective rule habits of their wives made Hector and Gunter perceive the problem(s) they faced as being more serious and pervasive in nature. This metacognitive aspect to risk appraisal raises an intriguing prediction. In relationships where both partners are inclined to connect, the shared habit to put one's outcomes in the other's hands should make it easier for partners to be responsive. In relationships

where both partners are inclined to self-protect, the shared habit to minimize dependence until it is safe could make it easier for partners to be
responsive in more limited, instrumental ways. In relationships where
one partner is inclined to connect and the other is inclined to self-protect,
the fate of the relationship may rest in which if–then rule habit prevails. In
such a relationship, partners are likely caught in the kind of conflict over
closeness (i.e., how much is too much) that underlies destructive interaction patterns (Christensen & Heavey, 1990). We further develop these
points in our final chapter on intervention and marital therapy.

The Context

Relationships do not take place in a vacuum. They take place in the context of surrounding family relationships, work responsibilities, health
concerns, and economic stressors. Such factors are also integral to the
relationship whole that fosters if–then habits of rule use. Research examining the effects of life stress on relationship functioning is notable in this
regard.

To this point, we have described risk as a property of the situation
(see Table 5.1). Riskier situations are ones in which the partner has a stronger temptation to be selfish, and as a result, putting one's outcomes in
a partner's hands creates greater risk of exploitation. Consider a conflict
Hector and Helena might have about how to spend the family's limited
Christmas budget (a "hot" issue for them both). When Hector has had a
good day at work, he can listen to Helena's litany of grievances about their
limited Christmas budget and not take the bait. He can effectively correct any impulse he has to respond to his hurt feelings by distancing and
instead try to assuage Helena's concerns. When Hector has had a bad day
at work, the conversation about how to allocate their resources is more
likely to deteriorate into a shouting match. On those days, he simply does
not have the self-regulatory capacity to correct.

This example suggests that partners who are mired in more stressful
circumstances might be prone to more self-protective if–then rule habits.
This could happen for three reasons. First, stressful circumstances might
increase the level of risk inherent in the situation. For instance, if money is
limited, one partner's spendthrift habits create a greater loss for the thrifty
partner and give that partner greater reason to protect against exploitation (perhaps by setting up a separate bank account). Second, stressful
circumstances might also decrease the threshold for perceiving the partner's rejection. For example, on days when Hector has received worrisome
feedback about his job security, he might be more likely to perceive Hel-

ena's offhand remark as a criticism of his capacity to be a good provider. Third, stressful circumstances could also limit the self-regulatory capacity even trusting partners have available to correct the automatic impulse to self-protect, as it did for Hector in the example we described above (Finkel & Campbell, 2001).

Impressive research reported by Neff and Karney (2009) illustrates such possibilities. These researchers assumed that marital satisfaction requires a kind of insensitivity. In even the best marriages, some days are better than others. Given the way the interpersonal mind works, it is easier for Gayle to be happy on days when Ron brings her flowers than on days when he criticizes her parenting or legal skills. To stay satisfied over the longer term, Gayle's daily satisfaction should be relatively immune to such variations in day-to-day events (Arriaga, 2001). Why would this be the case? In terms of our model of the interdependent mind, partners who are happy on good days and unhappy on bad days—that is, partners who are reactive to daily events—are excessively vigilant. For such partners, the if–then rules for vigilance in appraisal are hyperaccessible. Neff and Karney (2009) reasoned that such vigilance should be most evident among couples mired in stressful circumstances (e.g., financial stress, health problems, family conflicts, etc.) because such circumstances should both heighten the perception of risk and limit the opportunity to correct. Two studies using different measures of stress (one chronic, one daily) supported their hypotheses. Partners who were mired in stressful circumstances were happier in their relationships on good days and less happy on bad days. They seemingly failed to correct the if–then rules for vigilance. However, partners who were not mired in such stressful circumstances did correct. Their satisfaction was immune to the ups and downs in day-to-day events that are part and parcel of marital interactions.

Related research on stress conducted by Rauer, Karney, Garvan, and Hou (2008) echoes this theme. They conducted a representative survey of couples residing in Florida. Their results revealed that couples report less marital satisfaction the more external stresses they face (e.g., financial strain, poor mental health, lack of social support, substance use). Further findings suggested if–then habits of rule use could be implicated in this dynamic. Namely, exposure to multiple stressors (i.e., cumulative risk) compounded the detrimental effects of exposure to any individual stressor. This means that financial strain is more likely to be a source of marital dissatisfaction for Hector and Helena if it occurs in the context of multiple stressors (i.e., greater cumulative risk). Fortunately for them, it did not. Their children were healthy, neither of them had any kind of substance abuse problem, and they each provided reasonably solid support to each other most of the time. Things might have turned out quite differently had circumstances been different. Had Hector's job worries been compounded by his children's ill health, he might routinely succumb to the urge to lash out in response to Helena's "kitchen-sinking," setting their relationship on a downward rather than reasonably stable trajectory.

Summary

The if–then rule habits that define a relationship's personality stem in part from the dispositions and goals each partner brings to the relationship, compatibility in outcome preferences and rule habits that result from these dispositions and goals, and the surrounding life context. When money is in excess, a first baby has an easy temperament, and both partners aspire to a tidy house, two neurotics like Gayle and Ron might fare just as well in trust and commitment as two nonneurotic partners because the situations they face do not provoke chronically self-protective if–then habits of thought. But when money is tight, a first baby is colicky, and standards for household cleanliness are incompatible, one neurotic partner (like Sally) might be all it takes to put partners on a trajectory toward declining trust and commitment. This brings us to the most complex aspect of our analysis. How can the various pieces of the relationship whole explain why some relationships thrive while others falter?

WHY SOME RELATIONSHIPS THRIVE WHILE OTHERS FALTER

To answer this question, let's return to the patterns of mutual responsiveness and nonresponsiveness that characterize marital interaction for Ron and Gayle, Hector and Helena, and Harry and Sally. Ron and Gayle are highly responsive to each other's needs in multiple domains. They turn to each other first for socioemotional support. In even the most contentious domain in their marriage—their respective legal careers—Gayle ultimately sacrifices at least some of her professional ambitions to take Ron's needs into account. They take joy in being committed to each other; neither has ever seriously contemplated divorce.

Hector and Helena look like Ron and Gayle in most but not all respects. They too love spending time together as parents and provide valued sources of support to each other in this endeavor; they also easily coordinate their responsibilities because Hector is usually willing to give

Helena a break with child care. They also take great pleasure in shared recreational pursuits, like hiking and watching baseball; they usually find lots to laugh and joke about simply watching their kids play. But when discussions about Hector's job stresses come up, Helena's fearfulness can get the better of them. In these circumstances, Hector rarely gets the support he needs from Helena. She interprets his anxieties about his adequacy as a financial provider as resentment and anger with her and then "kitchen-sinks" in response. Her avoidance of the issue makes Hector feel unappreciated and misunderstood, which then prompts him to remind Helena (in a most insistent way) about everything he does do to provide for his family. Because he is normally so calm, his animation in such instances only confirms Helena's fear that he is upset with her and she becomes even more reluctant to provide support. To this point, this persistent conflict has had limited effects because the majority of their interactions are so rewarding. In most respects they are happily committed, but Helena takes some extra security in believing that Hector would never go against his religion and family by leaving her and their children.

Sally and Harry were not so lucky. Unrelenting exposure to high-risk situations made it difficult for them to find points of connection. They tread cautiously, guard their words, and talk mostly about how to coordinate their children's school and social activities (e.g., who will chauffeur to the ball game, who will take care of the doctor's appointment). When they do try to engage on other dimensions (e.g., Sally's aspirations to do more than part-time work, Harry's desire for his ailing mother to move in with them), discussions quickly degrade into arguments. They long ago gave up on being each other's confidants. Now they rely on each other in only the most superficial sense. Each knows the other can be counted on to fulfill established obligations to keep their household running, but that's it. Sally often thinks about divorce, but she knows she could not readily support her children on her own. Harry spends most of his time immersed in the television because it provides a necessary distraction from Sally's harangues.

Alternative Upward and Downward Trajectories: Implications from the Relationship Whole

How might such varying patterns of responsiveness (and nonresponsiveness) develop and then determine the trajectories trust and commitment take? As Figure 11.2 illustrates, our discussion of this issue begins and ends with situations. This figure abstracts the elements of our motivation management model (see Figure 2.1) central to our analysis here. It

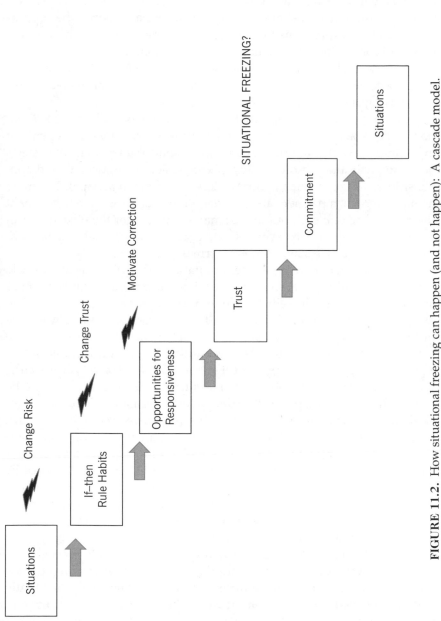

SITUATIONAL FREEZING?

FIGURE 11.2. How situational freezing can happen (and not happen): A cascade model.

assumes that situations and automatic if–then habits of thought open certain opportunities for behavioral responsiveness and close other opportunities. These expressions of responsiveness then reinforce the states of trust and commitment that generated them and thereby elicit more of the same types of situations. In explaining this cascade model of situation generation, we start with a theme that has permeated our analysis: Risk evokes congruent if–then rule habits.

Risk is a property of the situation as perceived (see Chapter 5). Situations vary in objective risk because partners are varyingly interdependent in life tasks (e.g., the number of domestic responsibilities to be allocated), personal goals and personality (e.g., extraversion, neuroticism), and relationship goals (e.g., having a more or less traditional marriage). The more domains in which partners are interdependent, and the more discrepant their preferences in each of these domains, the greater the objective situational risk they face. However, the perception of situational risk may differ from its objective state. Ron is so trusting that he perceives domains in which Gayle has a pretty strong temptation to be selfish as low in risk. Sally is so distrusting that she perceives domains in which Harry has only a small temptation to be selfish as high in risk. The situational risks typically perceived evoke Ron's automated will to connect and Sally's automated will to self-protect. The automatic behavioral strategies that come with these goals open up multiple opportunities for responsiveness for Ron and Gayle and limit such opportunities for Sally and Harry. For instance, Ron confides his worries about his parenting skills to Gayle because he expects her to be accepting. His dependence-escalating behavior gives Gayle the opportunity to demonstrate her responsiveness, which in turn strengthens Ron's trust in Gayle and his commitment to being responsive to her needs. In contrast, Sally rarely asks Harry for help around the house anymore because she expects him to be rejecting. She instead demands he do certain things and criticizes him at most every turn. Her dependence-minimizing behavior gives Harry little opportunity to prove her wrong, which reinforces her doubts about Harry's responsiveness and makes her more reluctant to be responsive to him.

The if–then rules Ron habitually practiced created self-perpetuating interaction cycles by selectively sampling situations that afforded opportunities to be responsive. By contrast, the if–then rules Sally habitually practiced created self-perpetuating interaction cycles by selecting sampling situations that limited opportunities to be nonresponsive. To delineate how such opposite cycles can develop, we return to the trust paradox. As we described at the beginning of this chapter, the paradox to trusting is that people cannot acquire objective and concrete evidence about their partner's trustworthiness without first taking the risk of trusting their partner (Holmes & Rempel, 1989). To gain objective reason to trust in Harry's responsiveness, Sally needs to expose herself to rejection. For instance, she might ask Harry to temporarily take over child care duties on his traditional poker night so that she could take an accounting seminar. Sally never takes these kinds of risks without insurance. She only asks Harry to take on a specific domestic chore if she has already taken some step (like granting him dispensation for a camping weekend with his friends) that guarantees that he "owes" her. Her automatic and habitual reliance on the "promote dependence" rule to extract Harry's responsiveness almost always gives her reason to discount his good deeds. Such external attributions only sustain her unease around Harry. Being less trusting limits her expressions of responsiveness to the types of behavior she anticipates in Harry. Her willingness to cook and clean, but not listen and emphasize, limits his trust in her and restricts his motivation to be responsive to her similarly low levels of interdependence.

Leverage Points for Changing Relationship Trajectories

For Sally and Harry to escape a downward trajectory, some piece of the relationship whole needs to change in a way that could break the habit to self-protect and foster a stronger habit to connect. We next examine how shifts in one piece of the relationship whole might put Harry and Sally's marriage on an upward trajectory (i.e., strengthening trust and commitment). For point of contrast, we also explore what pieces of the whole might need to change to put Ron and Gayle's marriage on a downward trajectory.

For Sally to trust enough to ask Harry to give up poker and for Harry to be committed enough to assent, at least one of them needs to treat the occasional high-risk situation as if it were low in risk. What might nudge behavior toward from approach in such situations? Our analysis of relationship personality reveals three points of influence for exacting change in the behavioral tendency to approach (vs. avoid) the partner. The lightening bolts in Figure 11.2 note these points of leverage in our cascade model of situational freezing. They include: (1) the situational landscape, both interior and exterior to the relationship; (2) trust as experienced in automatic evaluative associations to the partner (i.e., impulsive trust), deliberative expectations of responsiveness (i.e., reflective trust), and chronic personality dispositions to trust; and (3) motivation and opportunity to correct the leanings of the automated will. These points of influence can leverage behavioral change by dynamically shifting which if–then rule habits become habitual, which are readily corrected, and when new or specialized if–then rules gain influence. We illustrate each of the three points of leverage for exacting behavioral change by altering the personal and life context of Harry and Sally and Ron and Gayle in a way that affords different if–then rule habits.

Leverage Point 1: The Situational Landscape

Positive interactions outweigh negative interactions by a ratio of approximately 5:1 in satisfying relationships (Gottman, 1994). Such a ratio points to one critical point of leverage. Situations evoke congruent if–then rule habits. Therefore, it should be possible to nudge Sally's mind into perceiving high-risk situations as reasonably low in risk if many of the situations she faces are also low in risk and automatically elicit connectedness-promoting if–then rule habits. Conversely, it should be possible to nudge Gayle's mind into perceiving even low-risk situations as reasonably high in risk if many of situations she faces are also high in risk and automatically elicit self-protective if–then rule habits.

Harry and Sally's Happy Alter Ego. Imagine that Harry had shared Sally's desire that she work while raising her family, rather than wanting Sally to stay home. Feeling more supported in her core identity and values could have changed Sally's orientation toward a host of the domestic conflicts they ultimately faced. In such a circumstance, she might not have seen the empty ice tray as a symbol of Harry's laziness and selfishness. She might have instead laughed off the incident by reminding herself how Harry once forgot to diaper their daughter before dressing her (i.e., "if connect goal, then justify commitment"). Just this one change in the compatibility of their goals and values for the relationship could have had cascading effects on her experience of domestic chore negotiations. Rather than experiencing the allocation of dishwashing responsibilities as a zero-sum conflict, they might have approached such situations as coordination dilemmas. Such interactions might then have conditioned Sally's more positive automatic evaluative association to Harry. Being more impulsively trusting could then protect her optimistic expectations of his responsiveness against his occasional misdeeds. Being uniformly trusting as a consequence, she would evidence little sensitivity or vigilance to rejection. As a result, her commitment to meeting Harry's needs could have stayed strong despite daily ups and downs from ill-mannered children, work-related stresses, or forgotten dishes. Sally's willingness to commit by making sacrifices (Van Lange et al., 1997), being forgiving and accommodating (Rusbult et al., 1991), and providing emotional support (Collins & Feeney, 2004) would condition Harry's more positive evaluative associations to her and bolster his conscious expectations of her responsiveness. Being both impulsively and reflectively trusting would then secure his future commitment and responsiveness.

Ron and Gayle's Unhappy Alter Ego. Now imagine that Ron and Gayle were not well-off professionals with the financial largesse to pay housekeepers and nannies to take some of their domestic responsibilities off their hands. Compound this scenario by imagining that Gayle found Ron's fastidiousness overly controlling and that Ron hated that the gregarious Gayle so often put him in social situations he did not enjoy. In such a situational landscape, they would have faced more zero-sum conflicts over the allocation of household chores and in the goals they had for their relationship and life together. Inevitably, each would have witnessed more signs of the other's selfishness. Such behavior might condition Gayle's more negative automatic evaluative association to Ron. In such a climate, their neuroticism would have the chance to reveal itself fully. Each might have become vigilant and self-protective. Reflectively and impulsively distrusting, they would have been hesitant to rely on each other for anything but the most superficial favors, a pattern of responsiveness exactly opposite to the one they now inhabit.

Leverage Point 2: Trust

In each of these marriages, the objective situational landscape might not always need to change quite that radically for the perceived situational landscape to change. Such a shift in the perceived situational landscape could then set trust and commitment on different trajectories.

Harry and Sally's Happy Alter Ego. Imagine that Sally and Harry still had opposite preferences for the allocation of household tasks. This time both are secure in attachment style, high in self-esteem, and completely nonneurotic. Such a pairing of personalities lends itself to positive deliberative expectations for one another's responsiveness. Armed with trusting expectations, Sally might assume the best of Harry when they faced the occasional zero-sum conflict over household chores. Such an optimistic assumption would elicit connectedness-promoting rule habits and behavior in these high-risk situations (e.g., asking Harry to give up his poker night temporarily so she could attend her accounting seminar). The more often Sally took such risks, the greater the number of opportunities

Harry would have to prove his responsiveness. Because his faith in Sally made Harry resolute in his commitment, his communal behavior made Sally's automatic positive evaluation to him all the stronger. The congruence between her impulsive and reflective trusting sentiments might even stabilize trust and commitment in the face of Harry's desire to have his ailing mother live with them. In such new and risky situations, being so uniformly trusting might inoculate Sally against feeling hurt or rejected by Harry's attention to his mother, creating a self-reinforcing cycle for escalating trust and commitment.

Ron and Gayle's Unhappy Alter Ego. Now imagine that Gayle was not only neurotic, but also disinclined to trust Ron because he made the mistake of lunching with an old girlfriend early in their marriage. Such a pairing of Gayle's specific expectations and chronic dispositional sensitivity to loss might then elicit disproportionately self-protective if–then rule habits. It could make it difficult for her to anticipate Ron's responsiveness in the few domestic domains they had left to negotiate after the housekeeper and nanny took care of their respective tasks. Assuming the worst, she might take on child care tasks for herself (i.e., "if self-protect goal, then promote partner dependence") and come to resent Ron for impeding her career through his "laziness" with their children (i.e., "if self-protect goal, then withdrawn own dependence"). Ron might begin to develop a more negative automatic evaluative association to Gayle because her chronic accusations make him feel anxious and vulnerable in her presence. Early on, he might be reflectively trusting, still working to defend his commitment despite his growing impulsive unease. Should her behavior prove unrelenting, he might run out of excuses. Eventually his reflective and impulsive trusting sentiments might merge as his conditioned aversion to being together erodes his once-positive conscious expectations of her responsiveness. Declining trust might then weaken his commitment and motivation to be responsive to Sally's needs. Such shifts might change the coordination dilemmas they once faced into zero-sum conflicts because he was no longer motivated to transform conflicts of interest to take her needs into account. Like Gayle, he might become hesitant to sacrifice or provide support.

Leverage Point 3: Correction

Being more or less trusting might also change the trajectories each of these couples eventually took by changing their motivation to correct the leanings of the automated will.

Harry and Sally's Happy Alter Ego. Imagine that Sally trusts Harry consciously (if we imagine that she is not only secure in attachment style, but also because he has always been responsive to her). Being more trusting motivates her to correct the automated will to self-protect in high-risk situations (see Chapter 7). Imagine that Harry really blew it and went to his poker game on the night Sally had an important exam in her accounting seminar. Such a serious misstep automatically activates the goal to self-protect against future exploitation, perhaps by chastising Harry for his thoughtlessness. But being more trusting and having time to reflect on her feelings allows Sally to correct such an automated will. In fact, Harry is so forgetful that she has practiced such correction on more than one occasion. Now her inclination to forgive such transgressions is automatic. In fact, she typically substitutes a more forgiving response (a specialized "if Harry forgets, then laugh it off" rule). Being quick *not* to self-protect preserves her positive automatic evaluative association to Harry and stabilizes her commitment. It also gives Harry all the more reason to trust in her (once he realizes how forgiving she's been of what he's done).[2]

Ron and Gayle's Unhappy Alter Ego. Now imagine a Gayle and Ron who face domestic conflicts that are reasonably easy to negotiate, but Gayle is both neurotic and distrusting. Many of the situations Gayle faces (like asking Ron to take the kids to a movie he wants to see one weekend afternoon) are objectively low in risk. Such situations automatically activate her goal to connect and condition her more positive automatic association to Ron, making her more impulsively trusting, but being both neurotic and distrusting motivates her to correct such leanings. Instead, she decides to pay the nanny over-time rather than risk putting her outcomes in Ron's hands. This distrusting Gayle used to have to remind herself *not* to laugh at Ron's inability to comprehend basic rules of football early in her marriage. Given how often his questions interrupted her serene enjoyment of the game, she no longer has to correct her impulse to justify her commitment. Instead, the sight of the dishes itself is enough to remind her of Ron's more negative qualities. With time, she became so practiced at correcting her urge to connect that it no longer required much effort. Instead, when she felt herself wanting to get closer to Ron, she usually found a way to remind herself of how he had disappointed her in the past (a specialized "if feel close, then distance" rule). Once high in impulsive trust and low in reflective trust, she might then grow uniformly distrusting over time and successive interaction. As a result, even a secure Ron would have few opportunities (like the movie outing) to demonstrate his responsiveness. Imagine that their troubles were only compounded because Ron was relatively fearful in his attachment style. Even in easy coordination dilemmas, he was apprehensive about extending himself too much. With no signs of Ron's responsiveness forthcoming (and few opportunities to be responsive herself), Gayle grows even less trusting and less committed. With no signs of her responsiveness forthcoming, Ron also loses his motivation to be responsive.

Situational Freezing: How Trust and Commitment Become Self-Perpetuating

In each of the variations on Harry and Sally's and Ron and Gayle's marriages we described, trust and commitment take decidedly upward or downward trajectories. We believe this happens because the if–then rules partners practice, the rules they correct, and the specialized if–then rules partners develop freeze or narrow the situational field (see Figure 11.2). That is, the situations partners initially perceive create if–then rule habits that produce some expressions of responsiveness and commitment over others. By controlling how partners experience trust and commitment, such behavioral expressions ultimately elicit more of the same types of situations. Our "original" Sally and Harry confronted disproportionately more high- than low-risk situations early in their marriage. Such situation exposure made the if–then rules for vigilance and self-protection stronger and more accessible than the if–then rules for seeking connection. That is, the risks they correctly perceived made them vigilant to rejection and quick to distance and withdraw in response. Through such if–then rule habits, they grew less trusting. Being less trusting motivated each to curb or correct the automated will they had to connect, which only weakened their feelings of commitment to each other. Through the force of such shared habits, they became mired in the cycles of reciprocated negativity that typify distressed marriages (Gottman, 1994). Sally got all the more sarcastic and bitter and Harry got all the more recalcitrant and avoidant, a classic demand–withdraw interaction pattern (Christensen & Heavey, 1990). How did this happen?

Consider first the if–then rules they practiced. Each reacted to high-risk situations, such as needing the other's sacrifice, by avoiding and withdrawing dependence. Rather than telling Harry how much she needed and valued his help, Sally typically framed her requests for Harry's help as an angry accusation (e.g., "Why don't you ever lift a finger around here?"). This only made Harry more resistant to helping. Harry and Sally's shared and automatic inclinations to evade and avoid thus provided actual behavioral evidence of nonresponsiveness that eroded trust and made new situations seem inherently riskier. Now consider the if–

then rules each corrected. In the past, Harry often wanted to go to Sally for comfort when he had a bad day at work and she seemed to be in a receptive mood, laughing and joking with the kids. But in acting on this impulse he had gotten burned on occasion. In fact, Sally had sometimes responded to his legitimate complaints about his job stresses by regaling him with how difficult *her* day had been. Now his job woes have become a "hot issue" in their marriage. The failures to get the support he needed motivated Harry to curb his automatic urge to disclose to Sally when he had the opportunity to do so. Soon correcting such inclinations became automatic. He reverted to the TV when he got home and not even being tired or distracted was enough to motivate him to disclose. He essentially substituted a new and specialized "if desire support, then withdraw" rule for the default rule. Once correcting the automatic impulse to connect became second nature, it sealed his fate. Harry essentially foreclosed opportunities for greater trust by not talking to Sally, thereby limiting interaction to safe superficialities. Had he risked telling her about his day at least sometimes (i.e., succumbed to his automated will to connect), Sally might have surprised him on occasion. She might have been attentive and understanding. Such positive experiences could have conditioned a more positive automatic evaluative association to Sally, an impulsively trusting sentiment that might motivate him to approach her in risky situations again in the future.

In contrast to Harry and Sally's deteriorating fate, Ron and Gayle became more trusting and committed throughout their marriage. They initially encountered more low- than high-risk situations. Such situation exposure left them quick to perceive and act on signs of each other's acceptance. As they became more practiced in relying on each other for sacrifices, they grew more interdependent, more trusting, and more committed. They easily justified the costs they incurred as a result of being close. In fact, Ron had finally started to appreciate Gayle's obsession with sports as evidence of her great zeal and passion for competition. Growing more trusting also motivated Ron to correct his automated will to self-protect when Gayle criticized his legal acumen. Early in his marriage, her subtle insinuations that she was the more accomplished attorney provoked more than one argument. With time, Ron got enough practice at resisting her baiting that he now he forgives her boastfulness relatively automatically. He eventually learned a new and specialized rule (i.e., "if criticized, then increase closeness"). Such a transformation both strengthened his automatic and positive evaluative association to Gayle and being more impulsively trusting robbed this persistent conflict of its capacity to threaten his commitment to Gayle. Their interactions almost always unfold smoothly and harmoniously as a result.

Before we turn to the last part of this chapter, a caveat is in order. Each of these marriages experienced sharp downward and upward trajectories because the situations Harry and Sally and Ron and Gayle faced were disproportionately high and low in risk, respectively. Many more couples (like Hector and Helena and Gunter and Lastri) face a greater mix of low- and high-risk situations that are more likely to have gradual effects. We see this pattern next.

Motivational Interdependence Limits Satisfaction and Promotes Stability

As the four couples populating these pages illustrate, partners vary considerably in the ways in which they are responsive (and nonresponsive) to each other. That is, relationships vary considerably in observable phenotype. Ron and Gayle take joy in being each other's best friends and social supports; there is little they would not do for each other. Harry and Sally treat each other as necessary cogs in the machinery of domestic life. Such variations in responsiveness set the trajectory these marriages take by coordinating sentiments of trust and commitment across partners. Gayle has faith in Ron's responsiveness because his willingness to compromise his legal ambitions makes her feel like he truly values her as a person (sports and competition obsessed, warts, and all). Making such an intrinsic attribution for his commitment makes her all the more resolute in her own commitment. Immersed in the process of her commitment, she never imagines the possibility of divorce. Sally has comparatively little faith in Harry's responsiveness because working compulsively to promote his dependence makes her think he only does nice things for her because he "owes" her. Making such an instrumental attribution for his commitment makes her guarded in her own commitment. To keep a safe distance, she decides that she is only staying in the marriage because she has no choice. Because Harry cannot help but notice that she so rarely provides him the kind of emotional support he needs, he attributes his continuing commitment to his love for his children.

How do such acts of responsiveness (and nonresponsiveness) coordinate the experience of trust and commitment across partners? This question takes us back to the fourth level of interdependence introduced in Chapter 2: motivational interdependence. Partners are interdependent in the reasons they have for being more or less trusting and committed. Gayle can attribute Ron's commitment to any combination of intrinsic (e.g., his love for her sense of humor), instrumental (e.g., her skill in ironing), or extrinsic factors (e.g., fear of disappointing his parents). Gayle can also attribute her own commitment to more or less intrinsic (e.g., Ron's intelligence), instrumental (e.g., Ron's skills as a playmate to her children), or extrinsic factors (e.g., wanting her children to have a father at home). Similarly, Ron can attribute his trust in Gayle's commitment and his commitment to her to intrinsic, instrumental, and extrinsic factors.

Such possibilities impose three levels to motivational interdependence (see Table 8.2). First, Ron and Gayle can be more or less similar in the reasons each has for trusting in the other's commitment (i.e., similarity in trust motivations). Second, Ron and Gayle can be more or less similar in the reasons each has for being more or less committed (i.e., similarity in commitment motivations). Third, the reasons underlying Ron's trust in Gayle can match Gayle's reasons for commitment to a greater or lesser extent (i.e., understanding of commitment motivations). As we detail next, each partner's expression of responsive (and nonresponsive) behavior generally functions to instill and reinforce similarity in each partner's reasons for being trusting and committed. Such similarity in motivational interdependence reinforces mutually responsive interaction patterns and fosters relationship stability (although the type of responsiveness that results may not necessarily make the relationship highly satisfying).

Figure 11.3 models how behavioral interaction elicits similarity in motivational interdependence and mutually responsive (and nonresponsive) interaction patterns. Consider how Hector and Helena's marriage is likely to unfold as time goes on. At present, Hector has stronger if–then connect rule habits than Helena, whose if–then habit is to self-protect. Being secure in his attachment style and chronically motivated to connect, Hector was consumed with the task of implementing his commitment early in his marriage. He focused heavily on the qualities he adored in Helena, like her intellect and sense of humor. Intrinsically motivated in his commitment, Hector willingly sacrificed on Helena's behalf, from taking over her dishwashing responsibilities to forgiving her occasional attack of "kitchen-sinking" (Van Lange et al., 1997). Nonetheless, on days when he comes home from work stressed and looking for support, only to find Helena engrossed in her own issues, Hector does get pretty testy. Then he resents doing Helena any favors, even if it is something as mundane as helping Helena to bathe their children before bedtime. With layoffs impending at work, his need for support and coincident short temper are becoming more frequent. Despite his recent problems, the instrumental and extrinsic factors governing his commitment are not yet salient to him.

In the course of interaction, Hector's behavioral expressions of responsiveness shape Helena's reasons for being more or less trusting of him. Prone to be self-protective in her if–then rule habits, Helena weighs

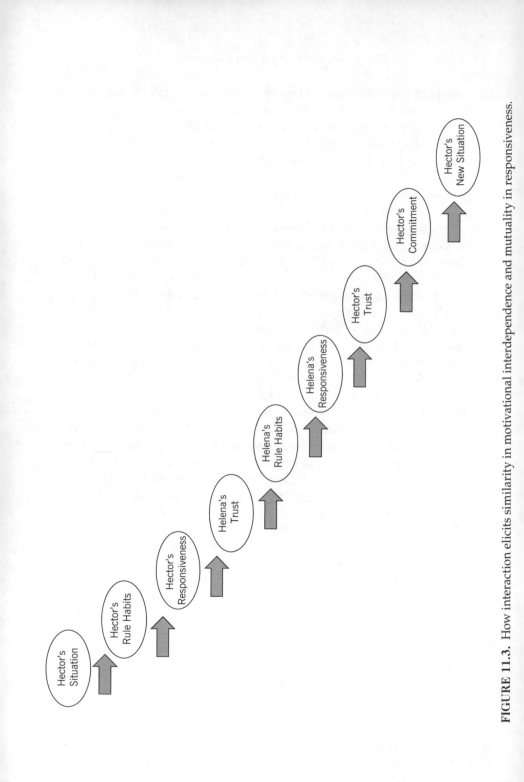

FIGURE 11.3. How interaction elicits similarity in motivational interdependence and mutuality in responsiveness.

Hector's recent irritability more heavily than his past generosity in gauging his current responsiveness. Her resulting increased uncertainty about his trustworthiness then elicits a complementary level of hesitance in her commitment. Now anticipating his rejection across multiple domestic domains, she engages almost compulsively in various tactics to promote Hector's dependence, from sewing his clothes, to packing his lunches, to enlisting the counsel of their parish priest on Sunday. Compounding matters, she becomes all the more reluctant to provide the emotional support he needs because she fears saying the wrong thing (and only escalating his anxiety and irritation). Her increasing instrumental behavior leads to Hector's realization that he cannot count on Helena for the emotional support in this time of acute crisis at work. Although he still values her sense of humor and intellect, he is starting to wonder whether it is safest to rely on her for the instrumental behaviors she gives so freely (and in which he does find value and comfort). In this way, Helena's instrumental expressions of responsiveness elicit a shift in Hector's experience of his commitment. This shift recalibrates his own expressions of responsiveness in a way that reinforces Helena's more limited level of trust in him. Now that the instrumental and extrinsic factors fostering his trust in Helena are more salient to him, he is still happy to trade dishwashing for vacuuming whenever Helena wants, but he keeps his biggest anxieties private. Rather than try to push her to engage in a free-for-all discussion of topics she clearly wants to avoid, he has also learned to limit conversations to the sports and recreational activities they still enjoy so much.

As the future unfolds, the long-term stability of Hector and Helena's marriage seems reasonably certain. They both realize they are in the relationship for the same reasons: to take care of their children, to have fun together whenever they can, and to respect their religion. In light of recent events, Hector's Catholicism has become just as important a constraint on his commitment as Helena's is for hers (Levinger, 1976). Despite greater similarity in their commitment motivations, their marriage now has the potential to become less satisfying than it once was. Satisfaction is a function of the rewards partners experience interacting (Kelley, 1979). Being instrumentally motivated puts an upper limit on the rewards to be gained from interaction because it puts on upper limit on responsiveness. Bathing the children together and exchanging dishes for vacuuming, while rewarding in some sense, nevertheless does not provide as great a source of reward as being each other's primary sources of social support, which they did so easily earlier in their relationship.

Contrast this scenario by imagining what might happen if Hector's intrinsic motivation for his commitment stayed steadfast, while Helena's grew more extrinsic. The future stability of such a marriage could be in peril because Hector would always be inclined to make major sacrifices that went unreciprocated by Helena. He might also continue to press Helena to make the kind of disclosures that she simply does not feel safe making. Such difficulties in behavioral coordination might lead Hector to conclude that Helena simply does not want the same things out of their marriage. Such a fundamental incompatibility in their relationship goals makes him question whether Helena really is the right person for him. The intrinsic basis for his commitment undermined (and with few instrumental or extrinsic factors salient enough to provide a plausible substitute), he starts to seriously consider the prospect of divorce. We explore interdependent mind–inspired interventions to avoid this eventuality in our final chapter.

SUMMARY

This chapter examined features of the relationship whole that make each relationship's personality distinct and set partners on a path toward relationship stability or dissolution. The relationship whole we described is composed of three parts: (1) the person: the preferences, attitudes, personality, and goals each partner brings to the relationship; (2) the pair: the degree of compatibility or fit between the preferences, attitudes, personality, and goals partners together bring to the relationship (e.g., Harry and Sally's divergent role preferences); and (3) the context: the life circumstances that surround the relationship (e.g., economic stress, religion). These three aspects of the relationship whole shape the if–then habits of rule use partners jointly practice. These shared if–then rules pull for different types of mutuality in responsiveness by controlling how partners respond to the paradox posed by trusting. To trust in Ron's responsiveness, Gayle first had to take the risk of putting her outcomes in Ron's hands. Despite her neuroticism, this was natural for Gayle to do because they faced multiple low-risk situations that made it easier for Ron to be accepting. Trust was much harder for Sally to come by because she and Harry faced multiple high-risk situations in which Sally often baited Harry into behaving nonresponsively. Consequently, Ron and Gayle came to rely on each other for most everything and they grew more trusting and committed with the passage of time. Harry and Sally instead came to rely on each other for very little and they grew less trusting and committed with the passage of time.

In the first half of this chapter we examined how each part of the relationship whole elicits particular if–then habits of rule use. We argued that the person, the pairing, and the context shape if–then rule habits by controlling the appraisal of risk, the interpersonal goals partners adopt in response to risk, and the tendency to correct the automated will.

First, we described how the person makes some if–then rules more of a habit. For instance, being high in self-esteem makes it easier for people to overlook the potential for rejection in specific conflicts of interest. In contrast, being high in attachment-related anxiety makes it more natural for people to self-protect in situations that tag the possibility of the partner's rejection. Being secure in attachment style instead makes it easier to correct the automatic impulse to self-protect in such situations. Second, we described how "pairing" makes some of the if–then rules more of a habit. In doing so, we defined partner compatibility in terms of both compatibility in outcome preferences and compatibility in if–then rule use. For instance, Ron and Gayle developed the habit to connect because they had compatible preferences for the allocation of domestic responsibilities (i.e., pay someone else to do most chores and then divvy up the rest). By contrast, Gunter and Lastri face conflicts in the future because Lastri's tendency to self-protect is making Gunter question her commitment to him. Third, we described how life context (e.g., economic stress) can make partners more likely to perceive risk and more likely to behave on the basis of the automated will to self-protect against such risks.

In the second half of this chapter we explored how the pieces of the relationship whole fit together in ways that allow some relationships to thrive while others falter. First, we argued that the situations and if–then rule habits that fall out of the relationship whole open certain opportunities for behavioral responsiveness and close other opportunities. That is, rule habits eventually provoke a situational freezing. In Gayle's case, being immersed in low-risk situations made it easy for her to put her outcomes in Ron's hands and take his outcomes in her own, despite her neuroticism. This created a mutually reinforcing cycle of escalating trust and commitment for both. Eventually, they came to rely on each other for progressively greater expressions of commitment despite Ron's cautious stance toward Gayle's competitiveness about their careers. Harry and Sally were not so lucky because Sally was both preoccupied in attachment style and immersed in multiple high-risk situations that only gave her even more to worry about. Her hesitance to put her outcomes in Harry's hands for anything but the most mundane of favors made it difficult for Harry to prove his responsiveness and confined their willingness to rely on each other to instrumental domains.

Second, we described how subtle changes in one piece of the relationship whole might be all that it would take to put Harry and Sally on an upward relationship trajectory and Gayle and Ron on a downward relationship trajectory. In particular, we described how the situational landscape, trust, and correction might all function as points of leverage in changing how Sally (and Harry) each responded to the paradox of trusting. Had Harry shared Ron's fastidious temperament, he might readily have shared responsibilities in the kitchen with Sally, turning the zero-sum conflicts they faced into coordination dilemmas. In such a low-risk climate, Sally might have had an easier time putting her outcomes in Harry's hands. She might have honestly explained to him just how very important it was for her to work outside the home, and he might have worked to find some way of making it happen as a result. By making this sacrifice, Harry might then have bolstered Sally's trust in him in a way that put commitment on an upswing.

We ended the chapter by returning to the attributional analysis of motivational interdependence we described in Chapter 8. We described how responsive (and nonresponsive) behavior generally functions to instill and reinforce similarity in each partner's reasons for being trusting and committed. Such similarity in motivational interdependence reinforces mutually responsive interaction patterns and fosters relationship stability, although the type of mutuality in responsiveness that results may not necessarily make the relationship highly satisfying. We also described how the interdependent mind fails to elicit mutuality when partners have incompatible if–then rule habits and consequently have dissimilar reasons for being committed and for trusting in the other's commitment. We continue to explore how such failures in behavioral and motivational coordination create relationship difficulties in our final chapter on intervention.

NOTES

1. We provided many examples of these effects in prior chapters, so we provide only select illustrative examples here to make our points.
2. We suspect that specialized rules are likely to be more localized to context, such that a specific eliciting trigger like Harry's forgetfulness-inspired transgressions elicit a contingent response to justify commitment. With time and experience across multiple situations in the relationship the specialized rule may become more general in that a broader class of transgress triggers may elicit the response (i.e., "if Harry transgresses, then justify commitment").

CHAPTER 12

A Practical Guide for Relationships

An ounce of prevention is worth a pound of cure.

In contemplating their current state of marital discontent, it's not likely that Harry or Sally would gain much comfort from Benjamin Franklin's advice. In their case, the time for prevention is past. The time for intervention and remediation is present. But Lastri and Gunter are now facing the largest test in their marriage to date—the incompatibility between Gunter's desire to have another child and Lastri's desire to return to school. Does our analysis of the interdependent mind provide any kind of "how-to" guide to keep their marriage on track in the face of this conflict?

In this chapter we begin to bridge the gap between theory and application. We start by acknowledging something up front. There's no one magic bullet that will keep a relationship satisfying and stable. As we saw in Chapter 11, such a magic bullet is likely to vary from couple to couple because situations vary across relationships. Harry and Sally faced much more difficult conflicts of interest in their marriage than Ron and Gayle. Sally wanted to go to school and work; Harry wanted her to stay home with their children. Ultimately, this incompatibility in their goals turned every discussion about dishes in the sink and toys on the floor into a power struggle. In such a competitive climate, it's no wonder that countless books Sally read on how to "fight fair" did them so little collective good. "Owning" her feelings did little to change the fact that Harry wanted something quite different out of their marriage than she did.

In the pages that remain, we hope to translate the major assumptions underlying our theory of the interdependent mind into preliminary recommendations for practice. Neither one of us is a clinical psychologist. The advice we offer here is informed by our understanding of the prevailing wisdom of the research literature. Our hopes are twofold. First, we hope that readers might find one or two practical tips for living happily in their own relationships. Second, we hope that clinical researchers and practitioners might find that natural translations of the advice we offer inform therapeutic intervention.

So where to begin? The first half of the chapter outlines factors that constrain the pursuit of relationship happiness. We start by considering two ways in which partners can be happy (or unhappy). First, partners can be more or less happy because of experienced successes and failures in behavioral coordination. Ron and Gayle are happier than Sally and Harry because they are responsive to each other's needs in more domains. Second, partners can be more or less happy because the domains in which they are responsive to each other's needs meet or fail to meet their expectations. For instance, Sally is so unhappy in her marriage in part because she wanted to be able to rely on Harry for much more than just his willingness to fulfill his role as provider and father. With this background, we review the features of our model that offer strengths and vulnerabilities in the pursuit of relationship happiness. These features revolve around the nature of situations and trust because these factors control which particular if–then rules become a habit.

The second half of the chapter builds on the first by offering prescriptions to make the most of the strengths and the least of the vulnerabilities. In offering such suggestions for the pursuit of relationship happiness, we take Benjamin Franklin's advice to heart. We assume that it is going to be much easier to intervene before the onset of serious distress than it is to alleviate such distress once it is entrenched. We offer two basic prescriptions for averting distress, given one hard and inescapable reality: Partners do not have complete control over the situations that will end up shaping their relationships.

The contentions of Internet matchmaking services aside, no single algorithm can guarantee the choice of a fully "compatible" partner (see Chapter 9). People can certainly try to limit the number of high-risk conflicts they might one day face by selecting partners who share compatible religious philosophies, desires for children, preferences for outside friends, and so forth. Nonetheless, no amount of forethought can circumvent uncertain knowledge of the future. Harry and Sally just did not foresee having a son with ADHD and the added stress that it would place on Sally's responsibilities at home. Because circumstances and people change, partners will inevitably find themselves questioning each other's responsiveness. Indeed, every relationship has at least one Achilles heel. This "hot" issue (or issues, as the case may be) has the power to irrevocably corrode trust. For instance, Ron and Gayle face persistent conflicts involving Gayle's greater competitiveness. Even though she's embarrassed to admit it, she feels better about herself when she's outperforming Ron professionally. Ron often finds himself on the receiving end of her digs at his courtroom finesse as a result. Nonetheless, this issue has not contaminated their relationship as a whole. Early on, Ron decided to accept Gayle's competitiveness for what it is—an expression of her own insecurity, not a comment on her feelings for him. Harry and Sally were not so lucky. Their early conflicts over household chores corroded Sally's trust in Harry in a way that made her suspicious of his motives inside and outside the kitchen.

Given that situations are not entirely within partners' control, our prescriptions for the pursuit of happiness focus on bolstering and sustaining trust (in its impulsive and reflective forms). We focus on trust because it is susceptible to influence. Trust can also turn an objectively difficult situation into a manageable one—the very transformation needed to keep destructive cycles of negativity from ever taking hold in the relationship.

Our first general prescription for influencing trust accedes preemptive power to the unconscious mind. As we saw time and again, people who are less trusting "know" the rules for seeking connection; the conscious mind simply gets in the way of their application. Therefore, bolstering trust in its impulsive form provides the "ounce of prevention" vulnerable people need to be happy. First, through experiential conditioning, one might strengthen automatic inclinations to approach by immersing partners in positive experiences, like sharing happy memories, watching a funny movie together, trying new food, or listening to a new band. Incidentally, these necessary positive experiences are precisely the ones that drop off precipitously in the first year of marriage. Second, through rule conditioning, one might strengthen automatic inclinations to approach by training people not to be overly vigilant and reactive to rejection—that is, by decreasing the accessibility of the if–then rules for self-protection.

Because once-isolated incompatibilities have the potential to snowball into escalating cycles of conflict, our second general prescription for influencing trusting expectations attributes recuperative power to the conscious mind. As we also saw time and again, people who stay trusting learn to correct the automatic urge to distance. Therefore, finding ways to make correcting self-protective impulses more automatic might also help keep trusting expectations intact and interactions responsive. First, through integrative thinking, partners might learn to accept incompatibilities that cannot readily be changed. In so doing, they might lessen their susceptibility to perceiving rejection when hot issues come up. Ron created just such an integrative "Yes, but" where Gayle's competitiveness was concerned. In situations where this incompatibility surfaces, he keeps a level and connectedness-promoting head by reminding himself that Gayle's warmth and intelligence more than make up for her competitiveness. Second, by exercising self-control, much as one might exercise a muscle, partners might build up executive resources (Muraven & Baumeister, 2000). Armed with greater self-regulatory capacity, trusting partners might more readily correct even the strong impulses to self-protect that hot issues can generate. In so doing, partners might short-circuit the negative, hostile behaviors that can make conflicts snowball.

In offering these prescriptions, we describe overlap with existing clinical interventions for the alleviation of distress where appropriate (drawing on a review by Bradbury & Karney, 2010). We end this book with a conclusion that may be unsatisfying to some, but seems inescapable to us. No one prescription for promoting resilience (or alleviating distress) is going to be universally effective. What works for one couple might not work for another because the ease of coordinating mutually responsive interactions depends on the person, the pairing, and the relationship context itself. In embracing this complexity, we hope to instill the reader and the therapist with hope for the myriad ways in which some form of happiness can be pursued.

THE PURSUIT OF HAPPINESS

Classic formulations of interdependence define happiness or satisfaction using basic algebra (Kelley, 1979; Thibaut & Kelley, 1959). In the happiness equation, satisfaction is a function of one's outcomes compared to one's expectations (what theorists describe as a comparison level). Gunter's outcomes refer to the overall balance of rewards and costs he experiences interacting with Lastri. His expectations refer to the balance of rewards and costs he thinks he deserves. His satisfaction increases when his outcomes exceed his expectations; it decreases when his outcomes fall short of his expectations. The translation of these ideas into our terms is straightforward. Satisfaction depends on partners' successes and failures in behavioral coordination *and* how the meaning of these successes and failures compare to their expectations.

Let's return to Harry and Sally and Ron and Gayle. Sally and Harry live an uneasy truce in which they rely on each other to fulfill their respective roles as caregiver and provider. In this sense, they are responsive, but they limit their interdependence to the realm of life tasks. Sally relies on Harry to pay most of the bills, take care of mechanical matters (e.g., car maintenance), and roughhouse with their children. Harry relies on her to cook and clean, coordinate their children's activities, and take care of his mother. They are hesitant to step outside of these clearly defined boundaries. Over the years, Harry learned not to go to Sally when he was feeling anxious about work because she never provided the kind of support he was seeking. Sally learned to avoid sharing her aspirations for a professional life outside the home with Harry. The successes and failures they experienced in behavioral coordination put an upper limit on satisfaction. The domains in which they found ways to be responsive (i.e., life tasks) confer lower levels of rewards than the domains in which they failed to be responsive (i.e., personality, relationship goals). They are as happy as partners who treat each other as cogs in the domestic machinery of life might expect to be (see Chapter 8). Sally's resentful yearning for a husband who truly understands her values and Harry's own aspiration for a more sympathetic wife only compounds their current malaise.

In contrast, Ron and Gayle are generally responsive to each other's needs. They rely on each other to coordinate household and child care responsibilities; they value each other's divergent personalities (e.g., Gayle's greater gregariousness); and they share convergent goals for their marriage (e.g., being friends and confidants first, parents second). The only exception to their general norm of responsiveness is that Ron hesitates to divulge his career anxieties to Gayle. Overall, they are highly satisfied because the domains in which they are most responsive to each other's needs confer great rewards. Gayle has always appreciated Ron's willingness to take late-night chauffeur duty, but she gains even more from his efforts to overcome his introversion to go to the office parties and other social events that she enjoys so much. From Ron's perspective, Gayle's warmth with their children, her intelligence, and her support for his leisure pursuits (e.g., his wine passion) more than offset her occasional tendency to be competitive about their careers. Their marriage largely meets their hopes. They each hoped for someone who would be a confidant and an intellectual equal and that's what they found.

Ingredients for Success (or Failure)

In each of these marriages, Ron and Gayle and Harry and Sally faced unique strengths and vulnerabilities in the pursuit of relationship happiness. These boons and pitfalls revolve around the situations they faced and the level of trust they brought to these situations. Together, situations and trust shaped the ways in which each partner experienced his or her commitment by controlling if–then habits of rule use. In Sally and Harry's case, the unfortunate combination of distrust and frequent high-risk situation exposure elicited self-protective if–then rule habits that created a shared sense of resignation in their commitment. They are not happy, but they are both committed because neither one can imagine managing their life responsibilities without the other's assistance. In Ron and Gayle's case, the fortunate combination of trust and frequent low-risk situation exposure elicited connectedness-promoting if–then rule habits that created a shared sense of higher purpose in their commitment. They are both committed and happy because neither one can imagine their life without the other in it. Given the formative power of situations and trust in shaping a relationship's personality, what path are Gunter and Lastri likely to take in the pursuit of marital happiness?

Table 12.1 updates Gunter and Lastri's profile with newly revealing details about their marriage. As we saw in Chapter 9, Gunter and Lastri did not decide to marry when they were in the blinding haze of infatuation. Instead, they married through the social engineering of their parents in Indonesia. This matchmaking ensured that they had been exposed to some of the same basic values growing up (e.g., similar religious beliefs, similar respect for family and tradition). But it did not guarantee their compatibility. In this sense, Gunter and Lastri are no different than any other couple. They turned out to be lucky in some respects and unlucky in others.

Situations

Let's start by considering their outcome preferences, because these outcome preferences determine the risk characteristics of the situations they encounter most often. They turned out to be lucky in the domain of life tasks because they have compatible preferences for household and child care responsibilities. For instance, Gunter likes to cook, but he hates doing dishes; Lastri hates to cook, but does not mind doing dishes. Consequently, preparing the evening's dinner simply involves coordinating their respective preferences to achieve an outcome they both desire—the prototypic

TABLE 12.1. Updating Our Couple Profiles

Couple	Basic demographics	Life task preferences	Personality preferences	Relationship goal preferences
Ron and Gayle	African American Lawyers Two young children	Ron likes cooking; Gayle likes washing dishes. Both enjoy child care. Gayle loves sports. Ron loves wine.	Gayle: More gregarious. Gayle: More competitive. Ron and Gayle: Neurotic.	Both value Gayle's working.
Harry and Sally	White Mechanic/customer service officer Three children, eldest 17	Harry dislikes all things domestic.	Sally: More gregarious. Sally: More fastidious. Harry: More reserved. Sally: More preoccupied.	Sally wanted to work; Harry wanted her at home.
Hector and Helena	Hispanic Factory worker/ homemaker Three young children Catholic Economically stressed	Largely compatible preferences.	Helena: Lower self-esteem; fearful in attachment style.	Both value family.
Gunter and Lastri	Indonesian PhD student/ homemaker One toddler	Gunter likes doing laundry; Lastri likes gardening. Gunter likes cooking; Lastri likes washing dishes.	Gunter: Enjoys outside social activities. Lastri: More prevention-oriented.	Gunter wants another baby; Lastri wants to return to school.

elements of a low-risk situation. They did not turn out to be nearly as lucky when it came to the domains of personality and relationship goals. In terms of personality, Gunter is more extraverted than Lastri. He often wants to have his friends over when Lastri would prefer that they spend quiet time alone with their child. In terms of relationship goals, Lastri acclimated to the United States more quickly than Gunter and now she has started to rethink some of her traditional values. She has started to want something more for herself than the traditional roles of wife and mother. She now wants to return to school. Gunter is having difficulty reconciling her new goal with his goal for a bigger family.

Such a high-risk conflict over relationship goals would be difficult for even the most resilient of couples to manage, but Gunter and Lastri turned out to be unluckier still. They have fundamentally different personality orientations toward risk. Gunter is more promotion focused, whereas Lastri is more prevention focused. In any given situation in her marriage, Lastri is more likely to be concerned about avoiding loss than Gunter is. This basic difference in their personality orientation lends itself to incompatible if–then rule habits in high-risk situations (see Chapter 11). The conversations they are now (not) having about Lastri's return to school are a case in point.

Because Lastri is strongly motivated to avoid negative outcomes, she cannot help but worry that another child is Gunter's biggest priority, not her happiness. Even though she tries to tell herself that Gunter does care about her, not being able to quash the fear that he might not care enough leaves her afraid to tell him how deeply she wants to return to school. Anticipating his rejection prompts her to self-protect; she now finds countless ways to avoid talking directly about the issue. Her favored means of avoidance is to criticize Gunter for being too indulgent with their child (i.e., "if self-protect goal, then withhold own dependence and distance"). Instead of engaging the baby issue, she's also taken over Gunter's cooking responsibilities and enlisted his work friends as her allies in the hopes of coercing him into being accommodating (i.e., "if self-protect goal, then promote partner dependence"). Her behavior frustrates Gunter because ensuring her happiness is just as important to him as having another child. He looks at her newly avoidant and manipulative behavior and now, for the first time in his marriage, starts to wonder whether his happiness is as important to Lastri as her happiness has always been to him.

Trust

The growing objective incompatibilities that Gunter and Lastri face are not trivial ones. Nonetheless, there are shades of gray to be had in the perception of such objective conflicts. Trust in the partner's responsiveness (in both its impulsive and reflective instantiations) fills in these shades of gray. So what does this mean for Gunter and Lastri? Until this possible crisis point in their marriage, life had been proceeding smoothly. With Gunter busy in his job and finishing his degree, they spent most of his free time at home with their child. Safe in these confines, they had an easy time meeting each other's needs because they have such compatible preferences for life tasks. In fact, they so rarely have time to invite friends over that Gunter's greater gregariousness seldom created any conflict. These experiences conditioned their reasonably positive automatic associations to each other (Murray, Holmes, & Pinkus, 2010). At least when it came to these easy issues, their joint impulse is to connect. Their conscious feelings of trust in each other largely reinforce these sentiments, but Lastri has never been quite as sure about Gunter's responsiveness as he has been of her responsiveness. Prevention-oriented by nature, she cannot help but sometimes worry about how Gunter might disappoint her, and those fears are taking over now.

Negotiating Reciprocal Commitment

So what is likely to happen to Gunter and Lastri now that they have reached a potential impasse in their marriage? Will they find a happy resolution to this conflict and return to a strengthened state of domestic bliss? Or might their current difficulties instead degenerate into reciprocated cycles of conflict? Ultimately, their fate depends on how the incompatibilities they now perceive come to shape the meaning of their commitment to each other. This returns us to the basic foundation for mutuality in responsiveness: commitment reciprocity. For Gunter and Lastri's interactions to stay reasonably fluid, how Gunter solicits and expresses responsiveness needs to mesh with how Lastri solicits and expresses responsiveness (see Chapter 4). Imagine that Gunter foregoes his desire for another child so that Lastri can return to school. Such a sacrifice would imperil his future happiness if Lastri ultimately failed to make similar sacrifices.

Because imbalances in commitment pull for destructive interaction cycles (Drigotas & Rusbult, 1992), the fate of most relationships rests in how situations, trust, and rule use combine to preempt or promote reciprocity. In this sense, the Achilles heel in Lastri and Gunter's marriage is not the fact that Lastri wants to return to school and Gunter wants another baby. This objective situation itself could provide just as much incentive for greater closeness as it does greater conflict. Their real vulnerability rests in their differing personality orientations toward risk. Because Lastri weighs the possibility of rejection so heavily, she has taken a self-protective stance whenever the topics of children or education come up (which they frequently do, given that their lives revolve around their child and Gunter's continuing education). Her self-protective and distancing behavior creates a pull for Gunter to reciprocate with similarly self-protective and distancing behavior (Gottman, 1994). Whether the difficulties they are having now escalate depends on Gunter's capacity to inhibit his automated impulse to retaliate against Lastri when she criticizes him for his indulgence with their child.

Two factors bode well for Gunter's capacity to inhibit his impulse to self-protect and instead connect in these situations. First—so far—he has always trusted that Lastri has his best interests at heart. Both his automatic evaluative response to Lastri and his explicit expectations for her behavior are positive. Such impulsively and reflectively trusting sentiments should blunt the impact of Lastri's criticisms, making him more likely to anticipate her acceptance than rejection the next time he tries to initiate a discussion about their conflicting desires for another child. Second, now that her recent behavior has become more intemperate—his promotion-oriented personality also helps him see the gains to be had in weathering a difficult period. One factor presents a serious obstacle to Gunter's capacity to correct his impulse to self-protect in response to Lastri's distancing behavior. He is in the midst of taking a series of challenging exams. Because he's stressed, he has limited self-regulatory capacity available to curb his impulse to self-protect (even though he is motivated to do so). To compound this pitfall, Lastri is now facing more stresses of her own. Because Gunter is so busy with school, she has been taking on more and more of his child care and household responsibilities. This stress further taxes her capacity to curb her strong impulse to distance from Gunter. As a consequence, she has responded to his occasional efforts to be understanding and supportive with suspicion. She's also starting to take his current shortfalls at home as further evidence that he might not care about her pursuing a life outside their home.

Their collective state is a precarious one. They are standing on the brink of distress. For Gunter, contrasting his efforts to draw closer to Lastri with her efforts to insert distance into the relationship leaves him wondering whether Lastri really cares about him as much as he cares about her. He thinks he is trying hard to be kind and supportive, and in his currently stressed state, Lastri's apparent indifference annoys and upsets him. He's even starting to lose sight of the qualities that drew him to her in the first place, such as her independence and strong will. Lately he's been left wondering whether she's really as committed to his happiness as he is to her happiness. This perceived imbalance in commitment is only exacerbating their problems interacting. Indeed, according to emotion-focused therapists, feeling insufficiently valued creates the feelings of anger that precipitate destructive cycles of conflict (Johnson, 2003).

Gunter is now in the position of "pursuer" in his marriage, and it's not a role he enjoys. He resents that he's "always" the one making the extra effort to solve the baby problem, whereas Lastri seems to be doing little to help change this unhappy state of affairs. Lastri is just as upset. She wants Gunter to understand how difficult it is for her to talk about her feelings, and he just doesn't seem to get it. Because they have mishandled the baby conflict so badly, it has now taken on a life of its own. This specific conflict is snowballing into a general conflict about how much closeness (vs. distance) each of them desires in the relationship (Christensen & Heavy, 1990). In this context, the slightest evidence of incompatibility is taking on greater significance. In fact, a recent disagreement over a TV show erupted into a full-blown argument—something that had never happened before. They used to laugh such things off.

BUILDING AND SUSTAINING TRUST: TWO GENERAL PRESCRIPTIONS

What tactics might we take (or recommend) to pull Gunter and Lastri back from the brink of relationship distress? We offer two general prescriptions. Both of these prescriptions involve the transformative power of trust. The first: Bolster the power of one's unconscious motivations to approach (because thinking too much is getting Lastri into trouble). The second: Bolster the power of one's conscious justification for approach (because losing the will to correct is getting Gunter into trouble).

Bolstering the Unconscious

To understand why bolstering the unconscious might have benefits, let's first step back and consider the effect being prevention oriented has on Lastri's orientation to her relationship. This feature of her personality makes her question her impulse to connect to Gunter. It's this capacity to second-guess herself that gets her into trouble. In fact, she might have avoided her current problems had she only trusted her automatic impulse to disclose her ambitions to Gunter. The perils of thinking are easiest to see when we look at the behavior of low self-esteem people. Take the most seemingly obvious demonstration of a partner's affections—a compliment. Although such avowals of affection should bolster feelings of trust (see Chapter 3), such compliments generally go unappreciated by lows (Marigold, Holmes, & Ross, 2007). To get low self-esteem people

to embrace such compliments, Marigold and her colleagues (2007) discovered they had to actively disable the defenses of lows. They did so by
subtly encouraging them to explain how much their partner's compliment
actually meant for their relationship.

Of course, researchers are not always going to be available to remind
vulnerable people not to second-guess an automatic impulse to approach.
For this reason, our first prescription for the pursuit of happiness focuses
on going "underneath the radar" to strengthen a vulnerable person's automatic impulse to approach. We recommend first bolstering the unconscious for two reasons. First, this tactic capitalizes on the fact that even
vulnerable people possess a resource for conditioning more positive evaluative associations to the partner. They generally have loving and committed partners. Low self-esteem people typically possess partners who
value and love them just as much as the partners of high self-esteem people (Murray et al., 2001). They just fail to appreciate this reality. Second,
stronger positive automatic evaluative associations to the partner disable
conscious defenses against rejection. As we saw in Chapter 10, low self-
esteem people who are more impulsively trusting can actually resist the
impulse to distance themselves from a seemingly rejecting partner (Murray, Pinkus, et al., 2010). We see two basic tactics for going under the radar
to bolster impulsive trust: (1) experiential conditioning and (2) rule conditioning. We discuss each in turn.

Experiential Conditioning

In his writing on couples therapy, Gottman (1994) locates the heart of
marital satisfaction in a 5:1 ratio of positive to negative affect. In satisfying
marriages, partners generally counter one negative display of irritation,
anger, or resentment with five positive displays of warmth, support, or
encouragement (Gottman, Ryan, Carrere, & Erley, 2002). This behavioral
perspective on marital therapy suggests that it's wise to have a "good
manners" policy in relationships because positive experiences provide a
reserve to counter negative experiences (Huston & Chorost, 1994; Rusbult
et al., 1991). From our perspective, it's wise to be civil because the impulsive barometer of trust keeps careful track of the quality of one's experiences.

The positivity of interaction unconsciously conditions one's general
habit to approach or avoid one's partner (Murray, Holmes, & Pinkus,
2010). This means that manipulating the behavioral rewards of interactions provides a viable means of increasing impulsive trust. Simply put,
the more often Lastri finds herself feeling good and safe in the presence

of Gunter, the stronger her automatic inclination to approach (and not avoid) him. The evidence for the relationship benefits of self-expanding activities is instructive in this regard (Aron et al., 2000). Associating the partner with positive experiences, like the laughter to be had in traversing a gym mat with ankles bound, increases state feelings of satisfaction in the relationship. Such findings suggest that the simple pleasure of shared enjoyments—like going to a new restaurant, watching a movie together, being physically intimate, laughing over a shared joke, or reminiscing about the past—might be invaluable for strengthening more positive automatic evaluative associations to the partner. Consistent with this idea, behavior-oriented couples therapists often encourage partners to treat each other better, or at the very last, to avoid particular negative behaviors like expressing criticism or contempt that are known to be related to dissatisfaction (Bradbury & Karney, 2010). With her positive automatic association to Gunter bolstered, Lastri might be better equipped to ignore her self-protective impulse to distance.

Rule Conditioning

Part of Lastri's current problems stem from the fact that she often misses Gunter's efforts to be supportive (and always notices when he falls short). In her case, reconditioning the negativity bias in her if–then vigilance rules might be part of strengthening her general habit to approach. Lastri basically needs to learn how to refocus her attention to focus on what Gunter does right, rather than what he might do wrong. A fascinating set of studies on how to recondition vigilance to social threat is telling in this regard (Dandeneau, Baldwin, Baccus, Sakellaropoulo, & Pruessner, 2007). These researchers reasoned that vulnerable people are reactive to social threats because their attention is oriented toward threatening (and away from reassuring) stimuli. Consequently, they reasoned that redirecting attention—for example, by training people to look for a smiling face in an array of rejecting faces—might lessen reactivity to social threat. It did. Low self-esteem participants who were trained to find the smiling face in an array of rejecting faces later evidenced less reactivity to rejection words in a Stroop task. This method for training people not to be sensitive to rejection even prevented low (and high) self-esteem people from being stressed by a classroom exam. Such findings suggest that it might be possible to condition Lastri not to be so sensitive to rejection.

In our view, the Dandeneau et al. findings speak to the power of using the if–then rules that the interdependent mind already has at its disposal to motivate approach (when circumstances warrant it). Two further examples make this point more directly. As we described in Chapter 6, Lydon and his colleagues revealed that women spontaneously protect their commitment when faced with an attractive and available alternative partner (Lydon et al., 2008). For instance, when primed with connection, women move away from an attractive suitor in a virtual reality environment. Men do not move away, but they can be trained to resist temptation by practicing the intention to protect their commitment. A simple self-instruction not to flirt did the trick. We suspect that forming this implementation intention worked because it co-opted the ready availability of the interpersonal mind's if–then rule for justifying commitment.

A follow-up to the Marigold et al. (2007) research on the power of compliments makes a similar point. In this study, Marigold, Holmes, and Ross (2010) subtly encouraged participants in the "intervention" condition to think about the grander meaning of a partner's compliment. They did so to give low self-esteem people in particular a reason to anticipate their partner's acceptance. Two weeks later the partner of the participant reported on the participant's behavior, identifying how often the participant had been critical or acted inconsiderately in the previous 2 weeks. The findings were striking. Low self-esteem people who were trained to generalize the meaning of their partner's compliment ultimately behaved less negatively (as reported by their partner)! How could the simple instruction to think about the meaning of a partner's compliment have such a transformative effect on interaction? We suspect that generalizing the meaning of the partner's compliment reconditioned low self-esteem people's if–then goal orientation rules. Anticipating acceptance left them newly primed to connect when they interacted with their partner, resulting in a decrease in negative behavior.

These collected findings suggest that relatively simple self-instructional techniques might help recondition vulnerable people's chronic if–then habits to self-protect. In particular, consciously forming the intention to focus on the partner's positive behaviors or making sure to stop and consider the broader meaning of a partner's compliment might foster the kinds of positive interaction experiences that could solidify more trusting unconscious sentiments.

Reinforcing the Conscious

Relationship problems are not limited to vulnerable people. Even the most personally resilient among us has at least one Achilles heel in their relationships—a hot issue that has the potential to trigger negative reciprocity cycles. Gayle's greater competitiveness is that hot issue in her marriage to

Ron. He might have taken Gayle's snipes at his career as a sign that she did not respect or value him as much as he did her. But he has worked at resisting this conclusion, and as a result this problem stays contained. What tactics might we recommend to keep Lastri's current intemperance from undermining Gunter's conscious feelings of trust in her? Correcting the automated will takes both motivation and opportunity (Olson & Fazio, 2008). These conjunctive prerequisites for correct suggest two interrelated tactics: (1) bolster trust and the motivation to correct by learning to integrate the good with the bad and (2) strengthen the capacity to correct through concerted practice exercising self-control.

Learning to Integrate

No partner is perfect. People inevitably discover that their partner has qualities they dislike. Some of these qualities are easily overlooked, like Gayle's odd aversion to finishing the last bite of food on her plate. Other qualities, like Gayle's competitiveness, are much harder to overlook because they present a barrier to responsiveness. In her marriage, Gayle's competitiveness makes it hard for her to be excited and happy for Ron when he succeeds—a lack of enthusiasm that has not escaped Ron's notice. Nevertheless, her competitiveness doesn't really bother him now because he has found a way to put this quality in its proper place. He sees her broader strengths as more than making up for this one admitted weakness.

In their writings on trust, Holmes and Rempel (1989) argued that people sustain trust in a partner's responsiveness through integrative thinking. Through the power of reflection, they develop "Yes, but" refutations that acknowledge a particular fault in the partner but simultaneously dispute its significance. These "Yes, buts" link the fault to a related, but greater virtue. In Ron's case, he sees Gayle's competitiveness as part of her ambition and intelligence, two qualities he values greatly in her. Having this "Yes, but" in hand effectively takes the sting away from episodes in which her competitiveness asserts itself. We found evidence for the relationship benefits of such integrative thinking in a longitudinal study of dating relationships (Murray & Holmes, 1999). In this study, we obtained three different measures of people's tendency to think about their partner's faults in the broader context of their virtues.

First, we asked participants to write a story about the development of intimacy in their relationships. We then coded these narratives for integrative thinking (e.g., finding a virtue in a partner's faults, making "Yes, buts"). Second, we asked participants to describe the meaning that their partner's "greatest" fault had for their relationship. We then coded these mini-narratives for integrative thinking. Third, we asked participants to sort their partner's qualities (both good and bad) into groups of categories they thought were related. This measure provided us with a mathematical index of integration (i.e., the degree to which participants put positive and negative partner qualities in the same as opposed to separate categories). Overall, the results revealed compelling evidence for the protective effects of integrative thought. Participants who linked their partner's faults to compensatory virtues reported greater satisfaction in the short term. They were also more likely to remain in their relationships over the course of a year!

These findings point to the power that integrative thinking might have to keep hot issues compartmentalized. The basic tenets of integrative behavioral couple therapy (IBCT) echo this theme (Jacobson, Christensen, Prince, Cordova, & Eldridge, 2000). The goal of IBCT is to help partners learn to accept aspects of each other's character that they find objectionable or upsetting because change is not always possible. It certainly wasn't in Gayle's case. She was a competitive child and she turned into a competitive adult. Once Ron accepted this quality as "part of the bargain" of being married to Gayle, it got a lot easier for him to be happy. A central component of IBCT is "tolerance building," wherein partners are encouraged to find something good in the qualities they find most objectionable (Bradbury & Karney, 2010). In Gunter's case, he might be encouraged to try to put Lastri's reluctance to talk about her ambitions in the context of her fear of eliciting his disapproval. Once he sees her avoidance in the context of her caring for him, this quality might lose much of its aversive punch.

Strengthening Self-Control

Overcoming an automatic impulse requires more than the motivation not to succumb to one's impulses (Olson & Fazio, 2008). It also requires opportunity. Namely, it requires executive strength, whether this capacity for self-control is afforded by the situation itself (e.g., not being distracted) or the personal resource of being high in working memory capacity (Hofmann et al., 2008) or high in self-control (Muraven & Baumeister, 2000). For instance, people high in working memory capacity resist the temptation to eat the M&M's they unconsciously covet, and instead adhere to their conscious intentions to diet (Hofmann et al., 2008).

Muraven and Baumeister (2000) conceptualize self-control as a muscle. This metaphor implies that self-control can be exhausted through exertion or strengthened through exercise (Baumeister, Vohs, & Tice, 2007). What insights does this metaphor offer for increasing Gunter's capacity to correct his impulse to distance himself from a criticizing Lastri (see Chapter 7)? Even though his automated will to self-protect conflicts with his general goal to connect, he's been acting out lately because he's depleted. In managing the demands of his job and his exam schedule, he uses up every available ounce of self-regulation before he even gets home. Although there's little to be done about his depleted state at the moment (short of a sugar high), over time, he might be able to build up his endurance by practicing self-regulation. For instance, he might increase his capacity to correct his impulses by foregoing the potato chips he craves or by doubling his 2-mile daily run. Greater practice in self-regulation in general might give him the strength to resist destructive temptations in his own relationship. Newly empowered, he might more readily correct the urge to return Lastri's criticisms in kind, thereby cutting negative reciprocity cycles short.

PUTTING THE PRESCRIPTIONS INTO PRACTICE

This brings us to our parting advice, the concrete steps that one might follow to allow the interdependent mind to do what it does best: promote mutual responsiveness.

1. *Be realistic.* This advice might seem curious, given that we started our collaborative research examining the relationship benefits of positive illusions. We advise "realism" because some situations are just hard. When the issue is tough—like Gunter and Lastri's baby versus education conflict—people would do well just to recognize this reality. In fact, newlyweds who face more intractable conflicts ultimately end up happier in their marriage if they tackle those problems head on (McNulty & Russell, 2010). We suspect all too often people miss that the problem itself is difficult, and instead conclude that the partner is difficult, selfish, or nonresponsive. As we have seen throughout this book, needlessly questioning the partner's responsiveness only makes it harder for the interdependent mind to elicit mutually responsive interactions.

2. *Be civil.* The unconscious trust barometer has a long memory. Gunter might consciously forgive Lastri's slights at his parenting skills, but his unconscious might not forget so readily. Instead, such slights can leave a lingering and negative associative residue, one that leaves him

sometimes feeling ill at ease in her presence. Adopting a "good manners" policy will go a long way toward preempting such negative associations (Gottman, 1994; Rusbult et al., 1991). This advice amounts to the simple prescription to treat one's partner well even when it is hard—indeed, especially when it is hard. Of course, this advice is much easier given than followed. That's why it is important to build up a reserve of positive experiences to inoculate against bad manners. Things as simple as taking a walk together, laughing over a movie, cooking a special meal, or delighting in a child's laugher will help buffer against times when tempers get short.

3. *Be optimistic.* The metaphor "you reap what you sow" captures something very basic about conflicts of interest. Assuming the best gives one's partner the opportunity to live up to one's hopes. Assuming the worst limits the partner's opportunity to do anything more than disappoint (Downey, Freitas, Michaelis, & Khouri, 1998). Because such self-fulfilling prophecies are basic to social life, there are gains to be had in entering conflict-of-interest negotiations with optimism. In Lastri's case, assuming that Gunter was going to at least try to understand her desire to return to school could have given him a better opportunity to demonstrate his responsiveness, setting them well on the way to find a mutually satisfying solution to the baby conflict.

4. *Be mindful of the rules.* The if–then rules that become one's habit regulate behavior without the intercession of consciousness, but that does not absolve partners of responsibility for their less-than-positive behavior. People can (and should) look at patterns of behavior in their relationships, and use this evidence to gain insight into their unconscious if–then rule habits from the behavioral fact. After all, the whole point of conscious reflection is to figure out how to behave more adaptively in the future (Baumeister, Vohs, DeWall, & Zhang, 2007). In reflecting on her interactions after the fact, Lastri might come to realize that she often criticizes Gunter's indulgence of their child before he even has a chance to explain himself. The insights gained from such reflections might then motivate her to bite her tongue in the future. Should distress get to the point of clinical interventions, therapists might also be advised to listen with a "third ear" to pick up the unconscious rules partners play by.

5. *Be selectively avoidant.* Because self-control is an easily depleted, but renewable, resource (Baumeister, Vohs, & Tice, 2007), there are good and bad times to engage difficult issues in the relationship. Experiences that tax self-control—like resisting the impulse to yell at one's boss or children, being distracted, or being stressed by acute financial problems—can

make it difficult to behave well in one's relationship. At the peak of such experiences, discretion is probably the better part of valor. When Gunter is feeling stressed or tired, not engaging the baby conflict is in Lastri's and his best interest because those are the circumstances under which he is less able to correct his automated will to self-protect. Consequently, those are the situations in which his interaction with a self-protectively disposed Lastri is more likely to escalate than deescalate the conflict.

EPILOGUE

The marriages of Ron and Gayle, Harry and Sally, Hector and Helena, and Gunter and Lastri each developed a unique personality and met unique fates. As the years wore on, Harry and Sally continued to rely on each other as instrumental cogs in the machinery of domestic life. Once their children left home, their need for this minimal level of interdependence left as well. Sally finally got the full-time job she wanted and she filed for divorce. Ron and Gayle had a much happier fate. Gayle's competitiveness still causes the occasional problem, but overall they each know that they make each other happy in far more ways than they make each other unhappy. As they imagine sending their children off to college in a few years, they relish the thought of it just being the two of them again. Hector and Helena's marriage faced a very rough patch when Hector lost his job. Their arguments got more heated and they separated. But being apart made Helena realize how much comfort she took simply in being with Hector. They reconciled and Hector now works even harder to take Helena's occasional insecurity in stride. Gunter and Lastri are still struggling to resolve their baby conflict. They recently decided to see a family counselor. Lastri is slowly becoming aware that Gunter really is trying to understand her and they are beginning to make headway on their problems. They both feel reasonably optimistic about the future.

FINAL THOUGHTS

Relationships are hard for a reason. Partners are never going to be able to anticipate the exact conflicts of interest they will encounter. The only absolute certainty is that differences will arise. This is what makes relationships risky, and it is a big part of the reason why so many relationships fail. But it is also why good relationships are so tremendously rewarding. Differences give partners the opportunity to provide and receive care and support. Because mutually responsive relationships satisfy the basic human need for connection, successfully negotiating conflicts of interest is indispensable to health and well-being (Baumeister & Leary, 1995).

The challenge all couples face in the pursuit of mutual responsiveness is that no one prescription can provide a cure-all. Each relationship has a unique personality, one shaped by the person, the pairing, and the context. Figuring out how to sustain a good relationship or fix a broken one requires understanding how each part of the relationship whole fits together. This complexity makes adult close relationships a fascinating topic of study. It also makes such study a social imperative because the knowledge to be gained will have a palpable impact on the relationships that people hold most dear in their lives. This book will fulfill its purpose if it helps inspire others with a passion for using the tools of science to disentangle the dynamics of close relationships.

References

Aarts, H., Custers, R., & Holland, R. W. (2007). The nonconscious cessation of goal pursuit: When goals and negative affect are coactivated. *Journal of Personality and Social Psychology, 92*, 165–178.

Aarts, H., Dijksterhuis, A., & De Vries, P. (2001). The psychology of drinking: Being thirsty and perceptually ready. *British Journal of Psychology, 92*, 631–642.

Abelson, R. P. (1983). Whatever became of consistency theory? *Personality and Social Psychology Bulletin, 9*, 37–547.

Acevedo, B. P., & Aron, A. (2009). Does a long-term relationship kill romantic love? *Review of General Psychology, 13*, 59–65.

Achtziger, A., Gollwitzer, P. M., & Sheeran, P. (2008). Implementation intentions and shielding goal striving from unwanted thoughts. *Personality and Social Psychology Bulletin, 34*, 381–393.

Ainsworth, M. D. S., Belhar, M. C., Waters, E., & Wall, S. (1978). *Patterns of attachment: Assessed in the strange situation and at home.* Hillsdale, NJ: Erlbaum.

Alexopoulos, T., & Ric, F. (2007). The evaluation-behavior link: Direct and beyond valence. *Journal of Experimental Social Psychology, 43*, 1010–1016.

Allport, G. W. (1935). Attitudes. In C. Murchison (Ed.), *A handbook of social psychology* (pp. 798–844). Worcester, MA: Clark University Press.

Altman, I., & Taylor, D. A. (1973). *Social penetration: The development of interpersonal relationships.* New York: Holt, Rinehart & Winston.

Andersen, S. M., & Chen, S. (2002). The relational self: An interpersonal social–cognitive theory. *Psychological Review, 109*, 619–645.

Andersen, S. M., Reznik, I., & Manzella, L. M. (1996). Eliciting facial affect, motivation, and expectancies in transference: Significant-other representations in social relations. *Journal of Personality and Social Psychology, 71,* 1108–1129.

Aron, A., & Aron, E. N. (1986). *Love as the expansion of self: Understanding attraction and satisfaction.* New York: Hemisphere.

Aron, A., Dutton, D. G., Aron, E. N., & Iverson, A. (1989). Experiences of falling in love. *Journal of Social and Personal Relationships, 6,* 243–257.

Aron, A., Fisher, H., Mashek, Strong, G., Li, Haifang, & Brown, L. L. (2005). Reward, motivation, and emotion systems associated with early-stage intense romantic love. *Journal of Neurophysiology, 94,* 327–337.

Aron, A., Norman, C. C., Aron, E. N., McKenna, C., & Heyman, R. (2000). Couples' shared participation in novel and arousing activities and experienced relationship quality. *Journal of Personality and Social Psychology, 69,* 1102–1112.

Aron, A., Paris, M., & Aron, E. N. (1995). Falling in love: Prospective studies of self-concept change. *Journal of Personality and Social Psychology, 78,* 1024–1037.

Arriaga, X. B. (2001). The ups and downs of dating: Fluctuations in satisfaction in newly formed romantic relationships. *Journal of Personality and Social Psychology, 80,* 754–765.

Arriaga, X. B., Slaughterbeck, E. S., Capezza, N. M., & Hmurovic, J. L. (2007). From bad to worse: Relationship commitment and vulnerability to partner imperfections. *Personal Relationships, 14,* 389–409.

Ayduk, O., Downey, G., Testa, A., Yen, Y., & Shoda, Y. (1999). Does rejection elicit hostility in rejection sensitive women? *Social Cognition, 17,* 245–271.

Baddeley, A. D., & Hitch, G. J. (1974). Working memory. In G. A. Bower (Ed.), *The psychology of learning and motivation* (Vol. 8, pp. 47–90). New York: Academic Press.

Balcetis, E., & Dunning, D. (2007). Cognitive dissonance and the perception of natural environments. *Psychological Science, 18,* 917–921.

Baldwin, M. W. (1992). Relational schemas and the processing of social information. *Psychological Bulletin, 112,* 461–484.

Baldwin, M. W., Fehr, B., Keelian, E., Seidel, M., & Thompson, D. (1993). An exploration of the relational schemata underlying attachment styles: Self-report and lexical decision approaches. *Personality and Social Psychology Bulletin, 19,* 746–754.

Baldwin, M. W., & Sinclair, L. (1996). Self-esteem and "if . . . then" contingencies of interpersonal acceptance. *Journal of Personality and Social Psychology, 71,* 1130–1141.

Bargh, J. A. (1994). The four horsemen of automaticity: Awareness, intention, efficiency, and control in social cognition. In R. S. Wyer & T. K. Strull (Eds.), *Handbook of social cognition* (Vol. 1, pp. 1–40). Hillsdale, NJ: Erlbaum.

Bargh, J. A. (2007). *Social psychology and the unconscious: The automaticity of higher mental processes.* New York: Psychology Press.

Bargh, J. A., Chen, M., & Burrows, L. (1996). Automaticity of social behavior: Direct effects of trait construct and stereotype activation on action. *Journal of Personality and Social Psychology, 71,* 230–244.

Bargh, J. A., & Ferguson, M. J. (2000). Beyond behaviorism: On the automaticity of higher mental processes. *Psychological Bulletin, 126,* 925–945.

Bargh, J. A., Gollwitzer, P. M., Lee-Chai, A., Barndollar, K., & Trotschel, R. (2001).

The automated will: Nonconscious activation and pursuit of behavioral goals. *Journal of Personality and Social Psychology, 81,* 1014–1027.

Bargh, J. A., & Huang, J. Y. (2009). The selfish goal. In G. B. Moskowitz & H. Grant (Eds.), *The psychology of goals* (pp. 127–150). New York: Guilford Press.

Bargh, J. A., & Morsella, E. (2008). The unconscious mind. *Perspectives on Psychological Science, 3,* 73–79.

Bargh, J. A., & Williams, E. L. (2006). The automaticity of social life. *Current Directions in Psychological Science, 15,* 1–4.

Bartels, A., & Zeki, S. (2000). The neural basis of romantic love. *Neuro Report, 11,* 3829–3834.

Baumeister, R. F. (1993). *Self-esteem: The puzzle of low self-regard.* New York: Plenum Press.

Baumeister, R. F., Bratslavsky, E., Finkenauer, C., & Vohs, K. D. (2001). Bad is stronger than good. *Review of General Psychology, 5,* 323–370.

Baumeister, R. F., Bratslavsky, E., Muraven, M., & Tice, D. M. (1998). Ego-depletion: Is the active self a limited resource? *Journal of Personality and Social Psychology, 74,* 1252–1265.

Baumeister, R. F., & Leary, M. R. (1995). The need to belong: Desire for interpersonal attachments as a fundamental human motivation. *Psychological Bulletin, 117,* 497–529.

Baumeister, R. F., Tice, D. M., & Hutton, D. G. (1989). Self-presentational motivations and personality differences in self-esteem. *Journal of Personality, 57,* 547–579.

Baumeister, R. F., Vohs, K. D., De Wall, C. N., & Zhang, L. (2007). How emotion shapes behavior: Feedback, anticipation, and reflection, rather than direct causation. *Personality and Social Psychology Review, 11,* 167–203.

Baumeister, R. F., Vohs, K. D., & Tice, D. M. (2007). The strength model of self-control. *Current Directions in Psychological Science, 16,* 351–355.

Baumeister, R. F., Wotman, S. R., & Stillwell, A. M. (1993). Unrequited love: On heartbreak, anger, guilt, scriptlessness, and humiliation. *Journal of Personality and Social Psychology, 64,* 377–394.

Beach, S. R. H., Tesser, A., Fincham, F. D., Jones, D. J., Johnson, D., & Whitaker, D. J. (1998). Pleasure and pain in doing well together: An investigation of performance-related affect in close relationships. *Journal of Personality and Social Psychology, 74,* 923–938.

Beach, S. R. H., Whitaker, D. J., Jones, D. J., & Tesser, A. (2001). When does performance feedback prompt complementarity in romantic relationships? *Personal Relationships, 8,* 231–248.

Bellavia, G., & Murray, S. L. (2003). Did I do that? Self-esteem related differences in reactions to romantic partners' moods. *Personal Relationships, 10,* 77–96.

Belsky, J., Spanier, G. B., & Rovine, M. (1983). Stability and change in the marriage across the transition to parenthood. *Journal of Marriage and Family, 45,* 567–577.

Berscheid, E. (1983). Emotion. In H. H. Kelley, E. Berscheid, A. Christensen, J. H. Harvey, T. L. Huston, G. Levinger, E. McClintock, L. A. Peplau, & D. R. Peterson (Eds.), *Close relationships* (pp. 110–168). New York: Freeman.

Berscheid, E., Dion, K. K., Walster, E., & Walster, G. (1971). Physical attractiveness and dating choice: A test of the matching hypothesis. *Journal of Experimental Social Psychology, 7,* 173–189.

Berscheid, E., & Regan, P. (2005). *The psychology of interpersonal relationships.* Upper Saddle River, NJ: Prentice Hall.

Berscheid, E., & Reis, H. T. (1998). Attraction and close relationships. In D. T. Gilbert, S. T. Fiske, & G. Lindsey (Eds.), *The handbook of social psychology* (Vol. 2, pp. 193–281). Boston: McGraw-Hill.

Berscheid, E., & Walster, E. H. (1969). *Interpersonal attraction.* Reading, MA: Addison-Wesley.

Bowlby, J. (1969). *Attachment and loss* (Vol. 1: Attachment). London: Hogarth Press.

Boyes, A. D., & Fletcher, G. J. O. (2007). Metaperceptions of bias in intimate relationships. *Journal of Personality and Social Psychology, 92,* 286–306.

Bradbury, T. N., & Karney, B. R. (2010). *Intimate relationships.* New York: Norton.

Braiker, H. B., & Kelley, H. H. (1979). Conflict in the development of close relationship. In R. L Burgess & T. L. Huston (Eds.), *Social exchange in developing relationship* (pp. 135–168). New York: Academic Press.

Brehm, S. S. (1988). Passionate love. In R. J. Sternberg & M. L. Barnes (Eds.), *The psychology of love* (pp. 232–263). New Haven, CT: Yale University Press.

Brickman, P. (1987). *Commitment, conflict, and caring.* Englewood Cliffs, NJ: Prentice Hall.

Buss, D. M. (1989). Sex differences in human mate preferences: Evolutionary hypotheses tested in 37 cultures. *Behavioral and Brain Sciences, 12,* 1–49.

Buss, D. M., & Schmitt, D. P. (1993). Sexual strategies theory: An evolutionary perspective on human mating. *Psychological Review, 100,* 204–232.

Cacioppo, J. T., Gardner, W. L., & Berntson, G. G. (1999). The affect system has parallel and integrative processing components: Form follows function. *Journal of Personality and Social Psychology, 76,* 839–855.

Campbell, L., Simpson, J. A., Boldry, J., & Kashy, D. A. (2005). Perceptions of conflict and support in romantic relationships: The role of attachment anxiety. *Journal of Personality and Social Psychology, 88,* 510–531.

Campbell, L., Simpson, J. A., Kashy, D. A., & Fletcher, G. J. O. (2001). Ideal standards, the self, and flexibility of ideals in close relationships. *Personality and Social Psychology Bulletin, 27,* 447–462.

Cantor, J. R., Zillmann, D., & Bryant, J. (1975). Enhancement of experienced sexual arousal in response to erotic stimuli through misattribution of unrelated residual excitation. *Journal of Personality and Social Psychology, 32,* 69–75.

Carr, L., Iacoboni, M., Dubeau, M. C., Mazziotta, J. C., & Lenzi, G. L. (2003). Neural mechanisms of empathy in humans: A relay from neural systems for imitation to limbic areas. *Proceedings of the National Academy of Sciences, 100,* 5497–5502.

Caughlin, J. P., Huston, T. L., & Houts, R. M. (2000). How does personality matter in marriage: An examination of trait anxiety, interpersonal negativity, and marital satisfaction. *Journal of Personality and Social Psychology, 78,* 326–336.

Cavallo, J., Fitzsimons, G. M., & Holmes, J. G. (2009). Taking chances in the face of threat: Romantic risk regulation and approach motivation. *Personality and Social Psychology Bulletin, 35,* 737–751.

Cavallo, J., Fitzsimons, G. M., & Holmes, J. G. (2010). When self-protection over-reaches: Relationship-specific threat activates domain-general avoidance motivation. *Journal of Experimental Social Psychology, 46*, 1–8.

Cesario, J., Plaks, J. E., & Higgins, E. T. (2006). Automatic social behavior as motivated preparation to interact. *Journal of Personality and Social Psychology, 90*, 893–910.

Chartrand, T. L., & Bargh, J. A. (1996). Automatic activation of impression formation and memorization goals: Nonconscious goal priming reproduces effects of explicit task instructions. *Journal of Personality and Social Psychology, 71*, 464–478.

Chen, M., & Bargh, J. A. (1999). Consequences of automatic evaluation: Immediate behavioral predispositions to approach or avoid the stimulus. *Personality and Social Psychology Bulletin, 25*, 215–224.

Christensen, A., & Heavey, C. L. (1990). Gender and social structure in the demand/withdraw pattern of marital conflict. *Journal of Personality and Social Psychology, 59*, 73–81.

Cialdini, R. B., & Trost, M. R. (1998). Social influence: Social norms, conformity, and compliance. In D. T. Gilbert, S. T. Fiske, & G. Lindsey (Eds.), *The handbook of social psychology* (Vol. 2, pp. 151–192). Boston: McGraw-Hill.

Clark, M. S., & Grote, N. K. (1998). Why aren't indices of relationship costs always negatively related to indices of relationship quality? *Personality and Social Psychology Review, 2*, 2–17.

Clark, M. S., & Mills, J. (1993). The difference between communal and exchange relationships: What it is and is not. *Personality and Social Psychology Bulletin, 19*, 684–691.

Collins, N. L. (1996). Working models of attachment: Implications for explanation, emotion and behavior. *Journal of Personality and Social Psychology, 71*, 810–832.

Collins, N. L., & Feeney, B. C. (2004). Working models of attachment shape perceptions of social support: Evidence from experimental and observational studies. *Journal of Personality and Social Psychology, 87*, 363–383.

Collins, N. L., & Feeney, B. C. (2010). An attachment theoretical perspective on social support dynamics in couples: Normative processes and individual differences. In K. Sullivan & J. Davila (Eds.), *Support processes in intimate relationships* (pp. 89–120). London: Oxford University Press.

Collins, N. L., & Miller, L. C. (1994). Self-disclosure and liking: A meta-analytic review. *Psychological Bulletin, 116*, 457–475.

Collins, N. L., & Read, S. J. (1994). Cognitive representations of attachment: The structure and function of working models. In K. Bartholomew & D. Perlman (Eds.), *Advances in personal relationships: Vol. 5. Attachment processes in adulthood* (pp. 53–90). PA: Jessica Kingsley.

Condon, J. W., & Crano, W. D. (1988). Inferred evaluation and the relation between attitude similarity and interpersonal attraction. *Journal of Personality and Social Psychology, 54*, 789–797.

Cottrell, C. A., Neuberg, S. L., & Li, N. P. (2007). What do people desire in others? A sociofunctional perspective on the importance of different valued characteristics. *Journal of Personality and Social Psychology, 92*, 208–231.

Cox, M. J., Paley, B., Burchinal, M., & Payne, C. C. (1999). Marital perceptions and interactions across the transition to parenthood. *Journal of Marriage and the Family, 61,* 611–625.

Cunningham, M. R. (1986). Measuring the physical in physical attractiveness: Quasi-experiments on the sociobiology of female facial beauty. *Journal of Personality and Social Psychology, 50,* 925–935.

Dandeneau, S. D., Baldwin, M. W., Baccus, J. R., Sakellaropoulo, M., & Pruessner, J. C. (2007). Cutting stress off at the pass: Reducing vigilance and responsiveness to social threat by manipulating attention. *Journal of Personality and Social Psychology, 93,* 651–666.

Davila, J., Karney, B. R., & Bradbury, T. N. (1999). Attachment change processes in the early years of marriage. *Journal of Personality and Social Psychology, 76,* 783–802.

Dennett, D. C. (2001). *Consciousness explained.* London: Penguin Books.

Derrick, J. L., & Murray, S. L. (2007). Enhancing relationship perceptions by reducing felt inferiority: The role of attachment style. *Personal Relationships, 14,* 531–549.

Diamond, L. M. (2003). What does sexual orientation orient? A biobehavioral model distinguishing romantic love and sexual desire. *Psychological Review, 110,* 173–192.

Diamond, L. M. (2004). Emerging perspectives on distinctions between romantic love and sexual desire. *Current Directions in Psychological Science, 13,* 116–119.

Dijksterhuis, A. (2004). I like myself but I don't know why: Enhancing implicit self-esteem by subliminal evaluative conditioning. *Journal of Personality and Social Psychology, 86,* 345–355.

Dijksterhuis, A., Chartrand, T. L., & Aarts, H. (2007). Effects of priming and perception on social behavior and goal pursuit. In J. A. Bargh (Ed.), *Social psychology and the unconscious: The automaticity of higher mental processes* (pp. 51–132). New York: Psychology Press.

Dijksterhuis, A., & Nordgren, L. F. (2006). A theory of unconscious thought. *Perspectives on Psychological Science, 1,* 95–109.

Dijksterhuis, A., & van Knippenberg, A. (1998). The relation between perception and behavior, or how to win a game of Trivial Pursuit. *Journal of Personality and Social Psychology, 74,* 865–877.

Doss, B. D., Rhoades, G. K., Stanley, S. M., & Markman, H. J. (2009). The effect of the transition to parenthood on relationship quality: An 8-year prospective study. *Journal of Personality and Social Psychology, 96,* 601–619.

Downey, G., & Feldman, S. I. (1996). Implications of rejection sensitivity for intimate relationships. *Journal of Personality and Social Psychology, 70,* 1327–1343.

Downey, G., Freitas, A. L., Michaelis, B., & Khouri, H. (1998). The self-fulfilling prophecy in close relationships: Rejection sensitivity and rejection by romantic partners. *Journal of Personality and Social Psychology, 75,* 545–560.

Drigotas, S. M., & Rusbult, C. E. (1992). Should I stay or should I go? A dependence model of breakups. *Journal of Personality and Social Psychology, 62,* 62–87.

Drigotas, S. M., Rusbult, C. E., & Verette, J. (1999). Level of commitment, mutuality of commitment, and couple well-being. *Personal Relationships, 6,* 389–409.

Dunbar, R. I. M., & Shultz, S. (2007). Evolution in the social brain. *Science, 317,* 1344–1346.

Dunning, D., Meyerowitz, J. A., & Holzberg, A. D. (1989). Ambiguity and self-evaluation: The role of idiosyncratic trait definitions in self-serving assessments of ability. *Journal of Personality and Social Psychology, 57,* 1082–1090.

Dutton, D. C., & Aron, A. (1974). Some evidence for heightened sexual attraction under conditions of high anxiety. *Journal of Personality and Social Psychology, 30,* 510–517.

Eastwick, P. W., & Finkel, E. J. (2008a). Sex differences in mate preferences revisited: Do people know what they initially desire in a romantic partner? *Journal of Personality and Social Psychology, 94,* 245–264.

Eastwick, P. W., & Finkel, E. J. (2008b). The attachment system in fledgling relationships: An activating role for attachment anxiety. *Journal of Personality and Social Psychology, 95,* 628–647.

Eastwick, P. W., Finkel, E. J., Mochon, D., & Ariely, D. (2007). Selective versus unselective romantic desire: Not all reciprocity is created equal. *Psychological Science, 18,* 317–319.

Egan, L. C., Santos, L. R., & Bloom, P. (2007). The origins of cognitive dissonance: Evidence from children and monkeys. *Psychological Science, 18,* 978–983.

Eidelson, R. J. (1980). Interpersonal satisfaction and level of involvement: A curvilinear relationship. *Journal of Personality and Social Psychology, 39,* 460–470.

Elliot, A. J. (2008). *Handbook of approach and avoidance motivation.* New York: Psychology Press.

Elliot, A. J., & Church, M. A. (1997). A hierarchical model of approach and avoidance achievement motivation. *Journal of Personality and Social Psychology, 72,* 218–232.

Elliot, A. J., & Maier, M. A. (2007). Color and psychological functioning. *Current Directions in Psychological Science, 16,* 250–254.

Elliot, A. J., Maier, M. A., Moller, A. C., Friedman, R., & Meinhardt, J. (2007). Color and psychological functioning: The effect of red on performance attainment. *Journal of Experimental Psychology: General, 136,* 154–168.

Elliot, A. J., & Niesta, D. (2008). Romantic red: Red enhances men's attraction to women. *Journal of Personality and Social Psychology, 95,* 1150–1164.

Endo, Y., Heine, S. J., & Lehman, D. R. (2000). Culture and positive illusions in close relationships: How my relationships are better than yours. *Personality and Social Psychology Bulletin, 26,* 1571–1586.

Enfield, N. J., & Levinson, S. C. (2006). *Roots of human sociality: Culture, cognition and interaction.* New York: Berg.

Etcheverry, P. E., & Le, B. (2005). Thinking about commitment: Accessibility of commitment and prediction of relationship persistence, accommodation, and willingness to sacrifice. *Personal Relationships, 12,* 103–123.

Fazio, R. H. (1986). How do attitudes guide behavior? In R. M. Sorrentino & E. T. Higgins (Eds.), *The handbook of motivation and cognition: Foundations of social behavior* (pp. 204–243). New York: Guilford Press.

Fazio, R. H., & Towles-Schwen, T. (1999). The MODE model of attitude-behavior processes. In S. Chaiken & Y. Trope (Eds.), *Dual process theories in social psychology* (pp. 97–116). New York: Guilford Press.

Feeney, B. C. (2004). A secure base: Responsive support of goal strivings and exploration in adult intimate relationships. *Journal of Personality and Social Psychology, 87,* 631–648.

Feeney, B. C., & Collins, N. C. (2003). Motivations for caregiving in adult intimate relationships: Influences on caregiving behavior and relationship functioning. *Personality and Social Psychology Bulletin, 29,* 950–968.

Feingold, A. (1988). Matching for attractiveness in romantic partners and same-sex friends: A meta-analysis and theoretical critique. *Psychological Bulletin, 104,* 226–235.

Feng, D., & Baker, L. (1994). Spouse similarity in attitudes, personality, and psychological well-being. *Behavior Genetics, 24,* 357–364.

Festinger, L. (1957). *A theory of cognitive dissonance.* Evanston, IL: Row Peterson.

Finkel, E. J., & Campbell, W. K. (2001). Self-control and accommodation in close relationships: An interdependence analysis. *Journal of Personality and Social Psychology, 81,* 263–277.

Finkel, E. J., Campbell, W. K., Brunell, A. B., Dalton, A. N., Scarbeck, S. J., & Chartrand, T. L. (2006). High-maintenance interaction: Inefficient social coordination impairs self-regulation. *Journal of Personality and Social Psychology, 91,* 456–475.

Fisher, H., Aron, A., & Brown, L. L. (2005). Romantic love: An fMRI study of a neural mechanism for mate choice. *Journal of Comparative Neurology, 493,* 58–62.

Fisher, H. E. (1998). Lust, attraction, and attachment in mammalian reproduction. *Human Nature, 9,* 23–52.

Fisher, H. E., Aron, A., Masheck, D., Haifang, L., & Brown, L. L. (2002). Defining the brain systems of lust, romantic attraction, and attachment. *Archives of Sexual Behavior, 31,* 413–419.

Fiske, S. T. (1992). Thinking is for doing: Portraits of social cognition from daguerreotype to laser photo. *Journal of Personality and Social Psychology, 63,* 877–889.

Fiske, S. T., Cuddy, A. J. C., & Glick, P. (2006). Universal dimensions of social cognition: Warmth and competence. *Trends in Cognitive Science, 11,* 77–83.

Fiske, S. T., & Neuberg, S. L. (1990). A continuum of impression formation, from category-based to individuating processes: Influences of information and motivation on attention and interpretation. In M. P. Zanna (Ed.), *Advances in experimental social psychology* (Vol. 23, pp. 1–74). New York: Academic Press.

Fitzsimons, G. M., & Bargh, J. A. (2003). Thinking of you: Nonconscious pursuit of interpersonal goals associated with relationship partners. *Journal of Personality and Social Psychology, 84,* 148–164.

Fletcher, G. J. O., & Kerr, P. S. G. (2010). Through the eyes of love: Reality and illusion in intimate relationships. *Psychological Bulletin, 136,* 627–658.

Fletcher, G. J. O., Simpson, J. A., & Thomas, G. (2000). Ideals, perceptions, and evaluations in early relationship development. *Journal of Personality and Social Psychology, 79,* 933–940.

Ford, M. B., & Collins, N. L. (2010). Self-esteem moderates neuroendocrine and psychological responses to interpersonal rejection. *Journal of Personality and Social Psychology, 98,* 405–419.

Forster, J., Liberman, N., & Friedman, R. S. (2007). Seven principles of goal activation: A systematic approach to distinguishing goal priming from priming of non-goal constructs. *Personality and Social Psychology Review, 11,* 211–233.

Frank, E., & Brandstatter, V. (2002). Approach versus avoidance: Different types of commitment in intimate relationships. *Journal of Personality and Social Psychology, 82,* 208–221.

Franzoi, S. L. (2009). *Social psychology* (5th ed.). New York: McGraw-Hill.

Gable, S. (2007, October). *Getting along or not arguing? Approach and avoidance goals in close relationships.* Paper presented at the Society of Experimental Social Psychology, Chicago, Illinois.

Gable, S. L. (2005). Approach and avoidance social motives and goals. *Journal of Personality, 74,* 175–222.

Gable, S. L., Gonzaga, G. C., & Strachman, A. (2006). Will you be there for me when things go right? Supportive responses to positive event disclosures. *Journal of Personality and Social Psychology, 91,* 904–917.

Gable, S. L., & Poore, J. (2008). Which thoughts count? Algorithms for evaluating satisfaction in relationships. *Psychological Science, 19,* 1030–1036.

Gable, S. L., Reis, H. T., Impett, E. A., & Asher, E. R. (2004). What do you do when things go right? The intrapersonal and interpersonal benefits of sharing positive events. *Journal of Personality and Social Psychology, 87,* 228–245.

Gagne, F. M., & Lydon, J. E. (2001a). Mind-set and close relationships: When bias leads to (in)accurate predictions. *Journal of Personality and Social Psychology, 81,* 85–96.

Gagne, F. M., & Lydon, J. E. (2001b). Mind-set and relationship illusions: The moderating effects of domain specificity and relationship commitment. *Personality and Social Psychology Bulletin, 27,* 1144–1155.

Gagne, F. M., & Lydon, J. E. (2003). Identification and the commitment shift: Accounting for gender differences in relationship illusions. *Personality and Social Psychology Bulletin, 29,* 907–191.

Gangestad, S. W., & Simpson, J. A. (2000). The evolution of human mating: Tradeoffs and strategic pluralism. *Behavioral and Brain Sciences, 23,* 573–587.

Gangestad, S. W., Simpson, J. A., Cousins, A. J., Garver-Apgar, E. E., & Christensen, P. N. (2004). Women's preferences for male behavioral displays change across the menstrual cycle. *Psychological Science, 15,* 203–207.

Gangestad, S. W., & Thornhill, R. (1998). Menstrual cycle variation in women's preferences for the scent of symmetrical men. *Proceedings of the Royal Society of London B: Biological Sciences, 269,* 975–982.

Garver-Apgar, C. E., Gangestad, W. W., Thornhill, R., Miller, R. D., & Olp, J. J. (2006). MHC alleles, sexual responsivity, and unfaithfulness in romantic couples. *Psychological Science, 17,* 830–835.

Gawronski, B., & Bodenhausen, G. V. (2006). Associative and propositional processes in evaluation: An integrative review of implicit and explicit attitude change. *Psychological Bulletin, 132,* 692–731.

Gilbert, D. T. (1989). Thinking lightly about others: Automatic components of the social inference process. In J. S. Uleman & J. A. Bargh (Eds.), *Unintended thought* (pp. 189–211). New York: Guilford Press.

Gilbert, D. T., & Malone, P. S. (1995). The correspondence bias. *Psychological Bulletin, 117,* 21–38.

Gilbert, P. (2005). Social mentalities: A biopsychosocial and evolutionary approach to social relationships. In M. Baldwin (Ed.), *Interpersonal cognition* (pp. 299–333). New York: Guilford Press.

Gillath, O., Mikulincer, M., Fitzsimons, G. M., Shaver, P. R., Schachner, D. A., & Bargh, J. A. (2006). Automatic activation of attachment-related goals. *Personality and Social Psychology Bulletin, 32,* 1375–1388.

Gillath, O., & Schachner, D. A. (2006). Goals, motives, and strategies: How do sexuality and attachment interrelate? In M. Mikulincer & G. S. Goodman (Eds.), *Dynamics of romantic love: Attachment, caregiving, and sex* (pp. 121–147). New York: Guilford Press.

Gollwitzer, P. M. (1990). Action phases and mindsets. In E. T. Higgins & R. M. Sorrentino (Eds.), *Handbook of motivation and cognition: Foundations of social behavior* (Vol. 2, pp. 53–92). New York: Guilford Press.

Gollwitzer, P. M. (1999). Implementation intentions: Strong effects of simple plans. *American Psychologist, 54,* 493–503.

Gonzaga, G. C., Campos, B., & Bradbury, T. (2007). Similarity, convergence, and relationship satisfaction in dating and married couples. *Journal of Personality and Social Psychology, 93,* 34–48.

Gottman, J. M. (1994). *What predicts divorce? The relationship between marital processes and marital outcomes.* Hillsdale, NJ: Erlbaum.

Gottman, J. M., Ryan, K. D., Carrere, S., & Erley, A. M. (2002). Toward a scientifically based marital therapy. In H. A. Liddle, D. A. Santisteban, R. F. Levant, & J. H. Gray (Eds.), *Family psychology: Science-based interventions* (pp. 124–174). Washington, DC: American Psychological Association.

Gregg, A. P., Seibt, B., & Banaji, M. R. (2006). Easier done than undone: Asymmetry in the malleability of implicit preferences. *Journal of Personality and Social Psychology, 90,* 1–20.

Greenwald, A. G., McGhee, D. E., & Schwarz, J. L. K. (1998). Measuring individual differences in implicit cognition: The implicit association test. *Journal of Personality and Social Psychology, 74,* 1464–1480.

Griffin, D. W., & Bartholomew, K. (1994). Models of the self and other: Fundamental dimensions underlying measures of adult attachment. *Journal of Personality and Social Psychology, 67,* 430–445.

Griffin, D. W., & Ross, L. (1991). Subjective construal, social inference and human misunderstanding. *Advances in Experimental Social Psychology, 24,* 319–359.

Grote, N. K., & Clark, M. S. (2001). Perceiving unfairness in the family: Cause or consequence of marital distress. *Journal of Personality and Social Psychology, 80,* 281–293.

Guichard, A. C., & Collins, N. A. (2008, February). *The influence of social support and attachment style on performance, self-evaluations, and interpersonal behaviors.* Poster presented at the meeting of the Society for Personality and Social Psychology, Albuquerque, NM.

Gunz, A., Sahdra, B., Holmes, J. G., Fitzsimons, G., & Kunda, Z. (2006). *Complementary and assimilative processes in automotive priming in relationship contexts.* Unpublished manuscript, University of Waterloo, Canada.

Haddock, G., Zanna, M. P., & Esses, V. M. (1993). Assessing the structure of prejudicial attitudes: The case of prejudice against homosexuals. *Journal of Personality and Social Psychology, 65,* 1105–1118.

Hall, J., & Taylor, S. E. (1976). When love is blind. *Human Relations, 29,* 751–761.

Hare, B. (2007). From nonhuman to human mind: What changed and why? *Current Directions in Psychological Science, 16,* 60–64.

Harmon-Jones, E. (1999). Toward an understanding of the motivation underlying dissonance effects: Is the productive of aversive consequences necessary? In E. Harmon-Jones & M. Mills (Eds.), *Cognitive dissonance: Progress on a pivotal theory in social psychology* (pp. 71–102). Washington, DC: American Psychological Association.

Harvey, J. H., & Omarzu, J. (1997). Minding the close relationship. *Personality and Social Psychology Review, 1,* 223–239.

Haselton, M. G., & Buss, D. M. (2000). Error management theory: A new perspective on biases in cross-sex mind reading. *Journal of Personality and Social Psychology, 78,* 81–91.

Hazan, C., & Diamond, L. M. (2000). The place of attachment in human mating. *Review of General Psychology, 4,* 186–204.

Hazan, C., & Shaver, P. R. (1987). Romantic love conceptualized as an attachment process. *Journal of Personality and Social Psychology, 52,* 511–524.

Hazan, C., & Shaver, P. R. (1990). Love and work: An attachment-theoretical perspective. *Journal of Personality and Social Psychology, 59,* 270–280.

Hazan, C., & Zeifman, D. (1994). Sex and the psychological tether. *Advances in Personal Relationships, 5,* 151–177.

Heimpel, S. A., Elliot, A. J., & Wood, J. V. (2006). Basic personality dispositions, self-esteem, and personal goals: An approach–avoidance analysis. *Journal of Personality, 74,* 1293–1320.

Heine, S. J., & Lehman, D. R. (1995). Cultural variation in unrealistic optimism: Does the West feel more invulnerable than the East? *Journal of Personality and Social Psychology, 68,* 595–607.

Henrich, J., Heine, S. J., & Norenzayan, A. (2010). The weirdest people in the world? (Target Article, Commentaries, and Response). *Behavioral and Brain Sciences, 33,* 61–83, 111–135.

Herrmann, E., Call, J., Hernandez-Lloreda, M. V., Hare, B., & Tomasello, M. (2007). Humans have evolved specialized skills of social cognition. *Science, 317,* 1360–1365.

Higgins, E. T. (1996). Knowledge activation: Accessibility, applicability, and salience. In E. T. Higgins & A. W. Kruglanski (Eds.), *Social psychology: Handbook of basic principles* (pp. 133–168). New York: Guilford Press.

Higgins, E. T. (1998). Promotion and prevention: Regulatory focus as a motivational principle. *Advances in Experimental Social Psychology, 30,* 1–46.

Higgins, E. T. (2000). Making a good decision: Value from fit. *American Psychologist, 55,* 1217–1230.

Higgins, E. T. (2006). Value from hedonic experience and engagement. *Psychological Review, 113*, 439–460.

Hofmann, W., Friese, M., & Strack, F. (2009). Impulse and self-control from a dual systems perspective. *Perspectives on Psychological Science, 4*, 162–176.

Hofmann, W., Gschwendner, T., Friese, M., Wiers, R. W., & Schmitt, M. (2008). Working memory capacity and self-regulatory behavior. Toward an individual differences perspective on behavior determination by automatic versus controlled processes. *Journal of Personality and Social Psychology, 95*, 962–977.

Holmes, J. G. (1981). The exchange process in close relationships: Microbehavior and macromotives. In M. L. Lerner & S. Lerner (Eds.), *The justice motive in social behavior* (pp. 261–284). New York: Plenum Press.

Holmes, J. G. (2002). Interpersonal expectations as the building blocks of social cognition: An interdependence theory perspective. *Personal Relationship, 9*, 1–26.

Holmes, J. G., & Murray, S. L. (2007). Felt security as a normative resource: Evidence for an elemental risk regulation system? *Psychological Inquiry, 18*, 163–167.

Holmes, J. G., & Rempel, J. K. (1989). Trust in close relationships. In C. Hendrick (Ed.), *Review of personality and social psychology: Vol. 10. Close relationships* (pp. 187–219). Newbury Park, CA: Sage.

Hoshino-Browne, E., Zanna, A. S., Spencer, S. J., Zanna, M. P., Kitayam, S., & Lackenbauer, S. (2005). On the cultural guises of cognitive dissonance: The case of Easterners and Westerners. *Journal of Personality and Social Psychology, 89*, 294–310.

Houts, R. M., Robins, E., & Huston, T. L. (1996). Compatibility and the development of premarital relationships. *Journal of Marriage and Family, 58*, 7–20.

Huston, T. L. (1983). Power. In H. H. Kelley, E. Berscheid, A. Christensen, J. H. Harvey, T. L. Huston, G. Levinger, E. McClintock, L. A. Peplau, & D. R. Peterson (Eds.), *Close relationships* (pp. 169–219). New York: Freeman.

Huston, T. L., Caughlin, J. P., Houts, R. M., Smith, S. E., & George, L. J. (2001). The connubial crucible: Newlywed years as predictors of marital delight, distress, and divorce. *Journal of Personality and Social Psychology, 80*, 237–252.

Huston, T. L., & Chorost, A. F. (1994). Behavioral buffers on the effect of negativity on marital satisfaction: A longitudinal study. *Personal Relationships, 1*, 223–240.

Huston, T. L., McHale, S. M., & Crouter, A. C. (1986). When the honeymoon's over: Changes in the marriage relationship over the first year. In R. Gilmour & S. Duck (Eds.), *The emerging field of personal relationships* (pp. 109–132). Hillsdale, NJ: Erlbaum.

Huston, T. L., & Vangelisti, A. L. (1991). Socioemotional behavior and satisfaction in marital relationships. *Journal of Personality and Social Psychology, 61*, 54–73.

Impett, E. A., Gable, S. L., & Peplau, A. (2005). Giving up and giving in: The costs and benefits of daily sacrifice in intimate relationships. *Journal of Personality and Social Psychology, 89*, 327–344.

Impett, E. A., Strachman, A., Finkel, E. J., & Gable, S. L. (2008). Maintaining sexual desire in intimate relationships: The importance of approach goals. *Journal of Personality and Social Psychology, 94*, 808–823.

Jacobson, N. S., Christensen, A., Price, S. E., Cordova, J., & Eldridge, K. (2000). Integrative behavioral couple therapy: An acceptance-based, promising treatment for couple discord. *Journal of Consulting and Clinical Psychology, 68,* 351–355.

James, W. H. (1981). The honeymoon effect on marital coitus. *Journal of Sex Research, 17,* 114–123.

Johnson, D. J., & Rusbult, C. E. (1989). Resisting temptation: Devaluation of alternative partners as a means of maintaining commitment in close relationships. *Journal of Personality and Social Psychology, 57,* 967–980.

Johnson, S. M. (2003). The revolution in couple therapy: A practitioner-scientist perspective. *Journal of Marriage and Family Therapy, 29,* 365–384.

Jones, E. E., & Gerard, H. B. (1967). *Foundations of social psychology.* New York: Wiley.

Jones, J. T., Pelham, B. W., Cavallo, M., & Mirenberg, M. C. (2004). How do I love thee? Let me count the Js: Implicit egotism and interpersonal attraction. *Journal of Personality and Social Psychology, 87,* 665–683.

Karney, B. R., & Bradbury, T. N. (1995). The longitudinal course of marital quality and stability: A review of theory, methods, and research. *Psychological Bulletin, 118,* 3–34.

Karney, B. R., & Bradbury, T. N. (1997). Neuroticism, marital interaction, and the trajectory of marital satisfaction. *Journal of Personality and Social Psychology, 72,* 1075–1092.

Karney, B. R., & Bradbury, T. N. (2000). Attributions in marriage: State or trait? A growth curve analysis. *Journal of Personality and Social Psychology, 78,* 295–309.

Karremans, J. C., & Aarts, H. (2007). The role of automaticity in determining the inclination to forgive close others. *Journal of Experimental Social Psychology, 43,* 902–917.

Kelley, H. H. (1967). Attribution theory in social psychology. In D. Levine (Ed.), *Nebraska symposium on motivation* (Vol. 15, pp. 192–240). Lincoln: University of Nebraska Press.

Kelley, H. H. (1979). *Personal relationships: Their structures and processes.* Hillsdale, NJ: Erlbaum.

Kelley, H. H. (1983). The situational origins of human tendencies: A further reason for the formal analysis of structures. *Personality and Social Psychology Bulletin, 9,* 8–30.

Kelley, H. H., & Holmes, J. G. (2003). *Interdependence theory: Situations, relationships, and personality.* Unpublished manuscript, University of California at Los Angeles.

Kelley, H. H., Holmes, J. G., Kerr, N., Reis, H., Rusbult, C., & Van Lange, P. A. (2003). *An atlas of interpersonal situations.* Cambridge, UK: Cambridge University Press.

Kelley, H. H., & Thibaut, J. W. (1978). *Interpersonal relations: A theory of interdependence.* New York: Wiley.

Kelly, E. L., & Conley, J. J. (1987). Personality and compatibility: A prospective analysis of marital stability and marital satisfaction. *Journal of Personality and Social Psychology, 52,* 27–40.

Kenny, D. A. (1994). *Interpersonal perception: A social relations analysis.* New York: Guilford Press.

Kityama, S., Markus, H. R., Matsumoto, H., & Norasakkunkit, V. (1997). Individual and collective processes of self-esteem management: Self-enhancement in the United States and self-depreciation in Japan. *Journal of Personality and Social Psychology, 72,* 1245–1267.

Klusmann, D. (2002). Sexual motivation and the duration of partnership. *Archives of Sexual Behavior, 31,* 275–287.

Kluwer, E. S., & Johnson, M. D. (2007). Conflict frequency and relationship quality across the transition to parenthood. *Journal of Marriage and Family, 69,* 1089–1106.

Knoblich, G., & Sebanz, N. (2006). The social nature of perception and action. *Current Directions in Psychological Science, 15,* 99–104.

Kunda, Z. (1990). The case for motivated reasoning. *Psychological Bulletin, 108,* 480–498.

Kunda, Z. (1999). *Social cognition: Making sense of people.* Cambridge, MA: MIT Press.

Kunda, Z., & Spencer, S. J. (2003). When do stereotypes come to mind and when do they color judgment? A goal-based theoretical framework for stereotype activation and application. *Psychological Bulletin, 129,* 522–544.

Kurdek, L. A. (1999). The nature and predictors of the trajectory of change in marital quality for husbands and wives over the first 10 years of marriage. *Developmental Psychology, 35,* 1283–1296.

Kurdek, L. A. (2002). Predicting the timing of separation and marital satisfaction: An 8-year prospective longitudinal study. *Journal of Marriage and the Family, 64,* 163–179.

Lakin, J. L., & Chartrand, T. L. (2003). Using nonconscious behavioral mimicry to create affiliation and rapport. *Psychological Science, 14,* 334–339.

Lang, P. J., Bradley, M. M., & Cuthbert, B. N. (1990). Emotion, attention, and startle reflex. *Psychological Review, 97,* 377–395.

Lawrence, E., Nylen, K., & Cobb, R. J. (2007). Prenatal expectations and marital satisfaction over the transition to parenthood. *Journal of Family Psychology, 21,* 155–164.

Lawrence, E., Rothman, A. D., Cobb, R. J., Rothman, M. T., & Bradbury, T. N. (2008). Marital satisfaction across the transition to parenthood. *Journal of Family Psychology, 22,* 41–50.

Le, B., & Agnew, C. R. (2003). Commitment and its theorizes determinants: A meta-analysis of the investment model. *Personal Relationships, 10,* 37–57.

Leary, M. R., & Baumeister, R. F. (2000). The nature and function of self-esteem: Sociometer theory. In M. P. Zanna (Ed.), *Advances in experimental social psychology* (Vol. 32, pp. 2–51). San Diego: Academic Press.

Leary, M. R., & MacDonald, G. (2003). Individual differences in self-esteem: A review and theoretical integration. In M. R. Leary & J. P. Tangney (Eds.), *Handbook of self and identity* (pp. 401–420). New York: Guilford Press.

Leary, M. R., Springer, C., Negel, L., Ansell, E., & Evans, K. (1998). The causes, phenomenology, and consequences of hurt feelings. *Journal of Personality and Social Psychology, 74,* 1225–1237.

Leary, M. R., Tambor, E. S., Terdal, S. K., & Downs, D. L. (1995). Self-esteem as an interpersonal monitor: The sociometer hypothesis. *Journal of Personality and Social Psychology, 68,* 518–530.

LeBel, E. P., & Campbell, L. (2009). Implicit partner affect, relationship satisfaction, and the prediction of romantic breakup. *Journal of Experimental Social Psychology, 45,* 1291–1294.

Lee, L., Loewenstein, G., Ariely, D., Hong, J., & Young, J. (2008). If I'm not hot, are you hot or not? Physical attractiveness evaluations and dating preferences. *Psychological Science, 19,* 669–677.

Lee, S., Rogge, R. D., & Reis, H. T. (2010). Assessing the seeds of relationship decay: Using implicit evaluations to detect the early stages of disillusionment. *Psychological Science, 21,* 857–864.

Lemay, E. P., & Clark, M. S. (2008). How the head liberates the heart: Projection of communal responsiveness guides relationship promotion. *Journal of Personality and Social Psychology, 94,* 647–671.

Lemay, E. P., Clark, M. S., & Feeney, B. C. (2007). Projection of communal responsiveness to needs and the construction of satisfying communal relationships. *Journal of Personality and Social Psychology, 92,* 834–853.

Levinger, G. (1976). A social psychological perspective on marital dissolution. *Journal of Social Issues, 32,* 21–49.

Levinger, G., & Breedlove, J. (1966). Interpersonal attraction and agreement: A study of marriage partners. *Journal of Personality and Social Psychology, 3,* 367–372.

Lockwood, P., Dolderman, D., Sadler, P., & Gerchak, E. (2004). Feeling better about doing worse: Social comparisons within romantic relationships. *Journal of Personality and Social Psychology, 87,* 80–95.

Lydon, J. E., Fitzsimons, G. M., & Naidoo, L. (2003). Devaluation versus enhancement of attractive alternatives: A critical test using the calibration paradigm. *Personality and Social Psychology Bulletin, 29,* 349–359.

Lydon, J. E., Menzies-Toman, D., Burton, K., & Bell, C. (2008). If–then contingencies and the differential availability of an attractive alternative on relationship maintenance for men and women. *Journal of Personality and Social Psychology, 95,* 50–65.

Lykken, D. T., & Tellegen, A. (1993). Is human mating adventitious or the result of lawful choice? A twin study of mate selection. *Journal of Personality and Social Psychology, 65,* 56–68.

Macrae, C. N., & Johnston, L. (1998). Help, I need somebody: Automatic action and inaction. *Social Cognition, 16,* 400–417.

MacDonald, G., & Jessica, M. (2006). Family approval as a constraint in dependency regulation: Evidence from Australia and Indonesia. *Personal Relationships, 13,* 183–194.

MacDonald, G., & Leary, M. R. (2005). Why does social exclusion hurt? The relationship between social and physical pain. *Psychological Bulletin, 131,* 202–223.

MacLeod, C., Mathews, A., & Tata, P. (1986). Attentional bias in emotional disorders. *Journal of Abnormal Psychology, 95,* 15–20.

Marigold, D. C., Holmes, J. G., & Ross, M. (2007). More than words: Reframing compliments from romantic partner fosters security in low self-esteem individuals. *Journal of Personality and Social Psychology, 92,* 232–248.

Marigold, D. C., Holmes, J. G., & Ross, M. (2010). Fostering relationship resilience: An intervention for low self-esteem individuals. *Journal of Experimental Social Psychology, 46,* 624–630.

Markman, H. J. (1979). Application of a behavioral model of marriage in predicting relationship satisfaction in couples planning marriage. *Journal of Consulting and Clinical Psychology, 47,* 743–749.

Markman, H. J. (1981). Prediction of marital distress: A 5-year followup. *Journal of Consulting and Clinical Psychology, 49,* 760–762.

Martz, J. M., Verette, J., Arriaga, X. B., Slovik, L. F. Cox, C. L., & Rusbult, C. E. (1998). Positive illusion in close relationships. *Personal Relationships, 5,* 159–181.

Matouschek, N., & Rasul, I. (2008). The economics of the marriage contract: Theories and evidence. *The Journal of Law and Economics, 51,* 5–110.

McGregor, I. (2003). Defensive zeal: Compensatory conviction about attitudes, values, goals, groups, and self-definition in the face of personal uncertainty. In S. Spencer, S. Fein, & M. Zanna (Eds.), *Motivated social perception: The Ontario Symposium* (Vol. 9, pp. 73–92). Mahwah, NJ: Erlbaum.

McGregor, I., Zanna, M. P., Holmes, J. G., & Spencer, S. J. (2001). Compensatory conviction in the face of personal uncertainty: Going to extremes and being oneself. *Journal of Personality and Social Psychology, 80,* 472–488.

McNulty, J. K., & Karney, B. R. (2004). Positive expectations in the early years of marriage: Should couples expect the best or brace for the worst? *Journal of Personality and Social Psychology, 86,* 729–743.

McNulty, J. K., & Russell, V. M. (2010). When "negative" behaviors are positive: A contextual analysis of the long-term effects of problem-solving behaviors on changes in relationship satisfaction. *Journal of Personality and Social Psychology, 98,* 587–604.

Mikulincer, M. (1998). Attachment working models and the sense of trust: An exploration of interaction goals and affect regulation. *Journal of Personality and Social Psychology, 74,* 1209–1224.

Mikulincer, M., Birnbaum, G., Woddis, D., & Nachmias, O. (2000). Stress and accessibility of proximity-related thoughts: Exploring the normative and intra-individual components of attachment theory. *Journal of Personality and Social Psychology, 78,* 509–523.

Mikulincer, M., Gillath, O., Halevy, V., Avihou, N., Avidan, S., & Eshkoli, N. (2001). Attachment theory and reactions to others' needs: Evidence that activation of the sense of attachment security promotes empathic responses. *Journal of Personality and Social Psychology, 81,* 1205–1224.

Mikulincer, M., Gillath, O., & Shaver, P. R. (2002). Activation of the attachment system in adulthood: Threat-related primes increase the accessibility of mental representations of attachment figures. *Journal of Personality and Social Psychology, 83,* 881–895.

Mikulincer, M., & Shaver, P. R. (2001). Attachment theory and intergroup bias: Evidence that priming the secure base schema attenuates negative reactions to outgroups. *Journal of Personality and Social Psychology, 81,* 97–115.

Mikulincer, M., & Shaver, P. R. (2003). The attachment behavioral system in adulthood: Activation, psychodynamics, and interpersonal processes. In M. Zanna (Ed.), *Advances in experimental social psychology* (Vol. 35, pp. 52–153). New York: Academic Press.

Mikulincer, M., & Shaver, P. R. (2007). Boosting attachment security to promote mental health, prosocial values, and intergroup tolerance. *Psychological Inquiry, 18,* 139–156.

Miller, M. V. (2008, September 1). After the beginning. *O, The Oprah Magazine.* Available at *www.oprah.com/omagazine/Getting-Over-Disappointment-In-a-Relationship.*

Miller, P. J. E., Caughlin, J. P., & Huston, T. L. (2003). Expressiveness and marital satisfaction: The role of idealization processes. *Journal of Marriage and Family, 65,* 978–995.

Miller, P. J. E., Niehuis, S., & Huston, T. L. (2006). Positive illusions in marital relationships: A 13-year longitudinal study. *Personality and Social Psychology Bulletin, 32,* 1579–1594.

Mills, J., Clark, M. S., Ford, T. E., & Johnson, M. (2004). Measurement of communal strength. *Personal Relationships, 11,* 213–230.

Mineka, S., & Sutton, S. K. (1992). Cognitive biases and the emotional disorders. *Psychological Science, 3,* 65–69.

Mischel, W., & Morf, C. C. (2003). The self as a psychosocial dynamic processing system: A meta-perspective on a century of the self in psychology. In M. R. Leary & J. P. Tangney (Eds.), *Handbook of self and identity* (pp. 15–46). New York: Guilford Press.

Mischel, W., & Shoda, Y. (1995). A cognitive–affective system theory of personality: Reconceptualizing situations, dispositions, dynamics, and invariance in personality structure. *Psychological Review, 102,* 246–268.

Monson, T. C., Hesley, J., & Chernick, L. (1982). Specifying when personality traits can and cannot predict behavior: An alternative to abandoning the attempt to predict single act criteria. *Journal of Personality and Social Psychology, 43,* 382–399.

Monteith, M. J. (1993). Self-regulation of prejudiced responses: Implications for progress in prejudice reduction efforts. *Journal of Personality and Social Psychology, 65,* 469–485.

Montya, R. M. (2008). I'm hot, so I'd say you're not: The influence of objective physical attractiveness on mate selection. *Personality and Social Psychology Bulletin, 34,* 1303–1314.

Muraven, M., & Baumeister, R. F. (2000). Self-regulation and depletion of limited resources: Does self-control resemble a muscle? *Psychological Bulletin, 126,* 247–259.

Murray, S. L. (1999). The quest for conviction: Motivated cognition in romantic relationship. *Psychological Inquiry, 10,* 23–34.

Murray, S. L. (2010). Unpublished data. State University of New York at Buffalo.

Murray, S. L., Aloni, M., Holmes, J. G., Derrick, J. L., Stinson, D. A., & Leder, S. (2009). Fostering partner dependence as trust-insurance: The implicit contingencies of the exchange script in close relationships. *Journal of Personality and Social Psychology, 96,* 324–348.

Murray, S. L., Bellavia, G., Rose, P., & Griffin, D. (2003). Once hurt, twice hurtful: How perceived regard regulates daily marital interaction. *Journal of Personality and Social Psychology, 84*, 126–147.

Murray, S. L., Derrick, J., Leder, S., & Holmes, J. G. (2008). Balancing connectedness and self-protection goals in close relationships: A levels-of-processing perspective on risk regulation. *Journal of Personality and Social Psychology, 94*, 429–459.

Murray, S. L., Derrick, J., Pinkus, R., Aloni, M., & Leder, S. (2008). *A daily diary study of newlyweds.* Unpublished data, University at Buffalo, State University of New York.

Murray, S. L., Griffin, D. W., Derrick, J., Harris, B., Aloni, M., & Leder, S. (in press). Tempting fate or inviting happiness? Unrealistic idealization prevents the decline of marital satisfaction. *Psychological Science.*

Murray, S. L., Griffin, D. W., Rose, P., & Bellavia, G. (2003). Calibrating the sociometer: The relational contingencies of self-esteem. *Journal of Personality and Social Psychology, 85*, 63–84.

Murray, S. L., Griffin, D. W., Rose, P., & Bellavia, G. (2006). For better or worse? Self-esteem and the contingencies of acceptance in marriage. *Personality and Social Psychology Bulletin, 32*, 866–882.

Murray, S. L., & Holmes, J. G. (1993). Seeing virtues in faults: Negativity and the transformation of interpersonal narratives in close relationships. *Journal of Personality and Social Psychology, 65*, 707–722.

Murray, S. L., & Holmes, J. G. (1997). A leap of faith? Positive illusions in romantic relationships. *Personality and Social Psychology Bulletin, 23*, 586–604.

Murray, S. L., & Holmes, J. G. (1999). The (mental) ties that bind: Cognitive structures that predict relationship resilience. *Journal of Personality and Social Psychology, 77*, 1228–1244.

Murray, S. L., & Holmes, J. G. (2008). The commitment-insurance system: Self-esteem and the regulation of connection in close relationships. In M. P. Zanna (Ed.), *Advances in experimental social psychology* (Vol. 40, pp. 1–60). Amsterdam: Elsevier.

Murray, S. L., & Holmes, J. G. (2009). The architecture of interdependent minds: A motivation-management theory of mutual responsiveness. *Psychological Review, 116*, 908–928.

Murray, S. L., Holmes, J. G., Aloni, M., Pinkus, R. T., Derrick, J. L., & Leder, S. (2009). Commitment insurance: Compensating for the autonomy costs of interdependence in close relationships. *Journal of Personality and Social Psychology, 97*, 256–278.

Murray, S. L., Holmes, J. G., Bellavia, G., Griffin, D. W., & Dolderman, D. (2002). Kindred spirits? The benefits of egocentrism in close relationships. *Journal of Personality and Social Psychology, 82*, 563–581.

Murray, S. L., Holmes, J. G., & Collins, N. L. (2006). Optimizing assurance: The risk regulation system in relationships. *Psychological Bulletin, 132*, 641–666.

Murray, S. L., Holmes, J. G., Dolderman, D., & Griffin, D. W. (2000). What the motivated mind sees: Comparing friends' perspectives to married partners' views of each other. *Journal of Experimental Social Psychology, 36*, 600–620.

Murray, S. L., Holmes, J. G., & Griffin, D. (1996a). The benefits of positive illusions:

Idealization and the construction of satisfaction in close relationships. *Journal of Personality and Social Psychology, 70,* 79–98.

Murray, S. L., Holmes, J. G., & Griffin, D. W. (1996b). The self-fulfilling nature of positive illusions in romantic relationship: Love is not blind, but prescient. *Journal of Personality and Social Psychology, 71,* 1155–1180.

Murray, S. L., Holmes, J. G., & Griffin, D. W. (2000). Self-esteem and the quest for felt security: How perceived regard regulates attachment processes. *Journal of Personality and Social Psychology, 78,* 478–498.

Murray, S. L., Holmes, J. G., Griffin, D. W., Bellavia, G., & Rose, P. (2001). The mismeasure of love: How self-doubt contaminates relationship beliefs. *Personality and Social Psychology Bulletin, 27,* 423–436.

Murray, S. L., Holmes, J. G., MacDonald, G., & Ellsworth, P. (1998). Through the looking glass darkly? When self-doubts turn into relationship insecurities. *Journal of Personality and Social Psychology, 75,* 1459–1480.

Murray, S. L., Holmes, J. G., & Pinkus, R. T. (2010). A smart unconscious? Procedural origins of automatic partner attitudes in marriage. *Journal of Experimental Social Psychology, 46,* 650–656.

Murray, S. L., Leder, S., McGregor, J. C. D., Holmes, J. G., Pinkus, R. T., & Harris, B. (2009). Becoming irreplaceable: How comparisons to a partner's alternatives differentially affect low and high self-esteem people. *Journal of Experimental Social Psychology, 45,* 1180–1191.

Murray, S. L., & Pinkus, R. T. (2008). The insecurity-inducing effects of upward social comparisons to romantic partners. Unpublished data, State University of New York at Buffalo.

Murray, S. L., Pinkus, R. T., Holmes, J. G., Harris, B., Aloni, M., Gomillion, S., et al. (2010). *When rejection loses its motivational sting: The power of automatic partner attitudes in close relationships.* Unpublished manuscript, State University of New York at Buffalo.

Murray, S. L., Rose, P., Bellavia, G., Holmes, J., & Kusche, A. (2002). When rejection stings: How self-esteem constrains relationship-enhancement processes. *Journal of Personality and Social Psychology, 83,* 556–573.

Murray, S. L., Rose, P., Holmes, J. G., Derrick, J., Podchaski, E., Bellavia, G., & Griffin, D. W. (2005). Putting the partner within reach: A dyadic perspective on felt security in close relationships. *Journal of Personality and Social Psychology, 88,* 327–347.

Murstein, B. I. (1970). Stimulus-value-role: A theory of marital choice. *Journal of Marriage and the Family, 32,* 465–481.

Neff, L. A., & Karney, B. R. (2002). Judgments of a relationship partner: Specific accuracy but global enhancement. *Journal of Personality, 70,* 1079–1112.

Neff, L. A., & Karney, B. R. (2009). Stress and reactivity to daily relationship experiences: How stress hinders adaptive processes in marriage. *Journal of Personality and Social Psychology, 97,* 435–450.

Nezlek, J. B., Kowalski, R. M., Leary, M. R., Blevins, T., & Holgate, S. (1997). Personality moderators of reactions to interpersonal rejection: Depression and trait self-esteem. *Personality and Social Psychology Bulletin, 23,* 1235–1244.

Ober, C., & Aldrich, C. L. (1997). HLA-G polymorphisms: Neutral evolution or novel function? *Journal of Reproductive Immunology, 36,* 1–21.

Olson, M. A., & Fazio, R. H. (2008). Implicit and explicit measures of attitudes: The perspective of the MODE model. In R. E. Petty, R. H. Fazio, & P. Brinol (Eds.), *Attitudes: Insights from the new implicit measures* (pp. 19–63). Mahwah, NJ: Erlbaum.

O'Mahen, H. A., Beach, S. R. H., & Tesser, A. (2000). Relationship ecology and negative communication in romantic relationships: A self-evaluation maintenance perspective. *Personality and Social Psychology Bulletin, 26,* 1343–1352.

Overall, N. C., & Sibley, C. G. (2008). When accommodation matters: Situational dependency within daily interactions with romantic partners. *Journal of Experimental Social Psychology, 44,* 95–104.

Overall, N. C., & Sibley, C. G. (2009). Attachment and dependence regulation within daily interactions with romantic partners. *Personal Relationships, 16,* 239–262.

Perunovic, M., & Holmes, J. G. (2008). Automatic accommodation: The role of personality. *Personal Relationships, 15,* 57–70.

Petty, R. E., Tormala, Z. L., Brinol, P., & Jarvis, W. B. G. (2006). Implicit ambivalence from attitude change: An exploration of the PAST model. *Journal of Personality and Social Psychology, 90,* 21–41.

Petty, R. E., Wegener, D. T., & Fabrigar, L. R. (1997). Attitudes and attitude change. *Annual Review of Psychology, 48,* 609–647.

Pierce, T., & Lydon, J. (1998). Priming relational schemas: Effects of contextually activated and chronically accessible interpersonal expectations on responses to a stressful event. *Journal of Personality and Social Psychology, 75,* 1441–1448.

Pietrzak, J., Downey, G., & Ayduk, O. (2005). Rejection sensitivity as an interpersonal vulnerability. In M. W. Baldwin (Ed.), *Interpersonal cognition* (pp. 62–84). New York: Guilford Press.

Pillsworth, E. G., & Haselton, M. G. (2006). Women's sexual strategies: The evolution of long-term bonds and extrapair sex. *Annual Review of Sex Research, 17,* 59–100.

Pinker, S. (2008, January 28). Crazy love. *Time, 171,* 82–83.

Rauer, A. J., Karney, B. R., Garvan, C. W., & Hou, W. (2008). Relationship risks in context: A cumulative risk approach to understanding relationship satisfaction. *Journal of Marriage and Family, 70,* 1122–1135.

Reis, H. T., & Aron, A. (2008). Love: What is it, why does it matter, and how does it operate? *Perspectives on Psychological Science, 3,* 80–86.

Reis, H. T., Clark, M. S., & Holmes, J. G. (2004). Perceived partner responsiveness as an organizing construct in the study of intimacy and closeness. In D. Mashek & A. P. Aron (Eds.), *Handbook of closeness and intimacy* (pp. 201–225). Mahwah, NJ: Erlbaum.

Reis, H. T., & Shaver, P. (1988). Intimacy as an interpersonal process. In S. W. Duck (Ed.), *Handbook of personal relationships* (pp. 367–389). Oxford, UK: Wiley.

Rempel, J. K., Holmes, J. G., & Zanna, M. P. (1985). Trust in close relationships. *Journal of Personality and Social Psychology, 49,* 95–112.

Rholes, S. W., Simpson, J. A., Campbell, L., & Grich, J. (2001). Adult attachment and the transition to parenthood. *Journal of Personality and Social Psychology, 81,* 421–435.

Rholes, W. S., Simpson, J. A., & Orina, M. M. (1999). Attachment and anger in an anxiety-provoking situation. *Journal of Personality and Social Psychology, 76,* 940–957.

Robins, R. W., Caspi, A., & Moffitt, T. E. (2000). Two personalities, one relationship: Both partners' personality traits shape the quality of their relationship. *Journal of Personality and Social Psychology, 79,* 251–259.

Roese, N. J. (1997). Counterfactual thinking. *Psychological Bulletin, 121,* 133–148.

Rubin, Z. (1973). *Liking and loving: An invitation to social psychology.* New York: Holt, Rinehart & Winston.

Rudman, L. A., Dohn, M. C., & Fairchild, K. (2007). Implicit self-esteem compensation: Automatic threat defense. *Journal of Personality and Social Psychology, 93,* 798–813.

Rusbult, C. (1983). A longitudinal test of the investment model: The development (and deterioration) of satisfaction and commitment in heterosexual involvements. *Journal of Personality and Social Psychology, 45,* 172–186.

Rusbult, C. E., & Buunk, B. P. (1993). Commitment processes in close relationships: An interdependence analysis. *Journal of Social and Personal Relationships, 10,* 175–204.

Rusbult, C. E., Martz, J. M., & Agnew, C. R. (1998). The investment model scale: Measuring commitment level, satisfaction level, quality of alternatives, and investment size. *Personal Relationships, 5,* 357–391.

Rusbult, C. E., & Van Lange, P. A. M. (2003). Interdependence, interaction, and relationships. *Annual Review of Psychology, 54,* 351–375.

Rusbult, C. E., Van Lange, P. A. M., Wildschut, T., Yovetich, N. A., & Verette, J. (2000). Perceived superiority in close relationship: Why it exists and persists. *Journal of Personality and Social Psychology, 79,* 521–545.

Rusbult, C. E., Verette, J., Whitney, G. A., Slovik, L. F., & Lipkus, I. (1991). Accommodation processes in close relationship: Theory and preliminary research evidence. *Journal of Personality and Social Psychology, 60,* 53–78.

Scinta, A., & Gable, S. L. (2007). Automatic and self-reported attitudes in romantic relationships. *Personality and Social Psychology Bulletin, 33,* 1008–1022.

Seligman, C., Fazio, R. H., & Zanna, M. P. (1980). Effects of salience of extrinsic rewards on liking and loving. *Journal of Personality and Social Psychology, 38,* 453–460.

Senchak, M., & Leonard, K. E. (1992). Attachment styles and marital adjustment among newlywed couples. *Journal of Social and Personal Relationships, 9,* 51–64.

Shah, J., Friedman, R., & Kruglanski, A. W. (2002). Forgetting all else: On the antecedents and consequences of goal shielding. *Journal of Personality and Social Psychology, 83,* 1261–1280.

Simpson, J. A. (1987). The dissolution of romantic relationships: Factors involved in relationship stability and emotional distress. *Journal of Personality and Social Psychology, 53,* 683–692.

Simpson, J. A. (2007). Psychological foundations of trust. *Current Directions in Psychological Science, 16,* 264–268.

Simpson, J. A., Ickes, W., & Grich, J. (1999). When accuracy hurts: Reactions of anxious-ambivalent dating partners to a relationship-threatening situation. *Journal of Personality and Social Psychology, 76,* 754–769.

Simpson, J. A., & Rholes, W. S. (2002). Attachment orientations, marriage, and the transition to parenthood. *Journal of Research in Personality, 36*, 622–628.

Simpson, J. A., Rholes, W. S., & Phillips, D. (1996). Conflict in close relationships: An attachment perspective. *Journal of Personality and Social Psychology, 71*, 899–914.

Sinclair, L., & Kunda, Z. (1999). Reactions to a Black professional: Motivated inhibition and activation of conflicting stereotypes. *Journal of Personality and Social Psychology, 77*, 885–904.

Sinclair, S., Huntsinger, J., Skorinko, J., & Hardin, C. D. (2005). Social tuning of the self: Consequences for the self-evaluations of stereotype targets. *Journal of Personality and Social Psychology, 89*, 160–175.

Snyder, M., & Stukas, A. A. (1999). Interpersonal processes: The interplay of cognitive, motivational, and behavioral activities in social interaction. In J. T. Spence (Ed.), *Annual review of psychology* (Vol. 50, pp. 273–303). Palo Alto, CA: Annual Reviews.

Sommer, K. L., & Baumeister, R. F. (2002). Self-evaluation, persistence, and performance following implicit rejection: The role of trait self-esteem. *Psychological Bulletin, 28*, 926–938.

Sprecher, S. (1988). Investment model, equity, and social support determinants of relationship commitment. *Social Psychology Quarterly, 51*, 318–328.

Sprecher, S. (2001). Equity and social exchange in dating couples: Associations with satisfaction, commitment, and stability. *Journal of Marriage and the Family, 63*, 599–613.

Sprecher, S., Schmeeckle, M., & Felmless, D. (2006). The principle of least interest: Inequality in emotional involvement in romantic relationships. *Journal of Family Issues, 27*, 1–26.

Sprecher, S., Sullivan, Q., & Hatfield, E. (1994). Mate selection preferences: Gender differences examined in a national sample. *Journal of Personality and Social Psychology, 66*, 1074–1080.

Strack, F., & Deutsch, R. (2004). Reflective and impulsive determinants of social behavior. *Personality and Social Psychology Review, 8*, 220–247.

Surra, C. A., & Hughes, D. K. (1997). Commitment processes in accounts of the development of premarital relationships. *Journal of Marriage and the Family, 59*, 5–21.

Swann, W. B., Hixon, J. G., & De La Ronde, C. (1992). Embracing the bitter "truth": Negative self-concepts and marital commitment. *Psychological Science, 3*, 118–121.

Taylor, S. E., & Brown, J. D. (1988). Illusion and well-being: A social psychological perspective on mental health. *Psychological Bulletin, 103*, 193–210.

Taylor, S. E., & Gollwitzer, P. M. (1995). Effects of mind-set on positive illusions. *Journal of Personality and Social Psychology, 69*, 213–226.

Tennov, D. (1979). *Love and limerence.* New York: Stein and Day.

Tetlock, P. E. (2002). Social functionalist frameworks for judgment and choice: Intuitive politicians, theologians, and prosecutors. *Psychological Review, 109*, 451–471.

Thibaut, J. W., & Kelley, H. H. (1959). *The social psychology of groups.* New York: Wiley.

Thornhill, R., & Gangestad, S. W. (1999). The scent of symmetry: A human sex pheromone that signals fitness? *Evolution and Human Behavior, 20,* 175–201.

Todd, P. M., Penke, L., Fasolo, B., & Lenton, A. P. (2007). Different cognitive processes underlie human mate choices and mate preferences. *Proceedings of the National Academy of Science, 104,* 15011–15016.

Tomasello, M., Carpenter, M., Call, J., Behne, T., & Moll, H. (2005). Understanding and sharing intentions: The origins of cultural cognition. *Behavioral and Brain Sciences, 28,* 675–691.

Tooby, J., & Cosmides, L. (1996). Friendship and the banker's paradox: Other pathways to the evolution of adaptations for altruism. *Proceedings of the British Academy, 88,* 119–143.

Triandis, H. C. (1995). Individualism-collectivism and personality. *Journal of Personality, 69,* 907–924.

Tucker, J. S., & Anders, S. L. (1999). Attachment style, interpersonal perception accuracy, and relationship satisfaction in dating couples. *Personality and Social Psychology Bulletin, 25,* 403–412.

Twenge, J. M., Baumeister, R. F., DeWall, C. N., Ciarocco, N. J., & Bartels, J. M. (2007). Social exclusion decreases prosocial behavior. *Journal of Personality and Social Psychology, 92,* 56–66.

Twenge, J. M., Baumeister, R. F., Tice, D. M., & Stucke, T. S. (2001). If you can't join them, beat them: Effects of social exclusion on aggressive behavior. *Journal of Personality and Social Psychology, 81,* 1058–1069.

Van Lange, P. A. M., & Rusbult, C. E. (1995). My relationship is better than—and not as bad as—yours is: The perception of superiority in close relationships. *Personality and Social Psychology Bulletin, 21,* 32–44.

Van Lange, P. A. M., Rusbult, C. E., Drigotas, S. M., Arriaga, X. B., Witcher, B. S., & Cox, C. L. (1997). Willingness to sacrifice in close relationships. *Journal of Personality and Social Psychology, 72,* 1373–1395.

Vohs, K. D., Mead, N. L., & Goode, M. R. (2006). The psychological consequences of money. *Science, 314,* 1154–1156.

Vorauer, J. D., Cameron, J. J., Holmes, J. G., & Pearce, D. G. (2003). Invisible overtures: Fears of rejection and the signal amplification bias. *Journal of Personality and Social Psychology, 84,* 793–812.

Waller, W. (1938). *The family: A dynamic interpretation.* New York: Gordon.

Walster, E., Walster, G. W., & Berscheid, E. (1978). *Equity: theory and research.* Boston: Allyn & Bacon.

Wegner, D. M. (2002). *The illusion of conscious will.* Cambridge, MA: MIT Press.

Wentura, D., Rothermund, K., & Bak, P. (2000). Automatic vigilance: The attention-grabbing power of approach- and avoidance-related social information. *Journal of Personality and Social Psychology, 78,* 1024–1037.

White, G. L. (1980). Physical attractiveness and courtship progress. *Journal of Personality and Social Psychology, 39,* 660–668.

Whitfield, M., & Jordan, C. H. (2009). Mutual influence of implicit and explicit attitudes. *Journal of Experimental Social Psychology, 45,* 748–759.

Wieselquist, J., Rusbult, C. E., Foster, C. A., & Agnew, C. R. (1999). Commitment, pro-relationship behavior, and trust in close relationships. *Journal of Personality and Social Psychology, 77,* 942–966.

Wilson, T. D. (2002). *Strangers to ourselves: Discovering the adaptive unconscious*. Boston: Harvard University Press.

Wilson, T. D., Lindsey, S., & Schooler, T. Y. (2000). A dual model of attitudes. *Psychological Review, 107,* 101–126.

Wood, W., & Neal, D. T. (2007). A new look at habits and the habit–goal interface. *Psychological Review, 14,* 843–863.

Zayas, V., & Shoda, Y. (2005). Do automatic reactions elicited by thoughts of romantic partner, mother, and self relate to adult romantic attachment? *Personality and Social Psychology Bulletin, 8,* 1011–1025.

Index